Wordsworth's Poetry of Repetition

Wordsworth's Poetry of Repetition

Romantic Recapitulation

SARAH HOUGHTON-WALKER

Great Clarendon Street, Oxford, OX2 6DP,
United Kingdom

Oxford University Press is a department of the University of Oxford.
It furthers the University's objective of excellence in research, scholarship,
and education by publishing worldwide. Oxford is a registered trade mark of
Oxford University Press in the UK and in certain other countries

© Sarah Houghton-Walker 2023

The moral rights of the author have been asserted

All rights reserved. No part of this publication may be reproduced, stored in
a retrieval system, or transmitted, in any form or by any means, without the
prior permission in writing of Oxford University Press, or as expressly permitted
by law, by licence or under terms agreed with the appropriate reprographics
rights organization. Enquiries concerning reproduction outside the scope of the
above should be sent to the Rights Department, Oxford University Press, at the
address above

You must not circulate this work in any other form
and you must impose this same condition on any acquirer

Published in the United States of America by Oxford University Press
198 Madison Avenue, New York, NY 10016, United States of America

British Library Cataloguing in Publication Data
Data available

Library of Congress Control Number: 2022947957

ISBN 978–0–19–287048–3

DOI: 10.1093/oso/9780192870483.001.0001

Printed and bound in the UK by
Clays Ltd, Elcograf S.p.A.

Links to third party websites are provided by Oxford in good faith and
for information only. Oxford disclaims any responsibility for the materials
contained in any third party website referenced in this work.

For my family

Preface

Wordsworth's 'I wandered lonely as a cloud' routinely tops polls of favourite English poems. Widely recognized by its nickname, 'The Daffodils', it is of course not really about flowers, but about recalling and reflecting upon a prior occasion: Wordsworth's best-known poem is actually a description of the experience of repetition in the mind formulized in the 'Preface' to *Lyrical Ballads*. Alongside the recollection it describes, the poem enacts this description through a variety of forms of repetition: most obviously, its marked metrical regularity, and its insistent, mainly monosyllabic rhyme; but also, through numerous more subtle instances of repeated sound. As stanza one directs us 'Beside the lake, beneath the trees', for example, structural repetition is established through a balanced pair of prepositions reiterating the 'be-' prefix. By stanza three, Wordsworth's original action is itself represented as a repeated one, which in turn can only be communicated adequately through a stridently repeated word: in the original moment, the poet simply 'gazed—and gazed'. The poem stutters as it encounters through its recollection the transfixed Wordsworth, before it moves on to assert the power of events recapitulated through tranquil reflection. In the way that it commands attention to formal and thematic repetitions, 'I wandered lonely as a cloud' is typical of Wordsworth's work: recapitulation persistently dominates themes and subjects explored through experimentation with formal and lexical reiterations. This book surveys instances in which recapitulation pushes most prominently to the fore.

What does it mean to repeat something? Philosophers and psychologists differently have wondered how repetition works within the mind, neurologically, imaginatively, and psychologically. Psychoanalytic criticism (and the psychoanalysis which preceded it) depends upon the capacity of the mind to repeat experience, in order to effect a changed relation to it. Memory is self-evidently a type of repetition; in eighteenth-century models of the mind and imagination, so is thought itself. Thinking about forms of repetition in art easily becomes entangled with discourses surrounding originality generally, and with debates about influence more specifically: one might repeat others, just as easily as oneself. Descriptive literary traditions have engaged with realism (effectively, the repetition of the real in their respective forms), whether by aiming for it, experimenting with it, or denying its possibility; such realisms depend upon the conviction that 'the real' *might* be repeated in art. Ideas of repetition have a particular relevance to formal literary critical traditions: rhyme, metre, and form are all types of repeated structure. Rhetoric exploits copious fundamentally repetitious devices.

All of these examples, and numerous more, could easily sit within a study of repetition; many of them will be raised in this book. Yet whilst some of them exert irresistible pressure, my discussion centres on the explicit engagement of Wordsworth with ideas of repetition, and on actual instances of recapitulation: repeated words and phrases; textual echoes and reiterations which function in particular ways, and the figuring of revisiting (imaginatively, textually, and literally) places and experiences. Significantly, it asks how those recapitulations accommodate changing ideas and perceptions, through their relationships to one another.

This study is most interested in the idea that Wordsworth explores the limits of recapitulation—of saying things again—and that in doing so he tests ideas of repetition *with difference*. Literally repeating things, within individual poems or across different versions of the same text, allows Wordsworth to navigate towards an awareness of the importance of retaining in some sense a prior form, whilst also suggesting a changed attitude or understanding. Repeating experience, whether recollecting within his own mind or physically revisiting a place or text, is an amalgam of two (or several) experiences, and attention to textual repetition can be harnessed to reflect this. The subtle (and sometimes not so subtle) use of repetition is one way in which this interest is manifest. But recapitulation is also achieved within texts, literally and conceptually, through the use of the conjunctions 'and' and 'or', allowing the presentation of alternatives which might turn out not to be as different as they first appeared. A consideration of the operation of these two little words will therefore have an important part to play here. I will argue that the connections Wordsworth understands to exist between different recapitulations of the same thing are integral to their significance. This book, then, surveys and analyses instances of repetition and the conjunctions which similarly facilitate recapitulation within Wordsworth's writing. More than simply cataloguing, examples from Wordsworth's poems are enlisted in the service of an argument about the importance of the element of difference within even apparently 'pure' repetition: difference might be in perception, attitude, or understanding, but for Wordsworth, the subtle relationship between instances of what seems to be the same experience illuminates the potential for poetry to portray simultaneously the specific and the universal: to hold within its lines both immediate and general truths at the same time. Poetic texts are particularly well fitted to this task, I shall argue, because they themselves draw on a range of types of repetition in their structure and form, and these characteristics ultimately allow recapitulation to enable the ideal of Romantic sincerity at which Wordsworth explicitly aimed.

Acknowledgements

A significant portion of this book was written during a research sabbatical which coincided with the national lockdowns of the Covid-19 pandemic. I am hugely indebted to the staff of the Gonville and Caius College Library, Mark Statham, Neil Kirkham, Jo Carter, and Lauran Richards, and of the Cambridge University Library, who made every effort to make materials available for consultation despite the difficult situation. I am even more grateful to all the teachers who did as much as was humanly possible to engage my children, and therefore saved me from totally drowning in home-schooling distractions. Another significant portion of the book was written whilst I was under an exceptionally heavy administrative burden. The staff of the Admissions Office at Caius at the time, and in particular Andrew Bond and Paul Wingfield, proved good friends as well as supportive colleagues, who kept the wheels from falling off throughout a very challenging period. I am grateful to Karen Raith and Emma Varley at OUP who made working on this project extremely straightforward, and to the generous anonymous readers for OUP whose comments were both thoughtful and insightful. My thanks also go to colleagues and students in the Cambridge English Faculty and in Caius, whose interest and enthusiasm fortified and inspired me on numerous occasions. In particular, I am grateful to Alex Oliver and Peter Mandler, who provided reading suggestions for particular subjects, and to the 'Finellows', most especially Ruth Scurr, who make Finella so very conducive to the pleasures of research.

Lastly, I'd like to thank my lovely family, the dedicatees of this book: my parents, whose support makes possible any research at all, and my husband and three daughters, who put up uncomplainingly with my antisocial working hours, and gave me (some) peace and space to get my work done, even when we were all confined in the house together for months on end.

Contents

PART I. INTRODUCTORY: REPETITION IN THE ROMANTIC PERIOD

1. The Sense and the Sound of Repetition in Romantic-Period Poetry   3
   The Idea of Repetition   3
   The Sound of Repetition   12

2. The Workings of Repetition in Romantic-Period Poetry   24
   Repetition, Metre, and Form   24
   Recapitulation in the Act of Reading   27
   Repetition between and across Works   31

3. Contexts for Repetition in the Romantic Period   40
   Repetition, Art, and the Mind   40
   Repetition and the Higher Criticism   44
   Order, Disorder, Repetition, and Variation   49
   Repetition in an Industrial Age   53
   Political Revolution   64

PART II. WORDSWORTHIAN RECAPITULATION

4. Repetition and Conjunction: The Quiet Work of *And* and *Or*   69
   Connection and Conjunction   70
   And and *Or*   75

5. Conjunction, Expansion, and Sublimity   91
   'We Are Seven' and 'Tintern Abbey'   91
   Wordsworth's Boat-Stealing   98

6. Conjunctions, Repetition, and Revision   107
   Wordsworth and Revision   107
   Wordsworth and Translation   114
   Revision and the 'Logic of the *AND*'   117
   Still Now: Transcending Specific Moments and Places   124
   Reader as Reviser   129

7. Connection, Recognition, and Return   132
   Recognition, Connection, and Community   133
   Disjunction, and the Absence of Community   139

8. 'The Thorn', Tautology, and Tragic Repetition	156
Repetition in 'The Thorn'	156
Tragedy, Repetition, and Martha Ray	162
9. Crafted Repetition	170
10. Resounding Voices, Habitual Haunts: Recapitulation, Specifics, and Generals	190
Strains That Never Die	190
Recapitulation and the Unification of Specific and General	198
11. Echo and Response	212
Echo	212
Sing, Cuckoo	220
12. Coleridge and Repetition: A Comparative Case	227
Coleridge, Repetition, and the Mind	227
Repetition in Coleridge's Poetry	240
13. Conclusion: Recapitulation and Sincerity	254
Bibliography of Works Cited	265
Wordsworth's Works	265
Other Works	266
Index	281

PART I
INTRODUCTORY
Repetition in the Romantic Period

1
The Sense and the Sound of Repetition in Romantic-Period Poetry

The Idea of Repetition

Repetition provokes a seductive paradox. One the one hand, it might prompt a sense of frustration, boredom, or ennui: the elderly relative who constantly repeats the same old stories is a stock figure of mockery. At the extreme, it is a symptom of psychopathologies; of dementia and of neurosis. Critics have perceived a consonance between some of the repetition operating within Romantic poetry, and the repetition associated by psychoanalysis with trauma and grief.[1] Yet in other contexts, as Freud famously pointed out, 'repetition, the re-experiencing of something identical, is clearly in itself a source of pleasure'.[2] Rehearsal makes perfect. In an incantatory, religious context repetition can achieve calm, comfort, or even ecstasy. And then again, a verbal stutter causes frustration, and repetition can over-exaggerate; taken too far, it can even cause meaning to be lost, as a word repeated ad infinitum starts to turn into nonsense.[3]

In various art forms, repetition is exploited for particular, desirable effects: mimetic theories of the plastic arts demand the attempt at a form of perfect reproduction;[4]

---

[1] See for example Fritz Breithaupt, 'The Invention of Trauma in German Romanticism', *Critical Inquiry*, 32.1 (Autumn 2005), 77–101; Thomas Pfau, *Romantic Moods: Paranoia, Trauma, Melancholy, 1790–1840* (Baltimore: Johns Hopkins University Press, 2005), and Thomas J. Brennan, *Trauma, Transcendence and Trust: Wordsworth, Tennyson, and Eliot Thinking Loss* (New York: Palgrave Macmillan, 2010).

[2] See *The Standard Edition of the Complete Psychological Works of Sigmund Freud, Volume 18 (1920–1922): Beyond the Pleasure Principle, Group Psychology and Other Works*, trans. and ed. by James Strachey and others (London: Hogarth Press and the Institute of Psycho-Analysis, 1955), pp. 1–64 (p. 36).

[3] Repeating any word to oneself can generate this effect; it is a feature of language recognized since at least the Ancient Greeks. Stephen Kidd points out that in the *Antidosis* 'a statement loses its force through its being repeated. Something similar to this idea is articulated in Plutarch's *De Garrulitate*... Such repetitive excess is not along the lines of the positive use of repetition for rhetorical force (anaphora, anadiplosis, etc.), or the positive use of repetition for magic and religious incantations. Rather what is being suggested is the negative effect of excessive repetition—that... in Isocrates' term (as language which *does* nothing), it becomes nonsense (ληρεῖν). Related is repetition not of the same words, but of the same idea' (Stephen E. Kidd, *Nonsense and Meaning in Ancient Greek Comedy* (Cambridge: Cambridge University Press, 2014), pp. 36–7.)

[4] On this subject generally (and on the nuances regarding which generalized version of the 'real' the reproduction was supposed to represent), see M. H. Abrams, *The Mirror and the Lamp: Romantic Theory and the Critical Tradition* (Oxford: Oxford University Press, 1971), esp. Chapter 2.

Andy Warhol's 'apathetic reiteration'[5] is one of the iconic styles of the twentieth century. Musical scores have symbols to mean 'now do exactly what you have just done, all over again', and these appear with intimate frequency throughout musical history: they are a million miles from remarkable.[6] Poetry, though, is different from the visual arts (the relationship with music is more complicated, as I shall discuss later), in that unless the intention is deliberately perverse, reading a poem almost always remains a process in which the reader is obliged to repeat the progress of the writer, to make sense. Whilst writers do not really write spontaneously in perfect lines, the idea of the reader retracing the evolution of the poem, following the path the poet took across the page, remains vivid. In a painting, we don't usually know which bit the artist did first; visual effects govern the eye's movement, but only within certain limits. Through the process of reading, repetitions in verse come to us sequentially; we cannot read them all at exactly the same moment in the way in which, if we step back, we can choose to see Warhol's soup tins simultaneously (regardless of whether we choose to look at smaller details as well).

A list of the most obvious contributors to the philosophical tradition which has dwelt upon repetition might run through Plato and Ecclesiastes to Hegel, Kirkegaarde, Wittgenstein, Nietzsche, Freud, Lacan, and Deleuze and Guattari. As has long been recognized, pure repetition is literally impossible in the written text; because the linear motion of reading leads us to encounter the repetition necessarily secondarily, a second instance of a word is different to a first by virtue of its *being* a repetition.[7] Plato's allegory of the cave is already concerned that a repetition is a representation, intrinsically different from the original, perfect form, and cannot therefore be a perfect repetition at all. In the eighteenth century, Hume breaks away from this preoccupation, arguing in a different direction in his discussion of necessary connection: 'repetition neither discovers nor causes any thing in the objects, but has an influence only on the mind'.[8] Hume decisively re-orientates our focus to the effect of the observing consciousness, rather than dwelling upon the inherent qualities of repeated objects. Deleuze's *Difference and Repetition* cites Hume, going on to assert that repetition involves elements that are

---

[5] The phrase is Kate Armstrong's; see her *Crisis and Repetition: Essays on Art and Culture* (Michigan: Michigan State University Press, 2001), p. 15.

[6] Peter Kivy's *The Fine Art of Repetition: Essays in the Philosophy of Music* (Cambridge: Cambridge University Press, 1993) surveys the different symbols musical notation uses to demand repetition.

[7] See for example Bruce Kawain: 'The growth of the work, even from one identical line to another, makes exact repetition impossible' (*Telling It Again and Again: Repetition in Literature and Film* (Ithaca: Cornell University Press, 1972), p. 7). Elizabeth Hellmuth Margulis cites David Huron's work on expectation in music, which argues that repetitions can appear new to listeners of music because whatever we hear between one hearing and another alters our expectations. See David Huron, *Sweet Anticipation: Music and the Psychology of Expectation* (Cambridge, MA: MIT Press, 2006), cited in Margulis, *On Repeat: How Music Plays the Mind* (Oxford: Oxford University Press, 2014), p. 23.

[8] *The Clarendon Edition of the Works of David Hume: A Treatise of Human Nature, Vol. 1: Texts*, ed. David Fate Norton and Mary J. Norton (Oxford: Oxford University Press, 2007), p. 112.

absolutely identical (if they are not identical, then there is no repetition), but yet must also be different (if they are not distinguishable, then there can be no repetition, because only one phenomenon exists). As Deleuze notes, in the apprehension of repetition, 'a change is produced in the mind which contemplates: a difference, something new *in* the mind'.[9]

Accepting the impossibility of perfect repetition, Bruce Kawain argues that we should aim to understand instead 'the aesthetics of near-repetition', because 'Repetition is a non-verbal state; it cannot be committed to any art that occurs in time.'[10] Kawain distinguishes the repetitious (when a word, action or experience loses impact through its repetition) from the repetitive (when a word, action, or experience equals or gains in force at each repetition).[11] He concedes that 'Ordinarily we consider those events that are capable of being repeated, or those functions that insist on being repeated, lower or more boring than those "once in a lifetime," extraordinary, unrepeatable experiences that we consider the true or interesting material of our life histories.'[12] A later chapter of this book will suggest that Wordsworth seems to disagree on this point. But Kawain goes on: 'Every day the sun comes up, stays up, goes down. We experience this cycle of light and warmth 26,000 times in an average lifetime, and find that not enough. What is more important... we do not find the cycle boring'; we do not 'wish our heartbeat would change color to keep us amused'.[13]

Our content with our repetitively beating hearts pertains, of course, to life. Life is repetitive: life writing is an art because it finds aesthetically pleasing ways to avoid listing the mundane reality and Shandyesque hyper-plenitude of the quotidian. But significant challenges attach to the negotiation of repetition in texts; there are pitfalls to avoid. For Kawain, 'the most destructive effect of repetition [is] the doing of things over and over, each time with less energy and less interest, [and this] is the root of repetitiousness in literature—on the way to anaesthesia: the cliché we do not even notice, the dead word, the dead work, the zombie.'[14] This recalls (repeats, perhaps) the problem from which, the Russian Formalists asserted in the early twentieth century, art can rescue us: for Viktor Shklovsky, art

> exists that one may recover the sensation of life; it exists to make one feel things, to make the stone *stony*... The technique of art is to make objects 'unfamiliar,' to make forms difficult, to increase the difficulty and length of perception because the process of perception is an aesthetic end in itself and must be prolonged.[15]

---

[9] See Gilles Deleuze, *Difference and Repetition* [1968], trans. by Paul Patton (London: Continuum, 2004; 2007), p. 90.
[10] Kawain, p. 7.   [11] Kawain, p. 4.   [12] Kawain, p. 1.
[13] Kawain, pp. 2–3.   [14] Kawain, pp. 20–1.
[15] Victor Shklovsky, 'Art as Technique' [1917], in *Russian Formalist Criticism*, trans. by Lee T. Lemon and Marion J. Reis (1965), repr. in David Lodge, ed., *Modern Criticism and Theory: A Reader* (London: Longman, 1988), pp. 16–30 (p. 20).

In another almost-paradox, insofar as it catches at us, halts us, trips us up in all sorts of ways, repetition (the basis of the familiarity which breeds insensitivity) turns out to be one of the most significant tools a poet has: the familiar is easily overlooked, yet a new instance can be striking *because* it is a repetition which causes us to look with fresh eyes. The stone re-becomes stony, even as it remains the same stone. The traces and implications of Shklovsky's defamiliarization effect glimmer through and animate a subsequent century of literary theory: as Paul Valéry maintains that art 'consists in a development of sensations tending to repeat or prolong what the intellect tends to eliminate or transcend', for instance;[16] or in Derridean 'différance', which is centrally concerned with ideas of 'iterability', of repetition and difference; or in the arguments about metaphor advanced by Lakoff and Johnson, which pursue the 'dead words' of Kawain.[17]

A strong theoretical tradition has argued that instances of repetition inevitably function doubly: they are registered both as original and as replica at once. Elizabeth Margulis draws on the work of musicologists who have argued that 'changing context' denies the possibility of 'true redundancy in music'. She goes on to concede to Peter Kivy's insistence that 'still, it repeats', and concludes that 'context reconfigures sound such that no repetition is truly redundant, but... we do experience many reoccurrences as "repetition."...Repetitions are always repetitive in one sense, and divergent in another.'[18] Kawain takes another course: repetition might either be a problem or a saviour for language, depending on the skill with which it is employed, but it is just as impossible to repeat a life in text as it is to repeat anything else: 'The falsification of reality in art or memory comes about from the *attempt* at repetition, the action of voluntarily remembering; by trying to "perceive" the event again, we change it.'[19] Wordsworth understood this only too well.

Already it is clear that ideas about repetition loop and pull through and across a range of different discourses, which understand the nature and operation of repetition in sometimes competing senses. The very idea of repetition is complex: its primary senses according to the *OED* are to do with words, not action (action comes a long way down the list). But to repeat in language might be to do one of very many things, as repetition's bulging lexicon suggests. Handbooks of rhetoric contain pages of definitions of forms of repetition: those of letters, syllables, and

---

[16] Paul Valéry, 'The Idea of Art' [1935], from *Aesthetics*, in *The Collected Works of Paul Valéry*, ed. Jackson Matthews, 15 vols [1958–75], xiii, trans. Ralph Manheim (London: Routledge & Kegan Paul, 1964), pp. 70–9 (p. 75).

[17] Lakoff and Johnson argue that metaphors shape all perception: 'the way we think, what we experience, and what we do every day is very much a matter of metaphor.' (George Lakoff and Mark Johnson, *Metaphors We Live By* (Chicago: University of Chicago Press, 1980; 2003), p. 3). Metaphor is fundamentally a form of recapitulation, a repetition with difference.

[18] Margulis, p. 32, citing Kivy and D. A. Hanninen, 'A Theory of Recontextualization in Music: Analyzing Phenomenal Transformations of Repetition', *Music Theory Spectrum*, 25 (2003), 59–97.

[19] Kawain, p. 31.

sounds; repetitions of words; repetitions of clauses or phrases, and repetitions of ideas. Poetry expands this toolkit, with a legion of effects of versification dependent upon the repetition of structures, sounds, or both. To risk truism, the most obvious, stridently repetitive features of poetry are rhyme, rhythm, and form, and all three can be conspicuous by their absence as well as their presence. Rhyme and rhythm occur in various arrangements at multiple places in poems, often leapfrogging over and jostling with different instances of themselves in the same line or stanza.

Rhyme has been called 'historically [the] single most consistent characteristic' of English poetry,[20] and it is encountered aurally as a form of repetition: Peter McDonald's compelling account of its presence in nineteenth-century verse points out that 'rhyme carries with it inescapably the burden of repetition, for a rhyme does repeat a sound.'[21] These repetitions suggest corresponding connections between the words which contain them, whether or not such connections exist outside of the particular text. The repetition involved in rhyme is never, of course, even when it is formed through the repetition of exactly the same words, perfect: as in all repetitions, the second occurrence is different to the first because of its being a repetition, and the awareness of that repetitive status which it bears. The idea of a directly linear relationship between rhyming features (that there is a first sound which is then repeated by a secondary one) is contentious. Already in the sixteenth century, Puttenham's *Arte of English Poesie* was addressing the pleasure of the 'report' and 'return' of rhyme: 'we make in th' ends of our verses a certaine tunable sound: which anon after with another verse reasonably distant we accord together in the last fall or cadence: the eare taking pleasure to heare the like tune reported and to feele his returne'.[22] In its necessary backwards glance, rhyme thus involves a split form of repetition. This is captured by Robert Douglas-Fairhurst's account of it as a 'double movement', possessing a 'forked tongue'.[23] Gillian Beer has pointed out that we do not rhyme progressively; rather, 'we rhyme backwards.'[24] Or, as she puts it elsewhere, rhyme

> does not begin to exist until the second term appears to *make* a rhyme... Rhyme always looks back and forward at once, janus faced, propelling our ears ahead to

---

[20] T. V. F. Brogan, *English Versification, 1570–1980* (Baltimore and London: Johns Hopkins University Press, 1981), p. 77.
[21] Peter McDonald, *Sound Intentions: The Workings of Rhyme in Nineteenth-Century Poetry* (Oxford: Oxford University Press, 2012), p. 18.
[22] George Puttenham, *The Arte of English Poesie* [1589], ed. Edward Arber (Westminster: Constable, 1895), p. 90.
[23] Robert Douglas-Fairhurst, 'Alexander Pope: "renown'd in Rhyme"', in David Womersley and Richard McCabe, eds, *Literary Milieux: Essays in Text and Context Presented to Howard Erskine-Hill* (Newark, NJ: University of Delaware Press, 2008), pp. 230–57 (p. 239).
[24] Gillian Beer, 'Rhyming as comedy: body, ghost and banquet', in Michael Cordner, Peter Holland, and John Kerrigan, eds, *English Comedy* (Cambridge: Cambridge University Press, 1994), pp. 180–96 (p. 181).

listen for the *chime* that has not yet arrived while giving us a cluster of sounds like a ground bass.[25]

In excavations of the nature of rhyme like these we can see that the echo–repetition involved in rhyming is always a repetition with difference: the ear finds something both identical and new at the same time by virtue of the rhyme's sound being exactly the same as something that we have already heard, but also existing in its own, independent instant. For Garrett Stewart, the chiming of rhyme is 'an effect, not a fact... No single inscribed word can rhyme in and of itself. It must appeal (rather than peal) across a distance defined by difference even when processed under the sign of similarity.'[26] Hegel takes this relationship further when he describes rhyming as a kind of flirtation: 'it is as if the rhymes now find one another immediately, now fly from one another and yet look for one another... the ear's attentive expectation is now satisfied without more ado, now teased, deceived, or kept in suspense owing to the longer delay between rhymes, but always contented again by the regular ordering and return of the same sounds.'[27] The repetitions of rhyme sounds call back to one another in a pattern which may be unpredictable in its variation, but whose seductions are satisfied in its eventual chiming reconciliation.

The Greeks and Romans did not use rhyme in their serious verse. A century before Wordsworth's birth, Milton's 'Preface' to *Paradise Lost* leaves his reader in no doubt as to his reasons for similarly shunning it, damning rhyme as 'the invention of a barbarous age.'[28] These are weighty influences, yet rhyme retained its dominating hold on the English poetic imagination. Since the Renaissance, various writers and traditions had, nonetheless, been exploring its limitations, and in particular its awkward tendency to determine sense by requiring a rhyme-word regardless of semantic propriety. This is the sort of debased poetry John Wilson Croker famously accused Keats of writing, in a review of *Endymion*: Keats's habit, Croker suggested, was to 'write a line at random', and then to follow 'not the thought excited by this line, but that suggested by the *rhyme* with which it concludes'.[29] Susan Wolfson, the foremost late twentieth-century scholar of Romanticism and form, recognizes that rhyme's 'double force' has potentially negative as well as positive effects, 'restricting how lines have to end'. Yet rhyme in

---

[25] Gillian Beer, '"Another Music": Rhyming and Transformation', for the George Herbert in Bemerton Group (2006), pp. 1–8 (p. 2), https://www.georgeherbert.org.uk/docs/Another%20Music%20-%20Rhyming%20and%20Transformation.pdf, accessed 2 June 2022.

[26] Garrett Stewart, *Reading Voices: Literature and the Phonotext* (Berkeley and Los Angeles: University of California Press, 1990), p. 98.

[27] *Hegel's Aesthetics: Lectures on Fine Art*, trans. T. M. Knox, 2 vols (Oxford: Clarendon Press, 1975), ii, 1030–1.

[28] See John Milton, *Paradise Lost*, ed. Alastair Fowler (London and New York: Longman, 1971; 1992), p. 38.

[29] Unsigned Review [John Wilson Croker], *Quarterly Review* (1818), in G. M. Matthews, ed., *Keats: The Critical Heritage* (London: Routledge & Kegan Paul, 1971), pp. 110–14 (p. 112).

her account also functions more helpfully, 'allying sound and sense, figure and reference.'[30] However the tussle between benefit and hindrance works out, the Romantic Period is of specific significance to its progress: various critics have found its poetry to be characterized by a new attention to rhyme. McDonald, for example, argues that whilst 'the use of rhyme can scarcely be anything other than self-conscious on a poet's part',

> a sense of the creative possibilities of this necessary self-awareness (and, in turn, a sense of its potential liabilities) distinguishes much poetry from Wordsworth onwards... The pre-determined nature of rhymes ('stream' rhymes with 'dream' before Wordsworth comes along, and certainly not *because* of him) presents poets with a test of their own authorial powers of determination.[31]

End-rhymes naturally achieve particular prominence in verse, not only from their own obviousness (their visual as well as aural claims on the attention), but also through the pressures of convention: despite the twentieth century's best efforts, we are rarely surprised to encounter rhyme in a poem; once established within a particular work, it strikes us because we have been expecting it, straining for it, as well as simply because it exists.

To trace the subtleties of rhyme in its many forms beyond end-rhyme (assonant, alliterative, half-, para-, internal, etc.) through lines of verse can appear to fall into over-reading: scholarship is sometimes accused of listening too hard for purely coincidental rhymes which exist simply by virtue of the finite number of sounds in the English language. Yet as Beer points out, rhyme 'specialises in the hidden parts of words, not the front they show the world. Rhyme has to do with words' back parts. Initial letters vanish, shift, collapse before our eyes... a first, apparently rationally sanctioned word, is tripped and changed (both semantically and aurally) by the rhyme word.'[32] Sixty years before Wordsworth's birth, Pope was stridently declaring (albeit in a passage ironically stuffed with tuneful, musical poetic effects) that those who pay too much attention to the sound of verse are 'tuneful fools', as ridiculous as those who 'to church repair, | Not for the doctrine, but the music there.'[33] Here again, McDonald's work is importantly elucidatory. In the Romantic Period specifically, he argues, writers were clearly aware that 'habits of listening were in the process of change... the capacity for close, attentive listening was taking hold, both in poetry itself and among the admirers of poets like Wordsworth and Keats.'[34] This awareness mutually feeds from and nourishes

---

[30] Susan J. Wolfson, *Formal Charges: The Shaping of Poetry in British Romanticism* (Stanford: Stanford University Press, 1997), p. 46.
[31] McDonald, p. 21.   [32] Beer, 'Rhyming as comedy', p. 181.
[33] *An Essay on Criticism*, in *Pope: Complete Poetical Works*, ed. Herbert Davis (Oxford: Oxford University Press, 1978), pp. 62–85 (ll. 340–3).
[34] McDonald, p. 27.

attention to the minute effects of verse, including the many, more subtle forms of rhyme we find buried within it; at just this point in literary history, sensitivity to the effects of rhymes of all types was enhanced and indeed harnessed. Wordsworth's interest in this type of attention to the repeated sounds of verse can be inferred from, for instance, his exposition of 'impressions of sound', in the 'Preface' to the 1815 *Poems*. In an account which explores 'that love of sound which the Poet feels', the poet describes the stock-dove's expression: it is 'said to *coo*, a sound well imitating the note of the bird; but, by the intervention of the metaphor *broods*, the affections are called in by the imagination to assist in marking the manner in which the bird reiterates and prolongs her soft note'.[35] Wordsworth's emphases draw visual and aural attention to the way in which the bird's own br*oo*ding repetition here reaches so strongly to her c*oo*ing sound that it is impossible to ignore the sounds repeating in one another, and impossible to think that Wordsworth has not registered the same consonance, so perfectly does it coincide with his point. And Wordsworth goes on to explain that these are

> images independent of each other, and immediately endowed by the mind with properties which do not inhere in them, upon an incitement from properties and qualities the existence of which is inherent and obvious. These processes of imagination are carried on either by conferring additional properties upon an object, or abstracting from it some of those which it actually possesses, and thus enabling it to re-act upon the mind which hath performed the process, like a new existence.[36]

The emphasis achieved by the hyphen in 're-act' is significant; this is a form of repetition involving change, resulting in novelty, and it explicitly depends on our ability to notice 'inherent and obvious' 'properties and qualities'. Wordsworth demands our attention to the sounds of his words, as he discusses words which mimic sound.

Isobel Armstrong has argued that 'The movement of Romantic poetry is one of slow, cumulative growth through repetition which can take many forms'; 'the poem *discovers* itself through repetition'.[37] McDonald argues that a specifically self-conscious sense 'of rhyme as a kind of repetition' is a key feature of the early nineteenth-century literary landscape, and 'fundamentally Wordsworthian in origin'. According to McDonald,

---

[35] 'Preface' to *Poems... in Two Volumes* [1815], repr. in *The Prose Works of William Wordsworth*, ed. W. J. B. Owen and J. W. Smyser, 3 vols (Oxford: Clarendon Press, 1974), iii, 32.

[36] *Prose*, iii, 32.

[37] Isobel Armstrong, *Language as Living Form in Nineteenth-Century Poetry* (Brighton: Harvester, 1982), p. 35.

largely owing to Wordsworth, the boundary between rhyme (the repetition of the same sound in different words) and repetition itself (allowing the same word to sound over again, whether in rhymed or unrhymed verse) tends to blur... After Wordsworth, the knowledge that 'all rhymes are repetitions' is implicit in the rhyming verse, and in some of the unrhymed verse, of many nineteenth-century poets.[38]

McDonald's model of repeated sounding here is complicated only by an analysis of the experience of poetry. W. H. Auden suggested that 'The ear tends to be lazy, craves the familiar and is shocked by the unexpected; the eye, on the other hand, tends to be impatient, craves the novel and is bored by repetition.'[39] Poetry as we currently encounter it in the West usually sits at the juncture between Auden's 'ear' and his 'eye'. We know, because we are often told by literary historians and because we ourselves experience it, that poetry has a fundamental basis in an oral/aural tradition. It has; but (despite the continuing, increasing popularity of readings, slams, and festivals) it has more recently in history been shared and enjoyed predominantly through personal, silent reading. Experience is personal and widely various, but most readers, reading verse, more or less self-consciously listen to it with an inner ear, as well as seeing it on the page. John Hollander points out that 'speaking and writing are both language... it is the region between them that poetry inhabits.'[40] Eric Griffiths has explored this relationship in nineteenth-century poetry; Angela Leighton's *Hearing Things* conducts a still fuller survey and contemplation (suggestively resistant to an overarching argument) of those who have covered similar terrain on the complexities of sound and listening, and 'voicing' and hearing.[41] Stewart turns the same dynamic more firmly inward, when he finds rhyme '*founded* through the activity of the inner ear... the processing of any kind of literary text, involves our passive auscultation, a listening *in* on our own latent articulation.'[42] The passivity registered here is important: poetry calls to the inner ear which these accounts rely upon whether we choose to prick it up deliberately, or not. At its most fundamental, that call comes from repetitious effects. Children register the effects of Dr Seuss or 'London's Burning' without worrying about whether (as Hume and Deleuze argue) the perceiving mind is changed by the experience of repetition; when they fill in gaps left by someone reading a familiar poem aloud, they instinctively match the rhythm and metre which belongs to the poem (and might even be able to guess an omitted

---

[38] McDonald, p. 11; p. 26.
[39] W. H. Auden, *The Dyers Hand* (New York: Vintage, 1989), p. 100.
[40] John Hollander, *Vision and Resonance: Two Senses of Poetic Form*, 2nd edn (New Haven: Yale University Press, 1985), p. x.
[41] Eric Griffiths, *The Printed Voice of Victorian Poetry*, 2nd edn (Oxford: Oxford University Press, 2018); Angela Leighton, *Hearing Things: The Work of Sound in Literature* (Cambridge, MA: Belknap Press, 2018).
[42] Stewart, p. 98.

rhyme-word), because they are patterned by those repeated features. Hence in part the cultural significance of song, whose co-existence as a literary and a musical form in turn demonstrates the unstable boundary between poetry and music.

The Sound of Repetition

Elizabeth Margulis's study *On Repeat* highlights the prominence and effects of repetition in music. She draws on musical analysis, neuroscience, and her own experience as a pianist in order to think about why such repetition is pleasing, rather than simply dull (as a story too-often repeated is dull), variously addressing internal repetition within individual pieces of music, and the repetition which occurs when we listen to familiar pieces multiple times. She begins her study by citing the long history of critics who have pondered the seduction of music's repetition; Victor Zuckerkandl, for example ('Music can never have enough of saying over again what has already been said'); and Ferdinand Praeger ('Since any whole part-repetition in poetry would be rejected as childish, or as the emanation of a disordered brain, why should it be otherwise with music?').[43] Although Margulis acknowledges early on that 'Repeatability is how songs become the property of a group or a community', and notes that various scholars have explored the question of when language might be processed musically,[44] her study is primarily focused on music understood as distinct from language. Looking back to Auden, however, we might insist that poetry *is* musical language; that the reason 'song' pushes its way into Margulis's account is because certain linguistic formulations—which are sometimes called poetry—share the characteristics of 'music' as Margulis understands it.

Drawing on the argument of Laurie Knox, that repetition in spoken discourse 'prompts the hearer to seek implicit meaning in utterances, by indicating that the speaker aims at a meaning different than that conveyed by uttering an expression only once',[45] Margulis does address what she calls the 'music-language divide',[46] but here she ignores the common ground in favour of distinguishing music from other art forms.[47] According to Margulis,

---

[43] Margulis, pp. 1–5. See Victor Zuckerkandl, *Sound and Symbol* (New York: Pantheon, 1956), and F. Praeger, 'On the Fallacy of the Repetition of Parts in the Classical Form', *Proceedings of the Royal Musical Association* (1882–3), 1–16.

[44] See Margulis, p. 6.

[45] Laurie Knox, 'Repetition and Relevance: Self-repetition as a Strategy for Initiating Cooperation in Nonnative/Native Speaker Conversations', in B. Johnstone, ed., *Repetition in Discourse: Interdisciplinary Perspectives* (Norwood, NJ: Ablex, 1994), p. 197, cited in Margulis, p. 14.

[46] Margulis, p. 15.

[47] See Margulis, p. 14. It isn't only users of language who, Margulis believes, experience repetition differently to listeners of music. For example, she suggests that whilst we revisit favourite paintings, we

> Poetry is perhaps the best comparative case... poetry unfolds sequentially and dynamically in time... just like music. Poems are reread, and re-enjoyed, but lack both the internal repetition characteristic of music, and the capacity to generate earworms (you don't get stuck in the shower reciting 'shall I compare thee to a summer's day?,' although if it were set to a pop tune you might)... Even if you love Robert Frost, you don't hear 'Two roads diverged' and think 'yes!' the way you might when you hear the opening notes of a favorite song.[48]

I am certain (not only from personal experience, but also from a quick survey of my own students and colleagues) that, in fact, poetry does generate earworms, and the discussion of Dorothy Wordsworth's notes on 'The Solitary Reaper' in a later chapter of this book will confirm this sort of persistence as an effect experienced by romantic-period listeners as well. I am equally sure that an encounter with a favourite poem can prompt *exactly* the same 'yes!' that a favourite song elicits. There are, of course, disparities between responses to music, and responses to poetry: semantic and melodic communication differ, and we are conditioned to approach them differently (Kawain, for example, makes the point that 'We enjoy choruses when they are sung and skip over them when they are printed'[49]). But despite the careful shrewdness of her study, there are more correspondences between the repetitions found in poetry (which, as this book will argue, can be encountered at a minute and unobtrusive level), and those belonging to music, than Margulis admits. As Oliver Sacks points out, '*The Iliad* and *The Odyssey*, famously, could be recited at length because, like ballads, they had rhythm and rhyme. How much such recitation depends on musical rhythm and how much purely on linguistic rhyming is difficult to tell, but these are surely related—both "rhyme" and "rhythm" derive from the Greek, carrying the conjoined meanings of measure, motion, and stream. An articulate stream... is necessary to carry one along, and this is something that unites language and music'.[50] The 'articulate stream' is one of sound: rhyme and rhythm are effects that we hear rather than interpret, and its music flows, eddies, and swirls with the characteristics of repetition.

Margulis demonstrates through experiment that introducing repetition to musical works, even when it is done entirely mechanically and without reference to composers' original intentions, makes listeners judge works more favourably, find them more interesting, and enjoy them more fully.[51] However, Margulis then invites her reader to

---

do so 'not with the degree of obsession we revisit musical works (or there would be a painting iPod)'. Yet for those who take pleasure in gazing at images, wall-hung reproductions (or even originals), books, and postcards do fulfil this function.
[48] Margulis, p. 14.   [49] Kawain, p. 9.
[50] Oliver Sacks, *Musicophilia: Tales of Music and the Brain* (London: Picador, 2008), pp. 259–60.
[51] Margulis, pp. 15–16.

note particularly that introducing the same manipulations into spoken utterances (additional repetition, without regard to linguistic sense) would *likely* not trigger elevated ratings of enjoyment, interest...quite the opposite, in fact. Repetition, *thus*, marks an important divider between the perception of music and language.[52]

Even setting aside the fact that Margulis's argument here dismisses forms of language which are structured according to repetition, this is an enormous 'thus' to base on a distinctly dubious 'likely'. It is telling that Margulis uncritically enlists the support of Cosmia Wagner's declaration, that 'in poetry, repetition is absurd, except when it is a refrain or when it has to produce a musical effect':[53] those exceptions are far from insignificant, and the assertion of absurdity is in turn absurd, as this book will demonstrate. The contention of this chapter, which lacks the scientific solidity of Margulis's grounding in neuroscience, but which I hope will be justified by attention to verse, is that the 'musical effects' of poetry, that is, the aural properties of language, separate from their purely semantic content, do generate the kind of effect Margulis measures with reference to musical experience. Margulis directs her comments on language to semantic meaning at the level of the word, but in their semantic capacity, words might well function differently to music, as Margulis asserts, whilst simultaneously functioning 'musically' through their sounded characteristics.[54] To say this is hardly controversial: John Hollander, for example, invokes the familiarity of the idea when he clarifies that 'By the "music of poetry" we generally mean all of the nonsemantic properties of the language of a poem including not only its rationalized prosody, but its actual sound on being read, and certain characteristics of its syntax and imagery as well.'[55]

Margulis's understanding of the distinction between poetry and music sounds very much like Adam Smith's:

> Poetry and Eloquence...produce their effect always by a connected variety and succession of different thoughts and ideas: but Music frequently produces its

---

[52] Margulis, p. 16 (my emphases). [53] See Margulis, p. 18.

[54] Cognitive science has not neglected the separation between the semantic and what I am calling the more musical content of language. Winnifred Menninghaus, for instance, has explored responses to patterns of repetition in poetry, including anaphora, metre, and various forms of rhyme. Such features, it has been demonstrated, facilitate perceptual processing, even though they make semantic processing more difficult. It has been found that these 'parallelistic' features intensify emotional response (see Winnifred Menninghaus and Sebastian Wallot, 'What the eyes reveal about (reading) poetry', *Poetics*, 85 (April 2021), 1–15, https://doi.org/10.1016/j.poetic.2020.101526, and Winnifred Menninghaus and others, 'The emotional and aesthetic powers of parallelistic diction', *Poetics*, 63 (August 2017), 47–59, https://doi.org/10.1016/j.poetic.2016.12.001, both accessed 2 June 2022). Menninghaus elsewhere argues that romantic-period aesthetics demonstrates an interest in nonsense which further suggests that the semantic content of literary works functions independently of the more 'musical' composition of the text: see Menninghaus, *In Praise of Nonsense*, trans. Henry Pickford (Stanford: Stanford University Press, 1999), especially pp. 1–9.

[55] *Vision and Resonance*, p. 9.

effects by a repetition of the same idea; and the same sense expressed in the same, or nearly the same, combination of sounds, though at first perhaps it may make scarce any impression upon us, yet, by being repeated again and again, it comes at last gradually, and by little and little, to move, to agitate, and to transport us.[56]

But words, even on the page, cannot escape their own aural properties. In their function as sound-carriers (often producing, even individually, multiple effects, both internal to the specific words, and in the way in which they enter into dynamic relationship with the other words around them through effects of rhyme, of contrast, etc.), words are essentially 'musical', as well as literally meaningful. We can see this if we push meaningfulness further, indeed, go beyond it, into nonsense. Jonathan Culler has demonstrated that 'Experientially it is often the case that that meaning is subordinate to rhythm' in verse, and he revisits Stephen Booth's analysis of the nursery rhyme 'Little Boy Blue' to extend his claim beyond rhythm to other repetitious effects: 'the rhyme horn/corn makes *corn* seem right; the parallelism between sheep and cow, and the fact that *Blue* of "Little Boy Blue" is the past tense of *blow*, all bolster the poem's ability to deafen us to the illogic of its claim about the sheep'.[57] In both Culler's and Booth's accounts, aural effects which rely upon repetition allow nonsense to be 'understood' in a special way. Surely, then, we must concede that similar musical effects create a similarly supplementary or separate 'sense', alongside the semantic content of texts (whether they are, to adapt Culler's phrase, intelligible collocations,[58] or are similarly nonsensical, or otherwise abstruse).

In fact, if we only shift very slightly the way Margulis understands 'word', so that the fuller potential of language as a carrier both of semantic meaning *and* musical effect is always recognized, much of Margulis's subsequent argument does seem to support exactly this understanding (even though she continues to assert difference). For example, drawing on recent, extraordinary work by Diana Deutsch, Rachael Lapidis, and Trevor Henthorn, Margulis demonstrates that repetition 'causes ordinary speech to be perceived as music'.[59] She even explicitly states, later on, that 'Repetition can encourage... interest to move away from explicit facts and ideas about a passage towards its actual sounding',[60] recognizing the musical capacity of words. Turning to earlier research, Margulis points out that 'repeated viewings, utterances, or hearings of the same word' can 'cause it to seem to degenerate into nonsense... in which the semantics vanish and are

---

[56] Adam Smith, 'Of the Nature of that Imitation which takes place in what are called The Imitative Arts' [1795], in W. P. D. Wightman, J. C. Bryce, and I. S. Ross, eds, *The Glasgow Edition of the Works and Correspondence of Adam Smith, Vol. 3* (Oxford: Oxford University Press, 1980), p. 192. (Margulis quotes from Smith at the start of one of her later chapters.)
[57] Jonathan Culler, *Theory of the Lyric* (Cambridge, MA: Harvard University Press, 2015), p. 168; p. 185.
[58] For Culler's 'subliminal collocations' see p. 185.   [59] See Margulis, pp. 16–17.
[60] Margulis, p. 18.

replaced by a sort of super-salience of the component parts—letters, phonemes, syllables.'[61] Highlighting the dominance of these 'component parts' of words leads Margulis thus almost to describe the way poetic language is distinct from everyday speech, according to many accounts. The difficulty of course is in any definition or diagnosis of anything we can really call 'poetic language' as distinct from 'everyday speech', and this is the point at which I do not envy Margulis's strongly scientific background: attentive readers of poetry don't need hard and fast borders around those terms to know that poets exploit the 'musical' effects of language even as they employ its potential to make meaning. Margulis argues that the shifting of focus to component parts of language is a function of 'attention', that 'Bored with repeated encounters with the same signified word, attention shifts to the only other available level—the constituent parts of the word.'[62] But we might easily suggest 'fascinated' as a replacement for 'bored' in this sentence. That sense of fascination more easily explains the next characteristic that Margulis notes: that 'Nuanced objects are more compelling on repetition... There is a sense in which the thing is known, yet constantly rediscovered—never grasped—and this may result in a satisfying pull towards the present moment—perhaps a prerequisite for the loss of self'.[63] Margulis's interest in the way in which listeners 'enjoy music more when they aren't given explicit information about it' concludes that 'the increased pleasure repetition can afford stems not from enhanced knowledge, but rather from something more implicit, a changed sort of orientation toward the work.' This might be 'a transportive, even transcendent kind of experience.'[64] Perhaps, then, the musical effects of verse similarly allow one form of 'getting lost' in poetry, even whilst still appreciating its 'meaning' in semantic terms. Where these effects are complementary, we might discover powerful verse indeed. Margulis thus seems to argue almost despite herself for the potential of language to achieve, though its aural qualities, the same sublimity she finds in music.

So far, my discussion has remained abstract; I want now to turn to an example, to demonstrate how even a relatively cursory reading can reveal numerous sound-repetitions functioning busily amongst the semantic properties of words. The following sonnet is chosen because it is *not* by Wordsworth, in order to argue for the wider point about the importance of repetitious techniques to romantic-period verse, though later chapters of this book will attend to Wordsworth's similar exploitation of them. Preoccupied as it explicitly is with the possibility of representing the breadth and multiplicity of a landscape, John Clare's 'A Scene' (first published 1820) seems an appropriate choice for this discussion. A thematic interest in expanse and unboundedness is introduced through the complicated repetition of 'wide'ness in the sonnet's opening lines. These two different forms of wideness powerfully appeal to the dominant critical discourses surrounding Clare,

---

[61] Margulis, p. 17. [62] Margulis, p. 18. [63] Margulis, p. 18. [64] Margulis, p. 15.

related to concepts of enclosure and liberty.[65] And beyond the sonnet's appeal to historical circumstance, it persistently exhibits the complex sonic repetitions I have been invoking, and suggests just some of the intricacies of their interaction in verse, even as it overtly focuses on a *visual* prospect:

> The landscapes stretching view that opens wide
> With dribbling brooks and rivers wider floods
> And hills and vales and darksome lowering woods
> With grains of varied hues and grasses pied
> The low brown cottage in the shelter'd nook
> The steeple peeping just above the trees
> Whose dangling leaves keep rustling in the breeze
> —And thoughtful shepherd bending oer his hook
> And maidens stript haymaking too apear
> And hodge a wistling at his fallow plough
> And herdsman hallooing to intruding cow
> All these with hundreds more far off and near
> Approach my sight—and please to such excess
> That Language fails the pleasure to express[66]

This sonnet bristles with rhyme. For twelve lines, it offers the reader a description of the scene before the poet's eye, and it then concludes by reflecting on the difficulty of expressing the pleasure that such a scene prompts. The poem displays often complex sequences of eye-, ear-, half-, or rich-rhyme, of assonant or alliterative effects; of repeated *sounds*. On top of these aural effects, reading the poem on the page introduces eye-rhyme which might not correspond with ear-rhyme (such as 'Please' and 'pleasure' in the final couplet), as well as examples of ear-rhyme which are not eye-rhymes (the first line's end-rhyme, 'wide', finds its corresponding rhyme in line 4's 'pied', for example; line 10's end-rhyme 'plough' rests in line 11's 'cow'). The heard poem and the silent poem therefore induce different effects, and the conjunction of these versions adds a further richness to both: these are multiple, simultaneous effects which enrich the poem, rather than drowning one another out. In some examples, repetition of sound works to consolidate sense in the poem: the longer, open vowel sounds of the first line, for example, might be said to enact the unfolding of the landscape to the eye, stretching indeed before the reader. But the sense enacted by the rhyme-sounds is implicit as well as semantic. For instance, the numerous 'ands' seem to spill out of

---

[65] I am grateful to the anonymous reader for OUP who wisely encouraged a fuller acknowledgement of the thematic interest in wideness, evinced through this repetition, which Clare is able to express through his own verbal and sonic repetitions.
[66] 'A Scene', in *John Clare: A Critical Edition of the Major Works*, ed. Eric Robinson and David Powell (Oxford: Oxford University Press, 1984), p. 11.

the second word of the poem, 'la*nd*scape', and down through its lines;[67] as they do so, each iteration of the 'and' sound recalls the fact that this is a view of the la*nd*scape, and also the more specific claim that these features belong *to* the landscape (it is the *landscape's* stretching view): there is no commanding, picturesque 'I' here, though the 'varied hues' quite deliberately participate in picturesque convention. In the polysyndetic rush unfolding before the reader, we are assured of the plenitude and variety that the sonnet itself works to communicate: the effect of the 'ands' themselves being repeated supplements the sense of quantity which each particular aspect they preface suggests. In this way, they manage the problem of capacity in the poem: not everything can be included, but the repetitions here recognize, highlight, and thus negotiate that truth, even though they can't solve the problem.

The sonnet form is similarly highly enabling, because the vast array we understand to be tumbling before the viewing poet necessarily needs containment. But the way in which repeated sounds reach across the poem to recall one another persistently functions on another level to disrupt the integrity of the form (this effect is particularly powerful in this sonnet with its particular subject). These properties of the poem function musically, and further effects might be described as 'musical', too: the onomatopoeia of the herdsman's hallooing (emphasized by the punning hypermetric beat), and Hodge's whistling, for example. Characteristically, Clare's landscape is a living, functioning rural economy. Activity dramatizes the view we are offered, literally, in the working individuals described, the movement of the water, and the behaviour of animal and plant life, but also aurally. Here is stretching, dribbling, lowering, peeping, dangling, rustling, bending, haymaking, whistling, hallooing, and intruding, simply to list the present participles. The [ɪ] which is the bouncing, active sound of do*ing* things catches at the ear elsewhere, too. It recurs in both nouns and the adjectives which describe them (in line 2, for example, it is part of 'dr*i*bbl*i*ng' and 'r*i*vers'), as well as in prepositions ('w*i*th' in line 4, for example; '*i*n' in line 5) which orientate the reader as to the relations and the dispositions of the features being described. There is thus a lightness to the sound which bubbles through the poem, and in its repetition it calls to the ear as a sustained, common feature of the verse, firmly associating features of the scene and the poet's attempt to suggest their relationship.

Granted space and time, one might catalogue numerous different examples of the way in which sounds are repeated through the poem in what seem to be more-than-coincidental instances. Given the limited number of sounds in English, it is

---

[67] Visually, the dominance of the 'and' is heightened in *The Early Poems of John Clare, 1804–1822*, ed. Eric Robinson, David Powell, and Margaret Grainger, 2 vols (Oxford: Clarendon Press, 1989), i, 413, where the ampersands of Clare's MSS replace the words, though the correspondence with la*nd*scape is correspondingly less obvious. The first published version, in *Poems Descriptive of Rural Life and Scenery* (London and Stamford: Taylor, Hessey and Drury, 1820), p. 198, printed 'and's.

inevitable that some repetition will occur in any given work, but where such repetitions have demonstrable effects, they become significant. Rather than begin endless listing, I shall take, as an example, the couplet lines 6–7:

> The steeple peeping just above the trees
> Whose dangling leaves keep rustling in the breeze

Here, the dominant repeated aural and visual repetition is the [iː] found in 'ee'. The sound appears in 'steeple', 'peeping', 'leaves', and 'keep', and it also constitutes the end-rhyme of the lines (these are notably self-contained in the poem: they form a couplet in accordance with the rhyme scheme, though even this is complicated because the C rhyme of nook/hook is aurally close and visually identical to the B rhyme, floods/woods, which itself is not a perfect rhyme[68]). Straightforwardly, the accumulated detail of the poem coalesces: this is part of the same thing, Clare's sonnet suggests, the same overarching scene, even as each element is individuated and made distinct. Other sounds contribute to this effect: as I've said, 'peeping', 'dangling', 'rustling', and 'in' exploit the [ɪ] sound strikingly close to the [iː] they accompany: in fact, ten of the twenty syllables of this couplet are either an [iː] or [ɪ] sound. This enhances the sense of accumulation with subtle difference; of a piling up even within the differentiation of features. The aural effect is complicated by the reading eye: 'leaves' is an ear- but not an eye-rhyme. And of course, to the extent that the lines describe something which is persistently happening (the leaves 'keep rustling', presumably throughout the time of the poem, before we get to them and after we have read on), this sonic repetition is entirely fitting, and enacts that continued action. So strong is this repetition that it almost drowns out the more obvious echo of the rustling leaves which Clare threads through the lines in a more straightforwardly onomatopoeic touch, as the 's' and 't' sounds found in 'steeple', 'just', 'trees', 'leaves', 'rustling', and 'breeze' whisper through the couplet. When we get to 'rustling' itself, it clearly calls backwards to the previous line's 'just'. Both 'ust' sounds occupy the stressed beat of the third foot of their line, and because of their difference from the dominant repeated [ɪ] and [iː] sounds, they strike the ear almost as strongly as an end-rhyme. The rhyme-sound is, we might say, *just*ified, coming almost as a relief, its status as the main verb of the sentence coinciding with the metrical and rhyme effects almost to blur the rigidity of the sonnet; its structure, reiterated by strong, monosyllabic end-rhymes, is thus undermined by its aural rendering. And yet, the saturating [iː] sounds fight back and do manage to retain the sense of the line ending to the ear.

---

[68] This analysis, of course, is dependent upon individual accent (my own is from Northamptonshire, though a different part of the county to Clare's).

At the same time, other repeated sounds are working busily away to particular ends. In amongst the recurrent [iː]s of line 6, for instance, 'j*u*st ab*o*ve' stands out because it is different to them. Despite not being an eye-rhyme, the pairing is an aural one, an [ʌ] which corresponds with the idea of *up*wardness suggested semantically by the steeple's peeping up above. The description of it calls upon a consonant idea of creeping, too, which is confirmed when in the next line '*keep*' calls back to the end-emphasized '*trees*', so that '*creep*' is superimposed on to the soundscape; the lines are ghosted by words which don't even appear in the poem, but nonetheless support its semantic sense. In line 7, it is 'dangling' which stands outside of the repeated, dominant rhyme sounds. Following the dragging of the eye upwards in line 6, the 'd' of dangling might be argued to encourage a downwards look: the 'd' is habitually vocalized as a lower note than the open [ʌ] of 'j*u*st ab*o*ve', performing a literal descent as the reader moves along the lines. We never hear the word 'down' in the poem, but we know that down is where/how leaves dangle, so that the image is completed, and the movement of the eye vertically is encouraged, without Clare's needing to introduce the word explicitly. (The attentive reader might here even recall, consciously or otherwise, 'brown' from line 5: striking because it is an eye- but *not* an ear-rhyme with its preceding word, 'low', 'brown' reverberates just enough, I think, to confirm the ghost of 'down' which haunts line 7.) Repetition in these cases is important because it allows these distinct sounds, which are outside of the dominant repeated sounds, to stand out *because* they are different. In this reading, 'just' is doing quite a specific aural job. But then, as it meets 'rustling' in the following line, as I have described, 'just' at the same time becomes part of a different track in the poem; the word/sound is performing different functions simultaneously. All trails lead to the overall description, but they take us through the landscape in different directions *at the same time*, beautifully communicating the multiplicity and activity but also the independence and simultaneous interdependence of the elements of the scene described (mimicked by the way that the human characters form a collective as aspects of the scene, and yet are individualized through their introduction in grammatically relatively self-sufficient lines).

As I. A. Richards argues, 'sound gets its character by compromise with what is going on already... The way the sound is taken is much less determined by the sound itself than by the conditions into which it enters'.[69] The final lines of the sonnet introduce a different set of 'conditions', a new sonic landscape, as the poem moves from description to reflection. The new rhymescape of these lines is enabled by the sonnet form: although the pre-penultimate line reaches across and breaks the standard scheme, the final couplet draws away from the rest of the

---

[69] I. A. Richards, 'Rhythm and Metre', in *Principles of Literary Criticism* [1924] (London and New York: Routledge, 2002), pp. 122–33 (p. 125).

poem in its dominant sounds, though it is no less full. In these lines, the [ɪ] sound which danced through the previous lines of the poem is absent, and the [iː] radically diminished. Here, again, the sound supports the meaning of the poem, insofar as the key, ironic failure of language is there in the deceptiveness of the repeated 'eas' in 'please' (l. 13) and 'pleasure' (l. 14): the letter sequence does not repeat sound; it is the same word-root, but it *sounds* different (recalling again, and disrupting the recollection of, the dominant [iː] sound from line 6). This happens in the very line in which Clare is criticizing the ability of language to express the *pleasure* the word denotes, though notably not its inadequacy to express the *scene* itself. In fact, the 'ea' of 'appear/near', the rhyme-word of lines 9 and 12, has already offered another pronunciation of the vowel combination. After the first few lines, the [ʌɪ] sound of 'sight' has been relatively rare in the poem, and [əʊ] of 'approach' has not predominated either, so that 'Approach my sight' delivers a refreshing turn. The word 'Language' itself is pretty stridently different, rhyming with nothing; the 'ess' sound with which lines 13 and 14 end is unique to these instances. The echoes of earlier lines of the poem do not vanish completely: 'That Language fails' mimics 'And hills and vales' from line 3; the sonnet manages the balance of novelty and repetition so that it retains integrity as a sonnet, rather than collapsing into atomized units. But the distinctive end-rhyme of the closing couplet is so strong, the words supporting it so similar, that it almost eclipses the sense of the lines: 'excess' and 'express' seem to be what the whole poem has been about, as indeed it turns out that it has: it is the pleasure Clare says he cannot articulate, not the scene itself.

The lines I've discussed here offer multiple examples of the way repeated sounds are picked up between and across lines, animating a form of meaning which is supplementary to the semantic sense of the words which contain it. The thematic gesture towards breadth and openness in the scene, found in that early repetition ('wide'/'wider', ll. 1–2), indicates the intense suggestiveness of ideas of repetition for the sonnet's interest in unbounded vision, and its delighted resistance to itself being enclosed. A discussion of the repetition in the poem thus might well have followed a different path; that it has not done so is explicitly not a resistance of the historically grounded reading which this sonnet so obviously invites, but simply a desire to establish for this book a habit of attending to sound as much as sense in texts. Even such a delimited reading might go much further: there are other repetitious sound effects on which I have not dwelt; the paradox of close reading is that the more the poem surrenders, the further the reader moves from the possibility of anything approaching a comprehensive analysis. And readings like this depend on a kind of attention which might, but probably doesn't, consciously register on anything other than an intensive reading. Barbara Strang is attentive to the intense subtlety of Clare's writing when she points out that 'Clare's superficially simple use of language can be delicate and deceptive, full of complexity and sleight-of-hand as to pass generally unnoticed'.[70] J. Middleton Murry describes it as 'unobtrusive'.[71] The subtlety both invoke is, of course, the glory of the sonnet here discussed: these are effects which operate upon us both within and without the context of semantic sense. They thus allow Clare to suggest the very sublimity he attempts to communicate, without the deliberate articulation which would necessarily fail: *language* fails the pleasure to express, but the sound of the poem effectively gestures to a transcendent sense of pleasure, beyond the grasp of explicit meaning and linguistic containment, but dependent upon the scene the sonnet *can* describe. This is the power that sonic repetition (unobtrusive rhyming *sounds* in this example, rather than just more obvious *schemes*) exercises in poetry. Repetition has its own economy which can support and meet the challenge other forms of meaning in a poem might reach towards, and writers in the Romantic Period exploited this economy to its fullest potential.

Clare's 'A Scene' combines a recognizable sonnet rhyme scheme with multiple instances of rebellious, subtle micro-rhymes. Milton's infamous headnote to *Paradise Lost* rejected more schematic rhyme altogether, as rhyme for rhyme's sake, and in doing so inaugurated multiple critical responses which have illuminated what might be possible through careful attention to forms of rhyme in particular works. Milton declares that his poem's measure 'is English heroic verse without rhyme', declaring rhyme to be productive of 'vexation, hindrance, and constraint'.[72] Rejecting 'the jingling sound of like endings', Milton asserts that in his great work, the 'neglect then of rime so little is to be taken for a defect, though it may seem so perhaps to vulgar readers, that it rather is to be esteemed an example set, the first in English, of ancient liberty recovered to heroic poem from the troublesome and modern bondage of rhyming.'[73] This statement's long tradition of citation has tended to focus on Milton's rejection of 'bondage' as a form of political liberty (a discourse which has been of real significance to Wordsworth scholarship too). But as O. B. Hardison has pointed out, there is more to it than this: Milton's pre-eminent concern in his own account is to avoid the same compulsion to include words merely for the sake of rhyme which Croker diagnoses in Keats; to avoid, that is, 'Changes forced on the poem by the need to preserve rhyme [which] falsify the words breathed into the poet by the Muse [...because] they make truth into a lie'.[74] Here, we find a vital interest in ideas of poetic sincerity and its relationship to rhyme which is central to the ultimate argument of this book.

---

[70] Barbara Strang, 'John Clare's Language', Appendix to *John Clare: The Rural Muse*, ed. R. K. R. Thornton (Ashington: Carcanet and the Mid Northumberland Arts Group, 1982), pp. 159-73 (p. 159).

[71] 'J. Middleton Murry on Clare and Wordsworth' [1924], in Mark Storey, ed., *Clare: The Critical Heritage* (London and Boston: Routledge & Kegan Paul, 1973), pp. 359-64 (p. 361).

[72] See *Paradise Lost*, pp. 38-9.   [73] *Paradise Lost*, p. 39.

[74] O. B. Hardison, Jr, *Prosody and Purpose in the English Renaissance* (Baltimore: Johns Hopkins University Press, 1989), p. 272.

Yet attention to the significance of Milton's avoidance of rhyme is counterbalanced elsewhere in the critical tradition by attention to his deployment of it: the enrichment of his verse by multiple, subtle internal rhymes. Christopher Ricks, for example, observes that 'it has long been remarked that *Paradise Lost* deploys rhymes, though fairly infrequently, with great skill';[75] Lawrence McCauley points out that, 'when one begins to examine the sound patterning in *Paradise Lost*, a systematic use of rhyming sounds is apparent'. He argues that, ultimately, *Paradise Lost* 'does not rhyme by rhyming subtly, irregularly, and in a variety of thematically and structurally meaningful ways', and that through numerous and subtle uses of rhyme, Milton alludes, for a fallen reader, to what might be transcendent: 'in his rhyming practices he strives, by various and subtle means, to give us an imaginative sense of a harmony that is beyond our knowing'.[76] These readings illustrate some of the many varieties of rhyme which the ear of the attentive listener might ascertain, more or less self-consciously, as well as the subtleties which might underpin the use of such rhyming. But beyond acting as an exemplar of some of the nuances of what it might mean for a poem to rhyme, Milton's rhyming is significant here insofar as he is a major influence upon Wordsworth, who in turn deliberates quite explicitly upon the utility and limitations of rhyming and repetition in verse. Numerous critics have explored the ways in which Wordsworth's verse exhibits a similar care for the poetic effects of rhyme, even when he ostensibly renounces it in his pronouncements upon poetical language.[77] This book will look closely at some examples of repetition within Wordsworth's work, in order to argue that such uses are far more than mere ornaments; that they are in fact the very feature which allow what Wordsworth considers to be 'sincere' verse.

---

[75] Christopher Ricks, 'John Milton: Sound and Sense in *Paradise Lost*', in *The Force of Poetry* (Oxford: Oxford University Press 1984; 2002), pp. 60–79 (p. 71).

[76] Lawrence H. McCauley, 'Milton's Missing Rhymes', *Style*, 28.2 (Summer 1994), 242–59 (p. 243; p. 249 and *passim*; p. 255; p. 257). McCauley is also convincing on the ways the poem is full of 'figures of narrative and thematic equivalence', and of 'thematic equivalence...manifested as textual echo' (p. 243), echoes which John Hollander has described as 'basic to the fabric of *Paradise Lost*, and... elements in what seems to be the poem's memory of itself.' John Hollander, *The Figure of Echo: A Mode of Allusion in Milton and After* (Berkeley and Los Angeles: University of California Press, 1981), p. 51.

[77] Listing examples of such a pervasive aspect of Wordsworth scholarship seems slightly superfluous, though by way of instance, one might take Susan Wolfson's *Formal Charges*, which set out to 'refresh...interest' in 'poetic form', understood to incorporate 'stanzas, verses, metres, rhymes, and the line' (all of these, of course, pertinent to a discussion repetition in verse): see Wolfson, pp. 1–3.

2
The Workings of Repetition in Romantic-Period Poetry

Repetition, Metre, and Form

Poetry is laden with significant recapitulative effects beyond rhyming sounds. Much of what is true of rhyme is true also of the repetitions inherent in the rhythms and forms of poetry. Standing in a long tradition of scholarship examining how rhythm and metre act upon readers,[1] Derek Attridge argues that

> Tension arises out of the twin tendencies of language, towards variety and towards regularity: the voice...enjoys its freedom to range over a finely gradated scale of intensities, timbres, pitches, and durations, but also feels the pull towards simple patterns and repetitions...metre marks off the language of poetry from the language of daily existence by formalising and controlling this natural tension.[2]

Elsewhere, Attridge proposes that 'reading always entails a continuous process of prediction, continuously modified as expectations are met, intensified, or disappointed.'[3] Detailing the sources of such anticipation and satisfaction, Attridge considers repetition, suggesting that 'the marked recurrence of an item of language in a poem repeats not just a series of sounds but also a meaning or series of meanings.'[4] But whilst repetition of meaning might be implied in such instances, it is not necessarily the principal effect. In his discussion of lyric patterning, Jonathan Culler argues for the seductive tendency of sound patterns:

---

[1] See for a romantic-period example Coleridge's description of 'the EFFECTS of metre': 'they act powerfully, though themselves unnoticed. Where, therefore, correspondent food and appropriate matter are not provided for the attention and feelings thus roused, there must needs be a disappointment felt; like that of leaping in the dark from the last step of a stair-case, when we had prepared our muscles for a leap of three or four.' (Samuel Taylor Coleridge, *Biographia Literaria*, ed. James Engell and W. Jackson Bate, 2 vols (London and Princeton, NJ: Routledge & Kegan Paul and Princeton University Press, 1983), ii, 66.)

[2] Derek Attridge, *The Rhythms of English Poetry* (London: Longman, 1982), p. 18.

[3] Derek Attridge, *Moving Words: Forms of English Poetry* (Oxford: Oxford University Press, 2013; 2015), p. 31.

[4] *Moving Words*, p. 32.

Nietzsche observes that 'even the wisest among us occasionally becomes a fool for rhythm—if only insofar as we feel a thought to be *truer* if simply because it has a metrical form and presents itself with a divine hop, skip, and jump.' Sound patterning gives lyric utterances authority that is neither justified not justifiable[.][5]

Moreover, variation *within* repetition turns out to be the most interesting aspect of the device, to which poets are acutely sensitive. This is again relevant to rhyme as much as metre, of course, but metrical *ir*regularity is especially necessary to vital verse. As I. A. Richard puts it, 'Verse in which we constantly get exactly what we are ready for and no more... is merely toilsome and tedious':[6] excessively rigid adherence to a metrical scheme results in flat, dull poetry. However, verse which is highly regular can engender a powerful effect from small deviations: even Pope's apparently meticulous regularity wriggles with minute rhythmic variations once we look closely enough.[7] At the other end of the scale, to turn again to Attridge, it is possible to argue that poetic language which 'fails to make any contact at all with an underlying rhythm... puts itself equally out of reach of the dynamic momentum afforded by sequences of tension and relaxation', which are what constitute poetry in his account.[8] This in turn recalls Roman Jakobsen's statement on the poetic function of language: according to Jakobsen, linguistic choices are made from the language available, choices 'produced on the base of equivalence, similarity and dissimilarity, synonymity and antonymity, while the combination, the build up of the sequence, is based on contiguity.'[9] Linguistic choices are made because terms in a sequence are in *some way* equivalent, but also in *some ways* different; this results in an effect of repetition with variation, and in Jakobsen's account, when this function is 'the dominant, determining function', the text can claim to be poetry.[10] This book will argue that the balance between similarity and dissimilarity is something which fascinates Wordsworth in his apprehension of experience, and it is something he embodies in the verse which represents that experience, according to his own criteria. Ideas of recapitulation—of saying things again, but possibly differently, depending on current perspective—are enlisted by Wordsworth as he tries to understand how revising or revisiting, and the changes they make to the apprehension of experience, can best be articulated.

Literary form governs instances of repetition including rhyme and rhythm within individual poems, as well as being standard across time, and variation from convention is often the site of interest or tension. The basic points made so

---

[5] Culler, p. 134.   [6] 'Rhythm and Metre', p. 128.
[7] See for example Attridge, *Rhythms of English Poetry*, pp. 352–6.
[8] *Rhythms of English Poetry*, p. 309.
[9] Roman Jakobsen, 'Closing Statement: Linguistics and Poetics', in Thomas Sebeok, ed., *Style in Language* (New York and London: The Technology Press of Massachusetts Institute of Technology and John Wiley and Sons, 1960), pp. 350–88 (p. 358).
[10] Jakobsen, p. 356.

far about repetition and rhyme and rhythm are relevant also to form; it would seem superfluous to repeat them. However, it is important here to acknowledge the significance of form to understandings of Romanticism specifically. Wordsworth's radical appeal to 'spontaneous overflow' in the 'Preface' to *Lyrical Ballads* almost invites the type of knowing, hyperbolic appraisal delivered by Hazlitt's infamous 1818 lecture on the 'new school', which declared that 'rhyme was looked upon as a relic of the feudal system, and regular metre was abolished along with regular government.'[11] Matthew Arnold's even more famous judgement of Wordsworth's verse ('It might seem that Nature not only gave him the matter for his poem, but wrote his poem for him. He has no style'[12]) further cemented the reputation of Wordsworth as having abdicated deliberative, poetic control over the content of verse in favour of the unformalized outpourings of emotion. Yet Stuart Curran resoundingly has put to bed the 'entrenched belief that Romanticism was inherently suspicious of, even hostile to, traditional literary forms', instead illuminating the rich and deep attention poets in the period paid to generic and formal issues, resulting in daring and sophisticated appropriations of literary conventions, allied with ideological preoccupations which temper and develop extant formal traditions to complex aesthetic effect.[13] The renewed interest in form has led to other shifts in the way Romanticism is understood.[14] In particular, the idea that poems from the Romantic Period are 'energized and subtilized by their consciousness of themselves as poems'[15] has become familiar and widely accepted:

> Much of the formal innovation in Romantic poetry is due to indirection, which we might define for the moment as a poetical playing with the sequencing of ideas... Even though the unit of the poem's script is the line... words often work 'versus' or against the linear notions of sequence of the line in which they appear.[16]

---

[11] William Hazlitt, 'On the Living Poets', in *Lectures on the English Poets: Delivered at the Surrey Institution* (London: Taylor and Hessey, 1818), pp. 283–331 (p. 321; p. 319).

[12] Matthew Arnold, 'Preface' to *Poems of Wordsworth* (London: Macmillan 1879), pp. v–xxvi (p. xxii).

[13] Stuart Curran, *Poetic Form and British Romanticism* (New York and Oxford: Oxford University Press, 1986; 1989), p. 5; p. 4, and *passim*.

[14] See for example Wolfson, *Formal Charges*; Curran, *Poetic Form and British Romanticism*; Michael O'Neill, *Romanticism and the Self-Conscious Poem* (Oxford: Clarendon Press, 1997); Tilottama Rajan and Julia M. Wright, eds, *Romanticism, History and the Possibility of Genre* (Cambridge: Cambridge University Press, 1998); David H. Richter, ed., *Ideology and Form in Eighteenth-Century Literature* (Lubbock: Texas Tech University Press, 1999); Isobel Armstrong, *The Radical Aesthetic* (Oxford: Blackwell, 2000), or Alan Rawes, ed., *Romanticism and Form* (Houndsmills: Palgrave Macmillan, 2007).

[15] O'Neill, p. xv.

[16] Paul M. Curtis, 'Romantic Indirection', in *Romanticism and Form*, pp. 1–22 (pp. 3–4).

Because they call to one another, instances of repetition (whichever shape they take) are profoundly available for this kind of indirection, pulling against the forms which constitute the poems that contain them. In this climate of enhanced self-awareness, poets play with the possibilities of repetition within form. Clare mimics the literal form of a bird's nest he observes, through the intricate, repetitive weaving of a poem's formal characteristics.[17] Susan Wolfson concludes that in Blake's 'To Summer', repetitions within the stanzaic form 'shape a phonic version' of the wreath his poem describes.[18] Wolfson also argues that in Coleridge's 'To Asra', 'In the still-visible Shakespearean scheme, we see formal limits impending and resisted—end-rhymes impressed by a flux of internal verbal repetitions and repetitive participles, as well as three enjambments into the preposition *Of*—all enacting the "overflowing" of Love.'[19] Here, types of repetition cause the poem to hover suggestively between category and originality; Wolfson goes on to argue that too heavy an occurrence of repetitious effects within a poem can function almost to obliterate the poem's form. In Keats's sonnet, 'The day is gone', she finds that the poem's 'very form reports the initial crisis with repetitions and anaphora that all but overwhelm the structure of the rhyme'.[20] Perhaps these effects are the 'Sandals more interwoven and complete | To fit the naked foot of Poesy' which Keats implores should be sought; playing across form like this might break and re-make the 'chains' Keats regrets in 'If by dull rhymes'. It is specifically the 'ear industrious, and attention meet' which Keats decrees must be put to work: a responsibility to listen carefully to the possibilities within 'sound and syllable', opening up the potential of forms of repetition within poetry; notably, Keats teases all of this out in an ultra-self-conscious sonnet about sonneteering.[21] Repetitions cooperate with form in each of these examples to heighten the sense of poetic self-consciousness; to draw attention to the possibilities of 'Romantic' poetry.

Recapitulation in the Act of Reading

Whilst rhyme, rhythm, and form are the preeminent examples of repetition in poetry, verse exploits a far wider range of recapitulative effects. One of these is the type of consonance which does not really exist in any material sense, but which our ears nonetheless identify. An example is the impact created when we attend to one word, but hear another altogether (as well, or instead), not in the sense of semantic ambiguity, but in a specifically aural effect. In such cases, the different aural phenomena bounce off each other, inducing a sense of recapitulation

---

[17] See Sarah Houghton-Walker, 'Forms of Repetition in "The Robins Nest"', *Romanticism*, 26.2 (2020), 139–52.
[18] See *Formal Charges*, p. 41.   [19] *Formal Charges*, p. 176.   [20] *Formal Charges*, p. 173.
[21] 'If by dull rhymes our English must be chained', in *John Keats: The Complete Poems*, ed. Miriam Allott (London: Longman, 1970), pp. 521–2.

through a type of echo, or doubled sound (we listen, and listen again to the alternative version). Homophones obviously can function in this way; a more sophisticated example of the effect is Garrett Stewart's 'transegmental drift', the outcome created when a phoneme becomes shared aurally between adjacent words. As well as forming the type of echo-effect I have just described, transegmental drift frequently creates supplementary rhyme, sometimes where none more obviously existed before, and sometimes when it did. Stewart points to the playfully serious interest of J. L. Austin in the possibility of reading 'iced ink' as 'I stink'; for Stewart, this is 'an extreme case' of a more common phenomenon: 'Poetic devices—rhyme, assonance, euphony—thrive ordinarily on something more like a middle ground, a hovering aural dispersion.' This is more than a simple ambiguity, because in literary texts, the blurring of words 'may operate as a more subliminal blending, a supple overlap without risk of lexical breakdown'; what emerges is 'a friction that may at any moment thaw the iced fixity of scripted lexemes.'[22] The reformings of sounds Stewart recognizes (which he finds occurring throughout the canon) can modify semantic meanings initially drawn, usually through the accretion or literal repetition of ideas or sense; in hearing something in two ways (on one level or another), the ear hears the same thing twice. The results are '[s]yntactically seditious, lexically anarchic: an arc of echo across unbonded, nonconfederate syllables—contaminating in the process that bastion of conservative poetics, the regularized forms of metered rhyme.'[23] Therefore, one must re-listen, even in the original moment of listening: this is recapitulation forced on the reader in the most understated manner.

Stewart describes many ways in which transegmental drifting occurs across lines, recalling words and parts of words.[24] In the examples he lists, with astonishing frequency, both of the options latent within the word-sounds are semantically relevant to the context in which they are found. Finding this to be a general feature of poetic language since Milton, Stewart cites Donald Wesling's work on modernist poetics to argue that the Romantic Period is of particular relevance to his study.[25] Noting that Wordsworth, Keats, Shelley, and Coleridge share a 'Romantic instinct for phonetic iteration',[26] he examines the momentary and meaningful complexities of a movement between 'sole self' and 'soul's elf' in Keats's 'Ode to a Nightingale'. Here, Stewart notes, 'an audition of the phrase explores in effect the underside of just the sort of critique leveled by Donald Reiman at "repetition of sounds" in even the "greatest poems" of Keats and Shelley'.[27] In this example, the centrality of repetition to later Romantic poetry is both recognized and rehabilitated from the negative connotations it sometimes has borne. But Stewart is most interested in what happens within the reading body. He remains constantly aware of the process of reading as something visual

---

[22] Stewart, p. 5.   [23] Stewart, p. 66.   [24] Stewart, p. 77.   [25] Stewart, pp. 81–2.
[26] Stewart, p. 150.   [27] Stewart, p. 83.

and aural (an aurality which itself might be internal or vocalized), so, for example, is happy to concede that 'there is a kind of rhyme that honors only the requirements of the ear, not the recognition of the eye.'[28] Moreover, as he points out, 'although audible phonetic sounds do not result from a text that is not read out loud, the "inner" articulation—or "endophony"—involved in silent reading... actuates the whole range of phonemic differentials'.[29] In this way, decisions about which is the right way to read a line are not necessary in the way they might be if reading aloud, interpreting, or translating verse. Perhaps the reader need not even consciously register such effects in order for them to operate at least to some degree. But transegmental drift represents a type of characteristic which encourages the attentive reader to re-think what it was they thought they had already read, even in the act of reading it: 'cognition subtly diverges from direct semantic processing; inked letters enunciated to oneself often take thinking by surprise.'[30] A doubled, or recapitulated form of 'hearing' expands the possibility of the text's meaning.

Another example of an effect encouraging such reconsideration is found in Christopher Ricks's analysis of Wordsworth's line endings: 'Lineation in verse creates units which may or may not turn out to be units of sense; the "flicker of hesitation" ([Donald] Davie's term) as to what the unit is—a flicker resolved when we round the corner into the next line—can create nuances which are central to the poet's enterprise.'[31] Such effects as these similarly operate precisely through a process of revision, or recapitulation to oneself; the reader becomes aware that one construal of a word, line, or other unit is potentially disrupted, even if it is not necessarily displaced, by another construal. Just as we 'rhyme backwards', so these effects involve not just the retention of earlier elements of the lines of verse, but a re-visiting and thus a repetition of them in the light of the new information which might make us 'read' them differently, or multiply. They rely on an effect similar to that induced by Stephen Pinker's 'garden path' sentences (so named because they lead readers up semantic 'garden paths', encouraging them to parse wrongly, and thus to need to reconsider). In Pinker's analysis, such sentences, which *require* readerly revision due to their ambiguities in a context of one particular, intended meaning, are 'one of the hallmarks of bad writing'.[32] But for Wordsworth, this book will demonstrate, they are the opposite, enriching the possibilities of meaningfulness, because they do not oblige the reader to privilege one meaning over another.

Both Susan Stewart and Angela Leighton have described reading as always, inevitably involved in a type of recapitulation, rooting the experience in the aural

---

[28] Stewart, p. 67. [29] Stewart, p. 7. [30] Stewart, pp. 43–4.
[31] *The Force of Poetry*, p. 98.
[32] Stephen Pinker, *The Language Instinct: How the Mind Creates Language* (London: Penguin, 1994), p. 213.

dimension of the written word: Leighton applauds Stewart's assertion that 'we are always *recalling* sound with only some regard to an originating auditory experience',[33] because, she insists, literary texts make constant claim 'on our ability to recall, not only the words we have just read but the sounds such words might make, read again, or read elsewhere, or heard somehow echoing from voices conjured from other remembered texts.'[34] For Leighton, poetic language is particular, because although a cursory reading of texts with the eyes can offer 'a nearly instant comprehension of their meaning', the poetic text is particularly invested in the fact that,

> if I try to read 'with the ears,' struggling to adjust my senses accordingly, I find myself going slower, no longer following the lines to the end in order to discover what is meant, but attending instead to any number of incidental rhythmic effects and sound combinations. [...As Robert] Frost explains, although the written word 'oh' looks identical to the eye, to the ear it has a wide spectrum of sounds and senses depending on the length and emphases of its voicing...To read 'oh' silently on the page is, first to hear all those possibilities jostling for attention, then to work at determining the most likely.[35]

Here again, actively returning to a text for a second encounter is not necessary for 're-reading'. Relatedly, if we accept Stanley Fish's model, all reading is essentially recapitulative, involving multiple minute readjustments of understanding as the eye moves along the line. In Fish's account, as reading is a process which takes place in time, so the reader is *always* obliged—even though it might be in an almost imperceptible manner—to revise the sense they are making as the sentence or page proceeds. Thus, words are constantly re-read, whether or not the eye looks at them more than once. The process of reading is one in which 'the terms of the reader's relationship to the sentence undergo a profound change' as the sentence's different elements, and the range of possibilities each of those elements variously opens up or restricts, are encountered. Significantly, 'most of [this] is going on so close up, at such a basic, "preconscious" level of experience, that we tend to overlook it.'[36] Such an understanding of the experience of reading insists that reading itself is subtly but fundamentally and continually recapitulative.

Nonetheless, some critics have found the recapitulative effects involved in reading verse to be potentially negative. In a discussion of other, more literal returns, Isobel Armstrong argues that revisitings and reduplications can offer 'addition', but her account is more keenly aware of the fact that they might also

---

[33] Susan Stewart, *Poetry and the Fate of the Senses* (Chicago: University of Chicago Press, 2002), p. 68, cited in Leighton, *Hearing Things*, p. 6 (emphasis original).
[34] *Hearing Things*, p. 6.   [35] *Hearing Things*, p. 2; pp. 6–7.
[36] Stanley E. Fish, *Self-Consuming Artifacts: The Experience of Seventeenth Century Literature* (Berkeley and Los Angeles: University of California Press, 1972), p. 385; p. 390.

prompt 'destruction': for Armstrong, effects which cause readers to look backwards can destroy the initial comprehension, by replacing or correcting it, as 'Repetition transforms meaning'.[37] Yet Ricks celebrates Wordsworth's ability to hold his reader in an interpretative suspension, and Garrett Stewart's focus convincingly remains firmly on a sense of supplement, in a way that might settle some of Armstrong's misgivings: 'Rethinking is not revision; the "last word" on a set of lines does not supplant, only subdues, our first impression; what *is* is not necessarily what was'.[38] These types of repetition in poetry do not over-write; it isn't like stepping in exactly the same footprint so that the most recent impression is the final or only impression. Rather, recapitulation enriches and deepens; perhaps in its resistance to conclusion it might even gesture to the sublime. The effect is related to that described by Eric Griffiths as the 'excellent awkwardness' of heterotonic rhyme: rhyme pairs with differing stress patterns can serve to 'outline the edges of the sublime and feel for a reality beyond our representations just by attending to the reality *of* our representations.'[39] Repetition does the same thing, by drawing attention to itself, and its own inadequacy (there would no need to repeat if the initial iteration had fulfilled its obligations perfectly). Kate Armstrong has argued that visual art can 'illustrate how that which is represented can be repeated to the point where it can actually transcend its representation and gesture to the unrepresentable', so that 'repetition introduces notions of the absent transcendent'.[40] It will become clear that the forms of repetition encountered within Wordsworth's poetry sometimes function in the same way, nodding in their repetitiveness towards a sublime fullness which could not ever adequately be transcribed.

Repetition between and across Works

So far, the attention of this chapter has been on recapitulative devices and effects within particular texts, but others are associated rather with the direct relationships between and across texts. The extensive Romantic scholarship which has explored ideas of influence, for example, raises another of repetition's ghosts. Such influence has been advanced as antagonistic in the dominant anxious model, propounded by Harold Bloom and Walter Jackson Bate,[41] but it can also be amicable, and embraced. Robert Douglas-Fairhurst points out that Bloom's

---

[37] *Language as Living Form*, p. 37.   [38] Stewart, p. 39.
[39] Eric Griffiths, 'Blanks, misgivings, fallings from us', in Katy Price, ed., *The Salt Companion to Peter Robinson* (Cambridge: Salt, 2007), pp. 55–82 (p. 4).
[40] Kate Armstrong, p. 9.
[41] Harold Bloom, *The Anxiety of Influence: A Theory of Poetry* (Oxford: Oxford University Press, 1973; 1997); W. Jackson Bate, *The Burden of the Past and the English Poet* (London: Chatto & Windus, 1971).

'understanding of composition as private trauma bypasses...those forms of memory which are willing to confront the truth of antecedents without revisionary flinching'.[42] It also ignores those engagements with extant texts which intend to be productive and friendly; a walking in another's footsteps as an aid to progress, rather than a worrying about the fit of second-hand boots. Writing about art history, and listing a vocabulary which evokes a complex and active engagement between influence and influenced, Michael Baxendall decisively refutes Bloom's model, describing it as 'shifty', and arguing instead that '"Influence" is a curse of art criticism primarily because of its wrong-headed grammatical prejudice about who is the agent and who the patient...If one says that X influenced Y it does seem that one is saying that X did something to Y rather than that Y did something to X. But...If we think of Y rather than X as the agent, the vocabulary is much richer and more attractively diversified.'[43]

Beyond this provocative idea, amongst the library shelves we also find more playful copying, which might tip into parody, or outright plagiarism or forgery: allusive, influenced and copied works exist on a spectrum whose gradations can be hard to discern. Plagiaristic copy is relatively easy to distinguish, in that 'the alluder hopes that the reader will recognize something, the plagiarist that the reader will not'.[44] Other forms of influence can be trickier to categorize; the criteria by which they might be judged are complicated. In his 'Letter about Mallarme', Valéry touches on their dominance and complexities: 'No word comes easier or oftener to the critic's pen than the word *influence*, and no vaguer notion can be found among all the vague notions that compose the phantom armoury of aesthetics. Yet there is nothing in the critical field that should be of greater philosophical interest or prove more rewarding to analysis than the progressive modification of one mind by the work of another.'[45] At one extreme, it is as Emerson declared not possible for any text to be 'perfectly unborrowed',[46] and the twentieth century did much to insist on the inherently quotational character of language itself. Robert Macfarlane's *Original Copy* observes that, in its most famous articulation, the idea of repetition *with difference* is central to the discourse of inescapable repetition:

---

[42] Robert Douglas-Fairhurst, *Victorian Afterlives: The Shaping of Influence in Nineteenth-Century Literature* (Oxford: Oxford University Press, 2002), p. 39.

[43] Michael Baxendall, *Patterns of Intention: On the Historical Explanation of Pictures* (New Haven and London: Yale University Press, 1985), p. 59.

[44] Christopher Ricks, *Allusion to the Poets* (Oxford: Oxford University Press, 2002), p. 1.

[45] Paul Valéry, 'Letter about Mallarmé', from *Leonardo, Poe, Mallarmé* [1956], in *The Collected Works of Paul Valéry*, ed. Jackson Matthews, 15 vols [1958–75], viii, trans. Malcolm Cowley and James R. Lawler (Princeton, NJ: Princeton University Press, 1972), 240–53 (p. 241), https://doi.org/10.1515/9781400873104, accessed 7 June 2022

[46] Emerson, cited in Robert Macfarlane, *Original Copy: Plagiarism and Originality in Nineteenth-Century Literature* (Oxford: Oxford University Press, 2007), p. 4.

Derrida coins the term *itérabilité* to describe the semantic drift which inevitably occurs between consecutive uses of the same text. His neologism exploits the derivation of the Latin verb *iterare* (meaning 'to repeat') from the Sanskrit word *itara* (meaning 'other'), an etymology which, Derrida notes, valuably emphasizes 'the logic which links repetition to alterity'. For Derrida, the repetition of a text inescapably involves its alteration: you can never step twice in the same poem, paragraph, or word.[47]

Creation in this context always turn out necessarily to be merely rearrangement, the making of verse inevitably to be merely recapitulation.[48]

Yet there is a fair distinction to be made between the general properties of language, and the deliberate or more passive engagement of writers with other, particular texts. Despite Coleridge's declaration that in his 'imaginative power' Wordsworth stood 'perfectly unborrowed and his own', the spectre of influence intrudes in the very same sentence, as Coleridge recognizes that Wordsworth 'stands nearest of all modern writers to Shakespear and Milton'.[49] Numerous studies have explored allusion in Wordsworth's writing, finding resonances with a range of other writers, and drawing a range of conclusions from them.[50] Not all the works alluded to are those of obvious canonical forebears. For example, Peter Manning has discussed the influence of the manuscript of Thomas Wilkinson's *Tours to the British Mountains*, to which 'The Solitary Reaper' is heavily indebted. (Wilkinson's text, which Wordsworth acknowledged as an influence on his poem, even includes the specific, haunting formulation, 'long after they were heard no more'.[51]) Susan Wolfson recasts the content of such moments of allusion or

---

[47] Macfarlane, p. 5.
[48] One might compare Gérard Genette's insistence that 'it is impossible to imitate a text *directly*; it can be imitated only indirectly, by practicing its style in another text... to imitate a text directly is... impossible because it is too easy, hence insignificant.' For Genette, 'direct imitation in literature or music, unlike what occurs in the visual arts, does not constitute a significant performance at all. Here, to reproduce is nothing, and imitating supposes a more complex operation, the completion of which raises imitation above mere reproduction: it becomes a new production'. (Gérard Genette, *Palimpsests: Literature in the Second Degree*, trans. Channa Newman and Claude Doubinsky (Lincoln: University of Nebraska Press, 1997), pp. 83–4.)
[49] *Biographia Literaria*, ii, 151.
[50] See most obviously Lucy Newlyn, *Coleridge, Wordsworth, and the Language of Allusion* (Oxford: Oxford University Press, 2001); Christopher Ricks, *Allusion to the Poets*, pp. 83–120; Robin Jarvis, *Wordsworth, Milton and the Theory of Poetic Relations* (New York: Palgrave Macmillan, 1991); Nicholas Roe, 'Wordsworth, Milton, and the Politics of Poetic Influence', *The Yearbook of English Studies*, 19 (1989), 112–26; Edwin Stein, *Wordsworth's Art of Allusion* (University Park: Pennsylvania State University Press, 1988), or more recently Richard S. Peterson, 'The Influence of Anxiety: Spenser and Wordsworth', *Studies in Romanticism*, 51.1 (Spring 2012), 77–88, or T. Somervell, 'Mediating Vision: Wordsworth's Allusions to Thomson's *Seasons* in *The Prelude*', *Romanticism*, 22.1 (2016), 48–60. The poet's allusions are also frequently noted by critics in the service of other central arguments (as in, for example, David Simpson's 'Minding the Poet's Trade', in *Wordsworth's Historical Imagination: The Poetry of Displacement* (New York: Methuen, 1987), pp. 25–42).
[51] See Peter J. Manning, *Reading Romantics: Texts and Context* (Oxford: Oxford University Press, 1990), pp. 243–54. For 'The Solitary Reaper', see *Poems, in Two Volumes, and Other Poems, 1800–1807*, ed. Jared Curtis (Ithaca: Cornell University Press, 1983), pp. 184–5.

reproduction as a form of memory, arguing that we don't necessarily need to understand textual memories as any different in type to 'real' ones: in the case of Wilkinson and 'The Solitary Reaper', for instance, 'The linked and imported material does not belie Wordsworth's mythology of recollection so much as collate poetic craft with an already textualized memory.'[52] Recapitulations of other writers' works might exist on a more minute scale than such echoes of recognized utterance. Demonstrating Wordsworth's 'Descriptive Sketches' to be derivative of Beattie's *Minstrel*, Jonathan Wordsworth argues that 'Resemblances go beyond paraphrase... to presumably unconscious repetition of sound'.[53] And, in a more straightforward way, the relationship between William and Dorothy Wordsworth invokes another, related form of repetition between writers: of collaboration, and of mutual borrowing with consent.[54] There is no space here to enter fully into the debate surrounding Wordsworth's use of other people's writing as a source of material, or to consider the various complexities of his allusions and borrowings; this book will focus mainly on lexical repetitions within particular works rather than the reconfigurings and reworkings of influential texts. However, it remains relevant to a bigger argument about the character and dominance of ideas of repetition in the period; repetition which results in the transformation of the original in some way, which might be more or less obvious (and therefore meaningful *because* of the awareness of its distinction from its origin) to the reader. The allusive or influencing process is fundamentally one of active recapitulation. As Lucy Newlyn puts it, '[i]nfluence is as much a process of revision as absorption... intertextual fluidity reflects the collaborative nature of Wordsworth's interaction with the audiences—past, present, and future—he imagines and addresses.'[55] The notion that allusion is a form of repetition or revision which accommodates as an inherent part of it the idea of difference, renders it essentially a form of translation.

Probed in Europe in the later seventeenth and eighteenth centuries most obviously (if far from exclusively) by Dryden and Pope, questions of translation continued to exercise minds through the 1790s and into the nineteenth century, a preoccupation exemplified in Alexander Fraser Tytler's *Essay on the Principles of Translation* (1791), or Schleiermacher's 'On the Different Methods of Translation' (1813). Denis Diderot's 1751 declaration of the impossibility of perfect poetic translation in his 'Letter on the Deaf and Dumb' ('I used to believe, like everyone

---

[52] Susan Wolfson, 'Wordsworth's Craft', in Stephen Gill, ed., *The Cambridge Companion to Wordsworth* (Cambridge, Cambridge University Press, 2003), pp. 108–24 (p. 113).

[53] Jonathan Wordsworth, *William Wordsworth: The Borders of Vision* (Oxford: Clarendon Press, 1982), p. 311.

[54] See Lucy Newlyn, *William & Dorothy Wordsworth: All in Each Other* (Oxford: Oxford University Press, 2013), *passim*.

[55] Lucy Newlyn, '"The noble living and the noble dead": Community in *The Prelude*', in *The Cambridge Companion to Wordsworth*, pp. 55–69 (pp. 60–1).

else, that one poet could be translated by another: that is an error'[56]) anticipates the position of twentieth-century New Criticism, as well as prefiguring Shelley's more contemporaneous insistence on 'the vanity of translation; it were as wise to cast a violet into a crucible that you might discover the formal principle of its colour and odour, as seek to transfuse from one language into another the creations of a poet'.[57] Shelley conducts this discussion specifically in a context of the aural quality of poetry, and what he defines as its repetitious character: 'the language of poets has ever affected a certain uniform and harmonious recurrence of sound, without which it were not poetry, and which is scarcely less indispensable to the communication of its influence, than the words themselves'.[58] This is a turn towards the musical nature of poetic language which returns us to the idea that the semantic and the aural properties of language are separable: that the aural properties can function 'musically', simultaneous with the accretion of semantic meaning. For Coleridge, the difficulty of translation inheres as much in organization as in phonetics. Coleridge's *Biographia* asserts that the language of poetry depends upon the ability of the poet to 'select and arrange his words':

> We do not adopt the language of a class by the mere adoption of such words exclusively, as that class would use, or at least understand; but likewise by following the *order*, in which the words of such men are wont to succeed each other. Now this order, in the intercourse of uneducated men, is distinguished from the diction of their superiors in knowledge and power, by the greater *disjunction* and *separation* in the component parts of that, whatever it be, which they wish to communicate. There is a want of that prospectiveness of mind, that *surview*, which enables a man to foresee the whole of what he is to convey, appertaining to any one point; and by this means so to subordinate and arrange the different parts according to their relative importance, as to convey it at once, and as an organized whole.[59]

According to this understanding, adequate translation of poetry is impossible, because the meaning of the 'organized whole' depends upon its consolidated totality, so that 'it would be scarcely more difficult to push a stone out from the pyramids with the bare hand, than to alter a word, or the position of a word, in Milton or Shakespeare, (in their most important works at least) without making the poet say something else, or something worse, than he does say.'[60] Ideas of originality, individuality, and genius circulating within the discourse of what we

---

[56] Denis Diderot, 'Lettre sur les sourds et muets' [1751], cited in Murray Krieger, *Ekphrasis: The Illusion of the Natural Sign* (Baltimore: Johns Hopkins University Press, 1992; 2019), p. 152.

[57] P. B. Shelley, 'A Defence of Poetry', repr. in *Shelley's Poetry and Prose*, ed. Donald H. Reiman and Sharon B. Powers (New York: W. W. Norton, 1977), pp. 478–508 (p. 484).

[58] Shelley, *Defence*, p. 484. [59] *Biographia Literaria*, ii, 58 (emphases original).

[60] *Biographia Literaria*, i, 23.

now call Romanticism might further indicate an inevitable debasement of translation, dependent as it is on a prior inspiration or source. Yet despite all this, the same Romantic writers were keenly engaged in translating a range of sources, and in reflecting on translation praxis.[61] Wordsworth was among them, and a later chapter of this book will argue that textual translation is conceived of by Wordsworth specifically as a form of revision, the poet deeply and self-consciously engaged in the technical demands, the advantages and limitations, of recapitulation.

Formal and thematic interests in recapitulation align in romantic-period verse in attention to issues of ekphrasis, itself a form of refined translation. Ekphrastic texts are inherently involved in the question of what it might mean to recapitulate an artwork in a different form (and, as that form is a poem, they adopt inherently repetitive devices like rhyme and metre to do so). Again, Shelley provides the most obvious example here, his self-aware, disputedly ironic 'Ozymandias' suffused in its form and content with ideas of repetition, quotation, translation, and persistence vs change; but the inevitably impossible premise of ekphrasis—the repetition of one artwork in another form—persistently declares its repetition to be inflected by difference: ekphrasis is essentially recapitulative, rather than 'merely' repetitious. Attention to the new life breathed into extant art through ekphrasis suggests some of the more fundamental implications of the discourse of recapitulation itself. An enquiry into ekphrasis, as Murray Krieger points out, 'goes to the very heart of the language—which is to say, the habit of metaphor—that, throughout its history, has shaped and directed our literary criticism.'[62]

Closely related to questions of translation in the period is this idea of metaphor. To remain with Shelley for now, his 1821 declaration of poetry as 'vitally metaphorical' depends on the idea that metaphor, instead of being a stale repetition, allows exactly a form of translation into an entirely new apprehension.[63] For Shelley, Jerold Hogle argues, poetry has its beginnings

> when the most primitive person uses 'language and gesture' to produce 'the image of the combined effect of... objects and his apprehension of them'. That primal moment is poetic because it is metaphorical. It is a transfer of something (a perception, itself metaphoric in being a transfer between reception and response) into something quite different (the verbalized image). Such a theory allows Shelley to make *deliberate* poetry, the reenactment of that earlier transfer,

---

[61] For further discussion of Romanticism and translation, see most obviously Timothy Webb, *The Violet in the Crucible: Shelley and Translation* (Oxford: Oxford University Press, 1976), and the wealth of critical response to Keats's 'On First Looking into Chapman's Homer'.

[62] Krieger, p. 3.   [63] Shelley, 'Defence', p. 482.

a transformation of existing forms of language into a re-envisioning of the world as we know it.[64]

This is precisely a recapitulation; a restatement via repetition. Shelley's famous conception echoes a sense previously articulated by Lowth's *Sacred Poetry of the Hebrews*, in the context of his discussion of metaphor and translation, that 'the associating principle is the true source of all figurative language'.[65] 'Poetical imagery', according to Lowth,

> frequently depends upon the use of certain terms, upon a certain association between words and things, which a translation generally perplexes, and very frequently destroys. This, therefore, is not to be preserved in the most literal and accurate version, much less in any poetical translation, or rather imitation[.][66]

Lowth's perception of association at the heart of the model thus moves the discussion of metaphor (a form of recapitulation, holding together both original and new version) into the realm of the conjunction, and the focus to an understanding of the connection between the two versions. Whilst Lowth's subject is scripture, a note to his text broadens the argument to encompass translation more generally, emphasizing the relevance of metaphorical language once more:

> It may be asserted of translations in general, and I am sure I have experienced the truth of the observation in this very attempt, that many of the minuter beauties of style are necessarily lost; a translator is scarcely allowed to intrude upon his author any figures or images of his own, and many which appear in the original must be omitted of course. Metaphors, synecdoches, and metonymies, are frequently untractable; the corresponding words would probably in a figurative sense appear harsh or obscure.[67]

The expression of the particular is rendered difficult if not impossible through the discrepancy in individual experience: metaphorical and other forms of translation are hampered by the need to express the autonomous self adequately (or 'sincerely'). This book will argue that it is by rendering individual experience through various forms of recapitulation that Wordsworth tries to attain poetic sincerity, and that it is by suggesting the interrelation of specific and general experience that repetition and conjunction are able to achieve it. Later chapters will return to Lowth, and his influence on Wordsworth in particular. This more introductory

---

[64] Jerrold E. Hogle, 'Language and Form', in Timothy Morton, ed., *The Cambridge Companion to Shelley* (Cambridge: Cambridge University Press), pp. 145–65 (p. 145).
[65] Robert Lowth, *Lectures on the Sacred Poetry of the Hebrews*, trans. G. Gregory, 2 vols (London: J. Johnson, 1787), i, 108, n. 4.
[66] Lowth, i, 182–3.   [67] Lowth, i, 182–3, n. 18.

chapter cannot aim to address the operation of translation, metaphor, and ekphrasis in any full sense, but they remain participants in a discourse of repetition which stridently declares their difference from an original; all, through the active demonstration of those differences, figure forth the complications behind their own functioning and thus become meaningful, and all three are of profound and explicit interest to Romantic poets.

In his *De Vera Religione*, written around 390, St Augustine described the necessarily chronological nature of linear verse:

> a metrical line is beautiful in its own kind although two syllables of that line cannot be pronounced simultaneously. The second is pronounced only after the first has passed, and such is the order of procedure to the end of the line, so that when the last syllable sounds, alone, unaccompanied by the sound of the previous syllables, it yet, as being part of the whole metrical fabric, perfects the form and metrical beauty of the whole.[68]

The way in which rhyme calls back to its corresponding sounds in a poem disrupts the solipsism Augustine attributes to individual words. The recapitulation rhyme demands (like that demanded by metre and form) creates expectations, whose fulfilment in turn creates networks across lines; it discovers connections retrospectively, which again spin filaments between disparate parts of a poem's language, binding it up into a less linear and far more sociable text than its flatness on the page might suggest. Poetic language is special because it is self-consciously aware of such possibilities, inviting us to listen for and to hear them as part of the purpose of the poem. Writing which does so too explicitly might become merely clumsy or tedious: it is often important to the success of repetition that it functions discreetly. Only in their perception (on some level) can the mind create the relationship of identity and difference between repetitions: as thinkers from Hume to Deleuze have argued, repetition doesn't change the object repeated at all; it alters instead something in the contemplating mind. But perception of the subtle recapitulations dwelling within verse is not always something of which we are conscious: as in music, the perception of the effects of poetry might be oblique, giving 'rise to some impression that registers as an expressive quality, rather than as explicit recognition of repetitiveness.'[69] This marks an important distinction between those repetitions which we might assume are supposed to be recognized, and those whose effects we might experience less self-consciously, though the picture is fundamentally complicated by the lack of any consensus about which

---

[68] St Augustine, *De Vera Religione*, XXII.42, cited in and trans. by A. D. Nuttall, *Two Concepts of Allegory* (New Haven and London: Yale University Press, 2007), p. 45.

[69] See Margulis, p. 35, and more generally her chapter 'From Acoustic to Perceived Repetition', which highlights significant cognitive responses to instances of repetition, and places them in a context of scientific study into the recognition (or otherwise) of such instances *as* repetitious.

instance might be which. Such perception remains ultimately personal, individual, and resistant to generalized analysis or tracking.

The potential scope of a study on different types of repetition is impossibly broad, and constantly tugs in new and alternative directions. Nonetheless, highlighting its powerful effects in a wide range of examples, this book contends that the presence and operation of repetition in Wordsworth's writing, even if variably discernible or interpretable in specific instances, is cumulatively compelling, and that it often sustains a particular function. Facing again the notion that repetition is impossible, because the representation draws attention to the fact that it is *not* the original or 'ideal', when Kierkegaard addresses the problem of the possibility of repetition, he concludes that consciousness itself originates in the collision between the ideal world and reality: without any distinction between ideal and real, things would repeat without variation, and consciousness would be arrested.[70] This is an important way of understanding the value of repetition which necessarily contains difference (not that Wordsworth formulates it in those explicit terms, though he explores similar terrain in 'The Thorn', and the note which he added to it). The repetition in which mimesis consists may have prompted Plato to banish 'poetical imitations' from his republic, but, in line with Kierkegaard's conclusion, this book argues that recapitulation is rehabilitated in Wordsworth's poetry, into the enabling condition of attending to the world, and that in its many textual forms it permits the expression of the results of that attention more adequately, or 'sincerely'. The fine textual detail of Wordsworthian repetition thus deserves a second look.

---

[70] See 'Constantine Constantius' [S. Kierkegaard], 'Repetition: An Essay in Experimental Psychology' [1843], in *Repetition and Philosophical Crumbs*, trans. M. G. Piety (Oxford: Oxford University Press, 2009), pp. 1–81, esp. p. 81. See also Attridge: 'meaning itself is grounded in repetition.' (*Moving Words*, p. 48.)

3
Contexts for Repetition in the Romantic Period

The recapitulative effects discussed thus far had been features of poetry, many of them exhaustively interrogated by theorists, long before the early nineteenth century, but various scholarly accounts have argued that a new relationship to repetition is specific to romantic-period verse. Just as McDonald's Wordsworth is self-consciously aware of the 'creative possibilities' of rhyme's repetition, so Isobel Armstrong asserts that, 'As with metaphor, Romantic repetition is often about the contradictory nature of repetition itself.' (In this sense, caught on the horns of contradiction, we can again glimpse the possibilities of repetitious techniques for poets reaching towards sublimity.) Armstrong declares repetition to be a fundamental aspect of the language of Romantic, idealist poetry, arguing that it is the very thing which 'renders the processes of a mind-creating world' with which its poets were concerned.[1] According to Armstrong, 'full meaning' is found in the relationship between two repeated things, grasped through a process of reflexive mental activity,

> accomplished by the simplest of things, repetition, within the line, the sentence, the paragraph, between episodes...For repetition acquires new meaning in the very act of being repetition...Repetition in a Romantic poem aims not to be a copy but a new thing every time it occurs: it *works* in the poem[.][2]

Persistently a feature of English verse since English verse existed, something particular happens in the Romantic Period to change writers' sensitivity to, and thus the possibilities of, repetition in poetry. This chapter will suggest some of the pertinent contextual factors which might be aspects of this change.

Repetition, Art, and the Mind

Aesthetic and philosophical ideas of repetition were under explicit pressure in the Romantic Period, as high art divorced mimetic repetition as its cornerstone, and

---

[1] *Language as Living Form*, p. 37; p. 34. [2] *Language as Living Form*, p. 35.

simultaneously liberated it from its Platonic inferiority complex. Plato inaugurated a tradition which understood artistic repetitions as increasingly debased: as each Platonic copy was inferior to its original, so each piece of mimetic art was inferior to its subject, a tradition revived and promoted in the early eighteenth century most obviously through the writings of Locke and Addison. Yet in the Romantic Period, new understandings of the artist, and therefore of art itself, had radically different implications. In 1770, Joshua Reynolds's third *Discourse* argued against 'mere imitation', asserting instead that 'the whole beauty and grandeur of the art consists' in 'being able to get above all singular forms, local customs, particularities and details of every kind.' Here, specific details function only to 'catch the sense and to divide the attention'. Being 'enabled to distinguish the accidental deficiencies, excrescences, and deformities of things, from their general figures', the true artist 'makes out an abstract idea of their forms more perfect than any one original'.[3] This argument finds the necessarily specific instance in the artwork only to be truly artistic—or truly 'true'—if it manages somehow to identify and represent that which transcends, by recognizing, the general. This of course reaches back again partly to the Platonic ideal. But Reynold's idea of a form 'more perfect than any one original' also depends on the capacity *of the artist* to discern what is common: to enter into an imaginatively active and discriminatory relationship with repetition. The same tension is found in Wordsworth's depiction of past events which are both unique and habitual, and in the revived memories of previous experience; later chapters of this book will look more closely at the operation and effects of this central negotiation in his work.

Beyond and before any particular content or form in which content might be expressed, the construction of Romantic models of the mind, and their implications for the representation of the world in art, is principally founded on changes to the understanding of the mind's essentially repetitive functioning. When Hume belittles the imagination in his *Treatise of Human Nature*, he does it in a form of words which emphasizes the necessity of repetition, in a mimetic sense, to its operation:

> neither the ideas of the memory nor imagination, neither the lovely nor faint ideas can make their appearance in the mind, unless their correspondent impressions have gone before to prepare the way for them...our second principle [concerns] *the liberty of the imagination to transpose and change its ideas*...in poems and romances...Nature there is totally confounded, and nothing mention'd but winged horses, fiery dragons, and monstrous giants.[4]

---

[3] See Joshua Reynolds, *Discourses on Art*, ed. Robert R. Wark (San Marino: The Huntingdon Library and Art Gallery, 1959), p. 41; p. 44; p. 50; p. 44.

[4] Hume, p. 12.

Relegating the imagination to the inferior occupation of jumbling up and rearranging actual memories of sensory experiences, both the memory and the imagination here clearly depend upon repetitions of the world in the mind of the artist. Charting the shift from Enlightenment 'mirror' to Romantic 'lamp', M. H. Abrams famously summarizes the radical transformation under which eighteenth-century ideas of the imagination were overturned:

> In any period, the theory of mind and the theory of art tend to be integrally related... for the representative eighteenth-century critic, the perceiving mind was a reflector of the external world... and the resulting art work was itself comparable to a mirror presenting a selected and ordered image of life. By substituting a projective and creative mind and, consonantly, an expressive and creative theory of art, various romantic critics reversed the basic orientation of all aesthetic philosophy.[5]

Abrams delineates the ways in which this astonishing transformation was manifest in the minds of critics and artists, forming 'an integral part of a corresponding change in popular epistemology'.[6] At the level of theory of mind, a specifically Romantic transition inflected the repetitions fundamental to the idea of art, according to the new conception of the imagination. Hence Paul de Man can declare that, for Wordsworth, 'While "fancy" depends upon a relationship between mind and nature, "imagination" is defined by the power of its language precisely not to remain imitatively and repetitively true to sense perception'.[7] Yet of course to some extent figurative art retained a hold on basically mimetic forms, reflecting the world even though now more obviously shaping it according to the will of the poet. That ideas of mimetic (essentially repetitive) art and eighteenth-century theories of the repeating mind give way to the creative imagination which privileges originality, might seem to diminish the value of repetition. This account does not set out to concern itself with the theoretical privilege of original or copy or to examine the stages along a trajectory which witnessed changing attitudes to both: all of these have been well explored elsewhere. Rather, it raises the possibilities that literal repetition might offer, *within* this context.

A variation on the idea of multiple copies is found in the repeated experience of an artwork by an observer. The Enlightenment cultivated the conditions for the widespread possibility of such a form of repetition in terms of visual art, through the expansion in the number of galleries and museums, for instance; via the contemporary popularity of the kind of house tour which takes Elizabeth Bennett to Pemberley long before she is its mistress; and, in terms of text, in the increasing production and dissemination of affordable print (whether via

---

[5] Abrams, p. 69.   [6] Abrams, p. 57.
[7] Paul de Man, *The Rhetoric of Romanticism* (New York: Columbia University Press, 1984), p. 53.

re-reading or re-hearing[8]). During the eighteenth century, reception theories which identify the reader or observer as the producer of the 'meaning' of an artwork, a meaning which is correspondingly individual, became established parts of aesthetic discourse. These can be traced back to an earlier eighteenth-century argument that a moment in time revisited immediately before or afterwards would be different; they announce the idea that there is no single apprehension of any given work, but multiple, potentially differing apprehensions, depending on the context and situation (or 'cognitive preconditions') of the individual doing the apprehending.[9] In this sense, repetition allows for a challenging but liberating sense that a repeat of an encounter will not necessarily lead to a repeat of experience, in another example of the capacity for repetition to contain variation which underscores its utility to Wordsworthian sincerity.

The burgeoning technological progress of the long eighteenth century, which facilitated mass production of objects identical to the eye, meets with these questions of mind and art most obviously in the twentieth-century work of Walter Benjamin. Benjamin's familiar argument is that the 'authority of the object' is lost through the process of mechanical reproduction: authenticity is abandoned when an art object is untethered from its proper position in time and space and situated away from its historical context and accumulative histories, as the reproduction 'permit[s] the reproduction to meet the beholder or listener in his own particular situation'.[10] Benjamin's ideas have been extended in various directions.[11] Such interventions tend to return us again to versions of the more mundane truism, that repetition intuitively suggests unoriginality, dullness, or artificiality. And yet, for Wordsworth, forms of repetition prove both conceptually and literally liberating. Within the realm of philosophical aesthetics, repetition is a significant component of the attempt to articulate the repossession and transformation of knowledge fundamental to Romantic theories of mind and art. Despite the perhaps instinctive sense that they might do so, later eighteenth-century changes in the literary and philosophical landscape do not diminish or degrade the role of repetition in verse for Wordsworth; rather, repetition pervades Wordsworth's poetry as something flexible, variable, and *useful*. Wordsworth was born into a world marked by the inventive spirit of the Enlightenment, characterized by the scientific method's dependence on the ability to repeat experiments,

---

[8] See David Perkins, 'How the Romantics Recited Poetry', *Studies in English Literature, 1500–1900*, 31.4 (Autumn 1991), 655–71, on the vitality of the 'oral delivery of verse' (p. 655) in the Romantic Period.

[9] See for example Richard Glauser and Anthony Savile, 'Aesthetic Experience in Shaftesbury', *Proceedings of the Aristotelian Society: Supplementary Volumes*, 76 (2002), 25–74 (p. 51).

[10] Walter Benjamin, 'The Work of Art in the Age of Mechanical Reproduction', in *Illuminations*, ed. Hannah Arendt, trans. Harry Zohn (London: Fontana, 1973), pp. 219–53 (p. 223).

[11] Perhaps their widest dissemination in the United Kingdom followed their acknowledged influence on John Berger's *Ways of Seeing* (London: The British Broadcasting Corporation and Penguin Books, 1972) (see esp. pp. 25–7). Berger agrees that because they lack Benjamin's *aura*, commercial reproductions of artworks are diminished.

and to identify knowledge by those experiments' repeated results. As Gadamer summarizes, in this type of science, 'experience is valid only if it is confirmed; hence its dignity depends on its being in principle repeatable. But this means that by its very nature, experiences abolishes its history and thus itself. This is true even of everyday experience, and much more so of any scientific version of it.'[12] Essentially, Romantic poetry emerges from a mindset which privileges repetition as the best and only form of 'truth'. However, if we accept Gadamer's claims about experience's abolition of its own history, we can immediately see problems for Wordsworth's attempt to chronicle personal experience in *The Prelude*: the poet must somehow sustain the individuality of lived experience even through the imaginative and textual repetitions of it (in Stephen Gill's sense of 'revisitings'[13]), required by poetry. The way that Wordsworth manipulates forms of repetition in his writing does, I will argue, indicate a shared awareness of the difficulty Gadamer identifies, but it strives party through its own experimentation with forms of repetition and recapitulation to address the impasse he suggests.

Repetition and the Higher Criticism

Gadamer's statements provide a short-hand definition for the way Enlightenment science decisively prioritized repeated experience as the basis for knowledge of 'truth'. This secular intellectual context was matched by a corresponding outpouring of theological scholarship (in the second half of the eighteenth century in particular), in which attention to repetition was similarly crucial, and whose importance to the way in which Romantic writers were to think about repetition is hard to over-state. Centuries of biblical hermeneutics had already established elements of the New Testament to be repetitions of aspects of the Old; Wordsworth's attempt to trace significance through the connections between his experiences and his works is conceptually indebted to this typological way of thinking. But ideas about literary style and form were also deeply marked by the conclusions of the Higher Criticism. The German biblical scholar, Johann David Michaelis, for example, defended the stylistic repetition found within the scriptures. Michael Legaspi summarizes Michaelis's position: 'Repetitions must not be treated as "offensive" or contemptible in such an old book, since they are a product of a more primitive time (*die Kindheit der Welt*) when repetition was thought to be useful, necessary, and pleasant. Homer, that great imitator of nature, made frequent use of repetition, and Virgil, in his own artful imitation of

---

[12] Hans-Georg Gadamer, *Truth and Method*, 2nd edn, rev. trans. Joel Weinsheimer and Donald G. Marshall (London: Continuum, 2004), p. 342. The implication of Gadamer's proposition for repetition is discussed by Howard Risatti, in *A Theory of Craft: Function and Aesthetic Expression* (Chapel Hill: University of North Carolina Press, 2007), pp. 192–3.

[13] See Stephen Gill, *Wordsworth's Revisitings* (Oxford: Oxford University Press, 2011).

antiquity, did the same.'[14] Other writers were more vigorous still in defending what was recognized to be a fundamental aspect of biblical writing, and modern scholarship has taken up some of their assertions. Kawain, for example, finds in the Old Testament 'some of the finest and most familiar examples of the beauty and strength of repetition.'[15] He highlights a thematic interest ('the very subject of Ecclesiastes is repetition'[16]), and moves on to the subtle way in which repetition can *avoid* dull sameness: Ecclesiastes depicts

> a deliberate activity of 'returning', re-examining a situation until a solution is discovered... Observations are repeated in an especially poignant way: Koheleth is pictured as continually *rediscovering* them... These returnings never threaten to become repetitious, because each rediscovery is preceded by a conclusion that, closing the matter for us, frees us to experience each repetition as something new.[17]

Modern theological thinkers interested in repetition have been keenly attentive to the possibilities of this idea of 'repetition as something new', cast in the form of repetition with difference. Their discussions derive in part from 'Lowth's eighteenth century reading of Hebrew poetry (in effect the Old Testament) though the figure of pleonasm, or repetition with variety',[18] an idea of the-same-but-different highly significant to Wordsworth. This effect is achieved through what Kawain calls 'some of the finest examples of parallelistic verse'.[19]

The formal characteristics of Hebrew verse were key to early nineteenth-century understandings of the structure of biblical writing, and thence for repetition and its possibilities in poetry more generally. In the 1815 'Preface', Wordsworth alludes directly to 'The grand storehouses of enthusiastic and meditative Imagination, of poetical, as contradistinguished from human and dramatic Imagination', which 'are the prophetic and lyrical parts of the Holy Scriptures, and the works of Milton'; Milton is 'a Hebrew in soul; and all things tended in him towards the sublime.'[20] Wordsworth's admiration explicitly stems from the fact that the Hebrew poets are 'preserved' from the 'bondage of definite form' to which the classical authors were subject; it is a recognition of the sublimity which (according to the eighteenth-century Higher Criticism) was exhibited within the Bible through its particular, repeated forms. Central to the cementing of this understanding of Hebrew texts were the works of Robert Lowth and Hugh Blair, respectively.

---

[14] Michael Legaspi, *The Death of Scripture and the Rise of Biblical Studies* (Oxford: Oxford University Press, 2010), p. 137.
[15] Kawain, p. 38.   [16] Kawain, p. 39.   [17] Kawain, pp. 39–41.
[18] Peter Larkin, 'Repetition, Difference and Liturgical Participation in Coleridge's "The Ancient Mariner"', *Literature & Theology*, 21.2 (June 2007), 146–59 (p. 153).
[19] Kawain, p. 39.   [20] 'Preface' to *Poems... in Two Volumes*, in *Prose*, iii, 34–5.

Robert Lowth's *Lectures on the Sacred Poetry of the Hebrews* (1753, translated into English in 1787) induced a radically new approach to the Psalms. Foreshadowing Benjamin's interest in the complexities of 'permitting the reproduction to meet the beholder or listener in his own particular situation', his astonishing, novel method encouraged readers actually to think themselves into the situation of texts' authors, and their original readers: 'he who would perceive and feel the peculiar and interior elegancies of the Hebrew poetry, must imagine himself exactly situated as the persons for whom it was written, or even as the writers themselves; he is to feel them as a Hebrew.'[21] Lowth explains that the Hebrew word 'Nabi' refers to 'a Prophet, a Poet, or a Musician, under the influence of divine inspiration'.[22] Poets and prophets are identical in Lowth's account: 'They had one common name, one common origin, one common author, the Holy Spirit',[23] and this claim was to revolutionize not only biblical criticism, but also to transform the status of poetry.[24] Prophecy is relevant to theories of repetition generally. Curtis explains that the idea of prophecy as a simple prediction of the future is flawed, because 'in effect the prophet repeats the words of' the divinity:

> the idea of repetition is crucial here in the sense that the utterance delivered by the prophet is a form of citation but without the quotation marks. Despite the apparent immediacy in the 'now' of a prophetic utterance, the temporal frame of the words uttered by the prophet belongs to some prior or past tense. Discourse pertaining to the future, through its repetition as a 'citation', is, therefore, a function of the past. 'Prophecy', Balfour summarises, 'is a call and a claim much more than it is a prediction, a call oriented towards a present that is not present'.[25]

This suggests an active contemporary interest in the possibility of the superimposition of different timeframes upon one another, which marks some of Wordsworth's most powerful writing. To remain for now with the legacy of Lowth's exposition of Hebrew verse, though, the conviction that a unique and 'delicate connexion' existed between the Hebrews' 'poetical imagery, and the peculiar circumstances of their nation'[26] led Lowth to declare that 'it is scarcely, or not at all, possible for any translation fully to represent the genuine sense of the sacred poets,' because it could not comprehend 'that delicate connexion':[27] in this derived his attention to metaphor and translation. But Lowth's position as

---

[21] Lowth, i, 113–14.   [22] Lowth, ii, 14.   [23] Lowth, ii, 18.
[24] On questions of poetry and prophecy in Lowth's writing, see also Yosefa Raz, 'Robert Lowth's Bible: Between Seraphic Choirs and Prophetic Weakness', *Modern Language Quarterly*, 81.2 (June 2020), 139–67.
[25] Curtis, 'Romantic Indirection', p. 12, citing Ian Balfour, *The Rhetoric of Romantic Prophecy* (Stanford: Stanford University Press, 2002).
[26] Lowth, i, 182.   [27] Lowth, i, 182.

professor of poetry at Oxford ensured that his attention was not purely thematic, and he most famously developed an account of the form and construction of Hebrew verse. Aware that the marking effects of rhyme and rhythm which distinguished European poetry were absent from Hebrew verse (including the Psalms, which were supposed to be songs), he identified structural parallelism as an alternative and distinctive feature of Hebrew poetry. Citing his own previous definition, he stated:

> The correspondence of one verse, or line, with another, I call *parallelism*. When a proposition is delivered, and a second is subjoined to it, or drawn under it, equivalent, or contrasts with it, in sense; or similar to it in the form of grammatical construction; these I call parallel lines; and the words or phrases, answering one to another in the corresponding lines, parallel terms.[28]

Lowth distinguished different forms of parallelism, and asserted that its origins could be traced to an earlier aural tradition. He thus donated to the critical tradition a way of thinking about the poet, and about repetition in poetic form, which struck a firm chord with similar, specifically aesthetic theories of repetition developing and circulating amongst his contemporaries.[29]

In 1783, Hugh Blair (then professor of rhetoric at Edinburgh University) devoted a chapter of his influential *Lectures* to a summary of Lowth's ideas. Blair's summary was a major source for their dissemination; it is where they were first encountered by Wordsworth, and it was a key influence on the extract from Wordsworth's 'Preface', quoted above. In their own form, but also in vicarious encounters like Wordsworth's with Blair, Lowth's ideas spread with quite dramatic effect. As Stephen Prickett describes it,

> By and large, the principal literary models in 1700 were classical; by 1800 they were more likely to be biblical. Lowth anticipates and sets the agenda for Wordsworth's theory of poetic diction...praising...the 'simple and unadorned' language of Hebrew verse, which gained its 'almost ineffable sublimity' not

---

[28] Lowth, ii, 32, n. 10.
[29] In 1778, for example, Joshua Reynolds wrote an admiring letter to Lowth, in which he thanked the bishop for a copy of his newly published translation of *Isaiah*, prefixed with a preliminary dissertation arguing that Isaiah had all of the characteristics of Hebrew verse, in which 'the Poetical and the Prophetical character of style and composition, though generally supposed to be different, yet are really one and the same' (Robert Lowth, *Isaiah* (London: J. Dodsley and T. Cadell, 1778), p. iii.) In his letter, Reynolds commented on the similarities between Lowth's principles of parallelism and his own notions of repetition in painting and architecture (see Joshua Reynolds to Robert Lowth, 7 November 1778, in *The Collected Letters of Sir Joshua Reynolds*, ed. Frederick Whiley Hilles (Cambridge: Cambridge University Press, 1929), pp. 63–7).

from artificially elevated diction, but from the depth and universality of its subject matter.[30]

Perhaps most significantly to Wordsworth, Lowth's establishment of parallelism as the distinguishing feature of Hebrew poetry led to the acknowledgement in the *Sacred Poetry* that the difficulties commonly understood to attach to the translation of European poetry (ancient and modern) which aimed to reproduce any sort of equivalence in tone or feeling were significantly diminished in translation of Hebrew poetry, *because* it was best translated into prose.[31] This was largely an intervention into a long-standing discourse relating to the propriety and difficulties of the translation of scripture, but as Prickett points out, it had another significant effect: 'that of blurring the traditional distinctions between prose and verse. To speak of a prose piece as "poetic" could now be much more than a metaphor.'[32]

It is hard to over-emphasize the effect of this breaking down of boundaries between prose and verse. In Wordsworth's 'Preface', the influence of Lowth's *Sacred Poetry* is direct and acknowledged, and critics have been quick to assess its wider impact. Mary Jacobus has explored Blair's assumptions about the origins of poetry in the context of Wordsworth's interest in the ballad tradition.[33] Alan Bewell argues that 'In "The Thorn," Wordsworth uses Hebrew poetry as a model for writing an experimental primitive ballad aimed at dramatizing the primitive origins of poetry'.[34] In her close attention to Wordsworth's 'Note' to 'The Thorn', Corinna Russell also has elegantly highlighted the significance of a specifically Lowthian tradition, which, Russell points out, Wordsworth knew through a translation which included a copy of a note by Michaelis.[35] Wordsworth's explicit reference in the 'Note' demonstrates the vital and transformative effect of Lowthian tradition on ideas about what literature was (and, reflexively, on what the Bible itself might be). For the purposes of this book, though, Lowth's central importance is found in his provocation of the re-assessment and re-valuing of repetition.

As critics including Stephen Prickett and Wesley Kort have made clear, attention to the way in which scripture should or could be read was widespread and heavily influential in the period, beyond the immediate boundaries of Lowthian

---

[30] Stephen Prickett, 'Biblical and Literary Criticism: A History of Interaction', in David Jasper and Stephen Prickett, eds, *The Bible and Literature: A Reader* (Oxford: Blackwell, 1999), pp. 12–43 (p. 28).
[31] See Lowth, i, 71.   [32] Prickett, p. 28.
[33] See Mary Jacobus, *Tradition and Experiment in Wordsworth's Lyrical Ballads (1798)* (Oxford: Clarendon Press, 1976), p. 8.
[34] Alan Bewell, *Wordsworth and the Enlightenment: Nature, Man, and Society in the Experimental Poetry* (New Haven: Yale University Press, 1989), p. 171; pp. 171–2.
[35] Corinna Russell, 'A Defence of Tautology: Repetition and Difference in Wordsworth's Note to "The Thorn"', *Paragraph*, 28.2 (2005), 104–18 (p. 109 ff.).

parallelism, and in other ways which bespeak an interest in species of repetition.[36] Friedrich Schleiermacher, for example, influenced by Herder and Schlegel, developed a theory of hermeneutics directed at readings of the Bible, but which was also significant for the way reading was thought about more generally. Centrally concerned with the intricate relationship between reader and text, Schleiermacher understood both to be situated within a complex cultural context which rendered each instance of that relationship individual. This necessitated an understanding of a form of reading which could not lead to a single 'meaning' or interpretation; rather, 'misunderstanding occurs as a matter of course, and so understanding must be willed and sought at every point'. Understanding thus becomes 'an unending task', perpetually subject to necessary revision.[37] Schleiermacher did not publish his lectures on hermeneutics; knowledge of his thinking on the subject was confined to vicarious communication through the notes and reports of his students. Nonetheless, this mindset induces a sense of revision in the period as vital and renewing, at odds with the tediousness of returning to and repeating things which Coleridge and Southey would attack as a character trait of Wordsworth's narrator in 'The Thorn'. It is moreover indicative of the extent to which an engagement with the concept of repetition persisted in various arenas throughout the early nineteenth century, and became central to the very possibility, in accounts like this, of truth, or 'sincerity'.[38]

Order, Disorder, Repetition, and Variation

Another cluster of eighteenth-century discourses which understood aspects of repetition as a means of knowledge of the world are connected by their shared fascination with ordering it. Literary disorder was increasingly admired in the period, but its accommodation within received traditions required some awkward critical wriggling. Artful irregularity was central to eighteenth-century picturesque theories, for example, yet although supposed to suggest sincerity, naturalness, spontaneity, and genius, the aesthetic was quickly problematized (and consequently politicized) by the artificiality necessary to the construction of its apparent

---

[36] See for example Stephen Prickett, *Romanticism and Religion: The Tradition of Coleridge and Wordsworth in the Victorian Church* (Cambridge: Cambridge University Press, 1976), *Origins of Narrative: The Romantic Appropriation of the Bible* (Cambridge: Cambridge University Press, 1996), and especially *Words and 'The Word': Language, Poetics and Biblical Interpretation* (Cambridge: Cambridge University Press, 1986; 1989); and also Wesley A. Kort, *"Take, Read": Scripture, Textuality, and Cultural Practice* (University Park: Pennsylvania State University Press, 1996).
[37] Friedrich Schleiermacher, *Hermeneutics: The Handwritten Manuscripts*, ed. Heinz Kimmerle, trans. James Duke and Jack Forstman (Atlanta, GA: Scholars Press, 1977), p. 110; p. 41.
[38] Repetition has interested modern theologians, and theological efforts to re-think the nihilistic conclusions of theorists such as Kierkegaard, Nietzsche, Freud, Derrida, and Deleuze have highlighted their linguistic elements, which has had some impact on literary studies: see for example a brief summary in Larkin, p. 147.

artlessness. Disorder concealed only a higher order, and problematically so, in that deception. Meanwhile, in the field of drama, the increasing entrenchment of Shakespeare as the representative of a specifically English excellence elevated the English style above the Ancient partly because of its disregard of classical rules and unities. For Byron, this was a cause for criticism,[39] but others celebrated the abandonment of tradition. Johnson's Shakespeare is gloriously disorderly, his work a mighty 'forest' incorporating 'weeds and brambles', in contrast to the work of the 'correct and regular writer', a 'garden accurately formed and diligently planted'. Whereas, for Johnson, 'Other poets display cabinets of precious rarities, minutely finished, wrought into shape, and polished into brightness', Shakespeare 'opens a mine which contains gold and diamonds in unexhaustible plenty, though clouded by incrustations, debased by impurities, and mingled with a mass of meaner minerals.'[40] Shakespeare's originality clearly indicates greatness, but Johnson's analysis cannot abandon its sense of 'debasement' and 'impurity', and the raising of Shakespeare to the status of English bard involves accepting this disordered character *as* the new order.

Attention to disorder also characterizes contemporary debate surrounding the structure of long poems. A simplified picture might portray the smooth polish and precision of Augustanism giving way to the apparently disorderly progress of Thomson's loco-descriptive verse, the enthusiastic meditations of the Graveyard School, and the formal innovations of Cowper's *Task*.[41] In 1785, John Scott argued in his *Critical Essays* that 'Modern poetry has, in general, one common defect, viz. the want of proper arrangement.'[42] Richard Terry describes long poems in the period as apparently 'generically polymorphous', and as a 'poetic gallimaufry'.[43] Contrary to this image of overriding, often chaotic irregularity, however, Terry asserts that poets did pay great attention to 'issues of continuity and rupture', suggesting that 'local discord becomes assumed beneath a total rationale of order'.[44] Regularity and repetition are obviously not synonymous, but they are related, and, moreover, within this environment of apparent discontinuity, repetition within literary texts was one way in which a comforting regularity was restored. Whilst certain forms of repetition might suggest a lack of care or poetical attention (a lazy re-use of a word or effect), repetitions tend to yoke together

---

[39] See Anne Barton, 'Byron and Shakespeare', in Drummond Bone, ed., *The Cambridge Companion to Byron* (Cambridge: Cambridge University Press, 2004), pp. 224–35.

[40] 'Preface to the Plays of William Shakespeare' [1765], in *Samuel Johnson: A Critical Edition of the Major Works*, ed. Donald Greene (Oxford: Oxford University Press, 1984), pp. 419–56 (p. 436).

[41] For a survey of opinions regarding the apparent lack of unity in Thomson's *Seasons*, for example, see Ralph Cohen, *The Art of Discrimination: Thomson's Seasons and the Language of Criticism* (London: Routledge & Kegan Paul, 1964), pp. 84–130.

[42] John Scott, *Critical Essays on some of the Poems, of several English Poets* (London: James Phillips, 1785), p. 251.

[43] Richard Terry, 'Transitions and Digressions in the Eighteenth-Century Long Poem', *Studies in English Literature, 1500–1900*, 32.3 (Summer 1992), 495–510 (p. 496).

[44] Terry, p. 498; p. 501.

disparate elements simply by virtue of their similitude: even as it performs a self-conscious disruption, repetition naturally lends a sense of connection and continuity. Yet what Terry identifies as local variation within overarching regularity is actually more important to the bigger argument about Wordsworth this book will seek to make. Through this characteristic, long poems become sites of negotiation seeking to achieve a balance of similitude and difference. The legacy of this is a model in which variation is possible within the whole, and which thereby goes some way to normalizing the idea of difference *within* repetition. It is this admittance of difference which, I shall argue, renders repetition available to Wordsworth for what he understands to be sincere poetic articulation.

The long poem's admittance of variation within the whole, the disorder within order of the picturesque, and the 'endless diversity' of Shakespeare's arrangements, find correlatives in contemporary scientific disciplines. For Terry, *Newton's Principia* (1686–87) offers 'strong conceptual paradigms providing external reinforcement of the notion, intrinsic to the organization of long poems, that unity and diversity could happily coexist in the same body…[T]he single most important analogue for understanding the compositional integrity of long works was…the spectrum.'[45] Newton had long remained undecided about how many distinct shades existed within the visible spectrum. Experimentation by seventeenth-century artists had clarified the idea of primary colours, and Newton had determined the number of uncompounded colours to be seven. Yet 'his investigations still stressed the stubborn near-indivisibility of the different hues', and in the *Second Book of Opticks* (1704), he advanced a perception 'that the colors grade into one another'.[46] This focus on the idea of distinction in Newton's writing is vital to questions of representation more broadly: how should the poet or artist distinguish, or perhaps even *un*distinguish, the specific, in order to assign the general character of something? How far can or should repetition in this sense of representation accommodate variation or difference? The discourse of poetic disorder thus runs parallel to notions of scientific gradation and the anxieties about particularity they inevitably raise. These issues together form a context which is fascinated by ideas of specificity and generality, and thus of how to represent accurately (or what Wordsworth would come to term 'sincerely') in verse. The experimental method of the scientific Enlightenment depends upon multiple repetitions of the same event to establish truth, just as Reynolds's artist achieves an 'Ideal Beauty' by representing an abstract general surpassing any individual original.[47] Chapter 10 of Samuel Johnson's *Rasselas* famously privileges the specific over the general:

---

[45] Terry, pp. 505–6.
[46] Terry p. 506. There are correspondences to be found here with the idea of 'transegmental drift' and similar aural effects in verse, discussed previously.
[47] *Discourses on Art*, pp. 44–5.

'The business of a poet,' said Imlac, 'is to examine, not the individual, but the species; to remark general properties and large appearances: he does not number the streaks of the tulip, or describe the different shades of the verdure of the forest. He is to exhibit in his portraits of nature such prominent and striking features as recall the original to every mind; and must neglect the minuter discriminations[.']⁴⁸

Rasselas's poet 'must disregard present laws and opinions, and rise to general and transcendental truths, which will always be the same'.⁴⁹ Yet even if one accepts the familiar Johnsonian dictum, how are these transcendental truths to be ascertained? How much repetition is *enough* repetition to signal generality? How might the natural historian (for example), seeking to describe, or the poet seeking to celebrate a natural scene, ever establish a reasonable line between the general and the specific?

The very 'knowledge' which is derived from repeated observation is challenged by what it means to repeat exactly. Edward Said finds intellectual historians continually preoccupied with the way in which ideas of an assumed-to-be-easy repetition (the type of generation discerned in numerous aspects of the natural world) founder with advances in knowledge:

> there is consensus of a very general sort: that from about the middle of the eighteenth century the problem of change, while customarily represented in many fields as the generation, reproduction, or transmission of life from parent to offspring, is intruded upon by forces troubling the continuity. In natural history written during the early nineteenth century—Cuvier's investigations are a case in point—such discontinuity is exemplified in the theory of geological disturbances...
> it is only as a kind of metaphorical nostalgia for early faith that the generative terms can be made to apply to the world of scientifically observable facts.⁵⁰

'Troubled continuity' is also a far broader effect of Romantic lyric verse, according to another dominant strand of scholarship. Christopher Miller summarizes the 'Greater Romantic Lyric' of M. H. Abrams's account as a form or genre in which, 'in the midst of some crisis, a solitary speaker stations himself in space, "departs" in a reverie of recollection or anticipation, and "returns" to his spot with a heightened awareness':⁵¹ in this model, the progress of the poem records a sense

---

⁴⁸ Samuel Johnson, *The History of Rasselas, Prince of Abyssina*, in *A Critical Edition of the Major Works*, pp. 335–418 (p. 352).
⁴⁹ *Rasselas*, p. 353.
⁵⁰ Edward Said, 'On Repetition', in *The World, the Text, and the Critic* (Cambridge, MA: Harvard University Press, 1983), pp. 111–35 (p. 119–20).
⁵¹ Christopher R. Miller, 'Coleridge and the Scene of Lyric Description', *Journal of English and Germanic Philology*, 101.4 (October 2002), 520–39 (p. 520). The essay Miller cites, M. H. Abrams's

of return—a repetition of sorts—and the poem must articulate that process of repetition as part of its being.[52] For Wordsworth, this same struggle dominates not just Said's natural historical observation, or the specific 'spots of time', but his attempt to write from experience at all; to capture the reality of lived experience as he sees it. In his work, ideas about specificity and generality and the perception and knowledge of the world in which they are involved take on a distinctly urgent cast. It is precisely *through* his many repetitions and recapitulations that Wordsworth faces and manages the eighteenth-century conflict between specific and general highlighted (differently) by Johnson, Reynolds, and Newton, in order to articulate experience, as he understands it, sincerely. Repetition allows Wordsworth to manage contemporary anxieties about order, disorder, and variation; about similitude and dissimilitude. Wordsworth evolves from his engagement with such anxieties a distinctive understanding of the nature of experience, and a means of representing it in verse which is fundamentally rooted in forms of repetition and recapitulation.

Repetition in an Industrial Age

One question about repetition which eludes conclusive answer relates to the extent to which perceptions of it might be historically variable. Can modern readers, living unselfconsciously in Walter Benjamin's 'Age of Mechanical Reproduction', appreciate repetition's effects in the same way that Wordsworth's first readers did (even assuming any kind of general, albeit unacknowledged, synchronic consensus)? Deidre Lynch points out that 'There are photographs of nearly every author whose writing is anthologized in the Victorian-period volume of *The Norton Anthology of English Literature*...By contrast, very few of the authors whose works comprise the romantic-period volume of the *Norton*...ever sat before a camera lens.'[53] Benjamin could assert that, by 1900, 'technical reproduction had reached a standard that not only permitted it to reproduce all transmitted works of art and thus to cause the most profound change in their impact upon the public; it also had captured a place of its own among the artistic processes.'[54] Benjamin

---

'Structure and Style in the Greater Romantic Lyric', appears in Frederick W. Hilles and Harold Bloom, eds, *From Sensibility to Romanticism: Essays Presented to Frederick A. Pottle* (New York: Oxford University Press, 1965), pp. 527–60.

[52] Miller's argument is that the passage of Coleridge's poems is along 'two simultaneous tracks: the internal melody of thought and the external harmony (or disharmony) of phenomena...the central philosophical challenge that preoccupied him [was] to give poetic form to the simultaneity of perceptions.' (Miller, p. 521) This is one of the features of repetition in verse to which this book pays particular attention: its ability to sustain similar *but different* things at the same time (though I remain unconvinced that Coleridge manages to surmount this challenge).

[53] Lynch, 'Matters of Memory: Response' in *Victorian Studies*, 49.2 (Winter 2007), pp. 228–40, p. 229.

[54] Benjamin, 'The Work of Art', pp. 221–2.

describes mass-produced objects as representing a strange combination: they are perfectly formed repetitions, yet lack the original work's 'aura':

> that which withers in the age of mechanical reproduction is the aura of the work of art... the technique of reproduction detaches the reproduced object from the domain of tradition. By making many reproductions it substitutes a plurality of copies for a unique existence.[55]

In a passage with important resonance for the discussion of sincerity which Wordsworth establishes as a criterion for good art, Benjamin argues that 'The presence of the original is the prerequisite to the concept of authenticity.'[56] A vivid preoccupation with originality, particularly as it is associated with authenticity and genius, runs through the eighteenth century and Romantic Period in various filiations. One associated anxiety is already evident in the middle of the seventeenth century, when Hobbes's *De Corpore* resurrects the classical thought-experiment of the Ship of Theseus. Discussion of this paradox rumbles through the seventeenth and eighteenth centuries, its most famous response remaining Plutarch's pronouncement that one cannot step twice into the same river. Yet stepping twice into the same river is exactly what Wordsworth tries imaginatively to do in his revisions to *The Prelude*, for example, even though he might have changed (and know that he has changed) his boots, and the discourse of repetition is directly pertinent to the Romantic negotiation of 'authenticity' and sincerity in this and related ways. Rooted in the individual artist rather than the legacy of a machine age, these are different anxieties to Benjamin's, but they spring from a common root, originating in a specific set of historical conditions.

Howard Risatti follows Benjamin in drawing a distinction between 'art' and 'craft', agreeing with Arnold Hauser that we should not 'under-estimate the value of uniqueness, of unrepeatable and individual form.'[57] In Risatti's account, as in Benjamin's, repetition can destroy our relationship with authenticity. He distinguishes copies and reproductions from the multiples of mass manufacture: multiples are problematic, because they 'undermine our idea of the original object as a philosophical concept and as a unique thing...atop a hierarchy of creative objects, they dissolve the hierarchy itself and with it our traditional basis for understanding the creative act through the physical object.'[58] Risatti traces the

---

[55] Benjamin, 'The Work of Art', p. 223.
[56] Benjamin, 'The Work of Art', p. 222. In the 'Essays upon Epitaphs', Wordsworth engages explicitly with the idea of 'a criterion of sincerity, by which a Writer may be judged' (see *Prose*, ii, 43–199 (p. 70)), discussed in Chapter 13 of this book.
[57] Risatti, p. 155, citing Arnold Hauser, *The Social History of Art Vol. 2: Renaissance Mannerism, Baroque*, trans. Stanley Godman (New York: Vintage, 1985), p. 197.
[58] Risatti, pp. 174–5. In a context of art and craft, the title of Wordsworth and Coleridge's collection *Lyrical Ballads* is interesting. Risatti begins his study with a quotation from Rose Slivka on the distinction between art and craft; a work 'is indeed craft unless "all links with the idea of function have been severed"' (Risatti, p. 1). According to this definition, a traditional ballad is craft, because it

shift towards problematical forms of impersonal reproduction to Wordsworth's lifetime: 'These changes began to occur when, for example, production factories like Josiah Wedgwood's Etruria opened near Stoke-on-Trent, England, in 1769... In later years it only became more acute as industrialization and automation increased.'[59] Risatti cites Georg Simmel and Hans-Georg Gadamer to illustrate the idea that:

> To say objects come from somewhere, in the old sense, was to say they come from someone's hand... They were not reduced to signs without reference to the meaningful practice that produced them. When one experienced such an object, one had an individual, autonomous experience... But in the machine age... Experience is flattened out—made uniform... This is such a drastic change from the way the world was encountered and understood in the past... [T]he scientific method objectifies experience to guarantee that it can be repeated and thus verified... experience, as an encounter with the world, gets flattened and made uniform by its repeatability. Repetition becomes the normal state of affairs, and it becomes not only the way we expect things to be but also how we judge what is creditable.[60]

This process 'began in earnest with the Industrial Revolution',[61] when, in Eric Hobsbawm's words, 'the shackles were taken off the productive power of human societies, which henceforth became capable of the constant, rapid, and up to the present limitless multiplication of men, goods, and services.'[62] Here, the Romantic Period is identified as historically significant for the very concept of repetition.

---

has widely recognized social functions. Later, Risatti returns to the definition of the terms: 'Following [Collingwood's] logic, the term "craft" ends up defining what can be called failed attempts at art or simply repetitive, rote work' (p. 13). The conventional ballad is complicated in this context, because it depends upon formally functional repetitions. The art/craft distinction is applied in Risatti's work to objects; yet it is not irrelevant here, because its diagnosis is attached specifically to the use of repetition in the creative process. For example, Risatti's discussion of the tools used in creating works argues that the 'application of the tool may be repetitive for the craft object, but the resulting object need not be if the tool is in the service of invention and the creative imagination' (p. 170). If we understand the poet's 'tools' as rhyme and metre, we can see that a distinction between poetic art and craft might rest on the successful manipulation of those tools, in the balance between the repetition vital to aspects of verse like metre and rhyme, and the variation which is understood to be necessary to good writing, to avoid the sort of 'toilsome and tedious' verse Richards criticizes, which lends itself too much to the kind of 'scanning by dumdies' criticized by William Empson (see Empson, 'Rhythm and Imagery in English Poetry', *British Journal of Aesthetics*, 2.1 (January 1962), 36–54, p. 43). But the really significant aspect of Risatti's discussion for this study is the assertion he makes about the way in which mechanical repetition affects the creative imagination: 'The point I am making is not a question of craft being different or better, nor is it a question of nostalgia for tradition and the past... Rather, it is about seeking ways to be in the world that recognize the importance of human values and human relations in order to counteract the "limitlessness" that mechano-techno-scientific culture encourages... [I]t has been so successful that the light it sheds onto the world is so strong it tends to blind us to all other ways of seeing and understanding' (Risatti, pp. 186–7). Unless, of course, repetition itself answers back, under the manipulation of the poet; this book argues that it does exactly this.

[59] Risatti, p. 177.   [60] Risatti, pp. 192–3.   [61] Risatti, p. 246.
[62] E. J. Hobsbawm, *The Age of Revolution 1789–1848* (New York: Mentor, 1962), p. 45.

In Book 5 of *The Prelude*, Wordsworth draws on the language of the industrial revolution in a context of intellectual method and teaching. He laments the action of the 'mighty workmen of our later age', who 'would confine us down, | Like engines', finding 'A wiser Spirit...at work for us' in intuition and emotion ('in the unreasoning progress of the world') than in mechanical response.[63] When he alludes in the 1800 'Preface' to *Lyrical Ballads* to 'great national events which are daily taking place, and the encreasing accumulation of men in cities, where the uniformity of their occupations produces a craving for extraordinary incident',[64] he seems to appeal to the type of repetitive mode of living and production which can be said to have characterized the new, industrial cities of the early nineteenth century, and to which Hobsbawm, Simmel, and Risatti refer: Susan Rosenbaum argues that Wordsworth's 'uniformity' actually 'connotes the repetitiveness or mechanical nature of daily tasks, suggesting a limiting of experience that accompanies the increasing specialization and mechanization of industry in the late eighteenth century...The worker performing a uniform task is forced to view time as a series of continuous presents, rather than as a narrative of growth from past to present.'[65] Various critics have attempted to outline Wordsworth's attitudes to increasing industrialism. W. Thomas Pepper's essay on 'Michael', a poem which centres on the loss of its protagonist's land caused by the industrial and agricultural revolutions, is not untypical. Pepper argues that Wordsworth's focus on domestic feeling disengages him from the processes which, he argues, re-shaped society: according to Pepper, for all he registered its social effects, Wordsworth was 'not trying to stop the industrial revolution'.[66] Instead, Pepper finds that 'The "evils" [Wordsworth] wants to stem are specifically the "rapid decay of domestic feeling among the lower orders of society"'.[67] In a more complex analysis (his account of Wordsworth's response to Marx's 'commodity'), David Simpson acknowledges that 'At first glance Wordsworth's poetry looks nothing like Blake's impassioned vision of dark satanic mills'. However, Simpson's unfolding argument places Wordsworth's writing in the context of the British 'expanding military-industrial complex'.[68] He unsurprisingly finds 'a resistance to modern massification', arguing that Wordsworth's poems 'most profoundly

---

[63] William Wordsworth, *The Prelude*, V.370–388, in *The Thirteen-Book 'Prelude'*, ed. Mark L. Reed, 2 vols (Ithaca: Cornell University Press, 1991), i, 107–324. Unless otherwise indicated, all quotations from the *Prelude* are taken from the 1805 AB-Stage Reading Text in this edition. Quotations from the 1850 *Prelude* are taken from the Reading Text in William Wordsworth, *The Fourteen-Book 'Prelude'*, ed. W. J. B. Owen (Ithaca: Cornell University Press, 1985).

[64] Wordsworth, 'Preface' to *Lyrical Ballads* [1800], in *Prose*, i, 118–89 (p. 128).

[65] Susan B. Rosenbaum, *Professing Sincerity: Modern Lyric Poetry, Commercial Culture, and the Crisis in Reading* (Charlottesville, VA: University of Virginia Press, 2007), pp. 39–40.

[66] W. Thomas Pepper, 'The Ideology of Wordsworth's "Michael: A Pastoral Poem"', *Criticism*, 31.4 (Fall 1989), 367–82 (p. 371).

[67] Pepper, p. 371.

[68] David Simpson, *Wordsworth, Commodification and Social Concern: The Poetics of Modernity* (New York: Cambridge University Press, 2009), p. 1; pp. 1–2.

explore the processes and consequences of modernization experienced at one of its most critical transitions.'[69] 'Modernization', in Simpson's account, is refracted through close attention to twentieth-century political theorists, but insofar as he asserts that Wordsworth 'had a profound poetic understanding of the condition of England around 1800, specifically of its evolution into a culture governed by industrial time, machine-driven labor and commodity form', his argument is relevant here.[70] Simpson argues for a huge expansion of commodity form in the period as a direct result of factors including 'automation and machine labor... and mass warfare, which brutally emphasized the general equivalence of everyone to everyone else', and he suggests that one of Marx's major insights was that 'it was not only those directly engaged in factory work (relatively few by 1800) who felt the changes'.[71] Clearly indicating the relevance of these factors for the whole of society, as well as compellingly asserting Wordsworth's explicit reflection on their operation and effects, Simpson's reading insistently affirms the relevance of the industrial context in which the poet wrote.

The term 'industrial revolution' has been heavily contested, but as Emma Griffin puts it, 'no matter how much we dispute the fine detail, it is clear that something momentous happened in Britain between the end of the eighteenth century and the middle of the nineteenth.'[72] The industrialization, and associated massification, which marked the British economy by 1800 are central aspects of the romantic-period context. The industrial revolution is directly implicated in the reproduction and transmission of art objects; an increasing preoccupation with ideas of perfect repetition in factory production and the processes of massification is self-evident. The processes of the revolution also more fundamentally pulled vast numbers of bodies into a more repetitive way of living and being. Whilst accounts such as Simpson's are convincing, it is impossible to ascertain with any degree of confidence the self-awareness of the period as a moment when life became more dominated than ever before by repetition, and particularly to surmise the extent to which this affected the way in which repetition was conceptually appreciated; yet, intuitively, it seems entirely plausible that ideas of revolution and replication could have contributed to an altered sense of what it might mean to repeat. Perhaps the early nineteenth-century period was one in which understandings of the very concept of repetition were subtly altered, as awareness of its changed obtainability and effects were heightened. As mechanized forms of repetition made apparently perfect duplication of objects a real and everyday possibility, and as mechanized processes introduced new, minutely regularized rhythms (the regular beats and thumps of engines, pistons, and wheels) into more

---

[69] *Poetics of Modernity*, pp. 3–4. [70] *Poetics of Modernity*, p. 4.
[71] *Poetics of Modernity*, p. 8.
[72] Emma Griffin, *Liberty's Dawn: A People's History of the Industrial Revolution* (New Haven: Yale University Press, 2014), p. 4.

and more aspects of everyday life, perhaps the very concept of 'repetition' became delicately refined, possibly even differently understood. It might be indulgent to pursue this theoretical possibility here, but equally it would seem remiss to ignore such a powerful aspect of the context of Wordsworth's writing.

That the Romantic age characterized itself by its repetitions is evident everywhere in contemporary sources. By 1832, Charles Babbage's *On the Economy of Machinery and Manufactures* was demonstrating that the repetitive, predictable nature of his titular machines and factories was totally entrenched. Extending to consider the economy of human effort and coordination, and also the mechanical foundations of the new industries, Babbage declares that 'NOTHING is more remarkable, and yet less unexpected, than the perfect identity of things manufactured by the same tool'.[73] Chapter 11 of his work is devoted to the different forms of 'copying' which machines enact, valuable pre-eminently as a source of 'excellence'.[74] Beyond the 'perfect identity' of manufactured goods, machines themselves depended on the achievement of more perfect repetition both for their own fabrication, and for the construction of the means of powering them. Modern histories of the industrial revolution turn time and again to the idea of power (generated by steam and water) as one of the most significant conditions which made the revolution possible. But the harnessing of that power depended on the machinery which channelled it, and in this sense again, repetition sat at the heart of the possibility of the revolution's scale. The development of the first industrial screw-cutting lathe by Henry Maudslay at the end of the eighteenth century, for instance, allowed for standard sizes of screw threads (and thus the production of interchangeable parts). The ability identically to replicate parts of machines enabled mass production on a previously impossible scale.[75] One transition underway in the early nineteenth century of obvious relevance to a literary context is the enormous advances made to printing technologies (Lord Stanhope's cast-iron press was in use by 1800; Koenig and Bauer's steam-powered rotary-motion cylindrical press was in development by 1802, and by the end of 1814 it was being used to print *The Times*). The effect of industrialization was also at work in the sphere of music which itself became increasingly mechanized during the eighteenth and nineteenth centuries (through the increased technological development of instruments and through forms of measurement); Arnold Pacey notes that 'only toward the end of the eighteenth century did composers begin to recommend metronome settings... So now music might be played... by the precise rhythms of a machine.'[76] Here we can see the margin for difference between

---

[73] Charles Babbage, *On the Economy of Machinery and Manufactures* (London: Charles Knight, 1832), p. 48.
[74] Babbage, p. 51.
[75] See Quentin R. Skrabec, Jr, *The Metallurgic Age: The Victorian Flowering of Invention and Industrial Science* (Jefferson: McFarland, 2006), esp. pp. 169–70.
[76] Arnold Pacey, *Meaning in Technology* (Cambridge, MA: MIT Press, 1999), p. 27.

separate, performed instances of a work narrowing, making 'repetition' more accurate (as Pacey points out, it was 'about this time also that people employed in the early factories were having to work to the rhythms of other sorts of machines, instead of to their own singing').[77]

These facilities for reproducing text and music augmented a situation in which, Walter Ong has argued, 'Knowledge conservation and retrieval was immeasurably helped... With knowledge fastened down in visually processed space, man acquired an intellectual security never known before.' Ong connects this specifically to the emergence of Romanticism: 'The enterprise of fixing knowledge in space reached a peak some three hundred years after the development of alphabetic letterpress print as, for example, in the *Encyclopedie*... It was precisely at this point that Romanticism could and did take hold. For man could face into the unknown with courage or at least with equanimity as never before.'[78] Ong also asserts the influence of broader technological developments, suggesting that Romantic poets (pre-eminently, Wordsworth) could rest secure in their interest in the unknowable *because* they had the reassurance of a technological age behind them: 'the feeling of control over nature quiets old fears of being swallowed up by nature.'[79] Perhaps. But the age of the factory led to a standardization not only of goods, but also of lives: to masses of people starting and finishing work at exactly the same time each day, regulated by clocks and mechanical alarms, returning to identical streets of identical houses thrown up to accommodate a rapidly expanding factory workforce. Days were governed by hooters, bells, and whistles, rather than variable natural light and meteorology. 1824 saw the passing of the 'Act for ascertaining and establishing Uniformity of Weights and Measures'; by 1840, the necessary standardization of 'railway time' had occurred.[80] Writing on 'The Tyranny of the Clock' a hundred years later, the anarchist George Woodcock posited timekeeping itself as the enabler and the result of industrial revolution: 'Men actually became like clocks, acting with a repetitive regularity which had no resemblance to the rhythmic life of a natural being'.[81] With the 'knocker up' doing his morning rounds, across households people rose at the same time, ate pretty much the same breakfast of increasingly mass-produced comestibles off similar, mass-produced plates, and followed a route through streets of identical slum housing to factories. Breaks were taken at predetermined times, for tightly

---

[77] Pacey, p. 28.
[78] Walter J. Ong, *Rhetoric, Romance, and Technology: Studies in the Interaction of Expression and Culture* (Ithaca: Cornell University Press, 1971; 1990), pp. 277–8.
[79] Ong, p. 280.
[80] See for example Christoph Asendorf: 'With industrialization... it became increasingly necessary to establish a division of time that could be conveyed from the individual clock towers into general applicability' (*Batteries of Life: On the History of Things and their Perception in Modernity*, trans. Don Reneau (Berkeley and Los Angeles: University of California Press, 1993), p. 141).
[81] George Woodcock, *The Tyranny of the Clock* (The Anarchist's Library, 1944), p. 2.

regulated periods. Even in the more enlightened manufactories, uniformity was dominant: Robert Owen, for example, designed standardized education and socializing programmes at his plant in New Lanark, which controlled the 'leisure' as well as the working time of the community he gathered there, setting out his theories in his *New View of Society* so that they might be shared and replicated.[82] Whilst individual lives, experienced as such, were obviously not uniform in any real sense, from a generalizing, bird's-eye historical perspective, urban life in the period 1790–1820 became increasingly repetitive.

The occupations which industrialization brought with it (even when machines were largely still the province of much smaller, more domestic outfits) were also more repetitive: workers performed the same action multiple times every day as a result of the specialization and division of labour, allowing greater productivity (both in factories and in other environments which sought cheaper alternatives to mechanization). Rural work could be dully and painfully repetitive too, but it continued to be governed by climate and season, and its purpose remained more obvious to those who lived close to the land they exhaustingly worked. Perhaps the most famous example of the impact of industrial processes on the individual worker is Adam Smith's description of pin making in *The Wealth of Nations*, where the creation of the pins is broken down into minute, repeated activities. Smith speculates about the effects of drudgery and repetition itself: repetition is negative insofar as it is physically wearisome and intellectually stultifying, but it remains positive as a driver of economic success.[83] David Landes describes 'the substitution of machines—rapid, regular, precise, tireless—for human skill and effort' as one of the three main principles of innovation in the period.[84] Raphael Samuel finds the idea of 'substitution' in this account problematic, because some workers 'were engaged in wholly new occupations which had no real analogy in previous times.'[85] However, Samuel's account does not take issue with the idea of the regularity and precision Landes describes, and in fact further emphasizes the repetitive action involved in the new industry: with the invention of new machines and processes (which were not necessarily factory-based), '[m]achinery takes over from man the role of tool-bearer, manipulating numbers of tools simultaneously, synchronising separate detail processes as one.'[86] Samuel's account emphasizes that mechanization, and especially the work which made mechanical processes possible, continued to depend upon human sweat and toil, including for instance

---

[82] See *A New View of Society and Other Writings* [1816], ed. Gregory Claeys (London: Penguin, 1991), and also *An Outline of the System of Education at New Lanark* (Glasgow: University Press, 1824).

[83] Adam Smith, *The Wealth of Nations: Books I–III* [1776], ed. Andrew Skinner (London: Penguin, 1970; 1999), pp. 109–10.

[84] David Landes, *The Unbound Prometheus: Technological Change and Industrial Development in Western Europe from 1750 to the Present* (Cambridge: Cambridge University Press, 2003), p. 41.

[85] Raphael Samuel, 'The Workshop of the World: Steam Power and Hand Technology in Mid-Victorian Britain', *History Workshop*, 3.1 (Spring 1977), 6–72, p. 7.

[86] Samuel, p. 12.

'the poor needlewoman's fingers'. In a world reliant upon the 'invisible hand', massification actually depends upon individuals, and yet in many contemporary accounts, human beings are at best forgotten in the focus on 'the simultaneous and repetitive operations of the machine.'[87] Christoph Asendorf takes the image further, charting a transition whereby 'the heartbeat, one of the elementary experiences of time, loses its autonomy to the beat of the machine—the latter makes the body into a *perpetuum mobile* that has to move with the regularity of a clock';[88] he appeals to Foucault to associate the prohibitions of factory life in the period with a shift to a linear and regimented sense of time.[89] The trope of child labourers as machines was entirely familiar.[90]

Changing fashions dictated that variation was a key part of the thriving economic climate. Mass production also meant more choice when it came to manufactured goods. However, particular models within runs of items were identical, and newly so. John Styles describes 'the manufacture of large batches of hundreds or thousands or tens of thousands of individual items to uniform specifications'; he goes on to argue that 'Developing specialized mechanical devices that would eliminate variability in products became an important preoccupation'.[91] The factory processes which plunged many into repetitive drudgery had positive social effects, leading in Jan de Vries's account to 'a steady rise, generation by generation, of the number, range, and quality of material possessions' amongst all sectors of society.[92] Yet whilst it thus made life more comfortable, proliferation and massification also caused anxieties: Roy Porter has highlighted the troubling association between metaphorical and symbolic undertones of consumption as both wasting disease, *and* a growing abundance of things, including, most troublingly, foodstuffs, in the period.[93] For better or worse, machine-made goods proliferated, being predictable and ostensibly duplicative in a way that hand-made objects struggle to be. In this new consumer society, the element of repetition is complex: praised for its economic advantages, in other quarters it was understood to be inferior, so that, by the end of the century, when 'the Bilston manufacturers began to go over to machine-stamped frying pans, they

---

[87] Samuel, p. 17; p. 14; p. 45.   [88] Asendorf, p. 144.   [89] Asendorf, pp. 146–7.
[90] See for example Andrew Wynter, *Our Social Bees; or, Pictures of Town & Country Life* (London: Robert Hardwicke, 1865), p. 189, or the discussion about 'little human machines' in Samuel, p. 49.
[91] John Styles, 'Manufacturing, consumption and design in eighteenth-century England', in John Brewer and Roy Porter, eds, *Consumption and the World of Goods* (Abingdon: Routledge, 1993), pp. 527–54 (p. 528; p. 534).
[92] Jan de Vries, *The Industrious Revolution: Consumer Behaviour and the Household Economy, 1650 to the Present* (Cambridge: Cambridge University Press, 2008), p. 124. De Vries cites Bruno Blonde: 'archaeological excavations in Antwerp have produced shoes from the sixteenth and eighteenth centuries. The former almost always show signs of repair; the latter almost never do.' (p. 145, n. 74). However, De Vries's account is not without its critics (see for example Frank Trentmann, *Empire of Things* (London: Penguin, 2017) pp. 74–5).
[93] Roy Porter, 'Consumption: disease of the consumer society?', in *Consumption and the World of Goods*, pp. 58–84.

took good care to do so in disguise. "The knowing housewife still looks for the marks of the hammer, so they are added afterwards."'[94] The capacity for perfect repetition was also a mixed blessing for the Royal Mint, whose disquiet was aroused by the possibility of too-perfect repetitions in the forgery of money which contemporary technologies made possible, but then also assuaged by the same industrial effort.[95] Such examples suggest a degree of self-awareness regarding the ambiguous desirability of the new possibilities for repetition, understood as such, and they connect the discourse of repetition to that of suspicious forgery as much as to that of desirable perfection.

The way of life depicted in John Clare's Northamptonshire village is predominantly pre-industrial, according to a seasonal cycle: he charts the presence in the community of the village of itinerant workers who perform tasks repetitively, but as craft, and who furthermore do so according to a predictable rhythm (predictable, but not particular: the knife grinder might come, for example, when harvest starts, rather than on 22 August at 2.30 p.m.). Yet Clare also often laments the decline in this traditional mode of living.[96] William Cobbett documents a similar transformation.[97] Beyond such accounts as Clare's and Cobbett's, though, is it reasonable to suggest that these changes were generally perceptible to those living through them? James Vernon has argued that the decline of ways of living more traditional to communities, concomitant with the shift to living in an industrialized society, 'generated a countermovement of attempts to reembed social, political, and economic relations in the local and personal'. Vernon discredits attempts to explain such phenomena as the survival of traditions, finding them rather to be 'attempts to localize and personalize new abstract systems.'[98] This suggests a persistent desire for continuity (which might also be called repetition). It also indicates that individuals and communities were aware of the decline of traditionally repeated aspects of life, trying to establish new ones being suggestive of heightened self-consciousness. E. A. Wrigley represents the summit of a tradition of historical argument which has maintained that the effects of the industrial revolution on societies were *not* evident to contemporaries ('The very fact that the term "industrial revolution" only came into common usage towards the end of the

---

[94] Samuel, p. 56, citing Arthur Shadwell's *Industrial Efficiency* (London, 1906), i, 150.

[95] Forgery was rife in the first decade of the century, but the forgers were thwarted by changes in the production of coins, 'made possible by Boulton's new steam-powered Royal Mint which, by ensuring the uniformity of these coins...finally put the counterfeiters out of business'. See James Vernon, *Distant Strangers: How Britain Became Modern* (Berkeley and Los Angeles: University of California Press, 2014), p. 113.

[96] See for example Sarah Houghton, 'The "Community" of John Clare's Helpston', in *Studies in English Literature, 1500–1900*, 46.4 (Autumn 2006), 781–802, or Sarah Houghton, '"Some little thing of other days / Saved from the wreck of time": John Clare and Festivity', in *John Clare Society Journal*, 23 (2004), 21–43.

[97] See for example his *Rural Rides* [1830], ed. Ian Dyck (London: Penguin, 2001), which records a perceived decline in the traditions and patterns of rural life (interpreted by Cobbett as such).

[98] Vernon, pp. 14–15.

nineteenth century is indirect evidence of this.'[99]) But others have disagreed: Paul Langford asserts that 'contemporaries had little doubt of the importance of what was taking place.'[100] Emma Griffin's *Liberty's Dawn* is particularly convincing in the way it draws on autobiographical writings to argue for a high degree of self-awareness amongst the labouring-class population, that something particular was going on at the time: 'The autobiographers never spoke of an "industrial revolution". But as they entered old age in the 1840s or 1850s... [they] did display an unmistakeable awareness that the times had changed.'[101] Griffin's meticulously documented account chimes here with E. P. Thompson's older argument, that 'it was not only the mill-owner but also the working population brought into being within and around the mills which seemed to contemporaries to be "new"', a novelty manifest in 'an essential change in the general character of the mass of the people', according to Robert Owen.[102] By 1842, William Cooke Taylor was writing that 'The manufacturing population is not new in its formation alone: it is new in its habits of thought and action, which have been formed by the circumstances of its condition', circumstances dominated by repetitions.[103]

In the *Jenaer Realphilosophie*, Hegel invokes Adam Smith's pin factory to argue that industrial production radically differs from handicraft manufacturing, and to highlight the shift towards specialization and division of labour he was witnessing in the first decade of the nineteenth century. According to Asendorf, such specialization results in 'a differentiating mode of perception of things',[104] a shift which 'causes the relation between the producers and things to lose its basis in repetitive experience, continuity, and an overview of the entire process of production.'[105] Such accounts are not directly focused upon repetition; it is merely one aspect of the new economy they trace, and in any case, tracking any sense of general consensus or awareness amongst a whole population is obviously problematic. But according to such conclusions, members of this new population are made and marked by the situation in which they live, characterized by new forms of repetition. Unverifiable in any empirical way, it therefore nonetheless intuitively seems plausible that a society flushed with products which were precise replicas of themselves in a way never before imaginable, produced through processes understood to be repetitive, by people living lives more regularized

---

[99] E. A. Wrigley, *The Path to Sustained Growth: England's Transition from an Organic Economy to an Industrial Revolution* (Cambridge: Cambridge University Press, 2016), p. 19.

[100] Paul Langford, *A Polite and Commercial People: England 1727–1783* (Oxford: Oxford University Press, 1989), p. 666.

[101] Griffin, pp. 242–4.

[102] E. P. Thompson, *The Making of the English Working Class* (London: Penguin, 1963; 1980), p. 208.

[103] W. Cooke Taylor, 'Notes of a Tour in the Manufacturing Districts of Lancashire' (1842), quoted in Thompson, p. 209.

[104] Asendorf, p. 2. Asendorf refers to Hegel's *Jenenser Realphilosophie II: Die Vorlesungen von 1805/06*, ed. Johannes Hoffmeister (Leipzig: Meiner, 1931).

[105] Asendorf, p. 3.

than ever, might reflect that context in some ways. And whether or not it is reasonable to abstract a specific *general* attention to or awareness of repetition from these ideas about massification and industrialization, it is in this context that Wordsworth dwells on the implications and possibilities of tautology, and wonders about the possibility of ever completing a multiply-revised poem about the growth of his own mind; that Coleridge wonders about the mind's self-reflection in the act of thinking; that Keats and Shelley experiment with ekphrasis and translation, and that Clare attempts to accommodate specificity within the general truths demanded by natural history. Recent scholarship has begun to wonder about the connections between the arts and industrial processes, in a more figurative sense.[106] The influence of the industrial context might never be knowable or measurable, but it is reason to be interested in, and attentive to the operation of, repetition in the Romantic Period.

Political Revolution

It would seem wilfully perverse to write about repetition in the Romantic Period without dwelling at least briefly on the historical and imaginative potency of other revolutions. Whether in writing about the immediate situation in 1790s France, or in the spinning-out of its broader significances for ideas of empire in works like Volney's *Ruins* or Shelley's 'Ozymandias', in its sharing of a vocabulary with slave revolutions in the Caribbean, or in the more domestic shock of Peterloo, the discourse of political revolution indelibly marks Romantic literature. Scholarship has described the ways in which revolutionary discourse spilled and spread, being legible in Wordsworth's work far beyond his engagement with events in France, even (for example) shaping his understanding of the fundamental structures of the earth itself.[107] Beyond the sheer breadth and extent of its relevance to writers in the period, revolution is important to ideas of repetition because of the beautiful paradox it contains: its sense of return, of coming round again, is balanced with the coterminous connotation of radical renewal, associated with entirely new beginnings. In this sense, it participates in the same definitional dilemma of repetition which always accommodates variation simply by virtue of its being repetitious, and is therefore *not* straightforwardly 'the same again'. Close comparative attention to repetition within the discourses of political revolution is beyond the scope of this book; here, I include it as an example principally to highlight that the contextual significances and relevancies of repetition to

---

[106] See John Gardner's research project, 'Engineering Romanticism', based in Anglia Ruskin University.
[107] 'By the 1790s, geology had assumed the status of the preeminent science of revolution... Wordsworth learned to read social revolution in terms of the language of geology' (Bewell, pp. 246–8).

romantic-period literature are manifold, stretching, and even at times contradictory. This chapter has certainly failed to contain them: whilst it has attempted to survey some of the historical aspects which exert pressure on the idea of repetition, and particularly those which impact upon contemporary thought about poetry and poetic praxis, it has necessarily been highly selective, because the focus of the remainder of this book is on local and specific effects of repetition in Wordsworth's poetry: on the idea of saying something again, which might involve variation, and on the texture of writing which results from that kind of repetition; and beyond this, on the connections which exist between such iterations. Whilst they cannot control the repetition of whole (or parts of) texts in the sense of re-reading, authors can control the effects of repetition on a far more minute scale, through its exploitation as a literary device with multiple modes. Looking closely at Wordsworth's work, placed lightly alongside the far broader contexts outlined in these introductory chapters, reveals an intense awareness in his writing of the challenges and possibilities of recapitulation and revision which the remainder of this book sets out to explore.

PART II
WORDSWORTHIAN RECAPITULATION

4
Repetition and Conjunction
The Quiet Work of *And* and *Or*

As a form of autobiography, Wordsworth's *Prelude* is preoccupied with looking back and repeating (emotionally, imaginatively, and textually) the events of Wordsworth's life. As a text which exists for the modern reader in multiple versions, *The Prelude* acts also as an exemplar of the repetition implicated in textual revision. Whilst all editing revises, the different versions of *The Prelude* articulate an awareness that the records of past events, feelings, and responses must be changed as the perspective of the poet changes, if they are to be accurate, or 'sincere'. Looking back on his experience of France in Book IX of *The Prelude*, in a passage which has been taken as exemplary of the way in which Wordsworth's changing opinion over time inflects his depiction of events and feelings, Wordsworth recalls an unsettled period when 'All things were to me | Loose and disjointed'. Explicitly attaching his disorientation to his inability adequately to discern connections between events, Wordsworth is 'left without a vital interest' (IX.106–7; l. 108). Yet the poem itself aims exactly to revitalize: to bring past experience to life. One way in which it does so is by negotiating the theoretical problems of disjunction it diagnoses, through the use of grammatical conjunctions. Coordinating conjunctions perform the physical work of joining, separating, and indicating relationship. They thereby assist in marking down on the page the results of the processes of memory, their difference from the present, and the connections between them in Wordsworth's mind. As they declare these connections, conjunctions simultaneously negotiate a particular form of recapitulation, allowing various versions of memories to exist without contradiction. Attending to the coordinating conjunctions *and* and *or* illuminates Wordsworth's attitude to connections and relationship in a literal sense; understood conceptually, they also offer revealing insights into Wordsworth's revisions and recapitulations, and they attest to Wordsworth's achievement of the 'sincerity' he prized. Examination of the unobtrusive conjunctions *and* and *or* and their function in literary texts thus bears significantly on the major preoccupations of this book.

Connection and Conjunction

> Along his infant veins are interfus'd
> The gravitation and the filial bond
> Of nature, that connect him with the world.
>
> (*The Prelude* II.262–4)

These lines celebrate the connection between mother and 'infant babe' as the blessing which cultivates the 'Poetic spirit' (l. 276); which confers upon Wordsworth the ability to be a poet. Yet, immediately previously, Wordsworth has announced the impossibility of locating such beginnings: it is

> Hard task to analyse a soul, in which,
> Not only general habits and desires,
> But each most obvious and particular thought,
> Not in a mystical and idle sense,
> But in the words of reason deeply weigh'd,
> Has no beginning.
>
> (I.232–7)

Holding together both the 'particular' and the 'general', Wordsworth asserts the impossibility of tracing the origin of the constitution of his own poetic selfhood as he confers an essentially circular character onto it. The theological resonance to line 237 suggests this sense of circularity, but it also implies an absence of perceptible connection. In Book VIII, Wordsworth's interest in conjunction in its broadest sense (in the connections between things, and the nature of such connections) is more apparent still:

> Thus sometimes were the shapes
> Of wilful fancy grafted upon feelings
> Of the imagination and they rose
> In worth accordingly.
>
> (VIII.583–6)

Wordsworth's poetic development has produced increasingly valuable results by putting things together in particular ways. A 'graft' is not an entirely new plant, sprung from seed, but part of one living plant joined to another. The lines thus evoke a deliberative and effortful form of reproduction dependent upon connection, in which the pun on the hard work of digging is not lost.[1] Having declared

---

[1] Contemporary definitions of 'graft' indicated a particular volume of earth dug, and, relatedly, a type of spade (*OED*, definition 3). Both suggest the origin of the term's association with labouring, as well as with growing by scion.

that his 'present Theme | Is to retrace the way that led me on | Through nature to the love of human Kind', Wordsworth admits that his mind has had fallible moments, but asserts nonetheless that, 'having been brought up in such a grand | And lovely region', and having 'At all times had a real solid world | Of images about me' (VIII.587–605), he has been preserved from the unanchored, disconnected thoughts of one unblessed by such an upbringing. In lines whose asyndeton draws attention to itself, he declares his sympathy for Coleridge's inevitable (as Wordsworth sees it) pining, as a city-bred child,

> in endless dreams
> Of sickliness, disjoining, joining things
> Without the light of knowledge.
>
> (VIII.608–10)

The connections Coleridge's mind has made are painted as haphazard, ignorant, and therefore unstable. Comforted by the advantages of being, in contrast, made 'steady' in his own thoughts, his composure conferred by his particular environment (VIII.599), Wordsworth insists on the necessity of mental balance: the random connections made by the unsteadied mind are not conducive to progress as a poet. But these lines preserve a degree of productive ambiguity which was lost when they appeared in print in 1850, invoking instead Coleridge's pining

> in endless dreams
> Of sickliness, disjoining, joining, things
> Without the light of knowledge.
>
> (1850 VIII.435–7)[2]

The different placing of the commas here makes the sentence mean something different.[3] Where in 1805 Wordsworth seems to refer to ideas ('things') which might be joined or disjoined according to a more-or-less disordered imagination, in 1850, the very activities of joining and disjoining are themselves the pitiable

---

[2] William Wordsworth, *The Prelude* (London: Edward Moxon, 1850), repr. in a facsimile edition, ed. Jonathan Wordsworth (Oxford and New York: Woodstock Books, 1993), p. 225.

[3] Punctuation of Wordsworth's works is notoriously controversial. This study assumes that the punctuation in the Cornell editions is accurate (on Mark Reed's editorial principles, applied to the 1805 *Prelude*, see *The Thirteen Book 'Prelude'*, pp. 99–104). Whilst the lack of a single text with settled punctuation inevitably leaves some readings more open to debate than might be desirable, I hope to draw on sufficient different examples to offset any anxiety about the arguable nature of one or two undetermined or contentious moments. In this particular example, some major modern editions preserve the punctuation which appeared in 1850: see *The Prelude 1799, 1805, 1850: Authoritative Texts, Context and Reception*, ed. Jonathan Wordsworth, M. H. Abrams, and Stephen Gill (London: W. W. Norton, 1979), or *The Prelude: The Four Texts (1798, 1799, 1805, 1850)*, ed. Jonathan Wordsworth (London: Penguin, 1995). However, the Cornell edition of the 1850 *Fourteen Book Prelude* retains the 1805 punctuation, omitting the relevant comma. (The scope for legitimate but differing editorial choices here is obviously itself significant.)

'things | Without the light of knowledge'. In 1850, that is, greater emphasis is shifted onto the way in which things are arranged and conjoined, moving away from the decipherable content of those constructions (whilst still asserting the steadying value of that content).

This interest in the *activity* of conjunction goes to the heart of *The Prelude*, in which Wordsworth draws attention to the capacity of the mind to 'disjoin' and 'join' things, as part of a process in which the constitution of the poetic mind is revealed. Another aspect of its legacy is found in Wordsworth's comments on the translation of Chaucer, where he identifies conjunctions as the only appropriate place in which to retain 'the ancient accent'.[4] It is also significantly evident in the poet's insistence that all of his works are connected. A letter written by the Wordsworths to Coleridge in December 1798 distinguished between the 'little Rhyme poems' and the 'descriptions' composed in blank verse it included.[5] For Hugh Sykes Davies, this letter's distinction between blank verse pieces (considered by the Wordsworths as 'serious'), and poems in ballad form (which they hoped would 'amuse' their friend), reflects an ongoing hesitation on Wordsworth's part relating to the propriety of these two broad formal categories for the ideals the *Lyrical Ballads* were founded upon. Yet even across this distinction, Sykes Davies notices subjects, themes, images, and phrases shared between poems: distinction is less remarkable, that is, than are affinities, similarities, and connections.[6] Recognizing such shared elements, Sykes Davies proves himself a dutiful reader: the relationship between part and whole in Romantic writing has become a critical cliché, but Wordsworth's conception of the interrelationship of his works, evidenced in the practical organization of his texts, and in the interfiliation between them he explicitly declares, bespeaks its centrality to the poet's self-conception. Wordsworth writes of *The Prelude* and *The Recluse* as having 'the same kind of relation to each other... as the Anti-chapel has to the body of a gothic Church', and, continuing the allusion, declares that his 'minor Pieces... when they shall be properly arranged, will be found by the attentive Reader to have such connection with the main Work as may give them claim to be likened to the little cells, oratories, and sepulchral recesses, ordinarily included in those edifices.'[7] Wordsworth's 'attentive' reader will be able to discern the entirety of his writing as a series of *and*s and *or*s, of supplementary things and alternative things which

---

[4] Wordsworth, 'Preface' to *The Prioress's Tale*, in *Translations of Chaucer and Virgil*, ed. Bruce E. Graver (Cornell University Press: Ithaca, 1998), p. 36.

[5] W[illiam] W[ordsworth] and D[orothy] W[ordsworth] to S. T. Coleridge, 14 or 21 December 1798, in *The Letters of William and Dorothy Wordsworth*, ed. Ernest de Selincourt, 8 vols, 2nd edn, rev. Mary Moorman, Alan G. Hill, and Chester L. Shaver (Oxford: Clarendon Press, 1967–93), *Volume 1: The Early Years 1787–1805*, ed. E. de Selincourt, 2nd edn, rev. Chester L. Shaver (Oxford: Clarendon Press, 1967), pp. 235–43.

[6] See Hugh Sykes Davies, *Wordsworth and the Worth of Words*, ed. John Kerrigan and Jonathan Wordsworth (Cambridge University Press: Cambridge, 1986), pp. 14–15.

[7] Wordsworth, 'Preface' to *The Excursion* [1814], in *Prose*, iii, 3–12 (pp. 5–6).

suggestively (though not definitively) declare their own connectedness, and whose very existence is necessary to the possibility of a 'main Work'. The act of discerning connection invokes a model of reading which is fundamentally recapitulative, the reader recalling and reassessing relationship as each new text is encountered.

Francis Jeffrey's scathing, path-setting review of *The Excursion* famously imputed a 'peculiar system' to Wordsworth's work.[8] The idea that an idiosyncratic order underpinned Wordsworth's writings had already appeared in responses to the 1807 *Poems*, and it persisted in the reception of the 1815 *Poems*, despite the fact that Wordsworth had denied any such scheme in the 'Preface' to *Lyrical Ballads*. Acknowledging this denial, modern critics have nonetheless followed Jeffrey, finding Wordsworth to be constructing a poetic system. Scott Hess, for example, offers one cogent account, arguing that Wordsworth 'attempted to reorganize print culture' with the intention of establishing an 'author-centered poetics',[9] specifically 'in order to construct his own poetic authority and identity'; in this undertaking, Hess suggests, the poet was enabled by the way in which Coleridge 'wove a new structure of authority' around the figure of the poet, 'a structure that transforms the decorum of class into...the decorum of the mind's act of reflecting on itself.'[10] Hess's vocabulary of reflection here indicates one way in which repetition inflects Wordsworth's poetic methodology, as well as the wider-reaching reconfiguration of literary culture he advances. But within this broader context of literary culture, Wordsworth's *Prelude* itself forces a rethinking of internal structural connection. Herbert Lindenberger points out that 'memoir is concerned chiefly with time in a mechanical sense: events follow one another because the calendar says they do. In *The Prelude* experiences are made to follow one another with a more inward inevitability'.[11] Such 'inward inevitability' demands a refined appreciation of what it means for events to be connected. In the 'Preface' to his 1815 *Poems*, Wordsworth recommits himself to a relational organization, dividing his works into 'classes': 'the small pieces of which these volumes consist, thus discriminated, might be regarded under a two-fold view; as composing an entire work within themselves, and as adjuncts to the philosophical Poem, "The Recluse"'. He recalls the hope of the 'Preface' to the latter poem, that

---

[8] Jeffrey's review of *The Excursion* appeared in the *Edinburgh Review* in November 1814 and is repr. in Robert Woof, ed., *William Wordsworth: The Critical Heritage, Volume I 1793–1820* (New York: Routledge, 2001), pp. 381–404.

[9] See Scott Hess, 'Wordsworth's "System," the Critical Reviews, and the Reconstruction of Literary Authority', *European Romantic Review*, 16.4 (2005), 471–97 (p. 471), https://doi.org/10.1080/10509580500303991, accessed 2 June 2022. Brian Bates's *Wordsworth's Poetic Collections, Supplementary Writing and Parodic Reception* (London: Pickering and Chatto, 2012) explores contemporary responses to Wordsworth; both Hess and Bates survey the discourse-shaping criticism surrounding Wordsworth's 'system'.

[10] Hess, p. 493.

[11] Herbert Lindenberger, *On Wordsworth's Prelude* (Princeton, NJ: Princeton University Press, 1964), p. 137.

the reader should perceive 'a meditated arrangement of [the] minor Poems', which are in 'connection with each other'.[12] Stephen Gill associates this mode of Wordsworthian 'classification' specifically with his habits of revision: 'Wordsworth had a sense of his whole *oeuvre*—published and unpublished—as interrelated and interdependent. His constant revision indicates a sense also that the evolving whole had both a historic existence, but, much more importantly, a being in the continuous present. Revisiting is... a live engagement with the past that reactivates it into conjunction with the present.'[13] Gill's use of the word conjunction here is obviously not intended to imply a grammatical sense, but grammatical conjunctions are vitally important to what Wordsworth wants to achieve through the establishment of these textual relationships.

Examining a passage from Thomson's *Spring*, Wolfram Schmidgen prefaces his analysis with a survey of the argument that modern society originated as a result of increasing differentiation in various spheres, yet he goes on to assert that the idea of a specialized and divided society has now transformed: 'We surely live in a period of weakening boundaries and increasing mobilities. The basic paradigm of our modernization narratives, differentiation, can no longer capture such a world.' Instead, Schmidgen argues, modern society is interested in hybridity, and 'explains culture not by highlighting the separation of kinds, spheres, and functions, but by stressing their blending'. He goes on to note that the word *or* has an essentially hybrid effect on Thomson's poem, because it allows multiple possibilities to exist at the same time.[14] Wordsworth was not possessed with such insight that he foresaw the preoccupation of the twenty-first century with intersections and fluidity, but he is acutely sensitive to the challenges involved in representing multiple possibilities (or versions) without necessary contradiction. Tellingly, Schmidgen finds the source of Thomson's *or* to lie in the predecessor whose influence Wordsworth shares: 'Thomson's reliance on the conjunction "or" is indebted to Milton, who realized the expansionist and inclusivist ambitions of his epic poetry in part through boundary-crossing shifts from one potential figure or scene to another.'[15] Expansion and inclusion, opening outwards and joining together, are fundamental capacities of the conjunctions *or* and *and*. These conjunctions are thus able to enact refined forms of recapitulation which are crucial to the quality of Wordsworth's writing. However, the operation of both conjunctions is more complex still than this, and their function was under close scrutiny in the second half of the eighteenth century.

---

[12] 'Preface' to *Poems... in Two Volumes* [1815], in *Prose*, iii, 28.
[13] *Wordsworth's Revisitings*, pp. 36–7.
[14] Wolfram Schmidgen, 'Undividing the Subject of Literary History: From James Thomson's Poetry to Daniel Defoe's Novels', in Kate Parker and Courtney Weiss Smith, eds, *Eighteenth-Century Poetry and the Rise of the Novel Reconsidered* (Lewisburg: Bucknell University Press, 2013), pp. 85–99 (p. 88).
[15] Schmidgen, p. 95.

And and *Or*

An interest in the technicalities of conjunction is evident in the flood of eighteenth-century grammars:

> The Connective parts of Sentences are the most important of all, and require the greatest care and attention: for it is by these chiefly that the train of thought, the course of reasoning, and the whole progress of the mind... are laid open; and on the right use of these the perspicuity, that is, the first greatest beauty of style, principally depends.[16]

Lowth's lines here exemplify the eighteenth-century desire for perspicuity, and the contemporary belief in 'Connective parts of Sentences' as central to perspicuous discourse. In 1690, Locke had stated that *'Particles connect Parts, or whole Sentences together'*, and that the functions of connectives is 'to express well... methodical and rational Thoughts.'[17] Sylvia Adamson demonstrates that throughout the eighteenth century, the perspicuity believed to be attainable through such expression retained its position as the 'dominant stylistic ideal';[18] following Locke, neo-classical writers 'deploy a greater range of connectives and differentiate their functions more precisely.'[19] Lowth's writing emerges from this context, and his attention to the importance and the potential of small, grammatically connective words like *and* and *or* finds echoes in the work of several twentieth-century readers of Wordsworth. In the middle of the century, John Jones argued that Wordsworth's achievement is 'an achievement shared... by the short words... [and] by language's humblest parts'. He specifically drew attention to the importance of *and*: '"And," more frequent in Wordsworth than in any poet, is the preserver of extreme structural simplicity through hundreds of lines of *Prelude* narrative... By its monotony, its insistence on the particular, *and* develops Wordsworth's expository style, in common with other words of modest function'.[20] This is convincing, but Jones is talking only about style. Specific issues of meaning also attach to these little words, especially to *and* and *or*.

Contemporary with Jones's study, Hugh Sykes Davis set out in *Wordsworth and the Worth of Words* to demonstrate the limitations of a certain type of

---

[16] Robert Lowth, *A Short Introduction to English Grammar: with Critical Notes*. 2nd edn (London: Millar and Dodsley, 1763), pp. 151–2, n. 2.

[17] John Locke, *An Essay Concerning Human Understanding* [1690], ed. Peter H. Nidditch (Oxford: Clarendon Press, 1979), p. 471; p. 472.

[18] Sylvia Adamson, 'Literary Language', in Suzanne Romaine, ed., *The Cambridge History of English Language Vol. IV: 1776–1997* (Cambridge: Cambridge University Press, 1998), pp. 589–692 (p. 595).

[19] Sylvia Adamson, 'Literary Language', in Roger Lass, ed., *The Cambridge History of English Language Vol. III: 1476–1776* (Cambridge: Cambridge University Press, 1999), pp. 539–653 (p. 607).

[20] John Jones, *The Egotistical Sublime: A History of Wordsworth's Imagination* (London: Chatto & Windus, 1964), pp. 206–7.

idiolectical approach to Wordsworth, criticizing Franklyn Bliss Snyder's 'Wordsworth's Favourite Words' as exemplary of it.[21] Snyder depended for his analysis on Lane Cooper's *Concordance*, which excluded what Sykes Davies called 'the really common words' (including for instance '*the, and, in*', the prepositions and conjunctions, and many other words arbitrarily selected); this omission is partly what led Sykes Davies to dismiss Snyder's scholarship as 'unfortunate', and 'meagre'.[22] Twenty years later, Christopher Ricks returned to the debate, agreeing that Snyder's methodological assumptions and his attribution of 'but little significance' to the omitted words, were wrong: 'little words can be, and often are, of the greatest significance.' Ricks compellingly argues that 'There is a sense in which prepositions constitute [the] "more philosophical language"' Wordsworth sought.[23] In various places, Ricks's spinning out of the operation of the preposition allows for a similar significance for the conjunction. Indeed, the first statement of his thesis is that:

> If as a poet you seek the simplest and most permanent form of language, you are bound to give special importance to prepositions *and conjunctions*... If as a poet you are concerned above all with relations and relationships, you are bound to give special importance to those words which express relationships: prepositions *and conjunctions*. Their importance for Wordsworth can hardly be overstated.[24]

Ricks's essay takes flight as it explores the operation and significance of Wordsworthian prepositions. But he leaves the conjunctions dangling, and never returns to weave them into the argument. A full consideration of the way in which relationships might be figured and explored must, however, offer an equivalent space to the conjunction, whose properties might be understood as even more vital than those of prepositions to the adequate expression of 'relationships', those joinings and disjoinings, and to the ways in which they can be made manifest on a page.

At the heart of Samuel Johnson's writing, Philip Davis finds a deeply troubling fear of ambiguity. Johnson, Davis explains, found it difficult to cope with 'mental gaps and vacuities, in experiencing contradiction or suffering passivity', and experienced 'in-between states of predicament, fallen uncertainty, and ambivalence' as painful. In Davis's account, syntax represents salvation, 'syntax being to Johnson the act of joining, with "syntactical" defined in the *Dictionary* as "conjoined, fitted to each other."' Eighteenth-century syntax, in this account, thus provides a way to manage and maintain Johnsonian sanity: 'the great work of

---

[21] Franklin Bliss Snyder, 'Wordsworth's Favourite Words', *Journal of English and Germanic Philology*, 22 (1923), 253–6.
[22] Sykes Davies, p. 51; p. 50; pp. 59–61.   [23] *Force of Poetry*, pp. 125–6; p. 121.
[24] *Force of Poetry*, p. 120 (my emphases).

human art is to put the separate phrases together', in order to sustain mental balance.²⁵ Wordsworth's writing finds Johnson's 'predicament' to be similarly inevitable, but very differently valued, and in the poet's work syntax (connectives in particular) becomes a means of communicating rather than avoiding the central truth about the indeterminate, changeable nature of human experience. In her account of alterations in the use of grammatical conjunctions across the Enlightenment and early nineteenth century, Adamson records that, amongst Romantic writers, 'opposition to the periodic sentence intensified':

> The formal features of a periodic sentence imply that the ideas it expresses have been pre-analysed into a hierarchy of importance. Periodic style leaves no room for the interruptions, digressions and new directions of spontaneous speech. Hence the breaking of a periodic sentence becomes an important figure in Romantic syntax... Underlying such frontal attacks on the periodic sentence is a more widespread shift in attitudes to connectivity, or, in syntactic terms, to the conventions governing clause-combining[.]²⁶

Adamson's account highlights the shift from a Johnsonian eighteenth century obsessed with hypotaxis, in which phrases or clauses are arranged in dependent or subordinate relationship, to a romantic-period veneration of parataxis. For Adamson, 'Where the period symbolised the virtues of unity and completeness, the parenthesis celebrates digression as a mode of discovery and the aside as the index of feeling and truth' (as she notes, the elevation of parataxis 'anticipates the Romantic genre of the fragment').²⁷ Adamson's history highlights two significant aspects of *and* and *or* for romantic-period writing. The first is that in literal, technical ways, what she emphasizes about writers' usage of conjunctions in the period is fascinating for reasons connected with well-recognized Romantic preoccupations and priorities: expression, spontaneity, and apparent faithfulness to feelings; that 'index of feeling and truth' often cast as 'sincerity'. The second is that in a conceptual sense, *and* and *or*, and the possibilities they imply for expressing things which might be incomplete, or more importantly things which might be seen in apparently contradictory ways *but* without any contradiction, are closely related to the Adamson's semantic 'interruptions, digressions and new directions'.

---

[25] Philip David, 'Johnson: Sanity and Syntax', in Freya Johnston and Lynda Mugglestone, eds, *Samuel Johnson: The Arc of the Pendulum* (Oxford: Oxford University Press, 2012), pp. 49–61 (p. 50; p. 51).

[26] Adamson, *Cambridge History of English Language Vol. IV*, p. 632-3. See also Adamson, *Cambridge History of English Language Vol. III*, pp. 607–8: 'Locke thus recognises no distinction between *cohesion* as a stylistic device and *coherence* as a semantic relation, or rather, he adopts an ideal view in which the one acts as a signal of the other... both Steele and Swift testify to the importance of connective strategies in the new stylistic idea, but where Steele does so by implementing Locke's recipe for "the clearness and beauty of a good Stile", Swift parodies it and puts in question the "methodical and rational" values with which it is associated.'

[27] Adamson, *Cambridge History of English Language Vol. IV*, pp. 638–9; p. 632.

Eighteenth-century grammarians increasingly came to recognize that the connectives they had relied upon for perspicuous discourse were capricious. In particular, they found *and* and *or* to be deeply problematic. Yet these very problems indicate particular ways in which a consideration of *and* and *or* lends itself to something more than an exercise in grammatical or logistical pedantry. The sense of possibility offered by the more conceptual *and*s and *or*s which hover behind Adamson's account, and the properties of conjunctions themselves where they do occur within texts, animate Wordsworth's writing. Because of their peculiarities, *and* and *or* offer exciting prospects to poets wanting to gesture to the impossibility of perfect expression even whilst expressing themselves, and particularly to Wordsworth as he revises and re-revises his work.

Certainly, it is the case that some of the trickiness inherent in *and* and *or* has always been exploited in verse. Pope's infamous zeugmatic sparkle, for instance, pivots on the conjunctions connecting disparate senses of his verbs.[28] Moreover, in numerous instances, Wordsworth himself employs *and* and *or* in what (for the sake of economy) one might call straightforward ways: *and* can be an invaluable marker of narrative progression or additional content; in discourse, *or* can express a simple choice or alternative; the phenomenon I am describing is not universally true of each use of these words. This qualification being acknowledged, the way in which theorists have grappled with *and* and *or* sheds light on the potentials within them, demonstrating that what I am proposing is more than a vague analogy for thinking about Romantic writing. Since classical times, the categorization of co-ordinating conjunctions has puzzled and fascinated both grammarians and philosophical logicians. Ian Michael traces the attempt back to the third century BC, noting that 'The classification of conjunctions continued as a customary practice, though its inadequacy was recognised.' He draws his tour to a close with Thomas of Erfurt's awareness 'of the unsatisfactory delimitation of the categories adverb and conjunction', adding only that 'the renaissance grammarians have nothing to add.'[29] The eighteenth century saw a renewed interest in the opportunities and difficulties presented by conjunctions, but grammarians seeking a schema fit for the Enlightenment were foxed by the operation of *and* and *or*. By 1771, James Harris was dismissive of them both, as words which refused to disclose the nature of the connection they asserted: *and*, he declared, 'does no more than barely *couple* Sentences', and *or*, being '*indefinite*', does 'no more, than *merely disjoin*'.[30] Whilst it might at first glance seem straightforward (*and* in general suggests a supplement, something *as well as*, whereas *or* posits an alternative, something *instead of*),

---

[28] See for examples *The Rape of the Lock*, in *Poetical Works*, pp. 86–109, III, ll. 7–8; II, ll. 107–9.
[29] Ian Michael, *English Grammatical Categories and the Tradition to 1800* (London: Cambridge University Press, 1970), pp. 103–6.
[30] James Harris, *Hermes; or, A Philosophical Inquiry concerning Universal Grammar*, 3rd rev. edn (London: John Nourse and Paul Vaillant, 1771), p. 242; p. 252 (emphases original). Harris is one of Adamson's examples in *Cambridge History of English Language Vol. III*, p. 607.

a harder push on their definition reveals the greater complexity which resulted in this interpretative disappointment.

Intuitively, *and* implies an addition; something more; by implication, something different, even if it is more of the same (I might read more *and* more poetry). But *and* can also suggest repetition (I might go on *and* on reading the same poem, over and over again). Discussing the semantic implications of coordination by *and*, the *Grammar of Contemporary English* states that:

> *And* denotes merely a relation between the clauses. The only restriction is the semantic one that the contents of the clauses should have sufficient in common to justify their combination... The implications of the combination vary and they depend on our presuppositions and our knowledge of the world.[31]

A list of the different types of implication follows, which (in brief) defines *and* as variously 'therefore'; 'then'; 'in contrast'; as 'a comment on' a previous statement; as a concession in which 'but' might actually replace *and*; as an indication of a condition; as an indicator of a point being similar to a previous point, and finally, as a so-called 'pure' addition to a previous point, the only suggestion being that the two points are in agreement or alike in some way.[32] The problem for grammarians, then, is that *and* doesn't reveal enough about the nature of the connection it implies to be definitive. Moreover, the list of potential implications also makes clear that only some uses of *and* imply a supplement; at least two of them suggest an alternative (something more like a *but*, or an *or*). In the most basic way, we can see one of these potential confusions played out on the title page of any modern edition of *Lyrical Ballads*: are they poems by Wordsworth and Coleridge, or are there some by each? What is the connection between the two writers, and between each and the text which follows? As Adamson points out, 'Writing that relies heavily on conjunctions like these thus poses continual problems of interpretation for its readers.'[33] The same peculiar character, however, offers rich opportunities for writers able to exploit it; deft handling of these characteristics holds a great deal of suggestive potential for a poet interested in different, but somehow simultaneously 'sincere' versions of the same narrative: for Wordsworth, for example, recording events at different distances which alter the way in which those events are understood, without wholly eradicating previous apprehensions of them.

Despite Lowth's confident tone in the earlier extract, his *Grammar* ignores the complexities of conjunctions. For Lowth, the operation of *and* as a conjunction is straightforward: 'The Conjunction connects or *joins together* Sentences; so as out

---

[31] Randolf Quirk, Sidney Greenbaum, Geoffrey Leech, and Jan Svartvik, *A Grammar of Contemporary English* (London: Longman, 1972), p. 560.
[32] *Grammar of Contemporary English*, pp. 560–2.
[33] Adamson, *Cambridge History of English Language Vol. III*, p. 607.

of two, to make one Sentence.'[34] But contemporaries were more sensitive to the complexities of *and* which the *Grammar of Contemporary English* spells out. Like Lowth, James Beattie (whose poetry Wordsworth imitated almost to the extent of plagiarism[35]) insists on the supremacy of the conjunction:

> Conjunctions are those parts of language, that, by joining sentences in various ways, mark the connections, and various dependencies, of human thought... where there is, in any discourse, a remarkable deficiency of connecting particles, it may be presumed, either that there is a want of connection, or that sufficient pains has not been taken to explain it... Nothing tends more to impress the mind with a distinct idea of a complex object, than a strict and natural connection of the parts.[36]

But Beattie is alert (as Lowth is not) to the complications hiding within the operation of *and*, and the difficulty of understanding the nature of its connection. Connection is repeatedly held to be a fundamental aspect of good Enlightenment writing in the eighteenth century, conveying a vital clarity, and acting as a demonstration of rational deliberation. But it proves slippery:

> Perhaps it may be thought, that Conjunctions, as well as prepositions, do sometimes connect words; as when we say, He is a learned *and* a wise *and* a good man. But this sentence, when analysed, will be found to consist of three distinct sentences;—he is a learned man;—he is a wise man;—he is a good man; or,—he is learned,—he is wise,—he is good: which three would forever remain distinct and separate, if we had no connection words to unite them in one sentence... [W]hen it is said, Peter and John went to the temple, it may seem, that the conjunction *and* connects only the two names *Peter* and *John*: but it really connects two sentences,—Peter went to the temple,—John went to the

---

[34] Lowth, *A Short Introduction*, pp. 98–9.
[35] In a letter of 1815, Wordsworth alludes to Beattie's interest in 'Syntax and *grammar*', with which he is evidently familiar. (See W[illiam] W[ordsworth] to R. P. Gillies, 14 February 1815, in *The Letters of William and Dorothy Wordsworth, Volume 3: The Middle Years, Part II: 1812–1820*, ed. Ernest de Selincourt, 2nd edn., rev. Mary Moorman and Alan G. Hill, pp. 195–8 (p. 196)). Although there is no reference to it in Duncan Wu's *Wordsworth's Reading 1770–1799* (Cambridge: Cambridge University Press, 1993), or his *Wordsworth's Reading 1800–1815* (Cambridge: Cambridge University Press, 1995), elsewhere Wu suggests Wordsworth 'had almost certainly encountered the philosophical writings of James Beattie... and probably read his *Dissertations Moral and Critical*', in which volume *The Theory of Language* was included. (Duncan Wu, *Wordsworth: An Inner Life* (Oxford: Blackwell, 2002; 2004), p. 16). The wider influence of Beattie on Wordsworth is explored in E. H. King, 'James Beattie's *The Minstrel* (1771, 1774): Its Influence on Wordsworth', *Studies in Scottish Literature*, 8.4 (1970), 3–29, and Kathryn Sutherland, 'The Native Poet: The Influence of Percy's Minstrel from Beattie to Wordsworth', *The Review of English Studies*, 33.132 (November 1982), 414–33.
[36] Beattie, *The Theory of Language*, new edn (London: A. Strahan, 1788), p. 355.

temple; for unless we suppose the words, *went to the temple*, to belong both to Peter and to John, the expression has no meaning.[37]

So far, so good: *and* actually connects sentences rather than words, helpfully uniting several separate sentences into a single, comprehensible one, in which the nature of the connection between the parts is clearly understood. But the picture is clouded by the complication that conjunctions are governed differently in the presence of certain prepositions, predicates, or semantics:

> conjunctions do sometimes connect words, and not sentences; as in examples, like the following: Saul *and* Peter are the same: This book cost a shilling *and* more: There is war between England *and* France. Each of these, no doubt, is one sentence, and, if we keep to the same phraseology, incapable of being broken into two. For, if instead of the first we say, 'Saul is the same—Paul is the same,' we utter nonsense... If we say, instead of the second, 'This book cost a shilling—this book cost more,' we speak with little meaning, or at least inaccurately. And, instead of the third, if we say, 'There is war between England—there is war between France,' we fall into nonsense as before[.][38]

Anna Wierzbika describes Beattie's work as 'amazingly reminiscent in form and content of what many twentieth century linguists have said';[39] Wierzbika revisits the problem, examining the solutions which grammarians and philosophical logicians have offered, demonstrating the faults inherent in each of them, and concluding that the problem remains 'an exceptionally intriguing and tantalizing dilemma'.[40] As for Beattie, referring to the passages from his *Theory of Language* quoted above, she declares:

> The last part of this passage is particularly interesting in that it shows Beattie's awareness of the fact that what is needed is a *uniform* analysis of the whole area under consideration... But the specific proposal Beattie made to meet this need—to regard all conjunction as 'sentential' conjunction—is totally unconvincing... The problem is indeed an intractable one.[41]

---

[37] Beattie, p. 346.   [38] Beattie, pp. 346–7.
[39] Anna Wierzbika, *Lingua Mentalis: The Semantics of Natural Language* (Sydney and New York: Academic Press, 1980), p. 223.
[40] Wierzbika, p. 223. An example of 'conjunction reduction', which illustrates the problem, is Wierzbika's sentence, 'I have learned an interesting fact: John and Mary are Mormons.' As Beattie's passage implies, and as Wierzbika spells out, *and* in this sentence can be understood as joining two ideas together: 'I have learned two interesting facts: first, John is a Mormon, and second, Mary is a Mormon.' But if we then put the sentence back together (perfectly logically) as 'I have learned two interesting facts: John and Mary are Mormons', we descend into the realm of the ridiculous. See Wierzbika, p. 226.
[41] Wierzbika, p. 224.

Here, though, the possibility of a solution is irrelevant. The important point is that *and* has a peculiar capacity to join together things without specifying precisely their connection, and to posit complexity beneath apparently straightforwardly conjoined ideas: 'It seems that wherever "and" appears at the surface, something is necessarily thought of in terms of addition, that is in terms of something being part of something else.'[42] That image of surface has a correspondent depth only hinted at through the relations implied in the rest of Wierzbika's sentence, a hint towards the possibilities for writers negotiating the expression of a 'sense sublime | Of something far more deeply interfused';[43] a hint, that is, towards the possibilities for the negotiation of the line between vital sublimity and less edifying obfuscation.

Just as *and* has fascinated linguists and philosophers, so the instability at the heart of *or* has been well explored. Jonson's 1640 *English Grammar* claims that 'A *conjunction* is a word without number, knitting divers speeches together: and is *declaring*, or *reasoning*. *Declaring*, which uttereth the parts of a sentence: and that again is *gathering*, or *separating*. *Gathering*,... which is *coupling*... as *And, also, neither*... A *separating conjunction* is... *severing*, or, *sundering*... when the parts are separated... so as more than one cannot be true as: *Either, whither, or*.'[44] But this is not strictly true: *or* can also be supplementary. Richard Jennings examines *or* as a matter of philosophical logic, listing numerous attempts by logicians to deal with its trickiness. Those he cites include Stephen Barker, who points out that 'Sometimes when we say "p or q," what we mean is "p or q but not both." This is called the *exclusive* sense of "or." More often when we say "p or q," we mean "p or q and perhaps both." This is called the *inclusive* sense of "or".'[45] After several pages of examples, Jennings concludes that

> Apart from the differences in the details of their accounts of the distinction, there are differences in their estimates of the relative frequency with which 'or' occurs in the two senses... Apart from the tangle of views on the exclusive/inclusive distinction... we find in some texts outright and in others near rejections of the distinction.[46]

Or, that is, is no easier to pin down than *and*.

---

[42] Wierzbika, pp. 232–3.

[43] 'Lines Written a Few Miles Above Tintern Abbey, On Revisiting the Banks of the Wye During a Tour, July 13, 1798', in William Wordsworth, *Lyrical Ballads, and Other Poems, 1797–1800*, ed. James Butler and Karen Green (Ithaca: Cornell University Press, 1992), pp. 116–20 (ll. 95–6).

[44] *The English Grammar: made by Ben Johnson [sic] for the benefit of all strangers out of his observation of the English language now spoken and in use* (n.pub, 1640), pp. 68–9.

[45] Stephen Barker, *The Elements of Logic*, 4th rev. edn (New York: McGraw Hill, 1985), p. 86, quoted in Richard Jennings, *The Genealogy of Disjunction* (New York and Oxford: Oxford University Press, 1994), p. 45.

[46] Jennings, pp. 47–9.

However, this problem at the centre of what *or* signifies—its ability to be both 'inclusive' and 'exclusive' *at the same time*—is potentially very powerful. Keats's 'Ode on a Grecian Urn' provides an example. Andrew Bennett suggests that its concluding couplet ('"Beauty is truth, truth beauty"—that is all | Ye know on earth, and all ye need to know.'[47]) sustains a 'finality emphasised by other forms of rhetorical closure', but he argues that Keats simultaneously thwarts a sense of closure, as any interpretation results in 'endless multiplication';[48] the refusal of the poem to concede an 'answer' thus productively provokes Keats's 'Negative Capability'. But this posture of certain uncertainty is something Keats has adopted as habitual, earlier in the poem, through his deliberately indecisive *or*:

> What leaf-fringed legend haunts about thy shape
> Of deities or mortals, or of both,
> In Tempe or the dales of Arcady?
> What men or gods are these?
>
> ('Ode on a Grecian Urn', ll. 5–8)

The 'or' that Keats uses here is an 'inclusive' one, allowing for multiple possibilities simultaneously; this is an effect of *or* which, as Sharon Cameron declares in the context of a different discussion, 'positively precludes choice'.[49] Such an *or* refuses to concede any single answer, as each possibility is equally full. At the same time, it remains the 'exclusive' signal of an alternative, suggesting that one possibility must be correct, even as the intensity of the interrogatives refuses to settle on a single, 'right' answer. In this way, the lines mimic the effect of the perpetually ambiguous closing of the 'Urn', in that they prepare us to be content with resolute irresolution. The different possibilities that remain in play act as a refined form of recapitulation: they represent different and equally cogent ways of apprehending or appreciating the same thing, differently.

In Wordsworth's 'Beggars', we encounter a woman apparently approaching the poet:

> She had a tall Man's height, or more;
> No bonnet screen'd her from the heat;
> A long drab-colour'd Cloak she wore,
> A Mantle reaching to her feet:
> What other dress she had I could not know;
> Only she wore a Cap that was as white as snow.

---

[47] John Keats, 'Ode on a Grecian Urn', in *Complete Poems*, pp. 532–8 (ll. 49–50).
[48] Andrew Bennett, *Keats, Narrative and Audience: The Posthumous Life of Writing* (Cambridge: Cambridge University Press, 1994), p. 137; p. 134.
[49] Sharon Cameron, *Choosing Not Choosing: Dickinson's Fascicles* (Chicago: University of Chicago Press, 1992), p. 23.

>   ...Such Figure had I never seen:
>   ...Fit person was she for a Queen,
>   To head those ancient Amazonian files:
>   Or ruling Bandit's Wife, among the Grecian Isles.[50]

Wordsworth's use of *or* in the first line here, the excess it points to emphasized through the stuttering rhyme 'or more', is metrically satisfying but semantically troubling. Whilst it doesn't undo the possibility raised immediately previously, allowing that the woman was about as tall as a tall man, though she might have been rather taller (in this sense acting as an 'inclusive' *or*), it simultaneously suggests a lack of clarity of vision, or interpretation. A brutal rebuttal might argue that she either looked like this, or like that, but can't have been both, and that Wordsworth should make up his mind. It might even be argued that the description teeters on the brink of the ridiculous: the woman's supernatural height is almost sublime in its vastness, but simultaneously rendered bathetic through Wordsworth's apparent hyperbole in the context of an impoverished woman he happened to meet, and about whom, he admits, he 'could not know'.

That Wordsworth returned to the subject of this poem in 1817, fifteen years after first writing about the woman, suggests the power that the event, or the *idea* of the event articulated in the poem, exercised over his mind. If we choose to believe that Wordsworth is simply making a sloppy or confused attempt to represent something, there is an obvious biographical reason why he might not have been sure about what he had seen: it was Dorothy Wordsworth who really met the woman, and an entry in Dorothy's journal which inspired the poem; as such, for Wordsworth, her figure can only ever be a product of the imagination. Actually, Wordsworth's version renders the woman less strange than Dorothy's journal does, and it is difficult to be sure whether or not he therefore intends a sense of alienation or familiarity (that is, he makes the woman very strange in her height, but he makes her less strange than it seems she really was, according to Dorothy). This is characteristic of a lack of certainty which troubles the poem, which as whole articulates a moral dilemma about the propriety of giving to the poor in the situation Wordsworth describes. Perhaps Wordsworth can't be sure, or can't decide, but *or* here allows for a more complicated effect, in which the sublimity of the vision Wordsworth establishes, juxtaposed with its demolition as the woman moves towards him and begs, powerfully directs the reading of the poem in a particular direction without closing down the potentials for interpretation: it remains possible that Wordsworth wants us to understand the difficulty of reading—people or poems—and the importance of continually recognizing the coterminous presence of different possibilities: apprehended in one way, the

---

[50] *Poems, in Two Volumes, and Other Poems, 1800-1807*, pp. 113-5 (ll. 1-12). The textual variants of the poem printed in this edition are not insignificant, but all retain this 'or'.

woman is merely very tall; apprehended in another, she is far more than this, and potentially the source of a sublime apprehension, just as she both is and isn't deserving of alms. To decide exclusively would be reductively to eliminate the very possibilities which constitute real experience for Wordsworth, and thus to write insincere poetry. Explaining his interest in the word 'concern', David Simpson points out that it captures 'the unresolved nature of the questions Wordsworth raises about suffering and sympathy. To be concerned usually means not having an answer...Concern means being involved and attentive and aware of oneself being so; aware also that concern is not of itself enough, that it does not solve anything...it is never enough.'[51] The refusal of conjunctions to completion, and their ability rather to open out possibilities, enables a similar resistance to ending; in the light of Simpson's account, their careful handling becomes a moral imperative for Wordsworth, specifically pertinent here to the fixed value judgements which he is anxious to avoid. *Or* in this poem allows Wordsworth to remain appropriately 'concerned'.

In his reminiscences, Henry Crabb Robinson recalls Wordsworth's remarking 'on the advantage which a mixed language like English has over one that is *single* like the German—in this, that the expressions do not so closely and palpably give the sensual image and direct sense, but convey indirect meanings and, faintly, allusions, by which poetry is favoured though philosophy may be injured.'[52] This is not to say that Wordsworth just wants to be vague or ambiguous, and a posture which faces the challenges of such indirect meaning has been identified and discussed by various critics. For example, Donald Davie identifies the particular quality of Wordsworth's diction in *The Prelude* specifically as being 'neither abstract nor concrete, but something between the two.'[53] According to Davie, this quality is achieved by an 'elaborately correct' syntax; the blank verse of *The Prelude* demands that we take it 'at a run, not pausing on the nouns for fear they congeal...but attending rather to the syntactical weave'.[54] Davie acknowledges that Wordsworth's 'moods, exultations, senses, sublimities and faculties will be no clearer at the end of *the Prelude*...yet the poem will not be a botch, for what will be clear at the end is the relationship between them'.[55] Our ability to find meaning in such words is, for Davie, dependent upon a posture of faithfulness, which the reader must adopt in order to proceed. The meaning we trustingly place in each word in the process of reading the poem does not tie those meanings down; everything depends upon the words' relationships between themselves. John Barrell notes Davie's argument with approval, transferring the discussion to

---

[51] *Poetics of Modernity*, p. 5.
[52] *Henry Crabb Robinson on Books and Their Writers*, ed. Edith J. Morley, 3 vols (London: J. M. Dent & Sons, 1938), i, 359.
[53] Donald Davie, *Articulate Energy*, published as *Purity of Diction in English Verse* and *Articulate Energy* (Manchester: Carcanet, 2006) [*Articulate Energy* first pub. 1965], p. 295.
[54] *Articulate Energy*, p. 297; p. 298; p. 298.   [55] *Articulate Energy*, p. 298.

'Tintern Abbey', and offering the difficulty of discerning the exact 'content' of the word 'thought' as an exemplar of a wider Wordsworthian tendency to depend on the reader's trust: 'Tintern Abbey',

> for all its ratiocinative appearance, its deployment, repeatedly, of all those conjunctions by which we seek to display the connections in a rational process of thought, is still continually concerned to suggest that it proceeds not so much by the logical accretion of propositions, but by leaps of faith and trust...the content of this meditation, and the state of mind it attempts to represent, can only be the objects of our trust: they are open neither to be proved or disproved.[56]

The lack of resolution which Davie identifies is no lazy abdication of poetic responsibility; as Barrell summarizes it, 'the power of the poem, the power it communicates to us, is somehow dependent upon the refusal of the poem to communicate fixed meanings.'[57] Barrell spells out the implication of Davie's argument as being 'that we will agree to trust the poet's understanding only under certain conditions', the first being

> that the poem will continually *attempt* to adopt a ratiocinative mode, as if attempting to produce a conclusion...and thus to acknowledge our sense that only when the attempt, made in good earnest, has failed, will we be disposed to accept that the meaning of those nouns is beyond clear definition.[58]

We must accept the sincerity of the attempt to define the indefinable, even as we acknowledge its futility. The other condition Barrell identifies is that the poem should call attention to itself 'as a representation of the poet's mental experience':

> all that is left to us thereafter is a ruminative mode, in which the mind proposes to itself, as its proper object of attention, not so much the meanings it seeks to generate, but its own movements in search of meaning.[59]

Conjunction is thus more important than actual content; success depends upon the ability of the poem to sustain different *potential* readings, as long as it does so 'sincerely' (any ambiguity cannot depend on the poet's just not trying hard enough). Davie's assertions similarly depend upon valuing syntax and connection *over* the fixed meanings of words; his argument is that 'Wordsworth is rendering the experience of being a child...in the only way possible, from inside the child's

---

[56] John Barrell, *Poetry, Language, and Politics* (Manchester: Manchester University Press, 1988), pp. 143-4.
[57] Barrell, p. 148.   [58] Barrell, p. 147.   [59] Barrell, p. 147.

mind, by rendering in his verse the movements of the child's consciousness'.[60] The use of conjunctions *and* and *or* (conceptually and literally), I suggest, allow 'movements of the mind'[61] to be represented, assert connection, and thus achieve rich ambiguity. And indeed, Barrell turns to *and* specifically as a way of expanding upon Davie's ideas of connection and relationship: 'brief lists of natural objects appear as islands of fixity and clarity in the troubled currents of Wordsworth's syntax, and among the objects in these lists, the simplest of all relationships is proposed—that made by the innocent conjunction "and". The simplicity of this connection is repeatedly emphasised'.[62] This is a good example of the way that criticism has tended to overlook the capacity of these little words: there is nothing at all 'simple' or 'innocent' about the way *and* problematizes clear understanding. Barrell sees these moments as offering respite, in which 'redescription' offers a grant of exactness in the face of instability.[63] But a fuller appreciation of the way that conjunctions operate suggests that the very characteristic of Wordsworthian language that Barrell (following Davie) is arguing for, the productive resistance to fixed meaning, actually pervades the far wider reaches of linguistic flexibility, in places which are often ignored.

Barrell's reference, above, to 'those conjunctions by which we seek to display the connections in a rational process of thought', is relevant here, too. Conjunctions facilitate the appearance of the attempt to connect, and to communicate and understand the relationship which Wordsworth relies upon. Yet they simultaneously quietly resist the articulation of certain relationship and connection. Davie's and Barrell's analyses are significant to this study in various ways: they acknowledge and address the way in which Wordsworth's use of language gestures towards the sublime by means far more sophisticated than simply describing or asserting its effects; they find Wordsworth's ability to resist fixed meanings to inhere in the particular qualities of his syntax, and particularly of the relationships between things (thus suggesting its relevance to a discussion of the operation of conjunctions, which share the same resistance to fixed meanings, even as they purport to define the nature of connections), and because the understanding of Wordsworth that they share depends upon a concept of 'sincerity', an idea of 'trust' in the poet's *intention* to be sincere (to which I shall return).

The ambiguity Davie highlights as characteristic of Wordsworth's verse is, as has been noted, not a simple throwing up of the hands. Connections are insisted on, even where precise referents are elusive. Yet their discernment does not belong solely to the poet: Wordsworth makes it clear that connections made must be

---

[60] *Articulate Energy*, p. 303.   [61] *Articulate Energy*, p. 303.   [62] Barrell, p. 148.
[63] See Barrell, p. 149: 'the act of redescription, serves to indicate how different this language is, whose proper objects are stable enough to be named with precision, from the language of moods, sublimities, presences.'

made actively by the 'attentive' reader, not simply passively given, if the literary work is to be of value. For Lucy Newlyn, 'The verb "work" is an important one' in Wordsworth's vocabulary; 'it crops up a number of times in *The Prelude* to describe imaginative process',[64] as well as suggesting the grind of editing and revision. This is related to Wordsworth's anxiety about the perception of his own industry: as Simpson remarks, particularly in the early part of his career, Wordsworth is 'a poet acutely anxious...about the public status of his "work" as a poet', and 'Wordsworth's poetry is constantly posing the question of its status as authentic labour.'[65] Wordsworth asks for similar effort on the part of his reader, upon whom it is incumbent always to *work at* reading, to avoid the 'savage torpor' distinguished in the 'Preface' to *Lyrical Ballads*.[66] This is almost an invitation to criticism: to 'repeat in order to produce difference' is what criticism does,[67] but it is the reader rather than the critic who sits on Wordsworth's shoulder, because response and responsibility remain personal and individual. Discussing the revisions to sense prompted by Wordsworth's line endings, Ricks notes the poet's frustration with readers who do not take their time: 'The obverse of his anger at such haste of pseudo-reading is his praise for the chastening dignity of the carver's slow art, at work upon a funeral inscription which is committed to reticence'.[68] This bespeaks the need to sit with lines of verse; to ponder slowly their fine and delicate effects; not to race to eliminate ambiguities, but to register and be slowed down by them; to allow meaning to be both this *or* this, and this *and* this. The characters of the conjunctions discussed here allow the strange posture of resolution *alongside* the activity of an indeterminacy; that is, both the spontaneous overflow of powerful feelings recollected in tranquillity, and the revised version of those recollections, at the same time. Conjunctions—in the example from 'Beggars', *or* specifically—enable Wordsworth to allow and perhaps even to *require* the possibility of the revision of sense without implying error, even in the very instant of reading. *And* and *or* offer a generous form of recapitulation, through a word one might not even really notice.

Or functions most interestingly when we consider its relationship to *and*. Whilst, intuitively, *and* and *or* would seem to have a contradictory effect, both

---

[64] 'The noble living and the noble dead', p. 50.
[65] *Wordsworth's Historical Imagination*, p. 41; p. 34.   [66] See 'Preface' to *Lyrical Ballads*, p. 129.
[67] Said, p. 124. Terence Hawkes discusses this passage from Said's essay in his discussion of 'Or' in *A Midsummer Night's Dream*. Reading Said, Hawkes is attentive to the expansive possibility *or* raises for literary critics: 'no commentary can simply repeat the text in its own terms, or lay claim to the discovery of its once-for-all "meaning"...All criticism, whether it intends to or not, effectively creates a potential space for "or".' Hawkes also notes Shakespeare's Ovidian legacy: that 'repetition, or the generation of more of the same, itself becomes the basis for change and the construction of difference.' (Terrence Hawkes, *Meaning by Shakespeare* (London and New York: Routledge, 1992), pp. 11–42 (pp. 38–9; p. 20; p. 22)).
[68] *Force of Poetry*, p. 116.

can confer an essentially repetitive sense on verse: both function as a supplement, in order to amplify description. *And* and *or* are thus crucial to the character of recapitulation. Much critical ink spilt over Wordsworth's *Prelude* by modern literary scholars originates in close attention to the nature of Wordsworth's revisions as he drafted and redrafted his poem. As a form of biography, *The Prelude* depends upon an additive *and* (in the sense of 'and then'). But it also simultaneously engages with the world of *or* ('and then again'), because in the very act of repetition Wordsworth is necessarily engaged in a re-ordering of memory, an inclusion of perspective which makes the original fundamentally different. This is reinforced through the fact that Wordsworth's attitude to events and experiences when he records them in 1799, for example, is different to his attitude by 1850, because Wordsworth himself has changed. The events being written about are both the same (in an empirical sense, the facts of history haven't altered) and different (that history only exists in the poem insofar as it is written down, and thus is inevitably inflected by the way in which it is written, and the person doing the writing). Hume insisted that 'repetition neither discovers nor causes any thing in the objects, but has an influence only on the mind';[69] in Wordsworth's hands, *and* acknowledges, and reflects on, that influence almost in action. *And* is an extra filter through which to view and re-write the past, yet its repetitive function is complicated by the fact that the repetition is always different by virtue of being a repetition. The little word itself implies that we are looking at the same thing, *and* that our perception of it has been transformed by the fact of our looking at it before (just like Wordsworth revising the *Prelude*).

The usual unobtrusiveness I've alluded to is a key feature of the conjunctions here discussed. Godfrey Dewey's 1918 survey of English prose found the most frequently used words to be 'The, of, and, to, a, in, that, it, is, I, for, be, was, as'.[70] Hugh Kenner describes the words on this list as 'our least-regarded', and 'our least definable.'[71] The *OED* entry for *and* reveals the extreme length of its definition. Kenner takes a similar look at the word 'set', remarking that 'The *OED* needed 60,000 words for *set*: easily the length of a Barbara Cartland novel. Ms Cartland, like the rest of us, has it easy. Neither she nor we, to get on with our talking, our writing, need think about the sense of *set*, the sense of *sense*.'[72] This idea of our not needing to *think* about these complex little words is important. Pervasive as they are, they work without the penetrative, disruptive attention-drawing and prompting of analytical thought which might be (for example) destructive of sublimity.

---

[69] Hume, p. 112.
[70] See 'Words', in Godfrey Dewey, *Relativ* [sic] *Frequency of English Speech Sounds* (Cambridge, MA: Harvard University Press, 1923), pp. 15–42 (p. 19), https://doi-org.ezp.lib.cam.ac.uk/10.4159/harvard.9780674419193, accessed 2 June 2022.
[71] Hugh Kenner, 'Further Thoughts: Little Words', in Christopher Ricks and Leonard Michaels, eds, *The State of the Language: 1990 Edition* (Faber and Faber: London, 1990), 62–5 (p. 64).
[72] Kenner, p. 65.

In this sense, such words perform a double bluff: we overlook their passing by, as we register bigger words, and the ideas they connote; but meanwhile, they are busily at work in all sorts of enabling ways. If 'Poetry should be great and unobtrusive, a thing which enters into one's soul, and does not startle or amaze it with itself, but with its subject',[73] *and* and *or* are thus perfect for the task of verse.

---

[73] John Keats to J. H. Reynolds, 3 February 1818, in *The Letters of John Keats*, ed. Maurice Buxton Forman, 4th edn (London: Oxford University Press, 1952), p. 95.

5
Conjunction, Expansion, and Sublimity

'We Are Seven' and 'Tintern Abbey'

Because they draw attention to the possibility of interpreting and expressing the same thing differently, *and* and *or* point to the difficulties inherent in the acts of perception and communication, but also, in the more conceptual sense I have described, to broader Romantic ideas about 'truth' and 'meaning'. As L. J. Swingle puts it,

> Romanticism proper is the state of being in the middle, surrounded... by the potent and even strident claims of multiple and competing systems of order... A mind oriented to the notion that truth should be a function of 'the nature of things,' and that systems are thus true or false in relation to that nature of things, confronts an intellectual situation wherein it appears that truth may refer only to coherence within a given system of thinking, and thus that contrary systems might seem to be equally 'true.'... Thus the cottage girl of Wordsworth's 'We Are Seven' has her own vision of things, and this vision refuses to accommodate itself to the contrary vision of her adult inquisitor.[1]

As the protagonists of 'We are Seven' debate, the poem participates in an early nineteenth-century discourse of census-taking and counting, exploiting the fruitful complexity of *and* and *or* to dramatize a clash between different ways of understanding.[2] In enumerating the siblings of the child he encounters, the speaker of the poem can only see the possibility of an *or*, in the sense of an exclusive alternative: there are either seven children, *or* there are five, in the family. He cannot see the possibility of a supplementary *or*; a different, but coherent way of looking at and understanding the world, which is closer to *and* (it is true that there are both seven children in the family, *and* five children, depending on how one counts the two dead infants). The speaker insists instead on another conjunction altogether, introducing an antagonistic *but*: 'But they are dead; those two are dead!' (l. 65). However, the child's repetitive *and*s serve a narrative function, but

---

[1] L. J. Swingle, 'The Romantic Emergence: Multiplication of Alternatives and the Problem of Systematic Entrapment', *Modern Language Quarterly*, 39.3 (September 1978), 264–83 (pp. 271–2), https://doi.org/10.1215/00267929-39-3-264, accessed 1 June 2022.
[2] 'We are Seven', in William Wordsworth, *Lyrical Ballads, and Other Poems, 1797–1800*, pp. 73–5.

also simultaneously lend a sense of legitimate certainty to her perception of the world: her conviction is demonstrated through her polysyndetic insistence:

> "And when the ground was white with snow,
> "And I could run and slide,
> "My brother John was forced to go,
> "And he lies by her side."
>
> (ll. 57–60)

Here is the 'cling[ing] to the same words' which Wordsworth diagnoses as indicative of the struggle to 'communicate impassioned feelings' in the 'Note' to 'The Thorn'.[3] But the repetition is more complex, because the repeated word is *and*. *And* here is literally additive rather than reductive, demonstrating the possibility of a multiple rather than a linear understanding of the world, which insists on the continuing, present truth of John's existence. Siegfried Kracauer has traced the way in which, as 'products of American distraction factories', moving, human bodies in a chorus line become 'no longer individual girls, but indissoluble girl clusters whose movements are demonstrations of mathematics... The regularity of their patterns is cheered by the masses, themselves arranged by the stand in tier upon ordered tier'; cumulatively, girls and audience constitute the 'mass ornament' of Kracauer's title.[4] To set this analysis directly beside Wordsworth's 'We are Seven' is certainly anachronistic, and might seem incongruous. But Kracauer's observation, that 'The structure of the mass ornament reflects that of the entire contemporary situation... Community and personality perish when what is demanded is calculability', is pertinent here.[5] 'We are Seven' underscores the idea that the same effect can result from a particular understanding of repetition: the interlocutor (representative of a contemporary mindset of empirical quantifying[6]) fails to recognize that the bonds of sibling affection are as much 'real things' as literally countable bodies. The little girl cannot see the possibility that they could be otherwise; her repeated *ands* yoke together previous playtimes and the state of death as coterminous; her understanding remains fundamentally multiple.

Repetition is also significant in the narrator's mouth:

> "But they are dead; those two are dead!
> "Their spirits are in heaven!"

---

[3] 'Note' to 'The Thorn', repr. in William Wordsworth, *Lyrical Ballads, and Other Poems, 1797–1800*, pp. 350–2 (p. 351).

[4] Siegfried Kracauer, *The Mass Ornament: Weimar Essays*, trans. and ed. Thomas Y. Levin (Cambridge, MA: Harvard University Press, 1995), pp. 75–6.

[5] Kracauer, p. 78.

[6] See James M. Garrett, *Wordsworth and the Writing of the Nation* (Aldershot: Ashgate, 2008) on Wordsworth's response to this context of counting and measuring.

> 'Twas throwing words away; for still
> The little Maid would have her will,
> And said, "Nay, we are seven!"
>
> (ll. 65–9)

In the anomalous extra stanzaic line here, the child continues to function according to the economy of *and* ('And said...'). But the speaker acknowledges no change in perspective, and simply gives up, believing any attempt at mutual communication to be an impossible waste; his limited insistence cannot allow space either for *and* or *or*. Instead, he relies on a direct repetition which fixes on the only certain aspect of the situation: the two siblings 'are dead'. But this does not offer the scope for their being dead to be an *and* state, with all the possibilities such multiple understanding might entail. His repetition allows escape from the impasse of the ambiguities of *and*, but only by deadening its more fruitful, expansive potentials, and ignoring the possibility that some things 'are open neither to be proved or disproved.'[7]

In Wordsworth's 'Ode: Intimations of Immortality', the poet invokes 'Fallings from us, vanishings; | ... Moving about in worlds not realiz'd'.[8] In 'We are Seven', the worlds *are* realized, through the little girl's perception of them: Wordsworth's manipulation of conjunctions allows, even forces, our awareness of the co-existence of different versions of the same thing; he does not share the speaker's blinkeredness. And in the first 'Essay upon Epitaphs', Wordsworth discerns contiguous relationship, drawing on an image of revolution to analyse

> feelings which, though they seem opposite to each another, have another and a finer connection than that of contrast.—It is a connection formed through the subtle progress by which, both in the natural and the moral world, qualities pass insensibly into their contraries, and things revolve upon each other. As, in sailing upon the orb of this planet, a voyage towards the regions where the sun sets, conducts gradually to the quarter where we have been accustomed to behold it come forth at its rising[.][9]

Here is the complex relationship of connection: apparent *or*s turn out to have been *and*s all along, and thus allow the reconciliation of apparently contradictory options without mental violence. Vitally, as Linda Brigham puts it, 'Wordsworth

---

[7] Barrell, p. 44.
[8] In *Poems, in Two Volumes, and Other Poems, 1800–1807*, ed. Jared Curtis (Ithaca: Cornell University Press, 1983), pp. 271–7 (ll. 146–8).
[9] *Essays upon Epitaphs*, p. 53.

does not advocate mixture': he still depends on conceptual and literal *and*s and *or*s, which allow differences to coexist without ironing out their complexity.[10]

Wordsworth's note to 'We are Seven' bases the poem on a real encounter; to this extent, it situates Wordsworth himself as the interlocutor (rather than interposing the kind of narrator-figure which the 'Note' to 'The Thorn' establishes), and we might assume therefore that the speaker's attitude is to be privileged over the stubborn persistence of the child. In the 1800 'Preface' to *Lyrical Ballads*, Wordsworth details his intent in the poem as being to show 'the perplexity and obscurity which in childhood attend our notion of death, or rather our utter inability to admit that notion',[11] and criticism has often taken this at face value: the child in the poem is simply ignorant of the real situation, which the incredulity of the narrator-poet, Wordsworth, exposes. However, the first stanza (which originated in a joke of Coleridge's) troubles the equation of poet and interlocutor. Still more challenging is the narrator-poet's stubborn deafness to what the child is saying, when his attitude is compared to Wordsworth's reflections upon ideas of death and community elsewhere. In the first 'Essay upon Epitaphs', for example, Wordsworth identifies the country parish churchyard as 'a visible centre of a community of the living and the dead'. Scholarly interest in mourning has established that, in Wordsworth's accounts, 'proper burial...comes to mark and identify...rural community, a community that includes the dead with and within the living';[12] the graveyard is conceptually valuable because it draws attention to the cycle of the life of members of the community. This is not a direct repetition, but through community, recapitulation is possible (individuals die; the community continues). Layered over this, is Wordsworth's belief in 'an immortal Soul'.[13] The notion that life continues after death requires a different understanding (or an acknowledgement at least of something beyond understanding) of what it means to 'live', one closer to the little girl's than to that of the narrator. Here lies the centrality of an idea of recapitulation which accommodates difference, even though specificity or clarity might be thus compromised. And indeed, in Wordsworth's image of 'sailing upon the orb of this planet', the voyage discovers

---

[10] Linda C. Brigham, 'Frail Memorials: "Essays Upon Epitaphs" and Wordsworth's Economy of Reference', *Philosophy and Literature* 16.1 (April 1992), 15–31, p. 22.

[11] 'Preface' to *Lyrical Ballads*, p. 126.

[12] Wordsworth, *Essays upon Epitaphs*, p. 56; see Michele Turner Sharp, 'The Churchyard Among the Wordsworthian Mountains: Mapping the Common Ground of Death and the Refiguration of Romantic Community', *ELH*, 62 (1995), 387–407 (391–2). See also for example Kurt Fosso, *Buried Communities: Wordsworth and the Bonds of Mourning* (Albany: State University of New York Press, 2004); David McAllister, *Imagining the Dead in British Literature and Culture, 1790–1848* (London: Palgrave Macmillan, 2018); Esther Schor, *Bearing the Dead: the British Culture of Mourning from the Enlightenment to Victoria* (Princeton, NJ: Princeton University Press, 1994); and Laura Clymer, 'Graved in Tropes: The Figural Logic of Epitaphs and Elegies in Blair, Gray, Cowper, and Wordsworth', *ELH*, 62 (1995), 347–86, on Wordsworth's attitudes to death, memorial, and the connections of community.

[13] *Essays upon Epitaphs*, p. 52.

the possibility that two events or states are simultaneously 'right' or possible: Wordsworth's passage towards the sunset explicitly analogizes the way West eventually becomes East, and night becomes day, and 'the contemplative Soul, travelling in the direction of mortality, advances to the country of everlasting life'.[14] The child's 'utter inability to admit th[e] notion' of death turns out to be entirely appropriate to the complex reality of death (at least, of death encountered in the connected context of the village community), as Wordsworth comes to understand it.

In the second 'Essay upon Epitaphs', Wordsworth describes the village churchyard as a 'faithful representation of homely life':[15] it is in such a place that the child in 'We are Seven' knits, plays, and eats supper amongst her dead siblings' graves, in moving imitation of Wordsworth's own children's activities.[16] Wordsworth repeatedly weaves living and dead into an interrelated community: the villagers in 'The Thorn', for example, believe that they hear cries coming from the mountain and interpret them as a kind of community choir in which 'Some plainly living voices were; | And others... | Were voices of the dead'.[17] When Anne Janowitz examines the narrator of 'Tintern Abbey', she concludes that 'no matter how much one knows about the particularities of Wordsworth's situation and locale in the poem, the "I" continually exerts its force as an abstraction or model of consciousness'.[18] The narrator of 'We are Seven' haunts the same abstraction. But if the stated intention in the poem was to cast light on the way death appears to children, it is difficult to ignore that Wordsworth elsewhere insisted that he had frequently shared a sense of total connection similar to that which the little girl implicitly adopts: 'I was often unable to think of external things as having external existence & I communed with all that I saw as something not apart from but inherent in my own immaterial nature. Many times while going to school have I grasped at a wall or tree to recall myself from this abyss of idealism to the reality.'[19] In her ability similarly to sustain a different way of apprehending the world, the capacity of the child in 'We are Seven' seems to meet the dictates of Romantic Idealism far more effectively than the pedantic empiricism of the

---

[14] *Essays upon Epitaphs*, p. 53.   [15] *Essays upon Epitaphs*, p. 64.

[16] See 'We are Seven', lines 36–48, and compare for example D[orothy] W[ordsworth] to Catherine Clarkson, 23 June 1812, in *The Letters of William and Dorothy Wordsworth, Volume 3*, pp. 31–6 (p. 32). Writing after the death of Catherine Wordsworth, Dorothy recalls that 'On the Sunday afternoon and the Monday I had been for several hours with Willy and [Catherine] in the Churchyard and they had run races and played on the very ground where now she lies'. The letter also contains an account, notable here, of Wordsworth's daughter Dorothy kneeling before her aunt, and praying 'for her Brothers and sister, I suppose without thinking of her. I said to her when she had done—My dear child you have no Sister living now—' (pp. 33–4).

[17] 'The Thorn', repr. in William Wordsworth, *Lyrical Ballads, and Other Poems, 1797–1800*, pp. 77–85 (ll. 172–4).

[18] Anne Janowitz, *Lyric and Labour in the Romantic Tradition* (Cambridge: Cambridge University Press, 1998), p. 18.

[19] *The Fenwick Notes of William Wordsworth*, ed. Jared Curtis (London: Bristol Classical Press, 1993), p. 61.

narrator. Anne Janowitz finds the man's incomprehension of the child to be 'inane', and Bewell asserts that 'it is the adult who needs to be educated' in the poem,[20] though an alternative reading might understand the child's attitude to be temporary, certain to alter with increasing maturity. But again, we are not supposed to choose, as much as to compare; to hold alternative perspectives simultaneously. And then again, all readers do have to choose in the act of reading, even as the poem simultaneously entertains different possibilities; in writing this book, I am inevitably participating (and failing to participate fully enough) in that economy of reading, by imposing my linear reading, unavoidably weighting and flattening the suggestiveness of the text as I attempt to describe it. Wordsworth seems to me to suggest that the best we can do is to be aware of that choosing, whilst remaining attentive enough as readers to acknowledge the persistence of other options. Admitting the intricacies of the text does not inhibit a wider view; there will always be more potential readings to be teased out. But whatever view might be taken (or 'chosen'), and however much a reader is or isn't aware of them, the formal effects of the poem still operate. The little girl's *ands* resist the interpretation of texts, because they always point outwards and beyond to other interpretative possibilities. The speaker of the poem cannot cope with the implications of this suggestive lack of definition which might be said productively to encourage thought; his mind muffles rather than delighting in the possibilities it offers, but it does nonetheless offer up graspable facts. Wordsworth's reader, on the other hand, is invited into the vital, energetic act of criticism through the abundant potential of the words of each, in juxtaposition with one another: syntactic connections on the page translate into synaptic connections in the mind of the reader, and thus the effort Wordsworth requires in the proper apprehension of poetry.

This abundance and richness of meaning is conducive to a particular type of sublimity which might seem to be at odds with the perspicuity which characterized stylistic perfection for Wordsworth's neo-classical predecessors;[21] Wordsworth's valuing of the sublime might be understood rather to privilege obscurity. But Romantic sublimity in fact emerges directly from perspicuous traditions. Despite the origins of its eighteenth-century revival in Boileau's French translation of Longinus's classical rhetorical treatise,[22] and its therefore being tempered by the rational values of the *Académie française*, the disparity between the ideal of perspicuity and the sublime obscurity was not lost on English writers and thinkers. Adamson identifies contemporary efforts to think through the problem and explains that the century found the solution in Milton.[23] But

---

[20] Janowitz, p. 42; Bewell, p. 196.   [21] See for example Lowth, i, 228–9.
[22] See for example Peter de Bolla and Andrew Ashfield, eds, *The Sublime: A Reader in Eighteenth-Century Aesthetic Theory* (Cambridge: Cambridge University Press, 1996), pp. 1–16.
[23] See Adamson, *Cambridge History of the English Language Vol. III*, pp. 619–20.

from a twenty-first-century perspective, only if we misunderstand the obscurity of Romantic sublimity as a somehow smudgy, blurred device does the concept of 'perspicuous sublimity' present a problem. Such an understanding misrepresents the profound insight available through the experience of the Romantic sublime, as exemplified by the concluding lines of 'Tintern Abbey':

> And I have felt
> A presence that disturbs me with the joy
> Of elevated thoughts; a sense sublime
> Of something far more deeply interfused,
> Whose dwelling is the light of setting suns,
> And the round ocean, and the living air,
> And the blue sky, and in the mind of man,
> A motion and a spirit, that impels
> All thinking things, all objects of all thought,
> And rolls through all things. Therefore am I still
> ... well pleased to recognize
> In nature and the language of the sense,
> The anchor of my purest thoughts, the nurse,
> The guide, the guardian of my heart, and soul
> Of all my moral being.
>
> (ll. 94–112)

The *and*s in this passage contribute a great deal to Wordsworth's gesturing towards the sublime *whilst* he is talking about it explicitly. They repeat with an insistence which itself speaks of excess, and the relative absence of conjunctions at the end of the extract is therefore similarly excessive, the final *and* fervently and misleadingly striking when it does come: the long-awaited *and* tugs the end of the line backwards, conjoining the soul with the heart, rather than tipping us forward into the next line, to which it properly belongs. According to Thomas Weiskel's definitions of the sublime, the *and*s in this extract incorporate an 'overdetermination' (which causes the signified thing to transfix us), and at the same time a Kantian mathematical sublimity through a repetition which induces a 'sense of *on and on*':

> The signifiers cannot be grasped or understood; they overwhelm the possibility of meaning in a massive underdetermination that melts all oppositions or distinctions into a perceptional stream; or there is a sensory overload. Repetition... in the signifier is a technique... for inducing the sense of on and on.[24]

[24] Thomas Weiskel, *The Romantic Sublime: Studies in the Structure and Psychology of Transcendence* (Johns Hopkins University Press, 1976), p. 26.

The *and*s, then, both overwhelm and overdetermine in the passage from 'Tintern Abbey'. But *and* functions so effectively here because it appears so insignificant; to be overwhelmed by a word which manages to be almost beneath notice and yet so sophisticated as to avoid the grasp of grammarians, and to have its slippery ungraspability highlighted merely by virtue of its repetition, renders the reader weaker than ever, but at the same time powerful in the opportunities conferred to self-make the connections between things. In many places (not only those in which the sublime is itself the subject) *and* is important because the surfaces and depths it possesses *at the same time* allow writers delicately to tread the line between the obscurity necessary to sublimity and a more simple obscurantism which cannot be conducive to it. *Or* is similarly efficient: Schmidgen isolates exactly this capacity, the unspecific generosity of *or*, when he expounds Longinus's explanation of 'the creation of sublime effects' in Sappho's verses, and finds that Homer's tempest is sublime for Longinus because it is 'allied with a logic of crowding that exceeds the boundaries of the probable because it collects and accumulates all the accidents that could describe a mental or a natural state.'[25] Schmidgen find it unsurprising that Longinus relies on the conjunction *or* to represent the poet's 'crowded lines', because his reading recognizes that *or* sustains multiple possibilities simultaneously, without engendering rivalry.[26] Little words like *and* and *or* fine-tune meaning even as they open up ever more possibilities for interpretation. Conjunctions ensure that comprehension is retained, although there is no demand for definitional decision. Excess is thus allowed, and sublimity admitted.

Wordsworth's Boat-Stealing

Numerous examples of Wordsworth's revisions to *The Prelude* suggest his sensitivity to the complex effects of *and* and *or*. For example, 'With triumph, and delight, and hope, and fear' (1805, I.501) becomes 'With triumph and delight, with hope and fear' in 1850 (I.474), a small change; but the loss of an *and* diminishes the escalating intensity of the line, and serves to delimit the emotional categories into neat pairings which disrupt the more passionate implication of the earlier version, in which the connections between emotions are richer, and more suggestive. In the same section of the poem, Wordsworth changes 'Ye Presences of Nature, in the sky | Or on the earth!' (1805, I.491–2) to 'Ye presences of Nature, in the sky, | And on the earth!' in 1850 (I.464–5), where *and*, despite its suggestive potentials, functions more to affirm Wordsworth's tight control and omnipotence than *or* did (substituting 'and' suggests he knows exactly where the 'presences' are,

---

[25] Schmidgen, p. 95.   [26] Schmidgen, p. 95.

rather than the hint 'or' gives that they might be here *or* there, *and/or* both). On the other hand, a few lines later, we discern in Wordsworth's retention of a strident *or* from 1805 confirmation of its continuing importance. Wordsworth figures the pleasures of childhood as a repeating pattern of joyful play 'to which the year | Did summon us in its delightful round.'[27] These are 'Unfading recollections' (1805, I.518; 1850, I.491) which Wordsworth almost, but not quite, perfectly re-experiences in the act of remembering:

> at this hour
> The heart is almost mine with which I felt
> From some hill-top, on sunny afternoons,
> The Kite high up among the fleecy clouds
> Pull at its rein, like an impatient Courser,
> **Or,** from the meadows sent on gusty days,
> Beheld her breast the wind, then suddenly
> Dash'd headlong; and rejected by the storm.
>
> (I.518–25)

Here is a sequence of specific occasions (one in which the kite flies high; one in which it crashes earthwards); these are memories of several events (plural afternoons and days, in contrast to the specific 'One evening' of the boat-stealing episode, for instance). Yet they are simultaneously part of one great amalgamated memory ('childhood'). Despite small alterations to the 1805 text by 1850, both share the *or* at line 523, on which pivots this sense. *Or* allows both versions of kite-flying to be true at the same time, and resists the possibility of deciding which is dominant or privileged: both memories contribute to the whole, and their details no longer *specifically* matter; they are lifted from the specific into being representative. As later chapters will demonstrate, this ability to sustain and evoke the individual and the general simultaneously constitutes the character of the poet.

The description in Book I of the boy-Wordsworth rowing out in a stolen boat offers further examples of *and*'s and *or*'s operation. The 1805 passage, beginning at line 372, opens with three sentences employing Wordsworth's characteristic, additive form of description. The lines seem straightforwardly to offer a recital of the details of the scene as they recur to the poet, structured by standard narrative markers: 'One evening'; 'I went'; 'No sooner . . .'. The only use of *and* in these first 11 lines is apparently straightforward, used in the context of a simple narrative of past events ('I unloosed her tether and embarked', l. 383); concluding the sentence, it also lends rhetorical finality to this stage of the description. In the next sentence of the poem, however, *and*'s effect is increasingly complex:

---

[27] See I.504–5. In 1850, 'its' becomes 'his', but the lines are otherwise identical (see 1850 I.477–8).

> The moon was up, the Lake was shining clear
> Among the hoary mountains: from the Shore
> I push'd, **and** struck the oars **and** struck again
> In cadence, **and** my little Boat mov'd on
> Even like a Man who walks with stately step
> Though bent on speed.
>
> (I.384–9)

Notably absent from the inventoried description of the first two lines here, three subsequent *and*s cluster together in lines 386–7. These *and*s maintain their narrative function, but they also enact the repetitive action they describe: their cumulative effect mirrors the effort of the boy-Wordsworth pulling the boat through the lake, catching at the rowing motion, with its thrusts of effort followed by the momentary stallings which the stutter of repetition generates. The effect is reminiscent of Coleridge's description of the water insect, who '*wins* its way up against the stream, by alternate pulses of active and passive motion'.[28] Some editions place a comma after 'oars', which exaggerates the effect, as each *and* follows punctuation marks which visually mimic the oar-dips into the water.[29] More than this, though, the sculling rhythm is described as a 'cadence'. This word's associations with rhythmical structure and verse self-consciously lend the physical activity a specifically poetic significance, associated with the 'growth of the poet's mind' the poem delineates. They also, however, call out to its etymological roots in an idea of *falling*. At this point in the poem, that falling is moral (here, the poem sustains a complex morality, grounded at once in its Miltonic, theological echoes, and in the sharp tension of the boy's awareness of his illicit but irresistible trip, and, additionally, in the adult poet's subsequent reflection upon it). But the cadence is also aesthetic: it begins the release of the narrative into a form of sublimity; it is a falling into the pathos of the sublime. In the *narrative*, the boy remains controlled, his action 'stately'; but the frantic repetition of *and* begins to perform the heightened emotion which the *poem* recollects. *And* thus indicates the additive experience of the boy, and the accumulating memory of the poet, inflected by perspective and simultaneously by poetic craft.

Even within this single sentence, the sense of *and* shifts about as we read. The third *and* tugs backwards to the repetitive striking of the oars; but, reading forwards as we must, it becomes a different *and*, functioning as a chronological and a descriptive aspect of the narrative: it is both 'and *then* (my boat moved on)', and a supplement to description (the boat in the scene is moving on). A similar

---

[28] See *Biographia Literaria*, i, 124. For further discussion of Coleridge's interest in the insect's peristaltic motion, see Chapter 12 of this book.

[29] See for example the Norton edition, ed. Wordsworth, Abrams, and Gill, or *The Prelude: The Four Texts*, ed. Jonathan Wordsworth, both of which include the extra comma described.

effect is in operation when Wordsworth characteristically repeats the lines, describing his rowing after the sublime shock of the cliff's appearance: 'I struck, and struck again, | And, growing still in stature...' (ll. 409–10). This is not the only typically Wordsworthian play with the idea of *still*ness in this section of *The Prelude*. Here, as in the previous example, the repetitions of *and* allow the boy-Wordsworth to be the subject of the growth of stature described in the lines: he (with the recollecting poet) seems to swell with the intensity of the verse before we are abruptly brought to acknowledge that it is the cliff which is really the subject ('the huge Cliff | Rose up', ll. 410–11). *And* thus performs the recollection of the poet, recalling the sublimity of the experience, as well as the child's frightened, dislocating response; this ambivalence in turn imitates the adult poet's complicated and repeated reflection upon that experience.

The sentence following Wordsworth's first striking, and striking again his oars, 'It was an act of stealth | And troubled pleasure' (ll. 389–90), explicitly reinforces the prior allusion to his guiltiness, but also to the emotional paradox which characterizes sublime experience. As Wordsworth turns briefly to 'the voice | Of mountain echoes' (ll. 390–1), the *and*s drop out of the poem, to return in line 397, as 'And now...'. Here, *and* again serves a narrative function vital within the context of a long poem, suggesting 'and then...'. But it is also at this point *and* in the sense of 'right now that I am thinking about and reflecting on the scene': attached to 'now', it redoubles the inherent complexity of 'now'.[30] Together, the two meanings contribute more strongly than they singly could to the sense of escalation in the passage. The fact that we might not even notice these small words, being distracted by weightier concepts and vocabulary, makes this all the more effective, *because* it is so subtle and yet so powerful. When Ricks talks about the similarly 'unobtrusive surprise of the prepositions' in 'Tintern Abbey', he explains that it is 'a matter of our being tacitly aware of how they might have been expected to figure.'[31] Complicating this in the case of the conjunctions *and* and *or*, though, is that although we might experience a similar surprise at their functioning, we can't ever *really* know 'how they might have been expected to figure', insofar as they refuse to disclose a precise operation in advance, and perform different functions simultaneously.[32]

---

[30] Chapter 6 of this book further explores the ways in which 'still' and 'now' permit a similar flexibility to *and* and *or*.

[31] *Force of Poetry* p. 121

[32] The potential of *and* to be unobtrusively but powerfully affective is evident elsewhere in the passage. For instance, some versions of the 1805 text exclude a second comma in the line which characterizes Wordsworth's energetic rowing: 'lustily | I dipped my oars into the silent lake, | And as I rose upon the stroke my boat | Went heaving through the water' (I.401–4). In 1850, this becomes 'lustily | I dipped my oars into the silent Lake, | And, as I rose upon the stroke, my Boat | Went heaving through the Water'. The addition of the comma reduces *and* to a more purely a narrative marker, diminishing the passage ('and, as I was doing one thing over here, the boat was doing another over there...'), rather than containing within it the more-than-temporal sense that all of these things were true and are true at once, and that they are part of the escalation of feeling already initiated through the

In the 1805 text, the sublimity of Wordsworth's experience can almost be charted by the frequency of this simple conjunction, swelling first as the boy sets off on his stolen boat, and rising again as the image of the striking oars returns; and as it returns, the *and*s proliferate:

> I struck, **and** struck again,
> **And**, growing still in stature, the huge Cliff
> Rose up between me **and** the stars, **and** still,
> With measur'd motion, like a living thing,
> Strode after me.
>
> (I.409–13)

Just as in the previous iteration, these *and*s are doing many things at once. In part, the effect is simple: insistent repetition lends a sense of heightened emotion. But beyond this, as before, the second *and* tugs backwards to the repetitive rowing action, and also drives forwards chronologically and descriptively in the narrative. Despite the experience of the previous lines (when the apprehension of the cliff shocked both the rowing boy and any reader assuming that the child, rather than the landscape, was the subject of the verse), the 'still'ness of line 411 clings to the boy, frantically trying to make his escape, and lending his effort a sense of futility. Yet, it turns out, 'still' is again attached to the recollection of the cliff, and *not* to the boy. Repeated several times in the passage, in its openness to interpretation, 'still' functions in a similar way to *and*, being potentially adjective and adverb, suggesting continuing action *and* stalling it, enriching the dimensions of the experience described. In the 1799 *Two-Part Prelude*, Wordsworth had dipped his oars 'twenty times';[33] in 1805, he dips them 'lustily'. The alteration marks a change from an idea of quantifiable repetition to one which is qualified, thus drawing attention to the *nature* of recapitulation in the poem. The passage is concerned with the present recollection of a past event, involving significantly repeated action, which itself became a constant psychological repetition in the mind of the boy-Wordsworth: 'huge and mighty Forms' which 'mov'd slowly through my mind | By day and were the trouble of my dreams' (ll. 426–8). In this

---

earlier repetitions of *and*. The punctuation on which this effect depends is notoriously difficult to resolve. The Norton and the *Four Text* editions omit this second comma, though Reed's *Thirteen Book Prelude* prints it (and it is clearly visible in the facsimile of MS A Reed reproduces); Gill's 1970 edition of *The Prelude: The 1805 Text*, based on de Selincourt's earlier edition (Oxford: Oxford University Press, 1933; 1970), includes it. In Stephen Parrish's *The Prelude, 1798–1799* (Ithaca: Cornell University Press, 1977), transcriptions offer a precedent for both versions. Wordsworth's later amendments to his text reduce the impact of lines immediately following the uprearing of the huge 'peak' (1850, l. 378)/ 'Cliff' (1805, l. 407): in both versions, immediately upon the sublime encounter, Wordsworth 'struck, and struck again', but the 1850 version omits the earlier lines, 'I push'd, and struck the oars and struck again | In cadence, and my little Boat mov'd on' (ll. 386–7), so that the striking of the oars is no longer a repetition, significantly diminishing the effect.

[33] See *The Prelude, 1798–1799*, ed. Parrish, I.103.

context, the revisions discussed here, alongside the number of word-repetitions in the poem and the effects of Wordsworth's reaching for *and* (and 'still') so often, allow us to glimpse Wordsworth's thinking through of the role and function of recapitulation. His discernment is nourished by a conceptual *and* which recognizes multiple rehearsals of the same event as valuable and necessary, but also that those different recollections must contain (ideally, must somehow acknowledge) that the changing perspective of the poet has in turn changed, in a way, the occasion. *And* enables this. Moreover, in revisions to the poem, the significance of the poetic act itself is amplified, compared to the significance of memory: as Gill points out, 'In *1799* Memory was the redeeming agent; in *1805* it is Poetry that will preserve'.[34] This episode, with its specific interest in recapitulation (in the dreams and imagination of the boy, and in the poet's creative return to the memory), and its particular attention to repeated instances of *and*, manages to negotiate exactly this problem: by representing it as an *and* event in the conceptual sense (exposing its own limitations but still allowing for a profoundly complex, affective readerly experience), the description might be properly 'sincere'.

At line 411, *and* in 'me and the stars' is straightforwardly grammatically connective, though it also hints at a more fundamental connection in Wordsworth's mind between poet and cosmos.[35] However, the subsequent *and*, 'and still, | With measur'd motion', is more complex: it is narrative ('this thing was continuing to happen'), but equally echoes that preceding *and* which links Wordsworth and the stars, so that all three (boy, cosmos, cliff) are associated. It also interacts with 'still' to complicate response yet further: 'and still' is both an extension of the narrative sense of 'this was still happening', and a play with the idea of a thing being both *and* (more than), and 'still' (the same as); this punning is picked up in the fluid movement of the line ending, which is not still at all, and in the 'measur'd motion' which immediately follows it, which also refuses to allow 'still' to *keep still*. In this way, *and* is almost turned inside out. The verse needs the fervency the repetition of *and* lends, but under pressure it is transformed, concurrently to function semantically more as a 'but'. Having these different possibilities of *and* in close proximity in the line fills the little words with almost too much meaning for their size; the overload of meaning contributes to the subtle performance of disturbing sublimity the boy experiences in his boat.

The boat-stealing passage is explicitly about a powerful memory. It enacts on the page as far as is possible the experience of recollecting that memory: both the poet's, and the boy-Wordsworth's (the additive and the exclusive senses of *and* are both necessarily present in the self-aware act of recollection). In another direct repetition, Wordsworth's poem returns to the 'cavern of the Willow tree' (l. 415):

---

[34] *Wordsworth's Revisitings*, p. 46.
[35] On Wordsworth's correlation of himself with the stars, see David Simpson, *Wordsworth's Historical Imagination*, pp. 22–55.

here, too, the boy's going 'Back' physically, just as the poet goes back mentally, is self-consciousness. But the *and*s continue to occur through the passage, and to function complexly:

> I left my Bark
> **And**, through the meadows [homeward] went with grave
> **And** serious thoughts: **and** after I had seen
> That spectacle, for many days my brain
> Work'd with a dim **and** undetermin'd sense
> Of unknown modes of being.
>
> (ll. 416–21)

And is such a common word that it is difficult to argue for patterns of use, except to say that when it occurs in *The Prelude*, it often does so in proximity with at least one other *and*. But Wordsworth does particularly like this triple construction, employing it often, habitually exploiting the possibilities of the left-hand margin. It appears in the very first sentence of the poem:

> Oh there is blessing in this gentle breeze
> That blows from the green fields **and** from the clouds
> **And** from the sky: it beats against my cheek
> **And** seems half conscious of the joy it gives.
>
> (I.1–4)

It occurs again in the passage from line 272, in lines which began the Two-Part *Prelude* of 1799. To return to the boat-stealing episode, *and* in 'and after I had seen | That spectacle' (ll. 418–9) is grammatically redundant; following the colon, it is perhaps admitted as a metrical filler, or to satisfy Wordsworth's preference for the construction I have just described. But it continues the driving sense of repetition, and carries both the narrative sense of *and*, bolstered by 'after' ('and then ... '), and a more capacious *and* which asks us to gather everything we have been reading about and glimpsing (irrespective of its temporal or logical place in the actual story) and to hold all of that whilst moving on to think about the next thing too, because that is what Wordsworth is doing in the act of recollection and writing. The *and* belongs both to the time of the child in the narrative, and to the thought-process of the poet recalling and structuring it, and it is also passed on to the reader who must attempt actively to appreciate the text. The reiterated *and*s draw attention to the mechanics of the poem, even as each individually functions semantically as well: we are not allowed to forget that this *is* a recollection of the scene crafted by a supplementary figure, not there at the time (the adult Wordsworth); the poem forces us to confront the fact that, as readers, we share aspects of that posture of active calling to mind.

Through their repetition, these *and*s refuse to relinquish the performed experience of the previous lines. When they subside in the poem it is to be replaced by the similar complexity of *or*:

> in my thoughts
> There was a darkness, call it solitude,
> **Or** blank desertion, no familiar shapes
> Of hourly objects, images of trees,
> Of sea, **or** sky, no colours of green fields...
>
> (ll. 421–5)

The first *or* here links two different explanations, but (entirely in line with the tendency of the poem) it allows those two things to be the same thing. Solitude, elsewhere an essential ingredient of the egotistical sublime, is here powerful, but also utterly, depressingly vacant. The 'or' in line 425 fights hard to reassert the connection which allows Wordsworth to be 'steady' (VIII.599). However, it is overwhelmed, as the predominantly asyndetic lines silence the repeated *and*s of the foregoing passage, failing to generate anything beyond a series of negative possibilities which lack the connections syntactical conjunction confers. Of course, the crisis is redeemed; the nightmarish sublimity remerges victorious, as it shapes the poet's mind: in an example of experience to be reformulated in Book XI as a 'spot[s] of time' (XI.258), through recapitulation, the shock of the occasion itself and the nightmares it induces cultivate the poetic imagination. 'The elements of feeling and of thought' are 'purif[ied]', and 'pain and fear' are 'sanctif[ied], so that the 'Soul' is 'buil[t] up' (I.435–43) along with the poem's text.

The most significant direct repetitions within the 1805 boat-stealing passage (line 386 which returns as line 409; the willow tree; the stars; the water's silence; the instances of 'still' and '*and*') originate in the 1799 version. However, by 1850, many of them had been reduced, as part of a wider tendency towards cutting direct repetition in the weakened, later text. In 1850, for example, the 'huge cliff' recalled in lines 407 and 410 of the 1805 version has become 'a huge peak, black and huge' (1850, l. 388). Hugeness returns again in the 'huge and mighty Forms' which conclude the passage (1805, l. 426; 1850, l. 398). In both versions of the recollection, 'huge' is repeated three times, but in 1850, each repetition is modified. 'Black' and 'mighty' both attempt to ascribe even more sublimity to the vastness of 'huge'; in doing so, they attempt to expand its meaning, but they are simultaneously reductive: they function like the repetitions Wordsworth had discredited in the 'Note' to 'The Thorn', performing the redundancy of 'virtual tautology', rather than the passionate possibilities of perfect repetition (which according to the 'Note' bears within itself an awareness of the impossibility of adequate articulation, and is therefore highly appropriate to the description of sublime experience). Two of the *and*s which I have suggested work powerfully in

1805 (at lines 397 and 418) are changed to 'but' in 1850, losing the suggestive openness, and the ability to yoke past event and present response, that *and* allows. The resulting passage in 1850 is less ambiguous; less moving; less powerful. In his commentary on Proust, Walter Benjamin recognizes that, 'in his work Proust did not describe a life as it actually was, but a life as it was remembered by the one who had lived it. And yet... the important thing for the remembering author is not what he experienced, but the weaving of his memory, the Penelope work of recollection.'[36] This is pertinent to Wordsworth's *Prelude*, which is a record of events, but only as it is *re-membered*, literally put back together into a whole body, by poet and, in turn, reader. Because memory contains fluctuating emotional and factual responses, so Wordsworth's representations must be flexible and open, even once they are fixed on the page. Often in *The Prelude*, events described *are* acts of remembering. But Benjamin's mention of 'weaving' is also key: weaving involves the weft of textual effects being threaded through the warp of recollection; the texture is the resulting poem itself. *The Prelude* thus manifests a particular understanding not only of memory but of experience, in its explicit content, in its revisions, and in its very language. *And* and *or*, as parts of this linguistic tendency, and because they themselves constantly demand a revisionary, open act of reading, sit at the heart of *The Prelude*'s rich fabric.

---

[36] Walter Benjamin, 'The Image of Proust', in *Illuminations*, 203–17 (p. 204).

6
Conjunctions, Repetition, and Revision

Wordsworth and Revision

In *The Prelude,* Wordsworth describes the benefits available to those who are patient enough to bestow a second glance: 'But let him pause a while, and look again | And a new quickening shall succeed' (VIII.728–9). 'Quickening' is a powerful word here, implying life-giving, but also, in a more specialized sense, resurrection; it denotes arousal, inspiration, and growing brightness, but its principal connotation is specifically maternal, evoking the first movements of the baby within the womb. 'Quickening' is thus a profound image of poetical creation bursting into being. The rest of the line confirms these optimistic associations; to 'succeed' might be to follow, but it carries with it an inevitable sense of triumph. Looking again is here the opposite of redundant repetition: it is a generative, enlightening action whose result is perpetual intellectual and imaginative stimulation; it produces 'A Spectacle to which there is no end.' (l.741).

One corollary of Wordsworth's interest in the recapitulative second look is his attitude to textual revision:

> Wordsworth didn't just revise, he revised his revisions up to the margins of the printed page he was using as base text and if indecipherability threatened, he sent the printers separate sheets with cross-references to the printed text, for them to make sense of, if they could. As requested, the printers sent revises, only to get them back—revised.[1]

Wordsworth's poetic praxis depends on these obsessive acts of reflection, reworking, and self-repetition. Duncan Wu argues for a direct association between revision, and Wordsworth's rhetorical strategy. He extends a discussion of Wordsworth's interest in tautology, to track 'the psychological and emotional patterns embedded in the *Prelude*', finding that

> Tautology is integral to the spots of time; it is what makes them so valuable to the poet. Their distinguishing characteristic is that they are

---

[1] *Wordsworth's Revisitings*, pp. 13–14.

> spectacles and sounds to which
> I often would repair, and thence would drink
> As at a fountain.

Wu's Wordsworth is compelled to return and repeat, in order to understand himself. Wu finds Wordsworth deeply attentive to the act of perception involved in such moments, and suggests that the 'straining' to see or to perceive which characterizes them 'may be embodied in verbal repetition': tautology 'is capable of describing the operations of the mind at their deepest level'.[2] Repetition in this account is vitally constitutive of the man and, self-consciously, his poetry, in a way which recalls an Hegelian understanding of the growth of knowledge and the mind through a process of repetition. For Hegel, the mind consists in a process, or 'movement',

> of becoming an *other to itself*, i.e. becoming an *object to its self*, and in suspending this otherness. And experience is the name we give to just this movement, in which the immediate... becomes alienated from itself and then returns to itself from this alienation, and is only then revealed for the first time in its actuality and truth, just as it then has become a property of consciousness also.[3]

The reflective, self-contemplating mind transforms its content through repetition, in the act of perception and reflection upon it. In a description which could be seen as an analogue of Wordsworthian revisiting and revision, Hegel addresses the 'essential' business of philosophy as a process, and not a result:

> Where could the inner meaning of a philosophical work find fuller expression than in its aims and results[?]... Yet when this activity is taken for more than the mere beginnings of cognition, when it is allowed to pass for actual cognition, then it should be reckoned as no more than a device for evading the real issue..., a way of creating an impression of hard work and serious commitment to the problem, while actually sparing oneself both. For the real issue is not exhausted by stating it as an aim, but by carrying it out, nor is the result the actual whole, but rather the result together with the process through which it came about.[4]

Accumulative recapitulation in Hegel's conception is thus fundamentally necessary to the attainment of knowledge. 'The True is the whole', and 'the whole is nothing other than the essence consummating itself through its development.'[5]

---

[2] Duncan Wu, 'Tautology and Imaginative Vision in Wordsworth', *Romanticism on the Net*, 2 (May 1996), https://doi-org.ezp.lib.cam.ac.uk/10.7202/005717ar, accessed 1 June 2022 (not paginated).

[3] From G. W. F. Hegel, 'Preface: On Scientific Knowledge', in *The Phenomenology of Spirit* [1807], trans. A. V. Miller (Oxford: Clarendon Press, 1977), p. 21 [para 36].

[4] 'On Scientific Knowledge', p. 3 [para 3].   [5] 'On Scientific Knowledge', p. 11 [para 20].

Here is Wordsworth's 'look[ing] again', and the resultant 'Spectacle to which there is no end', reconceptualized specifically as philosophical truth.

Shortly before Christmas 1814, Wordsworth wrote to R. P. Gillies on the desirability of textual revision:

> do you simply mean, that such thoughts as arise in the progress of composition should be expressed in the first words that offer themselves, as being likely to be most energetic and natural?... My first expressions I often find detestable; and it is frequently true of second words as of second thoughts, that they are the best.[6]

Wordsworth's manuscripts frequently reveal third and subsequent thoughts as well. Whereas it might be assumed that a published version of a text is privileged, Wordsworth's praxis and his stated theory deliberately pull in another direction, denying the primacy of any 'final' text; recapitulation is necessary to the achievement of 'the best'. The coordinating conjunctions are relevant here because a second look is always *and* as well as *or*: unlike a simple palimpsest, it may supplement, or modify, but it doesn't overwrite the previous impression, and thus it can allow a changed perspective without a change of mind or heart, and without a loss of Hegel's 'serious commitment', or what Wordsworth calls 'sincerity'. If a text can declare its revisions subtly but explicitly (wearing them on its sleeve, so to speak), this might be achieved.

The 'Preface' to *Lyrical Ballads* places memory at the heart of poetic activity, when it declares recollection to be its necessary condition.[7] In content and form, Wordsworth's *Prelude* is deeply embedded, like all memories, in processes of repetition and of revision. In some of Wordsworth's major works ('Tintern Abbey', *The Prelude*, and the 'Intimations Ode', for example), the operations of memory are directly explored, such that memory might legitimately be described as their subject. The meaning of 'memory' to Wordsworth, its activity and vitality as a faculty, undoubtedly modulated over time, and as a focus of scholarship it has yielded rich and abundant insights far beyond the scope of this study. But memory is relevant here insofar as it is a type of repetition, particularly as a memory contains within it both the original experience, and the remembered version: its associated activity involves not only replication, selection, and organization, but also an awareness of *difference* from the original; with the passage of time, perspective and feeling inflect its operation and record. When he compares episodes from *The Vale of Esthwaite* which reappeared in *The Prelude*, Sykes Davies finds 'The discovery of the power of memory' in the later poem to be accompanied by

---

[6] Wordsworth to R. P. Gillies, 22 December 1814, in *Letters*, iii, 178–80 (p. 179).

[7] 'Poetry...takes its origin from emotion recollected in tranquillity': 'Preface' to *Lyrical Ballads*, p. 148.

a crucial change in literary technique: one which intimately and accurately reflects the role of recurrence in the life of feelings and thoughts, and of recurrence with constant variation as in memory itself... *The Prelude* version is clearly distinguished from that in *The Vale* by the repetition of the main elements in the crucial experience.

What makes this 'technique both new and effective' for Sykes Davies is 'as much attention to variation as to repetition'.[8] Looking at a specific example, Sykes Davies concludes that:

> Here, then, in descriptive technique is exactly the kind of repetition with variations which Wordsworth regarded as the vital process of the memory in building up the human personality... [W]e are shown the successive transformations within Wordsworth's own imagination, the shaping action of the memory in actual action. And what is more, the variation is deliberately presented: it is the very essence of the writing.[9]

When Hillis Miller cites Benjamin's description of the 'Penelope work' of recollection, he highlights Benjamin's insistence upon the activity, or 'weaving', of memory as more important than the actual experience of 'the remembering author'.[10] For Hillis Miller, there are two types of remembering:

> Daylight, willed memory works logically, by way of similarities which are seen as identities, one thing repeating another and grounded in a concept on the basis of which their likeness may be understood... The second, involuntary form of memory, which Benjamin calls 'the Penelope work of forgetting'... is woven also out of similarities, but these are called by Benjamin 'opaquely similar'. These similarities he associates with dreams, in which one thing is experienced as repeating something which is quite different from it, and which it strangely resembles[.][11]

Critics have found both forms of repetition in Wordsworth's memories. The interest of this study, however, is in the way that Wordsworth's poetry performs the 'Penelope work' of both. It does so through the negotiation of the problems of disjunction which result from the *differences* between memories of the same event experienced at different moments. Such problems are confronted and sometimes resolved through linguistic attentiveness to connections, expressed via conjunctions and forms of repetition.

---

[8] Sykes Davies, pp. 27–8. [9] Sykes Davies, p. 30.
[10] J. Hillis Miller, *Fiction and Repetition: Seven English Novels* (Oxford: Basil Blackwell, 1982), p. 5.
[11] *Fiction and Repetition*, pp. 7–8.

As I have already suggested, *and* and *or* are useful and interesting as parts of a process of revision which resists complete difference, whilst incorporating and accommodating changed perceptions, because of the instability grammarians recognize in them. Beattie did not conclude that their problematic nature made conjunctions undesirable:

> when an author thinks himself at liberty to write without connection... he is apt to be more intent upon the brilliancy of particular thoughts, than upon their coherence: which is not more wise in an author, than it would be in an architect to build a house rather of round, smooth and shining pebbles, than of stones of more homely appearance hewn into such figures as would make them easily and firmly incorporate[.][12]

The architectural metaphor here echoes in the 'straggling heap of unhewn stones' in Wordsworth's 'Michael', and the 'shapeless heap of stones' in 'For the Spot where the Hermitage Stood', both of which testify to the collapse of a particular community.[13] But these ideas about sensible connections are particularly interesting in the context of Wordsworth's writing a long poem which is *not* structured according to a straightforward plot-narrative. In Book I of the 1805 *Prelude*, Wordsworth is already attentive to the fact that a process of revision might be necessary to avoid a poem more like the heap of Beattie's 'round, smooth and shining pebbles' than an 'incorporate' account of the growth of a poet's mind:

> that with a frame of outward life,
> I might endue, might fix in a visible home
> Some portions of those phantoms of conceit
> That had been floating loose about so long,
> And to such Beings temperately deal forth
> The many feelings that oppress'd my heart.
>
> (I.129–34)

Conjunctions, of course, connect in a literal way, and in this sense offer a practical means for a poet to 'fix' parts of his autobiographical account in their right places, and right relationships to one another (or to articulate their problematic lack of discernible connection). But they also offer an opportunity for a more flexible form of portrayal and definition. They are able to 'fix' in a place expressions previously floating too freely, implicitly addressing some of the major anxieties which attended eighteenth-century discussions about the structure of long poems,

---

[12] Beattie, pp. 358–9.
[13] See 'Michael, A Pastoral Poem', in *Lyrical Ballads, and Other Poems, 1797–1800*, pp. 252–68, l. 17; and 'For the Spot where the Hermitage Stood', in the same volume, p. 181, l. 1.

whilst refusing to abandon more productive kinds of looseness, including those associated with resistance to decision, or of definite, conclusive interpretations of events.

Moreover, as Beattie puts it, 'conjunctions, while they *couple* sentences, may also express opposition, inference, and many other relations and dependencies.'[14] Conjunctions, that is, can figure forth far more complex relationships in a manner vital to the progress of *The Prelude* and the events and feelings it records, according to the perception held at different points in Wordsworth's career. Addressing Wordsworth's revisions, Jonathan Wordsworth suggests that 'If *The Prelude* had been merely an account of Wordsworth's early life, there would have been no need for [his] periodic updatings. But it was also an embodiment of views and values that had to be brought into line as times changed, and he himself responded to change. Revision was a responsibility.'[15] In their more conceptual senses, a*nd* and *or* operate helpfully in this context because they do not demand the obliteration of earlier versions: they allow changes to be supplements as well as corrections. It matters that this idea of correction is not understood to be definitive: as Susan Wolfson has argued, Wordsworth's imagination is perpetually one in which 'floating and fixing compete for priority. Despite an intent to form a work that, in the words of its last book, would show "in the end | All gratulant if rightly understood" (13.384–5/14.388–9), years of revision subverted the rhetoric of *if* from its temporal promise into a perpetually conditional desire.'[16] She continues: 'The process [of revision] is not always additive but often contrary.'[17] To put it another way, revision plays with the literal and the conceptual senses of *and* and *or*. Wolfson's account goes on to argue that 'Despite what Wordsworth himself optimistically described as his "theme | Single, and of determin'd bounds"', *The Prelude*'s 'several distinct but interrelated textual forms, as Jack Stillinger remarks, leave open to question whether revisions are in the business of "clarifying [an] original idea" or "expressing a different idea".'[18] Later, she concludes:

> Manuscripts as well as memories constitute his past, and textual revision reduplicates, perpetuates, and enters into recollection. In this involute, revision is not just compositional; it is the very trope of autobiography, a resistance, in events large and small, to arresting and fixing phantoms of conceit in a final frame of autobiographical argument. In this respect, to read the network of Wordsworth's texts is to extend his activity as a reader in the network of recollection... as Wordsworth himself admits,

---

[14] Beattie, pp. 359–60.
[15] Jonathan Wordsworth, 'Revision as Making: *The Prelude* and its Peers', in Robert Brinkley and Keith Hanley, eds, *Romantic Revisions* (Cambridge: Cambridge University Press, 1992), pp. 18–42 (pp. 20–1).
[16] *Formal Charges*, p. 101.   [17] *Formal Charges*, p. 101.   [18] *Formal Charges*, p. 103.

> I cannot say what portion is in truth
> The naked recollection of that time,
> And what may rather have been call'd to life
> By after-meditation.   (3.646–50/3.613–16)[19]

To this extent, *The Prelude* is always recording the site of actual and implied *and*s and *or*s: Wordsworth's lines here suggest that, like the speaker in 'We are Seven', he believes a 'truth' exists, even though he cannot access it: only version x, y, *or* z can be correct. But they simultaneously assert the validity of *and*s: these different 'times' might have represented 'truth' at different points in time and after different instances of 'after-meditation'; therefore, versions x, y, *and* z all exist as true. Elsewhere, Wolfson suggests that 'Revision is endlessly open, not simply because any field of vision is open to numerous, potentially infinite interpretations and organizations, but because each view discovers new motions, changes, and interchanges. With the promise of mastery, revision revives the originating inquiry.'[20] Relatedly, Jonathan Wordsworth argues that

> Wordsworth was not too much concerned with fact. Chronology is distorted in the *Excursion* Preface as contentedly as it is in the various poems that constitute his autobiography. Past events are reordered in the service of emotional and imaginative truth ... Wordsworth in his retrospect was telling his readers what might have happened, or what should have happened, not what did.[21]

And Gill points out that when 'Wordsworth remarked to Sir George Beaumont that he had thought he might have success in an autobiographical venture, "as I had nothing to do but describe what I had felt and thought [and] therefore could not easily be bewildered"', the poet's claim is 'breathtakingly ingenuous. Wordsworth had been bewildered. Writing in 1804–5 about events of a decade earlier was the primary way in which Wordsworth was attempting to rescue himself from what bewilderment persisted, and no aspect of the task was easy.'[22] Gill here echoes John Jones's assertion that 'at its best the late *Prelude* is urgently bewildered; torn between old certainties and new doubts, self-consuming in its efforts to deal justly with both.'[23] Blithely indifferent to actuality, or bluntly perplexed, *and* and *or* provide helpful ways of understanding and incorporating different possibilities for Wordsworth. The most important feature they possess, is

---

[19] *Formal Charges*, pp. 104–10.
[20] Susan J. Wolfson, 'The Illusion of Mastery: Wordsworth's Revisions of "The Drowned Man of Esthwaite," 1799, 1805, 1850', *PMLA*, 99.5 (October 1984), 917–35 (p. 932), https://doi.org/10.2307/462144, accessed 01 June 2022.
[21] See 'Revision as Making', p. 23.
[22] Stephen Gill, 'Introduction', in Stephen Gill, ed., *The Prelude: A Casebook* (Oxford: Oxford University Press, 2006), pp. 3–41 (p. 20).
[23] Jones, p. 129.

that they allow the different versions of events (real or not), which critics recognize as vital to the constitution of Wordsworth's poetry, to continue to exist alongside one another, without needing necessarily to replace each other, or to negotiate a rank or preferred order.

The first of Wordsworth's 'Essays upon Epitaphs' envisages the 'departed Mortal' calmly 'speaking from his own tomb-stone': He 'gives a verdict like a superior Being, performing the office of a judge, who has no temptations to mislead him, and whose decision cannot but be dispassionate.'[24] This form of ex post facto judgement is similar to the process we find in the revisions of *The Prelude*; Alan Liu finds a like process at work in the Revolution books in particular. Echoing Wordsworth's claim that through the epitaphic voice, affliction is 'unsubstantialised', Liu argues that in these books, through Wordsworth's voice, history also is 'unsubstantialised':[25]

> The function of Wordsworth's lyric return of the dead is to allow the voice of past history to utter again only in the service of leading us into a purer, eternal history ruled by a transcendent authority.[26]

A proper negotiation between specific and general, or rather a path from one to the other, results in a more true, sincere text, scripted by the 'new, transcendental authority of history: Wordsworth's "I."'[27] The sincerity Wordsworth depends upon is that of an 'I', but one which resists fixed ideas and is open to changed accounts. Relatedly, David Bromwich defines 'the work of memory' in Wordsworth's lines beginning 'There was a boy' as being 'to associate virtually separate selves and not to recollect the shadows of a self already unified.'[28] In this account again, the act of remembering and the process of translating the experience of memory into verse allow for the coexistence of simultaneous but different forms of the same thing.

Wordsworth and Translation

Similar questions of authority and revision are raised by Wordsworth's experimentation with translation, which therefore offers an interesting case study here. The attention of poets in the Romantic Period to theories of translation is paid in a conceptual currency shared with discourses of repetition and difference.

---

[24] *Essays upon Epitaphs*, p. 60.
[25] See *Essay upon Epitaphs I*, p. 60; Alan Liu, *Wordsworth: The Sense of History* (Stanford: Stanford University Press, 1989), p. 384.
[26] Liu, p. 384.   [27] Liu, p. 384.
[28] David Bromwich, *Disowned by Memory: Wordsworth's Poetry of the 1790s* (Chicago: Chicago University Press, 1998), p. 149.

Awareness of the need to navigate the demands of sameness through a process inherently involved with alteration rendered translation an important part of the contemporary discourse surrounding forms of textual repetition (including ekphrasis, influence, and metaphor) which depended on revised forms of an original. Yet to the extent that Wordsworth describes his own writing as already a form of translation ('as it is impossible for the Poet to produce upon all occasions language as exquisitely fitted for the passion as that which the real passion itself suggests, it is proper that he should consider himself as in the situation of a translator'[29]), and in that he compulsively revised his own works, the Chaucerian translations he worked on begin to challenge categories of verse. The status of 'translation' is also complicated by the fact that Wordsworth's 'translation' of Chaucer is only partial; as Chaucer's English is revered by Wordsworth, so he retains much of the source text (Michael Baron calls them 'bad translations' specifically 'because they are too reverential'[30]). In his 1820 headnote to 'The Prioress's Tale', Wordsworth writes:

> In the following Piece I have allowed myself no farther deviations from the original than were necessary for the fluent reading, and instant understanding, of the Author: so much however is the language altered since Chaucer's time, especially in pronunciation, that much was to be removed, and its place supplied with as little incongruity as possible.[31]

As Bruce Graver argues, here, Wordsworth seems to be responding to Leigh Hunt: Hunt had complained about the way in which Dryden and other modernizers of Chaucer 'divert attention from the illustrious original', insisting rather that changes should be made 'only just as much as is necessary for comfortable intelligibility'.[32] Whatever his impetus, unlike Dryden, his most obvious predecessor in this regard, Wordsworth aimed to preserve as much of Chaucer's diction and syntax and as many of his rhymes as possible, even where that rendered the work obviously archaic. Notably, 'the ancient accent' was to be 'retained in a few conjunctions' specifically; Wordsworth recognizes the role of these words in forming points of connection between ancient and modern readers, as well as functioning grammatically within the text. In the 'Preface' to *Lyrical Ballads*, Wordsworth repeats his claim that 'the affecting parts of Chaucer are almost

---

[29] 'Preface' to *Lyrical Ballads* [1850], p. 139.
[30] Michael Baron, *Language and Relationship in Wordsworth's Writing* (Harlow: Longman, 1995), p. 135.
[31] From *Translations of Chaucer and Virgil*, p. 36.
[32] See Leigh Hunt, *The Round Table*, cited in *Translations of Chaucer and Virgil*, p. 17. See also Graver's commentary in 'The Reception of Chaucer from Dryden to Wordsworth', in Ian Johnson, ed., *Geoffrey Chaucer in Context* (Cambridge: Cambridge University Press, 2019), pp. 419–28 (esp. pp. 424 ff.).

always expressed in language pure and universally intelligible even to this day'.[33] However, just as Wordsworth states his determination there to have 'purified' the diction of 'the language really used by men',[34] Chaucer's language is also to bear some modification. Wordsworth's approach to Chaucer thus involves a process of renovation via negotiation,[35] and the 'Preface' in this way casts Wordsworth as the direct heir of Chaucer, figured through centuries of literary tradition as a 'master who purified the English language'.[36]

In his aim of preserving the original *through* alteration, as his headnote to 'The Prioress's Tale' declares, Wordsworth draws attention to the character of true repetition as non-identical (to repeat Chaucer's words exactly in a nineteenth-century context is to render them different because the context of their reception necessarily changes the reader's apprehension of what those texts mean). For Wordsworth, alteration is necessary in order to accommodate historical variation, and thus adequately to preserve the originals *as themselves*.[37] Just as he continually revises his own work in order to remain 'sincere', so he takes on the mantle on behalf of Chaucer, figuring himself (as Jeff Espie argues) as the heir to Chaucer's reputation and praxis, and therefore eligible to perform such translation, or modernization, appropriately. Eric Griffiths describes translation as 'an exercise of skill in bringing about a series of recognitions', and this seems directly to recall Wordsworth's more typical mode of writing: Chaucer simply replaces more personal, remembered 'originals'. Moreover, it is clear that Wordsworth's translation, once it existed, was treated to the same process of return and revision as the poet's more original works. Espie charts the progress of Wordsworth's 'Prioress's Tale':

> Wordsworth began working on his translation in 1801 and the project was alive again two decades later: he returned to and revised his original manuscript draft in 1819, first published the poem in 1820, and republished it, after adding an important prefatory note, in 1827.[38]

In this project of preservation and purification, through its various recapitulations, Wordsworth's versioning of 'The Prioress's Tale' becomes both a revision of

---

[33] See footnote to the 'Preface' to *Lyrical Ballads* [1800], p. 124.

[34] 'Preface' to *Lyrical Ballads* [1850], p. 123.

[35] See Jeff Espie, 'Wordsworth's Chaucer: Mediation and Transformation in English Literary History', *Philological Quarterly*, 94.4 (Fall 2015), 377–403.

[36] David Matthews, 'Periodization', in Marion Turner, ed., *A Handbook of Middle English Studies* (Chichester: Wiley-Blackwell, 2013), 253–66 (p. 263). See also Jeff Espie: 'The process of purification places Wordsworth in a distinguished line of poetic descent, attesting his ability to assume and reinvent the linguistic legacy of England's first poetic purifier, Chaucer.' ('Wordsworth's Chaucer', p. 384).

[37] Beyond Wordsworth's explicit translation theory, in Graver's edition of Wordsworth's translations the editor's notes in several instances suggest that Wordsworth's choices are 'trying to preserve the full sense of' Chaucer. See for e.g. *Translations of Chaucer and Virgil*, p. 69.

[38] Espie, 'Wordsworth's Chaucer', p. 390.

Chaucer, and of himself. As it draws attention to its status *as* translation, Wordsworth's text self-consciously performs the work of the poet as it is outlined in the 'Preface' to *Lyrical Ballads*, encouraging the reader to *recognize*; deliberately to re-think, constantly, what the poem *is*, and to engage in the active form of reading recommended by Wordsworth. The status and character of the translation as, fundamentally, a repetition, nurtures this posture and the accompanying recognition of 'the text' of 'The Prioress's Tale' as always open for revision, never absolutely determined: as conceptually an *and* text, rather than a 'finished' work, and in this sense a model for all poetic endeavour.

Revision and the 'Logic of the *AND*'

The critical tradition I have invoked above has usually described the effect of Wordsworth's literal textual revisions taking place over time, but there are moments in Wordsworth's writings in which repetition functions to revise within versions of particular works. In a well-discussed section of Book XI of *The Prelude*, for example, Wordsworth recounts the experience of becoming lost in the hills as a small child, and encountering a murderer's gibbet (XI.279ff). Isobel Armstrong argues that 'the triple account of the experience (for the "spot" is given three times in succession) gives another sense of "turnings", the return of words upon themselves in repetition and the transformation of meaning through repetition. Wordsworth makes it clear that the passage is a recreation of experience in the present moment of writing and thus virtually a new experience—as all memory is.'[39] Subsequent chapters of this book will look more closely at the operation of specific forms of repetition in Wordsworth's writing, but Armstrong here describes an explicit version of something which happens implicitly throughout *The Prelude*. In Book 1 of *The Prelude*, Wordsworth's revisions accommodate the way in which the active writing of poetry is itself part of the cultivation of the poet; as the 'Preface' to *The Excursion* makes clear, Wordsworth deliberately sets out to 'take a review of his own Mind'.[40] In 1805, self-consciously dwelling on the act of remembering, he writes: 'Well I call to mind | ('Twas at an early age, ere I had seen | Nine summers)...' (I.310-12). By 1850, the lines have become 'There were we let loose | For sports of wider range. Ere I had told | Ten birth-days...' (I.305-7). Both of these versions differ from the 1799 Two-Part *Prelude*, where the memory is introduced with 'And afterwards, 'twas in a later day, | Though early...'.[41] In this version, *and* functions both as a narrative marker ('and the next thing I will

---

[39] *Language as Living Form*, p. 76.
[40] Repr. in *The Excursion*, ed. Sally Bushell, James A. Butler, and Michael C. Jaye (Ithaca: Cornell University Press, 2007), p. 38.
[41] *The Prelude, 1798-1799*, ed. Parrish, First Part, ll. 27-8.

talk about is...'), and as a signal towards the cumulative nature of the experiences in the creation of the poetic mind, but it does not suggest the more specific timeframe and attempt at fixing memory that the later versions include. The amendment to 'I had *told*' in 1850 contains the awareness that looking backwards incorporates the activity of previous re-*telling*, of memory itself: telling is both narrating, and counting. The alliteration of the verb suggesting narration, 'told', with the revised age, 'Ten', emphasizes the significance of recitation. By 1850, that is, Wordsworth had shifted his focus from the 1805 idea of life as a series of primary, sensory experiences ('I had seen | Nine summers'), to an idea of life as a series of stories related and reckoned with. The age specified is irrelevant; the important thing is that the telling is now part of the memory. No *substance* is added in the 1850 version of the poem; there is nothing more to tell in that sense, but Wordsworth's relationship to and recognition of the past has changed by virtue of his own development: telling past years is both cause and consequence of the growth of the poet's mind. The 1850 text renders a shared memory: 'In that beloved Vale to which erelong | We were transplanted—there were we let loose' (ll. 304–5); the more specifically personal 1805 memory is of 'that beloved Vale to which, erelong, | I was transplanted' (ll. 309–10). In the repetition of events in his mind and on the page, Wordsworth's increasing distance is marked not only in the way that events become a narrative which has been told, as well as real happenings which themselves inevitably change each time they are re-imagined; but also in the way in which they have become communal, and thus generalized. Generalized, but still intimate: Wordsworth's 'We' remains specific enough, and the lines' continuing susceptibility to further revision keeps them in the realm of history, rather than legend, in Auerbach's sense. In Auerbach's legendary, 'All cross-currents, all friction,...everything unresolved, truncated, and uncertain... has disappeared', whereas 'The historical event which we witness, or learn from the testimony of those who witnessed it, runs much more variously, contradictorily, and confusedly...and how often the order to which we think we have attained becomes doubtful again'.[42] It is of course these contradictions and confusions which *are* the life of *The Prelude*, as they indicate the 'Growth of the Poet's Mind'.

Herbert Lindenberger argues that *The Prelude* 'follows three separate principles of organisation':

> The most obvious of these is that of the conventional memoir: the events of the author's life in more or less chronological sequence...The second principle is... the traditional cycle of paradise, fall and redemption. The third principle is repetition. As a pattern controlling the poem it stands at odds with the other

---

[42] Eric Auerbach, *Mimesis: The Representation of Reality in Western Literature*, trans. Willard R. Trask (Princeton, NJ: Princeton University Press, 1953; 2003), p. 19.

two, for, unlike both of them, it recognizes no beginning, middle, or end... The repetitive pattern should perhaps be called a pattern of alternation—between moments of high and low intensity... But the difference is... something within the poet himself, his way of looking at things at different times.[43]

The poem in this account has only an arbitrary conclusion, because Wordsworth might indefinitely continue to experiment with new ways to articulate the inarticulable, infinite potential connections between parts of experience and memory. In their introduction to *A Thousand Plateaus*, Deleuze and Guattari partly echo the idea of the conventional memoir (Lindenberger's first principle of organization), when they complain that:

History is always written from the sedentary point of view and in the name of a unitary State apparatus, at least a possible one, even when the topic is nomads. What is lacking is a Nomadology, the opposite of a history... History has never comprehended nomadism, the book has never comprehended the outside. The State as a model for the book and for thought has a long history: logos, the philosopher-king, the transcendence of the Idea, the interiority of the concept, the republic of minds, the court of reason... as legislator and subject. The State's pretention to be a world order, and to root man.[44]

This is a helpful context in which to think about *The Prelude*, which proclaims itself to be a history (of a poet's mind) through memoir, but which in its evolution also reveals the impossibility of 'history' in any pure sense. As an escape from this difficulty more generally, Deleuze and Guattari propose the rhizome as a model:

A rhizome has no beginning or end; it is always in the middle, between things, interbeing, *intermezzo*. The tree is filiation, but the rhizome is alliance, uniquely alliance. The tree imposes the verb 'to be,' but the fabric of the rhizome is the conjunction, 'and... and... and...'. This conjunction carries enough force to shake and uproot the verb 'to be.'

In this account, 'Where are you going? Where are you coming from? What are you heading for?' are 'totally useless questions', because 'Making a clean slate, starting or beginning again from ground zero, seeking a beginning or a foundation—all imply a false conception of voyage and movement'.[45] Asserting that 'Multiplicities are rhizomatic',[46] they write of the capacity for literature instead to 'establish a

---

[43] *On Wordsworth's Prelude*, pp. 190–2.
[44] Gilles Deleuze and Félix Guattari, 'Introduction: Rhizome', in *A Thousand Plateaus: Capitalism and Schizophrenia* [1987], trans. Brian Massumi (London and New York: Bloomsbury, 2015), pp. 1–27 (pp. 24–6).
[45] *A Thousand Plateaus*, p. 26.   [46] *A Thousand Plateaus*, p. 7.

logic of the AND... *Between* things does not designate a localizable relation going from one thing to the other and back again, but a perpendicular direction, a transversal movement that sweeps one *and* the other away, a stream without beginning or end that undermines its banks and picks up speed in the middle.'[47] To some extent this recalls the third structure Lindenberg describes; both find partial echo in Book II of *The Prelude*, when Wordsworth resists the possibility of locating fixed and specific ideas, instead promoting a sense of works as forever in process, flowing and therefore constantly being revised ('Who that shall point, as with a wand, and say, | "This portion of the river of my mind | Came from yon fountain"?', II.213–15). But 'A logic of the AND' is what the conjunctions *and* and *or* already achieve, both as a way of thinking conceptually as a notion governing the whole poem, and where they appear literally within Wordsworth's lines. The functions of Wordsworth's *and*s and *or*s suggest that we should be less concerned with privileging or verifying different versions, and instead better readers if we see all different versions as simultaneously 'right': Wordsworth's different accounts of the French Revolution, for example, are both more *and* less radical, or more *or* less radical, just as there are both five *and* seven siblings in 'We are Seven', and also possibly five *or* seven, depending upon how we choose to look: different versions act constructively as supplements rather than as frustrating contradictions. To repeat a point made earlier on, this is not a matter merely of ambiguity or vagueness, but a productive and positive form of openness. We would be wrong and perverse to decide which version is 'better', because the different meanings or conclusions are vital to *The Prelude*.

Dorothy Wordsworth's journal entry for 15 April 1802 records the scene which was to inspire Wordsworth's 'I wandered lonely as a cloud'. Having embarked on a windswept walk, 'a few daffodils' are spotted:

> But as we went along there were more & yet more & at last under the boughs of the trees, we saw that there was a long belt of them along the shore, about the breadth of a country turnpike road. I never saw daffodils so beautiful they grew among the mossy stones about & about them, some rested their heads upon these stones as on a pillow for weariness & the rest tossed & reeled & danced & seemed as if they verily laughed with the wind that blew upon them over the Lake, they looked so gay ever glancing ever changing[.][48]

The use of '&' in this passage is telling: it demonstrates the cataloguing list-sense of 'and also'; but it also confers the but-at-the-same-time-ness that lends the passage its vivid life, so that the writing here both records and mimics not just the constant

---

[47] *A Thousand Plateaus*, p. 27.
[48] 'The Grasmere Journal' (15 April 1802), in *The Grasmere Journals, including the Alfoxden Journal*, ed. Pamela Woof (Oxford: Oxford University Press, 1991; 2002), p. 85.

revision of sensory impression Dorothy is writing about, but also the felt sensation of that revision itself. Here, as elsewhere, *and* is behaving like 'now' in its ability to suggest both simultaneity and sequence ('about & about' pulls in a similar direction). This effect expands still further the way in which *and* complicates its own meaning. The breathless lack of punctuation in Dorothy's lines and the artless immediacy this seems to suggest haunt her brother's re-working of them. Made two years later, the poem writes the presence of Dorothy out from underneath the occasion as it opens with a focus on the intense, glorious solitariness of the speaker, and concludes with a demonstration of the process specified by the 'Preface' to *Lyrical Ballads*: the revelation of a moment's importance taking place after a time of quiet reflection upon it:

> For oft when on my couch I lie
> In vacant or in pensive mood,
> They flash upon that inward eye
> Which is the bliss of solitude,
> And then my heart with pleasure fills
> And dances with the Daffodils.[49]

Here is the theory:

> For all good poetry is the spontaneous overflow of powerful feelings: and though this be true, Poems to which any value can be attached were never produced on any variety of subjects but by a man who, being possessed of more than usual organic sensibility, had also thought long and deeply. For our continued influxes of feeling are modified and directed by our thoughts, which are indeed the representatives of all our past feelings; and, as by contemplating the relation of these general representatives to each other, we discover what is really important to men, so, by *the repetition and continuance* of this act, our feelings will be connected with important subjects, till at length, if we be originally possessed of much sensibility, such habits of mind will be produced, that, by obeying blindly and mechanically the impulses of those habits, we shall describe objects, and utter sentiments, of such a nature, and *in such connexion* with each other, that the understanding of the Reader must necessarily be in some degree enlightened, and his affections strengthened and purified.[50]

Current feelings are shaped by thoughts, which are representative of past feelings; the contemplation of the *relation* of these past feelings to one another reveals

---

[49] 'I wandered lonely as a Cloud', in *Poems, in Two Volumes, and Other Poems, 1800–1807*, pp. 207–8.
[50] 'Preface' to *Lyrical Ballads* [1850], p. 127 (my emphases).

'what is really important'. Reflection and recollection must be filtered through the understanding of connection if we are to appreciate their true significance. And this in turn the reader must experience repeatedly and continually, to inculcate a form of learned instinct. The emphasis upon the nature of the relation distances Wordsworth decisively from the eighteenth-century Humean tradition which (interested as much as Wordsworth in repetition and habits of mind) had insisted on understanding 'necessary connexion' through purely empirical enquiry.[51] In Wordsworth's analysis, connection and conjunction are bound with an idea of repetition into a single activity which becomes so ingrained that, unexpectedly, it turns the individual almost into a machine, 'obeying blindly and mechanically': purification and enlightenment comes via a process of repetition and conjunction which dominates the mind. In 'I wandered lonely', as the poet 'gaz'd—and gaz'd', we find exactly this form of repetition which is also interested in connection: *and* allows Wordsworth's gazing to be both a looking at one thing after another, *and* at the same time the accumulation of all of the mass of daffodils, *and* all of the instances of gazing consecutively, and of reflecting on that accumulation. The inclusion of the dash here (as it holds the instances of the word repetition apart and binds them together, marking and eliminating a gap) seems almost playfully hyperaware of the way that *and* thus performs and implies connection as well as supplementarity.[52] The anaphoric repetition within the poem's final couplet, 'And then my heart with pleasure fills | And dances with the daffodils', calls back to the repetition of gazing in the previous stanza, sharing the sense of equivalence and difference: the heart's filling is its own experience, *and* an experience which is part of the apprehension of the daffodils, both originally, *and* now in the recollection of it.

A letter from Wordsworth to Lady Beaumont of 21 May 1807 reveals that he was prepared for contemporary reviewers to find the subjects of some of his *Poems, in Two Volumes* 'very trifling', and insisted it was 'impossible that any expectations can be lower than mine concerning the immediate effect of this little work upon what is called the Public'; but the excoriating responses which scorched the presses far exceeded his predictions.[53] Francis Jeffrey infamously mocked Wordsworth's habit of writing about things that the 'greater part of his readers will probably persist in thinking low, silly, or uninteresting' in poems which were a 'violation of the established laws of poetry'. Numerous reviewers

---

[51] See Hume, pp. 105–15.

[52] The correlation between *some of* the characteristics of *and* and *or*, and the more literal connective, the dash, is highlighted by scholarship interested in Emily Dickinson's use of hyphens and ellipses. For a brief survey, see Sharon Cameron, *Choosing Not Choosing*, p. 3.

[53] W[illiam] W[ordsworth] to Lady Beaumont, 21 May 1807, in *The Letters of William and Dorothy Wordsworth, Volume 2: The Middle Years, Part I: 1806–1811*, ed. E. de Selincourt, 2nd edn, rev. Mary Moorman (Oxford: Oxford University Press, 1969), pp. 145–51 (p. 150).

used the word 'puerile'. *The Satirist* explicitly targeted the 'Daffodils'.[54] Such a reception bespeaks a lack of recognition of the seriousness or sincerity which techniques like the use of conjunction and repetition can evoke, enabling the poet as they resist (or even deny) the necessity for interpretative decision. Wordsworth seems to have hit the nail on the head when he insisted that 'every great and original writer, in proportion as he is great or original, must himself create the taste by which he is to be relished'; in 1807, he had yet to create it.[55]

This book has indicated ways in which the conjunctions *and* and *or* allow refined forms of recapitulation, and thus the expression of rich and multiple forms of experience. Sylvia Adamson directly connects conjunctions and repetition:

> For many modern writers, the most important replacement for connectives has been the device of lexical or structural repetition. In eighteenth-century stylistics, repetition had been disfavoured, being regarded as a form of redundancy. Its status changed with the translation into English in 1787 of Lowth's *Lectures on the Sacred Poetry of the Hebrews*, which demonstrated the importance of repetition as a structural principle[.][56]

Adamson notes Lowth's direct influence on Wordsworth, but despite the new, general attitude, Wordsworth remained anxious about the poetic redundancy to which repetition was often allied, as an 1805 letter about *The Prelude* makes clear:

> I had nothing to do but describe what I had felt and thought... If when the work shall be finished it appears to the judicious to have redundancies they shall be lopped off, if possible. But this is very difficult to do when a man has written with thought, and this defect, whenever I have suspected it or found it to exist in any writings of mine, I have always found incurable. The fault lies too deep, and is in the first conception.[57]

Here, Wordsworth is pulled between his rational conclusion that rhetorical redundancy (meaning not only superfluity, but also more specifically repeating things, according to eighteenth-century rhetoric) is a 'fault' which should be eradicated, and the more instinctive awareness that it is a central part of his

---

[54] The relevant reviews are collected in Donald H. Reiman, ed., *The Romantics Reviewed: Contemporary Reviews of British Romantic Writers: Part A—The Lake Poets*, 2 vols (New York and London: Garland, 1972). For Jeffrey's comments in the *Edinburgh Review* (October 1807), see Reiman, ii, 429–38 (p. 431; p. 438); for *The Satirist* (November 1807), see Reiman, ii, 845–7.

[55] 'Essay, Supplementary to the Preface' [1815], in *Prose*, iii, 62–107 (p. 80). Wordsworth here repeats a claim previously made in the letter to Lady Beaumont of 1807: 'never forget what I believe was observed to you by Coleridge, that every great and original writer, in proportion as he is great or original, must himself create the taste by which he is to be relished' (*Letters*, ii, 150).

[56] Adamson, *Cambridge History of English Language Vol. IV*, p. 641.

[57] W[illiam] W[ordsworth] to Sir George Beaumont, 1 May 1805, in *Letters*, i, 586–8 (p. 587).

particular style, and necessary ('incurable') to the making of the poem, which is after all an accumulation of repetitions and differences ('what I had felt and thought'). Recapitulation conceptually addresses this conflict, and the idea of redundancy is one which Wordsworth faced head-on in his comments on tautology, in the 'Note' to 'The Thorn'.

Briefly, then, to summarize: despite the anxieties of eighteenth-century and more modern philosophical linguistics, in terms of reading praxis, thinking about Wordsworth's use of *and* and *or* is not a means of recovering fixed meanings. Rather, the poet's conjunctions actively resist them, exactly in line with his stated preference for a 'mixed' rather than a 'single' language. They attempt to imitate the multiple nature of lived experience, both as it is undergone and as it is subsequently remembered, and through the recapitulation this involves they also encourage a form of criticism which is thus part of the existence of the poem, as conceived by its poet. If *and* and *or* are particularly useful and interesting as parts of a process of revision which resists complete difference whilst incorporating and accommodating changed perceptions, they also bear on ideas of copiousness and, vitally, on key aspects of the discourse sublimity. In a context of repetition, the powerful work these little words carry out impinges on other concepts related to the sublime: there are plainly similarities in the capacities of *and* and *or* to sustain the sorts of invitation to expansion, and resistance to fixed meaning, that preoccupy deconstructive discourses. Discussing the distinction between Deleuze's 'platonic repetition' and his 'other, Nietzschean mode of repetition', Hillis Miller recognizes that Deleuze's account posits a world based on difference: 'It seems that X repeats Y, but in fact it does not... Each form of repetition calls up the other, by an inevitable compulsion. The second is not the negation or opposite of the first, but its "counterpart".'[58] He goes on: 'The relationship between the two forms of repetition defies the elementary principle of logic, the law of non-contradiction which says: "Either A or not-A"... The very word "deconstruction" is meant to undermine the "either/or" logic'.[59] Yet for Wordsworth, this capacity to undermine does not provide a commentary on the deferral of meaning as a feature of language so much as it articulates the complexity of lived experience and feeling, which is rarely singular and direct, and instead calls for a poetry which can *try* to register and enact the multiple nature of each inscribed moment.

Still Now: Transcending Specific Moments and Places

Discussing the organization of the eighteenth-century long poem, Wolfram Schmidgen argues that Thomson's use of *or* in *The Seasons* resists individuation by suggesting

---

[58] *Fiction and Repetition*, p. 6; p. 9.   [59] *Fiction and Repetition*, p. 17.

that we are in a potential rather than an actual scene, that we're witnessing a sequence that does not want to resemble actual behavior on a cloudy spring afternoon, but aspires instead to something like an ideal fullness in which various possibilities are realized, but without being tied to the 'here' and 'now' of a particular point in time, space, and development.

This is an 'embrace of the general and the abstract' in which *or* facilitates the structural coherence of the long poem, because it obviates the need for a 'coherent center of perception and experience':

> The 'or' that moves us so swiftly from touch to sight places the observer in different positions in the landscape, but without worrying about their geographic coherence. Instead, we're immersed in a dream-like scene of effortless alternation.[60]

Wordsworth's use of *or* is a refined extension of this more practical effect, which expands to include attention to the possibility of recording *active* remembering, and implying the effects of 'revisiting' within the texture of the verse itself. And the geographical splitting which, Schmidgen suggests, the conjunction enacts also has a powerful temporal counterpart. The discourse of ekphrasis suggests a similar desire for artistic forms which might resist categorization as either temporalized or spatialized. Considering the role of time in ekphrastic poems, Theresa M. Kelley notes that 'Whereas Lessing tried to suppress the permeability between works of art frozen in time and the poetic expression of temporality', in Keats's poetry, 'ekphrasis foregrounds how works of art are, like geological formations, made in time and out of matter.'[61] Particular words can function similarly, inducing consciousness of time and change (through their literal meaning) and matter (in their attention-drawing existence as part of the text of the poem). These are living words, which resist petrification and instead suggest and contain difference and motion. *And* and *or* can function in this way; 'still' and 'now' are also able to sustain the effect.

Several critics have commented on Wordsworth's careful use of 'still' as adjective and adverb. Simon Jarvis's tellingly titled chapter on 'Infinity' points out that '"Still among Streets" grasps this in one move: the primary sense, that however far we walk we are still walking among streets, also contains a secondary possibility, that however far we walk we are still, that is, motionless.'[62] Writing on ekphrasis, Murray Krieger pushes further, recognizing 'still':

---

[60] Schmidgen, pp. 90–1.
[61] Theresa M. Kelley, 'Keats and "ekphrasis": Poetry and the Description of Art', in Susan J. Wolfson, ed., *The Cambridge Companion to Keats* (Cambridge: Cambridge University Press, 2001), pp. 170–85 (p. 183).
[62] Simon Jarvis, *Wordsworth's Philosophic Song* (Cambridge: Cambridge University Press, 2007), p. 40.

as an adjective, adverb, and verb; as still movement, still moving, and more forcefully, the stilling of movement: so 'still' movement as quiet, unmoving movement; 'still' moving as a forever-now movement, always in process, unending; and the union of these meanings at once twin and opposed in the 'stilling' of movement, an action that is at once the quieting of movement and the perpetuation of it, the making of it... a movement that is still and that is still with us.[63]

Krieger specifically connects the effect of this punning word to repetition: 'through all sorts of repetitions, echoes, [and] complexes of internal relations [a poem] converts its chronological progression into simultaneity'; in Krieger's argument this is 'Central to a poem's becoming successfully poetic.'[64] As Derek Attridge points out, 'What is especially valuable about the concept of repetition is that it highlights temporality.'[65] As 'still' implies something *still* continuing to happen, and constantly simultaneously plays with the idea of time by freezing action *still*, it implies repetition in contradictory senses: both continuance and stasis. The word 'still' itself is thus a form of repetition which never but also always moves. Another exceptionally interesting little word (which can function variously as conjunction, adverb, or adjective), 'now' is a bit like 'still' in its ability to indicate immediacy, but also sequence. When Christoph Asendorf discusses Hegel's *Jenaer Realphilosophie*, asserting that the increasing specialization and division of labour in the early nineteenth century led to a life 'based on partial experience', he suggests that one result of this was that the 'sequential character of the work process, the "and then," disappears—what follows is always the same.'[66] For Asendorf, literature thus becomes necessary, as it is capable of saving us: 'The storyteller's time and the time of narration is, with its free choice between various temporal forms (memory, present, fiction), in a certain respect related to the unregulated time of the divine.'[67] Like 'still', 'now' enables a slippage between Asendorf's 'various temporal forms'. These words do for time what *and* and *or* do for more concrete description, because they acknowledge *at the same time* a sense of 'immediately in the same moment I am describing', and of an unfolding, one-after-the-otherness, more like 'and then'; and, in self-conscious verse in particular, they also lend a sense of *right now* in the present moment of reflection.

Gill describes Wordsworth's revision of his poems as lending a sense 'that the evolving whole had both a historic existence, but, much more importantly, a being in the continuous present. Revisiting is never an act of homage to past achievement... nor the memorializing of a long-gone experience, but a live engagement with the past that reactivates it into conjunction with the present.'[68]

---

[63] 'Ekphrasis and the Still Movement of Poetry; or *Laokoön* Revisited (1967)', in Krieger, pp. 263–88 (pp. 267–8).
[64] Krieger, p. 263.   [65] *Moving Words*, p. 38.   [66] Asendorf, p. 3.
[67] Asendorf, p. 146.   [68] *Wordsworth's Revisitings*, pp. 36–7.

And and 'now' in their shared operation hold these moments together particularly powerfully. In *The Prelude*, for instance, as the boy-Wordsworth rows out across Ullswater for Patterdale, Wordsworth writes, 'And now, as suited one who proudly row'd | With his best skill, I fix'd a steady view' (I.395–8): 'And now' here is not straightforwardly the same as a narrative 'And then...'; it does function in that way, but it also shares in the immediacy of the experience as it is encountered by the boy-Wordsworth doing the rowing *right now*, and momentarily it also manages to imply a self-conscious, lyric-voiced, 'now that I am writing about it'. In Book II, Wordsworth appeals to the familiar pattern of his childhood: the section itself is preoccupied with the passage of time being simultaneously dizzyingly, repetitively circular, *and* sedately linear ('the year span round | With giddy motion. But the time approach'd | That brought with it regular desire | For calmer pleasures', ll. 48–51). The lines 'When summer came | It was the pastime of our afternoons' (ll. 55–6) declare both the annual and the quotidian to pursue a habitual track; but of course, mere repetition would be tedium, and as the poem goes on to detail the different joys within that routine, 'now' again suggests sequence and synchrony in the description of playtimes:

> the selected bourne
> Was now an Island, musical with birds
> That sang for ever; now a Sister Isle,
> Beneath the oak's umbrageous covert...
> And now a third small Island...
>
> (II.58–63)

This is a recorded memory of imaginative activity, rooted in the reality of customary habit, and it offers Wordsworth a way of seeing both the specific and the general at the same time. The constitution of the poetic mind is found chorally in the original experience (which here is itself imaginative), and the remembering of that experience, and the crafting of that memory into poetry in the moment, *now*. As I have said, *and* can sustain a similar weight to 'now' in this sense. When Wordsworth remembers playing in a stream, he recalls that he 'Bask'd in the sun, and plunged, and basked again' (I.295). That Wordsworth is sensitive to such depictions of repeated, separate actions rendered singular and cohesive through memory is suggested by his amendment of the original line, 'Basked in the sun, or plunged into thy streams' (1799, First Part, l. 20): as well as omitting the word 'again', this previous iteration exploits an *or* rather than an *and*. Whilst *or* has its own complications (it allows the action of the diving boy to be both as well and instead of the sunbathing), it does not here engender the more specifically temporal effect; Wordsworth's addition of repetition and the triple *and* to the revised version suggests his delicate inclusion of the very particular impression of split multiple experience. In 'To the Cuckoo', we find the effect again: 'And I can listen to thee yet; | Can lie upon the plain | And listen':[69] the various literal repetitions in the lines here coalesce with the simultaneous-with-sequential effect of *and* to flood the reading with the experience the poem describes. Repetition in language is necessarily chronological, but these little words have the capacity partially to transcend chronology, or at least to draw attention to the *experience* of its transcendence.[70] Of course, time is a matter of past event and present perspective, but it is also something which is *kept*, in the rhythm of the poem itself. The pulse of the poem resists the stagnation which threatens when the need continually to 'revisit' (to borrow Gill's term) refuses to allow any sense of completion. At some point, after all, Wordsworth has to stop revising.

Wordsworth's 'To a Sky-Lark', composed in 1805, approaches its subject by patterning the text according to birdsong. The skylark's call is composed of extended, lingering repetitious phrases, which incorporate variation within their reprisals. Wordsworth's poem is deeply aware of this arrangement:

> Up with me! up with me into the clouds!
> For thy song, Lark, is strong;
> Up with me, up with me into the clouds!
> Singing, singing,
> With all the heav'ns about thee ringing,
> Lift me, guide me, till I find
> That spot which seems so to thy mind![71]

Full end-rhyme, internal rhyme, conduplicato, epizeuxis, identical rhyme, anaphora, epistrophe, mesarchia: the poem might provide a case study for rhetorical devices of repetition. Repeated structures and sounds cooperate to mimic, though they cannot truly imitate, the progress of the song. In the course of his repetitions, Wordsworth discovers inadequacy, renouncing his opening imperative control, replacing it with a plea to be allowed to be a follower, and giving himself up to the folding soundscape the bird creates. It is telling, then, that in its concluding lines, the 1805 *Prelude* declares itself to be a 'Song which like a lark | I have protracted' (XIII.380–381). Apparently at odds with the elation of its closing lines, when he completed his revisions of his long poem in 1805 (for a time at least considering that he had 'finished' it), Wordsworth wrote to Sir George Beaumont complaining of unsettling depression: 'it was not a happy day for me I was dejected on many accounts; when I looked back upon the

---

[69] Repr. in *Poems, in Two Volumes, and Other Poems, 1800–1807*, pp. 213–15 (ll. 25–7).

[70] Other words function similarly: in a discussion of Coleridge, Michael O'Neill points out that in 'the phrase "Was richly ting'd"... "Was" erases and recollects': because it puts the tree (which 'richly ting'd' describes) in the past, and revives it in the present of the description (*Romanticism and the Self-Conscious Poem*, p. 79).

[71] 'To A Sky-Lark', in *Poems in Two Volumes, and Other Poems, 1800–1807*, pp. 117–18.

performance it seemed to have a dead weight about it, the reality so far short of the expectation'.[72] To the extent that they facilitate refined forms of recapitulation, conjunction and repetition assist Wordsworth in the articulation of a sincere record of the growth of his own mind, allowing the articulation of a multiple form of experience; but even they cannot fully transcend the weight of the text, whose fixedness resists the possibility of verse absolutely 'sincere' to experience.

Reader as Reviser

We do not need eighteenth-century accounts of the imagination to recognize that, insofar as we make sense of the world by reference to our previous experiences, meaning itself depends on repetition: we understand and categorize experience according to what we already know. But experience itself is not a groundhog day: it allows forward movement, the assimilation or creation (depending on one's philosophical allegiance) of the new. Every time we encounter a word in a poem, if we are to understand it, we must either have met it before (it is a direct repetition), or, if it is new to us, understand it through a process of cognitive construction which relies on what we do already know, from the word itself or from the context in which it appears. Yet, at the same time, every repeated word *is* a new word, by virtue of its different context and placing, its meaning inevitably minutely (perhaps radically) redefined by its use. To this extent, Wordsworth's repetitions within his verse mimic the 'revisitings' of his life, in that they portray as new things which are inevitably old, *and* are fresh, in their new incarnation. They are both the same, and changed. But poetry itself interrupts this. Poems as Wordsworth understands them are not single use, and disposable. Poems are to be re-read, as well as re-written. The relationship of the reader to the poem thus introduces another level of encounter. The re-read text which contains repetition is particularly sensitive to this: a repeated word or phrase is never truly identical to its predecessor, *because* it is a repetition, and it carries the knowledge, the memory of its predecessor, as it sounds. And yet, the poem being re-read, the first occurrence of the word or phrase is now laden also with the knowledge that through the re-reading it too has become a repetition (or rather, that it always already was one).

Such revision is not confined to the *return* to pages of verse, and it goes well beyond Wordsworth's hope that the attentive reader would recall and be able to map out the plan of the metaphorical Gothic cathedral he imagines his entire corpus to constitute. It occurs in the moment of reading. Significantly, once registered, Wordsworth's pervasive use of forms of revision attracts a self-aware

---

[72] W[illiam] W[ordsworth] to Sir George Beaumont, 3 June 1805, in *Letters*, i, 593–5 (p. 594).

kind of noticing; but readerly revision is required by Wordsworth in various other ways too. Garrett Stewart's 'transegmental drift', and the possibilities of line endings described by Christopher Ricks, both (as discussed in Chapter 2) leave readers with two specific ideas which nonetheless usually pull in the direction of one reading. In Ricks's account, the effect is engendered in other ways too: discussing *Home at Grasmere*, he draws out the sophisticated way in which Wordsworth builds up sense:

> At which point there dawns upon us the calm splendour of the ambiguity of 'breathe in peace'. Does it mean breathe *in peace* or *breathe in* peace? Both ... The two meanings can co-exist with perfect 'inobtrusive sympathies'; no strain, no pressure, but an interfusion which is limpidly and lucidly at ease.[73]

One version does not replace the other; the second reading we reach when a sentence disrupts what we thought it had implied cannot be forgotten, just as Wordsworth's earlier versions of his writing are not rendered 'wrong', 'insincere', or eliminated by subsequent versions. And like the use of conjunctions to engender forms of recapitulation which allow Wordsworth to communicate the multiple form of experience, such effects are powerful *because* they are subtle and unobtrusive. In other, related ways, critics have found that making sense of Wordsworth's poetry involves a re-reading or revised reading, a second look, which is inevitably a form of recapitulation. Armstrong identifies one species of this, when she discusses lines from *The Prelude*, concluding that:

> Surprisingly, and against all expectations, the postponed verb here is 'was scattered love, | A spirit of pleasure and youth's golden gleam'... The shape of the sentence at first suggests a delayed verb of physical action... But when that verb discovers itself as a metaphor which has nothing to do with physical action it acts on and changes the proposal of the sentence almost in the moment that proposal is made.[74]

Entirely appropriately thematically, 'It retrospectively transforms the contours of the sentence from the rear, lighting up new possibilities in the syntax as if it were conferring on it the "gleam" of fresh experience'. The demands Wordsworth's lines make upon interpretative revision are identified again in Peter McDonald's delicate attention to Michael O'Neill's discussion of 'clock time' in *The Prelude*:

> O'Neill's interest in 'the past returning back upon the present' fails to take account of the way in which poetry's words come back upon themselves, most

---

[73] *Force of Poetry*, p. 116.   [74] *Language as Living Form*, p. 61.

arrestingly in the repetition of line-endings in '...would give' and '...can give'. What happens in this repetition is a kind of hold-up, a hitch in the verse, which makes the meaning of a simple word ('give') more difficult, as though it were being held in suspension, under suspicion, or in doubt.[75]

Wordsworth's language thus encourages revision in the act of reading, 'repetition establishing another kind of time'.[76] Repeatedly, critical attention finds that lexical repetitions demand a revision of sense: comprehension involves recapitulation. This is directed by the poem, but it literally involves the reader, who must revise their original understanding of the lines. Yet these are not ambiguities which ultimately must resolve one way or the other; the conceptual sense of *and* is in play again. Through these recapitulations, Wordsworth creates the perception of 'similitude in dissimilitude' upon which, his 'Preface' insists, 'depend our taste and our moral feelings'.[77]

---

[75] McDonald, p. 49.   [76] McDonald, p. 49.   [77] *Prose*, i, 149.

7
Connection, Recognition, and Return

> And now, with gleams of half-extinguish'd thought,
> With many recognitions dim and faint,
> ...
> The picture of the mind revives again
>
> (ll. 59–62)

Recognition; revival: these processes betray Wordsworth's fascination with going back over things. This poem's title, 'Lines Composed a Few Miles above Tintern Abbey, On Revisiting the Banks of the Wye During a Tour, July 13, 1798', highlights the significance of return before a word of the poem proper is read. Jeremy Prynne has observed the difference between the visit 'which might be partly the accident of its occasion', and the *re*-visit, 'which bears the mark of full deliberateness'.[1] Re-viewing is similarly selective: a second visit looks for something in particular, rather than just gazing around. David Simpson claims that within many of Wordsworth's poems, 'the "first sight" produces either confusion or misreading, and must be corrected by the second look.'[2] But Wordsworth's compulsion to revisit is rooted in something more fundamental than anxiety about getting things wrong on a first attempt: the value of the 'spontaneous overflow of powerful emotion' in the 'Preface' to *Lyrical Ballads* depends upon its recollection 'in tranquillity'.[3] Recognizing is a form of revision for Wordsworth; indeed, in the early nineteenth century, one of the established meanings of 'recognition' was 'the action of reviewing or revising something' (*OED*); Prynne argues that 'to recognise is to confirm by second looks'. Yet this confirmation is never absolute, as the 'many recognitions' of 'Tintern Abbey' imply: each recognition is influenced by the different contexts and agendas under which the visit, event, or feeling has previously occurred. The picture that Wordsworth revives can never be an exact reconstruction; recognition is an act of remembering which is filtered through the associations the mind bears.

---

[1] J. H. Prynne, 'Tintern Abbey, Once Again', *Glossator*, 1 (2009), 81–7 (p. 83), emphasis original.
[2] David Simpson, *Wordsworth and the Figurings of the Real* (Houndsmills: Macmillan, 1982), p. xviii.
[3] *Prose*, i, 149.

Recognition, Connection, and Community

Dorothy Wordsworth's sketch of another re-visit, which inspired Wordsworth's 'Stepping Westward' (1807), begins with an apparent denial of the possibility that she might change her earlier description. Dorothy depicts a consolidated, repeated experience: 'I can add nothing to my former description of the Trossachs...' Yet, shortly afterwards, she declares that 'it was much more interesting to visit a place where we have been before than it can possibly be the first time':[4] as 'Tintern Abbey' articulates, a revisit is more than the opportunity for a simple confirmation (or identification of difference). It is perhaps not a coincidence that the poem her brother subsequently wrote (which Dorothy copied into her journal entry) is animated by engagement with various forms of repetition.[5] 'Stepping Westward' is explicitly cast, via its preface, as a record of a revisit, and its text performs a kind of revisiting as well. It begins with two repetitions: its first line (*"What you are stepping westward?"—"Yea."*) echoes its title, and immediately restates the question which concludes the preface (albeit in an amended way: it is given an answer in the poem). The phrase 'stepping westward' is picked up again, in modified form, in line 11. In the course of the poem, however, reiteration changes the greeting, as it becomes separated from the woman who originally articulates it, and thus from its roots in the welcome of her 'native' place. It transforms instead into a 'sound' (l. 13), a word reasserted through its own emphatic repetition later in the poem as 'the very sound' (l. 20). The 'sound' is then recast again, as the 'echo' it has become (l. 23). The 'power' held by this reverberation resonating within the memory, changing itself and its auditor as it does so, is demonstrated through the profound affect the poem seeks to communicate:

> It's power was felt; and while my eye
> Was fixed upon the glowing sky,
> The echo of the voice enwrought
> A human sweetness with the thought
> Of travelling through the world that lay
> Before me in my endless way.
>
> (ll. 21–6)

The reader is prepared for the sublimity engendered by the coincidence of echoing sound and twilit sky by explicitly divine diction (*'heavenly* destiny'; 'spiritual right', l. 12; l.15). The sublimity is affirmed by the way that, rather than reinforcing something, the repetition breaks down certainty: despite the specificity of place

---

[4] Dorothy Wordsworth, *Recollections of a Tour Made in Scotland, A.D. 1803*, ed. J. C. Shairp (Edinburgh: Edmonston and Douglas, 1874), pp. 220–1.
[5] 'Stepping Westward', in *Poems, in Two Volumes, and Other Poems, 1800–1807*, pp. 185–6.

with which the poem began, the reiteration of direction ('westwards', l.11), and the recurrence of geographical indicators ('home', l. 4; l. 7; 'place', l. 5; l. 14; 'region', l. 16), Wordsworth is unable fully to locate or comprehend his experience; things can only 'seem (l. 11; l. 15)', or to be 'a kind of' (l. 12); to be 'something without place or bound' (l. 14).

Leslie Stephen describes 'Stepping Westward' as 'at once a delicate expression of a specific sentiment and an acute critical analysis of the subtle associations suggested by a single phrase',[6] deftly capturing the nature of the poem as it attempts to communicate one specific idea or feeling, but in doing so discovers a proliferation of potential meanings or resonances rippling and swirling within and beyond the text. In the very centre of the poem is the only fact Wordsworth can hang onto, and his direct, personal statement, 'I liked the greeting' (l. 13), throws into relief the sublime escape from certainty the rest of the poem evokes. In an echo of 'Tintern Abbey', of the 'eye made quiet by the power | Of harmony, and the deep power of joy' (ll. 47–8), so here the 'eye' is fixed, as the 'power' of the scene is viscerally felt as something separate from (though not totally independent of) the act of merely looking. What this power lends Wordsworth is based in another form of repetition: his 'spiritual right | To travel through that region bright' (ll. 12–13) renders him the legitimate heir of Milton. Earlier, scattered Miltonic echoes in the poem crystallize into the unmistakable allusion of the final lines, in which Wordsworth's 'right | To travel' returns in his 'travelling through the world that lay | Before me on my endless way' (ll. 25–6): the controlled infinitive is transformed into an extensive, limitless journeying which refuses to fix an end point (or meaning). Such 'travelling' is now both an imaginative recollection of Milton's poem, and Wordsworth's own response to it: a recognition, in all senses set out here, which fuels and legitimates his claim to be inspired by the simple statement with which the poem began. It is also a call to the reader to recognize: to comprehend a relationship between Wordsworth, Milton, and Milton's Adam. But the poem is underscored by anxiety: the woman asks a question because she is surprised to see the Wordsworths literally chasing the sunset. Is their adventure mistaken in some way? It is Satan, after all, who searches for 'place or refuge' in *Paradise Lost*,[7] who is 'roving still | About the world' in *Paradise Regained*.[8] Again, though, the reader is not obliged to decide whether Wordsworth is Adam or Satan, nor to lose sight of the fact that of course he is really neither; the binaries are collapsed into a more inclusive, conceptual *or* that supports the simultaneous possibility of both identities, and thus gestures to more.

---

[6] Leslie Stephens, 'Wordsworth's Ethics' [1876], in *Hours in a Library*, 3 vols (London: Smith, Elder, 1892), ii, 270–307 (p. 306).

[7] *Paradise Lost*, IX.119.

[8] *The Complete Works of John Milton, Volume 2: The 1671 Poems: Paradise Regain'd and Samson Agonistes*, ed. Laura Lunger Knoppers (Oxford: Oxford University Press, 2008), I.33–4.

The echo which runs through the poem draws attention to this characteristic, keeping alive, and multiplying, meaningful possibilities.

Like 'Stepping Westward', 'Tintern Abbey' is about memory, revisiting, connections, and reflection. The poem contains multiple recollections (even its subtitle gestures to the date of its writing, the eve of Bastille Day, as significant for retrospection), and literal repetitions. Marking a revisit, its lines speak to the certainty of future revisitings, in the form of memories and reconsiderations, and come to rest in another type of connection of enormous significance to Wordsworth: the enhancing pleasure of community. Wordsworth's benedictive conclusion, tracing the process of tranquil recollection described in the 'Preface', is confident that

> in after years,
> When these wild ecstasies shall be matured
> Into a sober pleasure, when thy mind
> Shall be a mansion for all lovely forms,
> Thy memory be as a dwelling-place
> For all sweet sounds and harmonies; Oh! then,
> ...with what healing thoughts
> Of tender joy wilt thou remember me...
> Nor wilt thou then forget,
> That after many wanderings, many years
> Of absence, these steep woods and lofty cliffs,
> And this green pastoral landscape, were to me
> More dear, both for themselves, and for thy sake.
> (ll. 138–60)

The poem ends on an idea of shared experience. The mutual nature of the memory will, ultimately, allow it to persist. As in 'Stepping Westward', the text is underscored by the absolute conviction that not only in the moment but also in this repeated memorial form, human connection and remembrance are the legacies of the revisit. Earlier in the poem, Wordsworth has declared that he should not

> Suffer my genial spirits to decay:
> For thou art with me, here, upon the banks
> Of this fair river; thou, my dearest Friend,
> My dear, dear Friend, and in thy voice I catch
> The language of my former heart, and read
> My former pleasures in the shooting lights
> Of thy wild eyes.
> (ll. 114–20)

Just as Wordsworth understood his written works to exist most fully in their connection with one another, as parts which constituted a whole, here, social bonds create a rich, nourishing, and unified network. Wordsworth can revisit not just former places, but his former self, through the echoes of that self which are reflected in his sister. For Wordsworth, full community extends to the living and the dead; the third 'Essay upon Epitaphs' finds him insisting that a proper epitaph allows 'a prolonged companionship', as it provides a locus to which 'the fancies of a scattered family may repair in pilgrimage; the thoughts of the individuals, without any communication with each other, must oftentimes meet here.' And the connection extends beyond the familial: 'it feeds also local attachment, which is the tap-root of the tree of Patriotism.'[9] In 'Tintern Abbey', the poet's relationship with his sister represents a perfect form of this community, and such connection is simultaneously a form of self-repetition, as Wordsworth literally hears and sees himself in Dorothy's voice and eyes, and longs for that to continue: 'Oh! yet a little while | May I behold in thee what I was once, | My dear, dear Sister!' (ll. 120–2).

Wordsworth's assertion of Dorothy's willingness to submit to and support her brother has aroused some unease. Several critics have refused to accept Wordsworth's turn towards Dorothy as sincere, seeing it merely as a selfish poetic opportunity. Yet we might with Soderholm wonder why such critics 'insist, contrary to all biographical evidence, that William secretly has it in for Dorothy when he writes a poem including and even celebrating her?'[10] For Soderholm, 'Tintern Abbey' and 'A slumber did my spirit steal' offer examples of the apostrophic address which (as he demonstrates through quotation of Jonathan Culler) poses 'a temporal problem':

> 'something once present has been lost or attenuated; this loss can be narrated but the temporal sequence is irreversible, like time itself. Apostrophes displace this irreversible structure by removing the opposition between presence and absence from empirical time and locating it in a discursive time. The temporal movement from A to B, internalized by apostrophe, becomes a reversible alternation between A' and B': a play of presence and absence governed not by time but by poetic power.' For Culler, the use of apostrophe works toward the elusive ideal of atemporal immediacy, a way of converting the temporal into an eternal present.[11]

---

[9] *Prose*, ii, 93. The natural metaphor is suggestive, because Wordsworth's idea of connection encompasses the natural world, as its repetitive rhythms provide models of 'types of renovation and decay' to 'the notice of the serious and contemplative mind.' (*Essay upon Epitaphs, I*, in *Prose*, ii, 54).

[10] James Soderholm, 'Dorothy Wordsworth's Return to Tintern Abbey', *New Literary History*, 26.2 (Spring 1995), 309–22 (p. 315), https://www.jstor.org/stable/20057284, accessed 2 June 2022.

[11] Soderholm, p. 320.

Such use of apostrophe resists the same kind of binaries that *and* and *or* resist, in order to facilitate a productive escape from the limitations upon understanding, experience, and poetic expression. Culler's more general argument, and Soderholm's extension of it into an account of the connection between Dorothy and William, lays bare Wordsworth's desire for an open, more fluid discourse, achieved though poetry. However they might sound to modern ears, Wordsworth's lines in 'Tintern Abbey' reflect a mutually enriching relationship: as Lucy Newlyn argues, 'It seems bizarre...that Dorothy is often regarded as playing an undervalued or exploited role [...when] the reality was otherwise... She shared with her brother a vision of the "ennobling interchange" between human beings and the natural world'.[12] Newlyn's study emphasizes *'the communal nature of their creative processes'*.[13] Alan Bewell notes that Wordsworth's lines addressing Dorothy have a scientific grounding in 'the Enlightenment idea that all people pass through the same stages of development': Wordsworth 'finds a way out of the impasse he had earlier reached, by reading *her* present experience as a "survival" of *his* past feeling'. Such a movement is, in Bewell's account, fundamentally mutual and generous: 'The relationship is reciprocal: if Dorothy has allowed her brother to recover an experience that he has passed beyond, Wordsworth offers his sister the possibility...of recovering in his absence her own history'.[14] And Soderholm argues that Dorothy's 'Thoughts on my sick bed' responds directly to the end of 'Tintern Abbey':

> Dorothy's poem echoes her brother's earlier works, borrowing from them as liberally as William once borrowed from her journals. The intermingling of poetic images helps us to reexamine the function of address and apostrophe: figural evocations of subjectivity produced by turning, and returning, to another person.[15]

Resolving on an image of connection and repetition, Soderholm's reading proposes a 'deeper understanding of a brother and sister who, with wandering steps and slow, left Tintern Abbey only to return, in memory'.[16]

This Miltonic allusion returns us to the end of 'Stepping Westward', a poem interested in the fact that in revisiting a place, a degree of recognition is necessarily at play, which reaches out to literary, imaginative, and literal echoes. The classic exploration of recognition is Aristotle's account of *anagnorisis*, which is widely translated as 'recognition' (literally, knowing something again), but which connotes a more complex change from ignorance to knowledge.[17] For Malcolm

---

[12] *All in Each Other*, pp. xii–xiii. [13] *All in Each Other*, p. xiii (emphases original).
[14] Bewell, pp. 38–9. [15] Soderholm, p. 309. [16] Soderholm, p. 321.
[17] See Aristotle, *Poetics*, trans. Malcolm Heath (Harmondsworth: Penguin, 1996), pp. 18–19, and Heath's 'Introduction' to the same text, pp. xxviii–xxix.

Heath, Aristotelian recognition reveals that 'because things are not what they seemed, what a person has done or is about to do is not what he thought it was'.[18] This appeal to the flexibility of interpretation suggests its attraction to Wordsworth, interested in endlessly revising his works as experience alters his perception of events and feelings, and in attempting to communicate the multi-layered nature of human experience. Terence Cave argues that Aristotelian recognition 'works against mimesis in Auerbach's sense of the word. The scar is a mark of treacherously concealed narrative waiting to break the surface and create a scandal; it is a sign that the story, like the wound, may always be reopened.'[19] Wordsworth's revisions re-open, but also insist that final, 'closed' versions are impossible; insofar as the reader can be made aware of the process of recognition, the work can thus enact its own predicament. Whether at the level of line endings whose 'fugitive suggestiveness' mock their pretension to finite meaning,[20] of textual details which are minutely revised over time, or of the understanding of an entire corpus which is necessarily constantly reshuffling and rearranging itself in relation to itself, Wordsworth's writing plays out this fact.

But Wordsworth's recognitions do not necessarily share in the violence implicit in Cave's (and Auerbach's) vocabulary of brutality and pain. Dorothy's account of 'Stepping Westwards' registers the reconciliation that recognition in a state of community can allow. Aristotle breaks recognition down into different kinds, the third of which is 'by means of memory, when someone grasps the significance of something that he sees'.[21] This is what happens to the Wordsworths in the Trossachs, specifically as a result of the greeting of the woman, even though they can't grasp its significance completely. Dorothy registers the failure of expression: 'I cannot describe how affecting this simple expression was'.[22] The result of the unsettling experience is not, however, disorientating:

> We went up to the door of our boatman's hut as to a home... It had been a very pleasing thought, while we were walking by the side of the beautiful lake, that, few hours as we had been there, there was a home for us in one of its quiet dwellings. Accordingly, so we found it... I slept in the same bed as before, and listened to the household stream, which now only made a very low murmuring.[23]

'[T]here was a home for us': Dorothy records a sense of belonging. Through the re-affirmation of the personal connection with her brother, reinforced by the textual connection worked out in the borrowing and copying of material, the sublime experience of the moment is rendered into contentment; a sense of

---

[18] Heath, 'Introduction', p. xxxi.
[19] Terence Cave, *Recognitions: A Study in Poetics* (Oxford: Oxford University Press, 1990), p. 24.
[20] *Force of Poetry*, p. 99.   [21] Aristotle, *Poetics*, p. 26.
[22] Dorothy Wordsworth, *Recollections*, p. 221.
[23] Dorothy Wordsworth, *Recollections*, pp. 222–3.

coming home, and rest; a sense of return, and peace. Both in Wordsworth's poem, and Dorothy's account of its genesis, recognition and return are forms of repetition which fundamentally reassure when they are experienced within the connective tissue of real community.

Disjunction, and the Absence of Community

The form of community epitomized by Wordsworth's mutually sustaining relationship with Dorothy, and the sense of anagnorisis its connections allow, finds a harsh, anonymous counterpart in the London of *The Prelude*. Book VII exemplifies Wordsworth's preoccupation with the vital necessity and the deep challenges of connection. The crowd which characterizes Wordsworth's 'Residence in London' is radically different, in its capacity to allow the poet to feel connected, to the intimate relationship discovered in the Wordsworths' siblinghood. Yet the poem exhibits the negotiation of those challenges in its display of self-aware *revisiting*, not only through the poetic reflection advocated in the 'Preface' to *Lyrical Ballads*, but also through the exploitation of literal conjunctions and repetitions in its text.

At the end of January 1801, Charles Lamb wrote to regret that he could not take up a 'very kind invitation into Cumberland' the Wordsworth's had issued; the journey was beyond the reach of his purse, and anyway, despite his affection for William and Dorothy, he explained, 'I don't mu[ch] care if I never see a mountain in my life.—I have passed all my days in London, until I have formed as many and intense local attachments as any of you **Mountaineers** can have done with dead nature.' A sensory medley follows in Lamb's densely packed description of London, which climaxes with

> the pantomimes, London itself, a pantomime and a masquerade, all these things work themselves into my mind and feed me without a power of satiating me. The wonder of these sights impells me into night-walks about her crowded streets, and I often shed tears in the motley Strand from fulness of joy at so much **Life**—. All these emotions must be strange to you. So are your rural emotions to me.[24]

Figuring London as a vast theatre (for Lamb, the slide from London-based pantomime to London *as* pantomime is seamless) was a familiar trope in the early nineteenth century. In Deborah Epstein Nord's account of it, this city stage is equally for performance as for observation, and it is primarily a means of achieving 'a distance and tentativeness in the relation between the spectator and

---

[24] Charles Lamb to William Wordsworth, Jan 30 1801, in *The Letters of Charles and Mary Lamb, 1796–1801*, ed. Edwin W. Marrs (Ithaca: Cornell University Press, 1975), pp. 265–8 (p. 267).

the action upon the stage.'²⁵ A flâneur *avant la lettre*, Lamb's posture as observer leads to intense 'attachment': because he understands himself as just one of the many interconnected elements he describes, he is controlled ('impel[led]') by the city's rhythms. But he recognizes that Wordsworth, who does not belong in the city (and therefore has no existing connection to it) 'must' be estranged by it. Lamb's multi-sensory chaotic listing, the idea of the observer as a walker *amongst* the life of the streets, and the idea of the overwhelming excess nonetheless being 'without a power of satiating', all prefigure aspects of *The Prelude*'s London. The difference between the two accounts, however, is that, totally at odds with Lamb's affectionate participation, Wordsworth's is rooted in discontinuity and a lack of relationship which he must confront textually and imaginatively in order to communicate anything meaningful at all.

The distance and the complicated relationship Epstein Nord describes as aspects of the experience of London in the 1820s and 1830s are already both necessary and problematic in Book VII of the 1805 *Prelude*. Wordsworth must be the observing eye in his depiction: he must be 'Still among Streets with clouds and sky above' (VII.160) in order to survey the scene, though the pun recognizes that he is both part of the moving pageant *and* separate from it. And to the extent that he must occupy the position of the lyric 'I', he is always able to separate himself from the ebb and flow of the tide of people. Wordsworth, that is, falls back on the capacity claimed in Book I, where he is 'singled out' (I.62) by his ability to observe, reflect, and offer back. But in 'Residence in London', Wordsworth exists on a fragile edge between his separation from the rest of the life of the city, and his situation within it. This positioning turns him, effectively, into a lone audience-member, part of the theatre but not of the play, witnessing the continuous performance of the city in pantomimic scenes which exemplify the metaphor Epstein Nord explores. In the translation of lived experience to poetry, Wordsworth's being 'singled out' creates the possibility for his processing of the spectacle of the world. Spectacles are exciting things to look at, but they are also means of seeing more clearly. And of course, Wordsworth's poem is never really 'about' the 'raree show' of dancing dogs and antic monkeys: described in explicitly theatrical terms, the spectacle becomes merely the stimulus to the imagination; Wordsworth, through his struggle to create meaning in the absence of a sense of connection, remains the star of his own show.

Distance affords the necessary vantage point of any description at all. In *The Prelude*, though, it also enacts the atomization London's streets troublingly suggest, rendering observations 'random sights' (VII.233), without the poet at the centre of them to make them cohere: Wordsworth's is an oddly displaced lyric self. The city is a swirling mass of spectacles which melt into one another, with the

---

[25] Deborah Epstein Nord, 'The City as Theater: From Georgian to Early Victorian London', *Victorian Studies*, 31.2 (Winter 1988), 159–88 (p. 160).

disintegration of identity or unity. Apparently paradoxically, the general mass is generated through the proliferation of specifics. The paradox is resolved through the recognition that the particular characters are categories, rather than individuals. Because the depths of personhood are replaced by the superficial labels of types, occupations, and nations, Wordsworth is unable to read into his fellow citizens, and thus to understand their connection to one another, or to himself. Introduced first to 'A travelling Cripple' and one 'in Sailor's garb', the reader is surely meant to infer that these begin the 'range | Of written characters' over whose description Wordsworth is taking control (VII.219–22). But the lines run on in an unsubtle wordplay: these characters are merely more illegible words, 'with chalk inscribed | Upon the smooth flat stones' (ll. 222–3; by 1850, the extended pun is laboured still further, introducing 'a range | Of well-formed characters...', 1850, VII.205–6). Instead, we meet a cast of anonyms: 'Nurse', 'Bachelor', 'military Idler', 'Dame', 'Italian', 'Jew', and 'Turk' (ll. 223–31). All of these labels are preceded by the definite article, implying a fixed typology, generally representative, but individually or specifically empty. A type is the opposite to that which Wordsworth delineates in the third 'Essay upon Epitaphs' as the best of epitaphic descriptions: a headstone bearing simply name and dates. This tombstone moves Wordsworth so deeply because, as Brigham points out,

> The proper name, in the absence of the interfering substitution of a more intrusive and less private language, summons no icon but the deceased itself... A language which renders locality and character abstract and universal undoes the mystery, and with it social incentive. The result is a transient, alienated people, Wordsworth's indictment of modernity.[26]

These 'transient, alienated people' are those we find in Wordsworth's London; whilst their presentation as types might seem to render them catalogable, and therefore comprehensible, the 'Essay upon Epitaphs' makes clear that it actually does the opposite. Individual specificity is lost, and with it departs Wordsworth's ability to enter into community.

In the middle of his list of characters, Wordsworth's poem pauses, as the sight of the Turk induces a momentary reflection:

> Briefly, we find, if tired of random sights,
> And haply to that search our thoughts should turn,
> Among the crowd, conspicuous less or more,
> As we proceed, all specimens of man
>
> (1805, ll. 233–6)

[26] Brigham, p. 28.

This momentary, abstractive, analytical effort reaches towards a generalizing impulse in 'all specimens of man', but almost immediately collapses back into its non-exhaustive listing. The 1850 version emphasizes the moment, inserting the expostulation 'Enough;—' (1850, l. 219), yet still going on with the catalogue despite itself. Although the description in this later version remains tied together with present-tense verbs and imperatives ('is here'; 'See', etc.), Wordsworth in 1850 casts his deliberation into the past: 'I surveyed...'.[27] The in-the-moment, collective effort to turn 'our thoughts' (1805, l. 234) has become a reflection on how, 'with no unthinking mind', Wordsworth solipsistically *was* 'well pleased to note' (1850, l. 220). The shift to thoughts and thinking prefaces another verbal repetition, as Wordsworth returns to the idea of 'character' (1805, l. 238; 1850, l. 223). But the attempt at active reflection fails; in both the 1805 and the 1850 *Prelude*, the line returns Wordsworth to his catalogue, and his litany continues with 'The Swede', 'the Russian', 'The Frenchman and the Spaniard', 'the Hunter Indian', and finally 'Moors, | Malays, Lascars, the Tartar and Chinese, | And Negro Ladies in white muslin gowns.' (1805, ll. 239–43). The multicultural array remains steadfastly superficial, despite Wordsworth's directing us to 'See' them, and despite the fact that these are relatively vivid amongst the even 'less distinguishable shapes' of a 'thickening hubbub' which directly recalls Milton's Chaos (1805, ll. 228–9). Londoners are only recognizable and thus only understandable by the poet as costumes, or representatives: in a period still fixated on Lavater's physiognomical deduction of inner self from outward appearance, it is striking that nothing is manifest by these exteriors apart from their difference from other exteriors, all of which flood past with no discernible relationship to one another.

The problem at the heart of Wordsworth's attempt to survey, which prevents him from moving beneath mere ciphers, is one of connection: of how to distinguish and put together (to order and conjoin) the overwhelming sights into something that can be comprehended and thus properly *known*. London is

> An undistinguishable world to men,
> ...the same perpetual flow
> Of trivial objects, melted and reduced
> To one identity, by differences
> That have no law, no meaning, and no end;
>   (1805, ll. 700–5)[28]

As John Jones explains, Wordsworth here insists that 'the impression made by objects depends upon the distinctness with which they are individually

---

[27] See 1850, ll. 207–19.
[28] In 1850, Wordsworth deletes 'An undistinguishable world to men,' but changes 'flow' to the yet more chaotic, directionless 'whirl'.

imagined... Wordsworth is involved in a huge, sustained argument from solitude to relationship, from the points "where all stand single" to their connexions'.[29] Ricks summarizes this as 'Wordsworth's commitment to those ample relationships which yet do not swamp or warp the multiplicities which they accommodate'.[30] In describing London thus as a composite of 'differences | That have no law, no meaning, and no end', Wordsworth specifically attributes his chaotic sensory experience to the lack of a grammar of city life: London's streets are places of endless conjunction which resist inferable relation, deny Jones's 'connexions', and thus refuse the appreciation of 'relationship'. In Locke's seminal account of the operation of the mind, difference is necessary to create contrastable concepts and, thereby, understanding; but the lack of discernible connection in Wordsworth's London leads to differences that melt and reduce into a mass which cannot be logically separated out. The semi colon both follows and resists the 'end' at line 705. It is replaced in some modern editions by an idiosyncratic dash which makes the point more forcefully,[31] because it highlights the observer's sense of the impossibility of terminating such an undifferentiated stream, and yet also the practical need to call a halt.

The same editions also instate a dash at line 418 when Wordsworth describes his shock at first hearing 'The voice of Woman utter blasphemy—'. This dash is similarly busy, mimicking the conventional omission of blasphemous speech, as it simultaneously fulfils its teasing grammatical function: a double moment of articulation-through-denial. The editorial decision to employ a semi colon reduces, though it does not eliminate, the effect of the passage; and even where it is included, the dash does not fulfil its other possibility (the quasi-colonic promise to reveal the woman's profanity). Instead, we are told that the poet

>   Saw Woman as she is to open shame
>   Abandon'd, and the pride of public vice.
>   ...a barrier seem'd at once
>   Thrown in, that from humanity divorced
>   The human Form, splitting the race of Man
>   In twain, yet leaving the same outward shape.
>   (1805, ll. 418–27)

Wordsworth's return to these lines in 1850 suggests that he was dissatisfied with the terms available adequately to express his meaning, becoming tangled in a vocabulary of personhood, fellow-feeling, and figure (1850, ll. 386–91). Both versions of the passage, though, remain dominated by the diction of separation, barrier, divorce, and splitting, which decisively breaks innate connections and

---

[29] Jones, p. 33.   [30] *Force of Poetry*, p. 91.
[31] See for example the Norton edition, ed. Wordsworth, Abrams, and Gill.

alienates a humanity which *had been* whole, which is no longer so, yet which still looks the same. This is the problematic 'one identity' of line 704 (1805); not the kind of harmonious unity Wordsworth celebrates in *The Recluse*, for example, but a bulk which resists the attempts of the poet to penetrate it enough to know and to understand (the same anxiety emerges when Wordsworth encounters some gypsies who fascinate and in many ways resemble him, yet whose 'knot' utterly resists his penetration.[32]) London offers a throng which exhibits 'all the strife of singularity' (1805, l. 574): the 'living shapes they wear' can offer only deception, 'Lies to the ear, and lies to every sense' (ll. 575–6). Moreover, 'Of these ... | There is no end.' (ll. 576–7). Again, the punning conclusion to Wordsworth's sentence, falling mid-line, insinuates that the torrent of multiple singularities cannot stop, that the poet cannot still it, because they remain unconnected and therefore beyond adequate comprehension and syntactic representation. This is in direct contrast with the images of perfect, and recognized, connection we find in depictions of ideal communities elsewhere in Wordsworth's writing, pre-eminently in *Home at Grasmere*, in passages which affirm his assertion that 'a parish-church, in the stillness of the country, is a visible centre of a community of the living and the dead'.[33]

Yet if a conjunctive grammar of the city eludes Wordsworth, throughout Book VII, the way words are connected at a grammatical level reflects the capacity of the mind and the text to connect and therefore cope with the phenomena they represent. Wordsworth's anxiety, that the absence of any apprehension of relationship and connection refuses to offer him a grasp of the whole metropolis, extends also to the microcosm:

> Above all, one thought
> Baffled my understanding, how men lived
> Even next-door neighbours, as we say, yet still
> Strangers, and knowing not each other's names
>
> (1805, ll. 117–20)

Wordsworth's first experience of London as he offers it to the reader here is at second hand, via the report of a school friend, though he acknowledges that his own interpretation pre-determines the vicarious experience of the city's attractions. The suggestion is enhanced in the 1850 text, in which Wordsworth augments his address, 'Oh wondrous power of words', adding 'Licensed to take the meaning that we love!' (ll. 119–20). First, Wordsworth imaginatively tours aspects of the city scene which are deliberately created to be fanciful:

---

[32] See Sarah Houghton-Walker, *Representations of the Gypsy in the Romantic Period* (Oxford: Oxford University Press, 2014), pp. 135–54.
[33] *Essays upon Epitaphs*, p. 56.

> Vauxhall and Ranelagh! I then had heard
> Of your green groves, and wilderness of lamps,
> Yours gorgeous Ladies, fairy cataracts,
> And pageant fire-works
>
> (1805, ll. 123-6)

Notably, in the 1850 revision, Wordsworth rendered the delights more obviously supernatural as he made the lines fuller, the elements of his enhanced description being more prominently tied together by conjunctions. The lamps are now 'Dimming the stars', with

> fire-works magical,
> And gorgeous Ladies under splendid Domes
> Floating in dance, or warbling high in air
> The Songs of Spirits!
>
> (1850, ll. 121-6)

Here, the conjunctions do their work to sustain a sense of plenitude and richness: these things are all happening at once, but they can still be discriminated individually by the eye which looks directly at them, at a distance. The connections between them are governed by the poet who selects them for inclusion. These are the incarnation of 'airy Palaces, and Gardens built | By Genii of Romance' (1805, ll. 82-3) imagined by Wordsworth as a boy. The pleasure gardens exist for sheer experience, and so they satisfy in this regard; moreover, fundamentally being products of the imagination, they ultimately remain within the control of the poet. As the poem moves on to 'Those other wonders, different in kind' (l. 127)—the architecture and statuary of civic life—Wordsworth's description abandons conjunction for lists held together by semi colons which do not disclose any relationship other than a narrative one, and within a few lines the poet is acknowledging that these ideas were replaced by real experience: 'These fond imaginations, of themselves, | Had long before given way,... | And now I look'd upon the real scene' (1805, ll. 136-9). 'Real' experience here is already actually theatrical; it is always recognized and confronted *as* a 'scene'.

Immediately, Wordsworth introduces his 'disappointment' (l. 142), but he nevertheless looks on, dwelling rhetorically on the desirability or propriety of 'Copying the impression of the memory' (l. 146). These lines read more as a sort of desperate settling in, than a serious moment of philosophy: given the disjointed nature of the subject, where should the poet begin? Yet begin he must, and suddenly he plunges: '—And first, the look and aspect of the place...' (l. 154). Wordsworth's opening conjunction smudges over the fact that there is no right place to start; 'And' (along with the dash which introduces it) implies running-on, but it is really just poetical throat-clearing. The endlessness of the 'illimitable' walk

(l. 159) inhibits the possibility of ordering: Wordsworth is overwhelmed as he looks 'On Strangers of all ages; the quick dance | Of colours, lights and forms; the Babel din' (ll. 156–7), and on a stream of further images stacked in clauses yoked predominantly by commas, until his poetic eye lights upon

> The Comers and the Goers face to face,
> Face after face; the string of dazzling Wares,
> Shop after Shop, with Symbols, blazon'd Names...
>
> (1805, ll. 172–4)

Conjunctions, which functionally aim to clarify the nature of the connection between elements of the scene, are eclipsed by a rash of punctuation marks which simply link elements together as a mass. The moment of real surrender here is figured through repetition: as 'face to face' becomes 'Face after face', the correction buttresses the significance of the line just as any sense of personal connection falls away; this is an unceasing torrent of humanity which cannot recognize itself, let alone pause to find a vantage point for reflection.

Here, Wordsworth's experience prefigures the work of historians who trace the emergence of the modern condition to the ability of the urban crowd to render inhabitants strangers to one another,[34] echoing contemporary fears. Thomas de Quincey finds 'utter loneliness' to be the only response to a first experience of London: 'in the centre of faces never-ending, without voice or utterance for him; eyes innumerable, that have "no speculation" in their orbs which *he* can understand; and hurrying figures of men and women weaving to and fro, with no apparent purposes intelligible to a stranger'.[35] Here is the lack of purpose, abstraction, and inability to see beyond the part to the whole which has been teased out by historians of industrial life. Christoph Asendorf argues that 'The city multiplies human contacts and at the same time removes from them the quality of persistence, which they had, for example, in the village community (*Gemeinschaft*). Continuity and individual characteristics disappear in the circulation of human beings and commodities'. Asendorf points out that Walter Benjamin

> works with opposing concepts of experience, *Erfahrung* and *Erlebnis*. *Erfahrung*, grounded in the domain of the epic tale, the storyteller, and the craftsman, is bound to notions of continuity, habitat, and sequence. Its opposite is *Erlebnis*, the discontinuous experience of the city[.][36]

---

[34] See for example Vernon, *passim*.
[35] From 'The Nation of London', in *Autobiographic Sketches, Vol. I* [1853], repr. in *The Works of Thomas De Quincey, Vol. 19: Autobiographical Sketches*, ed. Daniel Sanjiv Roberts (London: Pickering & Chatto, 2003), pp. 109–31 (pp. 111–12).
[36] Asendorf, pp. 4–5.

Wordsworth's London crowd is a figuration of just this discontinuous strangeness, and the connection to commodity Asendorf raises is implied in the structural repetition immediately beneath 'Face after face' at line 173: 'Shop after Shop' visually and semantically transfers the sense of a mass of perpetual, isolated motions to the fabric of the city itself. The poet can now only point randomly 'Here' and 'There' as direction (l. 176; l. 179): construing connection between aspects of the cityscape is abandoned, even as the possibility that they *should* be literally readable is enforced through their similitude to 'title-page[s]', allegories, and long-forgotten personages (ll. 176–83).

Later, Wordsworth's contemplation of the potential of a beautiful child he meets in the theatre 'to live | To be, to have been, come and go' (ll. 402–3) half-echoes Hamlet's wondering whether 'To be or not to be', as it recalls at the same time his own 'Comers and [...] Goers face to face, | Face after face'. The intensity created by Wordsworth's double allusion, to his own writing and to Shakespeare's dwelling on the very possibility of existence, invokes the idea of *being*; of who the poet *is*, in this context and in writing about it. As Lionel Trilling remarks, 'It is impossible to exaggerate the force that the word "be" has for Wordsworth. He uses it as if with the consciousness that it makes the name of God'.[37] The double echo here powerfully indicates the depth of feeling prompted by both encounters, but also the fact that, Hamlet-like, Wordsworth as poet ultimately can and must choose his posture within the city. And, simultaneously, Wordsworth does gain control, through his repetition of 'face to face' in 'Face after face'. According to Peter Kivy, musical repetitions are a way of 'allowing us, indeed compelling us to linger ... they allow us to grope so that we can grasp':[38] whilst it cannot entirely still the swirling world, repetition slows both poet and reader down, enough at least to begin to see those connections between faces and architecture, and at least momentarily to recognize the character and effects of the experience. Repetition cannot cure Wordsworth's dizziness here, but it can steady him, and us, *enough*, which is all that can be asked for. In the 1850 version, Wordsworth reduced this passage, and attempted to seize direction of the scene through imperatives:

> Rise up, thou monstrous Ant-hill on the plain
> Of a too busy world! Before me flow,
> Thou endless stream of men and moving things!
>
> (1850, ll. 149–51)

But he retained the key elements of the 1805 text (as they are key to this discussion), and the passage sustains the same effect of running away from poetic

---

[37] Lionel Trilling, *Sincerity and Authenticity* (London: Oxford University Press, 1972), p. 91.
[38] Kivy, p. 356.

prescription, despite its relative brevity, even as it communicates profoundly at the level of affect.

As Wordsworth turns into a 'sequestered nook' for respite from the disturbing surge of urban humanity, *ors* proliferate. Conjunctions indicate connection, but the indecision of *or* implies that this description has lost the correspondence to real sights it previously claimed (it bespeaks a *lack* of connection). However, *or* does effectively communicate the effect of the city. The lineation of the poem suggests a particular, contained sight: 'another Street | Presents a company of dancing Dogs,' (1805, ll. 191-2). But the following line offers a more exotic possibility, which spills into the next line again: 'Or Dromedary with an antic pair | Of Monkies on his back' (ll. 193-4). Then Wordsworth encounters 'a minstrel Band | Of Savoyards, or, single and alone, | An English Ballad-singer.' (ll. 194-6). *Or* in both of these instances encapsulates Wordsworth's struggle to focus, in order to articulate anything; it allows both things potentially to be present, and yet for their interchangeability to indicate that neither, both, or indeed anything else might be objectively *there*, but that such objective truth is barely relevant. These sights are hardly equivalent, but *or* suggests that the purport of the passage is no longer to describe specifics: this has become impossible, because the connections between parts of the scene are not discernible. Instead, to describe as accurately, or 'sincerely' *as possible* is to acknowledge that a dog might as well be displaced by a dromedary, or a foreign choir with a solo native singer, with no cognitive disruption, because the detail is not the point; the effect of the city is dissonance; phenomena are so overwhelming that all or none of anything particular might or might not actually be there. The important thing is the *effect* that the possibility of their (and multiple, expanding numbers of other phenomena's) being there has on the mind attempting to put them in some sort of order, in order to achieve comprehension (in both senses). *Or* brilliantly sustains this effect, even as it still allows Wordsworth to slide in the details which after all fascinate and distract him, and which form the scaffolding of his poem, through which he can explore and represent the more pressing subject of the poet's mind.

Aubrey De Vere reports Wordsworth's saying that 'the soul and essence' of poetry was 'truth in its largest sense, as a thing at once real and ideal, a truth including exact and accurate detail, and yet everywhere subordinating mere detail to the spirit of the whole'.[39] This suggests the importance of the dynamic between specific and the general, and also the idea of accuracy to Wordsworth; and of course, in another way, even in the city, the detail (the reality of the content) does matter. Ironically, this becomes evident in lines from Book VII which focus on the theatre. Wordsworth acknowledges the pleasures of theatrical spectacle in more than one place (see for example VII.436 ff.). Being a real member of a real

---

[39] Aubrey De Vere, 'Recollections of Wordsworth', in *Essays Chiefly on Poetry*, 2 vols (London: Macmillan, 1887), ii, 275-95 (pp. 278-9).

audience represents his 'delight'. However, having described his enchantment, he immediately admits a sort of apology: 'The matter which detains me now will seem | To many neither dignified enough | Nor arduous'. He admits that

> When, wrought upon by tragic sufferings,
> The heart was full; amid my sobs and tears
> It [the imaginative power] slept...
> For though I was most passionately moved,
>   ...yet all this
> Pass'd not beyond the suburbs of the mind.
>
> (VII.489–507)

The lines acknowledge Wordsworth's susceptibility to spectacle, but insist that he is not seduced into a total renunciation of his mental faculties; rather, this is a momentary relaxing into a pastime separate from those activities which are, by implication, arduous, and which do, by the same implication, pass (in a tellingly municipal metaphor) beyond the suburbs of the mind.

The extended idea of theatricality is more than a metaphor for the changeability and superficiality of the city, though: what stands in opposition to its troubling flux is an idea of fixity located in the gaze, in looking steadily. Wordsworth has been called the 'poet in the English canon whose work [most] powerfully engages the simple act of looking'.[40] But when it slips beyond the poet's control, looking becomes spectatorship, and spectatorship (especially in the context of the Romantic attitude to performed tragedy) is a passive and helpless posture. Wordsworth's most detailed unearthing of its significance is tellingly found in his own stage-play, *The Borderers*, which, as David Marshall argues, deliberately places its spectators in a position where they are forced to *repeat* the hero's crime of leaving a man to die, as they too see it, and do nothing.[41] *The Borderers* is saturated in a preoccupation with observation, and with evidence: Reeve Parker points out that 'situations of seeing and beholding dominate the action from the outset of the Early Version', and in the essay on Rivers he wrote to accompany that version, Wordsworth repeatedly insists on Rivers' status *as* a spectator. The posture of spectatorship refuses the intellectual manipulations which redeem and even ennoble repetitions in 'The Thorn', for example; it is the inevitable lot of the audience member, not the director of the play.

Problematic spectatorship can, however, be redeemed if the spectator becomes a witness. To witness is to look, but also to testify; caught in the tangle of its

---

[40] Melynda Nuss; '"Look in My Face": The Dramatic Ethics of the Borderers', *Studies in Romanticism*, 43.4 (Winter 2004), 599–621 (p. 600).

[41] See David Marshall, 'The Eye-Witnesses of "The Borderers"', *Studies in Romanticism*, 27.3 (Fall 1988), 391–8.

meanings are ideas of response and report which connote more than a simple act of observation: active witnessing is a powerful form of recapitulation. Through its religious associations it reaches for the type of calling Wordsworth shares; indeed, in his prefatory note to the 1842 revision, Wordsworth identifies his position as an 'eye-witness' as a source of *The Borderers*.[42] In the London of *The Prelude*, Wordsworth remains distanced from the seductive laziness that might be associated with the merely spectacular, making spectacle the object of thought by witnessing (rather than just looking at) it, and turning it into his subject. Watching a production of 'The Maid of Buttermere', based upon a real woman Wordsworth had actually met, introduces a debased form of repetition into his experience which profoundly disturbs his posture as spectator, prompting him to become a witness. The disruption to Wordsworth's self-styling as audience member occurs when his knowledge of the eponymous maid forces him to recognize himself as part of the action he elsewhere imagines himself to remain apart from. The play represents an aspect of Wordsworth's real, past experience, but he has no mediating power over it. He is, thus, uncomfortably, the observer as well as the observed, and the rupture which occurs through his lack of control moves him to reassert himself. The Mary of Buttermere Wordsworth knows is of 'modest mien, | And carriage, mark'd by unexampled grace.' (ll. 333–4). The stage-Mary is a false representation; repetition is disrupted by violent inaccuracy, recognized because Wordsworth here *does* know what lies beneath the surface of the character: she is not to him a 'Maid', a 'type'; she remains 'Mary'. Wordsworth appeals to Coleridge, addressee of the poem, as an extra witness who can confirm the accuracy of his claim (l. 327); as Coleridge is figured as a critic of the poet's truthfulness,[43] Wordsworth's criticism of the falsity of *The Maid of Buttermere* asserts his preoccupation with sincerity, and with the way that *recognition* enables him to be steadied. The real Mary is identified as a mother whose 'new-born Infant' was buried 'Beside the mountain Chapel': the place, the 'Essays upon Epitaphs' explain, which is the symbol of true Wordsworthian community (ll. 355–6). The recollection of Mary's baby leads Wordsworth immediately back to the 'rosy Babe' he sees displayed at the theatre (l. 368; ll. 383–5); but this child's mother is no more than a painted, hollow spectacle herself: 'on the Mother's cheek', Wordsworth writes, 'the tints were false, | A painted bloom' (ll. 373–4). Wordsworth suggests that a life played out entirely amongst the false spectacle of the theatre might lead to a child looking 'With envy on [Mary's] nameless Babe, that sleeps, | Beside the mountain Chapel, undisturb'd!' (ll. 411–2). That early

---

[42] See 'The 1842 Note', in *The Borderers*, ed. Robert Osborn (Ithaca: Cornell University Press, 1982), p. 813.

[43] For discussion of this role for Coleridge, and Wordsworth's sense of audience, see E. de Selincourt, 'Wordsworth's Preface to "The Borderers"', in *Oxford Lectures on Poetry* (London: Oxford University Press, 1934), pp. 157–79, and David Perkins, *Wordsworth and the Poetry of Sincerity* (Cambridge, MA: Harvard University Press, 1964), pp. 143–75.

infant death might be preferable to a life as spectacle is a big and troubling claim, but it is part of a response to the falsity of what Wordsworth sees: this is no longer simply a question of superficiality, but an example of something he knows to be wrong, and thus insincere. Whilst a dromedary might be confused with a dog in terms of their relationship and connection within the city streets, the example of Mary of Buttermere insists that fact still matters. The indistinction of aspects of Wordsworth's language does not imply a failure to reach for precise meaning; it is the effort to connect which is significant. Simple inaccuracy does not provide the necessary basis for such connection, because there is nothing real or sincere to associate.

'For we were nursed, as almost might be said, | On the same mountains; Children at one time' (ll. 342–3): Wordsworth's recollection of Mary recalls the nature of bonds previously discussed, between properly communicant individuals (like himself and Dorothy). But the rushing London throng *cannot* communicate in a meaningful way. Wordsworth calls the alternative, preferable communication of which he is capable 'unconscious intercourse', which one drinks in (I.590–1). It is a form of fellowship with 'life and nature' (I.438), and it derives from the nourishment of upbringing; he is 'Bless'd' by the 'mute dialogues with [his] Mother's heart' (II.237 ff.), a blessing sustained by 'All that [he] beheld' (l. 296) in his native surroundings. It is not available in the city, which lacks the interaction necessary for communion. In a more solipsistic sense, this recalls Book II of *The Prelude*, in which the poet refers to his infant self as 'Bless'd', because 'his soul | Claims manifest kindred with an earthly soul, | Doth gather passion from his Mother's eye!' (ll. 237–43). The child is nurtured through the watchful look of his mother; this mutual looking cultivates the predisposition of the poet, who thereby acquires the ability to go into the world and observe 'kindred' truth. In yoking himself and Mary together with the same image of nourishment ('we were nursed . . . '), Wordsworth indicates that she, too, grew up in this environment; she is not a substitute for him, but she allows Wordsworth to articulate his idea of spectatorship and the nurturing of character through observation. Wordsworth's re-rendering of Mary attempts to wipe out her new, false identity and instead reassert an authentic emotional bond. The 'Preface' to *Lyrical Ballads* articulates Wordsworth's desire to use language which has arisen from 'repeated experience and regular feelings', as a reaction against those whose language use 'separate[s] themselves from the sympathies of men'.[44] These sympathies are an index of truth; as Perkins puts it, Wordsworth 'made the peculiar claim that he was speaking to human nature, that is, to a permanent and universal character that abides in all of us';[45] like a form of echo, such sympathies enable the recognition which allows true community, and thus sincere communication. In *The Prelude*, the poet

---

[44] 'Preface' to *Lyrical Ballads* [1800], p. 124.
[45] *Wordsworth and the Poetry of Sincerity*, p. 148.

attempts to restore Mary's status as a real person, rather than a spectacle, by overwriting the dramatic narrative of *The Maid of Buttermere* with the actual knowledge of her real existence. For Wordsworth, poetry has the capacity to remove the quality of spectacle by re-rendering Mary in an authentic language that speaks to the truth of ordinary life, because his 'memorial Verse | Comes from the Poet's heart, and is her due' (VII.340–1); it exemplifies the ideal epitaph described in Wordsworth's 'Essay', and in doing so demonstrates Wordsworth's movement from spectator to witnessing, empathetic observer, able to reflect: 'So have I thought of him a thousand times' (l. 408).

To some extent, Wordsworth's ability to respond to the challenge that the stage-Mary presents mirrors the way that the poet's mind is always better able to manage the city's plenitude when it is already restrained into artistic forms. In exhibitions, for instance, Wordsworth finds:

> Spectacles
> Within doors, troops of wild Beasts, birds and beasts
> Of every nature, from all Climes convened:
> And, next to these, those mimic sights that ape
> The absolute presence of reality,
> Expressing, as in mirror, sea and land,
> And what earth is, and what she hath to shew
>
> (VII.245–51)

With the awareness that 'The absolute presence of reality' is the artist's responsibility and not his own, Wordsworth seems to gain respite: his 'troop' literally seems more easily marshalled; the repetition of 'beasts' in the line implies time to reflect and modify; the contents of the lines are tightly woven together by the way that 'ape' recapitulates not only 'mimic' (its primary semantic sense), but also the 'beasts' of other 'Climes'. The exhibits' being 'convened' acknowledges their deliberate gathering and ordering, and Wordsworth is able to indicate a more specific relative physical position ('next to these...'). In an echo of the effects of London's pleasure gardens, the exhibition's artifice acts as a temporary crutch for Wordsworth's ability to organize. But he soon plunges back, into other theatrical delights, and on through court and conventicle, always aware of the limitations and partiality of his account: 'I glance but at a few conspicuous marks; | Leaving ten thousand others...' (ll. 567–8).

'Residence in London' embodies a turn towards listing as a means of demonstrating the attempt at, and failing of, adequate mimetic description. This listing participates directly in the semantic economy of conjunction: the sights Wordsworth includes induce a sense of more and more, but he cannot see everything at once, requiring an implied (sometimes a literal) *and* or *or*, helpful to him because of the complex way in which the little words function.

Predominantly asyndetic as it is, Wordsworth's list of sights at Bartholomew Fair suggests his inability to perceive their connection. Yet the poet's fundamental task is to order experience into verse, and so he must 'From those sights | Take one' (ll. 649–50), recognizing that the Fair will become an essentially arbitrary, synecdochic prop which will allow the poem to move on: 'O, blank confusion! and a type not false | Of what the mighty City is itself.' (ll. 696–7). Even so, Wordsworth admits defeat so far as to rely upon the imaginative stance the invocation of the Muse allows (l. 656). The *relative* absence of coordinating conjunctions is notable:

> 'tis a dream
> Monstrous in colour, motion, shape, sight, sound.
> Below, the open space, through every nook
> Of the wide area, twinkles, is alive
> With heads
>
> (ll. 661–5)

It is important that Wordsworth does not abandon conjunctions completely: that would draw attention to the strangeness of his writing more than the strangeness of the city. But when streams of nouns lack clear indications of their relationship, the reader is inevitably disorientated. This effect, rather than accurate knowledge, is what Wordsworth seeks to induce. The simultaneous grammatical consequence is to hasten the reading, so that the reader has no space or time to catch at an individual part of the rushing parade of ideas, in order to start to order or process in turn. In the above example, for instance, 'colour, motion, shape, sight, sound' inaugurates a habit of reading which ploughs onwards; in the following sentence, however, a similar manner of reading is halted by the sudden adjective: the reader is cast back into the previous line to understand exactly what 'twinkles', but is also driven on, through the subsequent comma.

A similar effect is encountered in Book 3 of *The Prelude*, in which the 'Cabinet | Or wide Museum' provides a simile for an excess of *things*, which defies comprehension: 'little can be seen, | Well understood, or naturally endear'd' (III. 653–6). Like London, this space for display is 'thronged' with overstimulating curiosities, and Wordsworth walks though it 'step' by step (l. 654; l. 657). *Or* allows the simile to be both cabinet and museum, any distinction irrelevant. This is a 'gaudy Congress, framed | Of things, by nature, most unneighbourly' (ll. 662–3): a tasteless assemblage of objects without relationship. As in the London passage, the lack of conjunctions in the first lines of the description bespeaks the inability of the mind to order the impressions it receives: here are asyndetic 'fishes, gems, | Birds, crocodiles, shells' (ll. 664–5). Yet the frequency and range of conjunctions and prepositions increases through the passage; connections begin in this way to be established by implication at least, as the viewing poet remains in control (if uncomfortably so) over the static catalogue. Wordsworth concludes in lines which look forward to Coleridge's account of the secondary imagination, as a faculty which 'struggles to idealize and to unify. It is essentially *vital*, even as all objects (*as objects*) are essentially fixed and dead':[46] the poetic mind might still redeem such exhibits, insofar as they ultimately contribute to the formation of the poet, when 'something to the memory sticks at last | Whence profit may be drawn in times to come' (ll. 668–9).

Faced with the living chaos of Bartholomew Fair, however, the poet fails to reach a similar potential redemption: where conjunctions do emerge, they build up the stock of images only to collapse again into disjointed lists: 'with buffoons against buffoons | Grimacing, writhing, screaming' (VII.672–3). The sheer excess, and particularly the suggestion of sickness and perversion with which the passage climaxes, is evoked through a splurging, runaway sentence form, whose rhetorical restraints (multiple commas; frequent tricolonic structures, for example) serve actually to throw further into relief the chaos they describe. Ultimately, they indicate only their own incapacity to contain and order the world being perceived:

> The Stone-eater, the Man that swallows fire,
> Giants, Ventriloquists, the Invisible Girl,
> The Bust that speaks, and moves its goggling eyes,
> The Wax-work, Clock-work, all the marvellous craft
> Of modern Merlins, wild Beasts, Puppet-shows,
> All out-o'th'-way, far-fetch'd, perverted things,
> All freaks of Nature, all Promethean thoughts
> Of man; his dullness, madness, and their feats,
> All jumbled up together, to make up
> This Parliament of Monsters: Tents and Booths,
> Meanwhile, as if the whole were one vast Mill,
> Are vomiting, receiving, on all sides,
> Men, Women, three years Children, Babes in arms.
>
> (ll. 683–95)

Humanity is blurred into a heap in the last line here, which even as it attempts to distinguish, only reinforces the impossibility of separating out its constituents.[47] As Simon Jarvis describes it, Wordsworth's city is

> a single ideality...of unchanging self-sameness: the same perpetual flow, one identity. The *rich variety* of city life is usually thought of as lying in its many

---

[46] *Biographia Literaria*, i, 304.

[47] This again recalls Wordsworth's 'knot' of 'Men, Women, Children, yea the frame | Of the whole Spectacle the same!' in 'Gipsies', in *Poems, in Two Volumes, and Other Poems, 1800–1807*, pp. 211–12; these figures constitute an 'unbroken knot' the poet is anxiously unable to unpick or penetrate (see *Representations of the Gypsy in the Romantic Period*, pp. 135–44).

differences. But here these 'differences' are not opposed to that blank identity. They establish it.[48]

And yet, despite this anxiety about a lack of discrimination, and the difficulty of therefore writing accurately, Book VII of *The Prelude* nonetheless gets written, and the blank verse retains its dominion, so that the poem never runs out of control: communicating the excessive, overwhelming experience of the city as much as its specific features is Wordsworth's eloquent response to the problem of its expression. And Wordsworth's poem even fights back against the apparent irony of this: the ending of Book VII is not, it turns out, final: in Book VIII he reverts to his 'Preceptress stern', granting 'London! to thee I willingly return.' (VIII.678–9).

The grip established on the shifting scenes of Book VII is directly connected by Wordsworth to his own abilities, conferred upon him by his past. 'The Spirit of Nature' allows Wordsworth 'Composure and ennobling harmony' (VII.736; l. 741), even 'in London's vast Domain', as he reiterated it more explicitly in 1850 (l. 766). The 'steadiness' acquired amongst the landscape of the Lakes ultimately 'Gives movement to the thoughts, and multitude, | With order and relation.' (VII.711; ll. 728–9). The streets 'weary out' the eye (l. 708) and cannot be ordered or related by the person caught within their flux, but the reflections of the poet can be. Wordsworth falls back on the habits of 'Attention... | And comprehensiveness, and memory' (ll. 717–18) conferred upon him by his upbringing, to establish the closest possible thing to an actual apprehension of wholeness: he 'who looks | In steadiness,... |... sees the parts | As parts, but with a feeling of the whole' (ll. 710–13): in the repetition enacted through tranquil, recollective contemplation, the recapitulation of the very differences he perceives (the *and*s and the *or*s of London's chaotic streets which are themselves microcosmic recapitulations) lead to at least a *sense* ('a feeling') of a whole. This is connection of a sort. It is the best that Wordsworth can acquire, and the best that he can hope to pass on to the reader. Wordsworth's use of recapitulative effects within his verse (conjunctions and forms of repetition and reflection) allows him to communicate this sense, if not the whole (which he fails to comprehend), and yet still to exploit all the detail he claims to be unable to grasp, and put it to work meaningfully in his poem.

---

[48] *Wordsworth's Philosophic Song*, p. 142.

8
'The Thorn', Tautology, and Tragic Repetition

Repetition in 'The Thorn'

In a letter to William Hamilton of 1831, Wordsworth emphasizes the meticulous, laborious, revisionary nature of his compositional process by slipping into an adamant tautology: 'Again and again I must repeat, that the composition of verse is infinitely more of an art than Men are prepared to believe, and absolute success in it depends upon innumerable minutiae.'[1] Acknowledging that 'Repetition and redundance' are 'general characteristics' of Wordsworth's style in *Home at Grasmere*, Kenneth R. Johnston steps quickly if cautiously to labelling such repetitions 'tautological': 'Wordsworth's description of Grasmere makes much of reflections in the lake. As a phenomenon, reflection is characterized by a quality of complementarity which might, with a little wrenching, be called circular or "tautological." Wordsworth does a lot of the wrenching himself.'[2] Moving beyond poetry, Corinna Russell identifies the 'tautologous energy' of Wordsworth's prose:

> Invoking a formula expressive of infinite reiteration ('the Reader cannot be too often reminded'), the motivation for poetic repetition is emphatically identified in the axiom 'Poetry is passion', but the return of the phrase upon itself immediately introduces a critical difference... The reformulation enacted here in a sentence is repeated on a larger scale by the note [to 'The Thorn'].[3]

The 'Note' to 'The Thorn' and the texture of the poem it accompanies constitute Wordsworth's most explicit commentary on repetition, and specifically on the idea of tautology (precisely a form of repetition with difference). Modern scholarship has pondered the effect of Wordsworth's appending the 'Note' after the first publication, and reflected in its light on the repetition which pervades the text (in Russell's alert account, for instance, as 'an inducement to... re-reading' which is

---

[1] W[illiam] W[ordsworth] to William Rowan Hamilton, 22 November 1831, in *The Letters of William and Dorothy Wordsworth, Volume 5: The Later Years, Part II: 1829–1834*, ed. E. de Selincourt, 2nd edn, rev. Alan G. Hill (Oxford: Clarendon Press, 1979), pp. 454–5.
[2] Kenneth R. Johnston, '"Home at Grasmere": Reclusive Song', *Studies in Romanticism*, 14.1 (Winter 1975), 1–28 (p. 18; p. 12).
[3] Russell, p. 105.

perpetually open to difference[4]). However, Wordsworth's contemporaries were less impressed, either by the prose defence, or by the poem which enacts its principles. For them, Wordsworth's use of repetition was a blunder.

In the *Biographia Literaria*, Coleridge makes a valiant attempt to defend lines in 'The Thorn' 'which have given, and which will continue to give universal delight'.[5] Yet even within the context of this praise, Coleridge maintains that 'it is not possible to imitate truly a dull and garrulous discourser, without repeating the effects of dullness and garrulity'.[6] Here, and despite previously expressing significant enthusiasm for the poem, Coleridge by 1817 is echoing the wider disparagement which greeted 'The Thorn' upon first publication.[7] Robert Southey, for example, singled out the poem even above the rest of his infamous attack on the *Lyrical Ballads* in the *Critical Review* in 1798, grousing that 'He who personates tiresome loquacity, becomes tiresome himself'.[8] Diagnosing the poem as conducive to tiresomeness directly connects Southey's attack to the narrator's repetitive manner (the *OED*'s first definition of 'tiresome' is 'Having the property of tiring by continuance, sameness...'). Southey might have counted himself lucky, then, that the published poem actually reduced the repetition found in the earliest version of the work, in which Wordsworth wrote of:

> A summit where the stormy gale
> Sweeps through the clouds from vale to vale—
> A thorn there is which like a stone
> With jagged lychens is o'ergrown
> A thorn that wants its thorny points,
> A toothless thorn with knotted joints...[9]

The reiterations of 'thorn[y]' cluster more thickly here than in the published version; 'vale to vale' establishes a rhetorical sense of balance and repetition which is displaced in the less certain published poem (though the repetition itself survived, appearing in the third stanza). On the other hand, the fact that 'thorn' becomes an end-rhyme in the opening stanza of the published version arguably raises the profile of the word there still further, so that the repetition is more obvious and pressing. It also advances the sense of wretchedness in the poem, as through the consonance of rhyme it renders the thorn itself 'forlorn', as the echo further picks up and redoubles the significance of the word.[10]

---

[4] Russell, p. 117.   [5] *Biographia Literaria*, I, 50.   [6] *Biographia Literaria*, I, 49.
[7] See Gordon K. Thomas, '"The Thorn" in the Flesh of English Romanticism', *The Wordsworth Circle*, 14.4 (Autumn 1983), 237–42, for an overview of the negative contemporary response to Wordsworth's poem (as well as an account of some of its twentieth-century defenders).
[8] Review of *Lyrical Ballads*, *Critical Review*, 2nd series, xxiv (October 1798), 197–204 (p. 200).
[9] Repr. in *Lyrical Ballads, and Other Poems, 1797–1800*, p. 283.   [10] See 'The Thorn', ll. 1–11.

Wordsworth aimed to address such criticism as Southey's through the careful exposition contained within the 'Note':

> There is a numerous class of Readers who imagine that the same words cannot be repeated without tautology: this is a great error: virtual tautology is much oftener produced by using different words when the meaning is exactly the same. Words, a Poet's words more particularly, ought to be weighed in the balance of feeling, and not measured by the space which they occupy upon paper. For the Reader cannot be too often reminded that Poetry is passion: it is the history or science of feelings: now every man must know that an attempt is rarely made to communicate impassioned feelings without something of an accompanying consciousness of the inadequateness of our own powers, or the deficiencies of language. During such efforts there will be a craving in the mind, and as long as it is unsatisfied the Speaker will cling to the same words, or words of the same character.[11]

Here, perfect repetition is more meaningful, more powerful, than paraphrase. Yet Wordsworth's passage endorses the philosophical idea that perfect repetition is in fact nothing of the kind. What appears to be an identical instance always carries a simultaneous sense of difference from the previous statement, *by virtue of its being a repetition*: 'pure' repetition is an impossibility. Whilst the 'Note' to 'The Thorn' is Wordsworth's most explicit comment on the desirability and effects of repetition, encouraged by editors' commentaries, he was experimenting with it as early as his undergraduate days. As Duncan Wu has observed, in Wordsworth's translations of Virgil's *Georgics*, Orpheus's grief at Euridice's death 'is no less passionate for his repetitions. The editions of Virgil from which Wordsworth was translating commended the technique'.[12] In 'The Note' to 'The Thorn', Wordsworth expands upon the idea of word-repetition, incorporating the repetitions which constitute 'lyrical and rapid Metre' into his description of the requirements for success in the poem, as a way of navigating the ability of the reader to relate to the character in the text.[13] (Wordsworth declares metre to be similarly enabling in 'Goody Blake, and Harry Gill'.[14]) Southey's accusation of 'tiresomeness' followed the 1798 publication of the 'The Thorn', when it was accompanied only by a brief 'Advertisement' which highlighted its status as a dramatic narrative. When the poem re-appeared in 1800, Wordsworth had added the 'Note', which significantly expanded his intentions in employing the mouthpiece of a *type*, of the kind of 'superstitious' men who 'cleave to such ideas'.[15] The 'Note' attaches Wordsworth's interest in repetition to discourses beyond theories of

---

[11] 'Note' to 'The Thorn', p. 351.
[12] Wu, 'Tautology and Imaginative Vision' (not paginated).
[13] 'Note' to 'The Thorn', p. 351.
[14] See 'Preface' to *Lyrical Ballads*, p. 150.
[15] 'Note' to 'The Thorn', p. 351.

classical translation, drawing on Lowth's account of biblical poetry to support his claim that 'the mind luxuriates in the repetition of words which appear successfully to communicate its feelings.' Lowth had declared that 'what in any other language would appear a superfluous and tiresome repetition, in [Hebrew] cannot be omitted without injury to the poetry.'[16] Lowth's use of the same word—tiresome—that Wordsworth's critics dropped in so lightly, only reinforces the argument that Wordsworth was making a subtle and sophisticated point about the use to which repetition might productively be put in a poem. Coleridge, however, and the many other nineteenth-century critics who shared Southey's low opinion of Wordsworth's narrative experiment, remained unmoved.

Twentieth-century readings of the poem, on the other hand, looked more closely, refusing to stop at the superficial repetitions which litter the text of 'The Thorn'. As well as drawing psychoanalytic conclusions based in theories of repetition compulsion and grief, many of them focused on the content of the poem as much as its style. Gordon K. Thomas extended this critical discourse still further, to argue that part of Wordsworth's originality lies in the fact that the poem 'is "a poem written about itself"... about poetry, about *telling*'. For Thomas, this is a 'reflective and introspective technique,' which, in its exhibition of Romantic Irony, makes the poem 'genuinely revolutionary', and thus (in Lilian Furst's terms) 'a part of the philosophical, aesthetic and literary re-orientation that is at the core of the Romantic movement.'[17] Indeed, the poem constantly reiterates that it is focused on 'telling', another form of repetition (telling is inherently *re*telling). But as the synonym 'recount' declares, 'telling' is also a form of reckoning which depends on concrete forms of evidence.[18] As in 'We are Seven', in 'The Thorn' the narrator and the poem itself explore different ways of reckoning and thereby knowing, acknowledging that things can be the same but appear differently: knowing what the truth is, is explored through the device of re-telling the tale in a particular way. The poem thus perfectly demonstrates and itself reflects upon the processes which Wordsworth believes to be central to poetic revision and poetic sincerity. Sincerity is a form of truth which allows us to dwell on what we are being true *to*; 'We are Seven' demonstrates that different ways of seeing and knowing can in fact challenge the idea of 'an' empirical, scientific 'truth'. In his desire to 'tell' in this mixed sense, Wordsworth needs both to communicate a narrative, and also to encourage deliberation upon the idea of

---

[16] Lowth's discussion of parallelism occupies Lecture 19 of his *Lectures*; in Lecture 4, Lowth had already established the significance of repetition to Hebrew poetry, recognizing that its characteristically terse statements were echoed in the 'recurrence of clauses', which amplified the sentiments and could therefore be a source of 'perpetual splendour' (See Lowth, i, 101. For further discussion, see Legaspi, p. 113).

[17] Gordon K. Thomas, p. 241.

[18] The *OED* connects recount's primary sense ('To relate, narrate; to give a full or detailed account of (a fact, event, etc.); to tell *to* a person') to the verbs 'count' and 'account', both of whose definitions include the idea of 'reckoning'.

accuracy, not in the sense of recording a scene like a photograph, but in the sense of sincerity to the fuller meaning or significance of it; what it means to experience the connective bonds of sibling affection in 'We are Seven', for example, or to communicate the habitual dearness of 'Winander' to the eponymous 'boy' of those lines, rather than the accuracy of knowing exactly where the boy is in relation to the lake or the trees. The sincerity in this sense evidently must be that of the poet, *not* the narrator.

The poem proper beings with a confident deictic, 'There is a Thorn', backed up by the strident claim to speak 'In truth' of line 2. But prefiguring the way that the text struggles to retain this confidence, here, immediately, it moves on to inference and supposition. The narrator remarks that the eponymous thorn '*looks* so old' (my emphasis) and supposes that 'you'd find it hard to say'; the poem next wonders 'how it could ever have been young', and its subsequent description is often via negatives ('Not higher than...'; 'no leaves it has, no thorny points'). The poem proceeds through a constant interplay between fact and speculation. The attempted objective measurement of the thorn, the hill of moss, and the pond, for example, and the way that the spatial relationship between them is mapped out with the meticulous exactitude of the picturesque guidebook ('Not five yards from the mountain-path, | This Thorn you on your left espy; | And to the left, three yards beyond...', ll. 27-9), and the record of what Martha Ray actually did and said when the narrator encountered her, are all juxtaposed with rumour ('They say'; ''Tis said'; 'some say'; 'I've heard'[19]). The interpretation of Martha's behaviour is common consensus, reached without evidence: 'all and each agree, | The little babe was buried there (ll. 218-19). Similar inferences are used to interpret the environment which contains Martha (the alleged burial site, for example, is said to have begun to shake when the community attempted to dig it up in investigation), though each instance could easily have a mundane explanation, and the narrator is careful not to commit to anything he does not know for sure. Nonetheless, it would be a perverse reading that ignored the way in which the reader (with, it is suggested, the rest of the rural community) is led to infer that Martha Ray's baby is buried under the hill of moss: it 'Is like an infant's grave in size | As like as like can be' (ll. 52-3). Just as the reiterated likeness here fervently insists on a similitude which is so blatant that it also always declares its *dis*similitude, so the poem's narrator is constantly reaching for measurements against his context of rumour, without ever definitively coming down on the side of scepticism or belief. The narrator comes with his sea captain's telescope,[20] but he can only look down it one way. The poem, however, can see more clearly, and it looks more closely, in different directions at the same time.

---

[19] See l. 133; l. 137; l. 216; l. 221.   [20] 'Note' to 'The Thorn', p. 350.

There are certainly many repetitions of words and phrases within the poem. To trace them all would be a superfluous exercise, so obvious and numerous are they, but for an example, one might take the first line, 'There is a Thorn; it looks so old': 'It looks so old' reappears in line 4, and the word 'Thorn' comes back in line 6 and (as 'thorny') in line 7 of the stanza. Or, one could take the last two lines of the first stanza, 'It stands erect, and like a stone | With lichens it is overgrown', which appear only slightly altered in the first lines of the second stanza ('Like rock or stone, it is o'ergrown | With lichens to the very top'). There is no doubt that Southey's criticisms rest significantly on such pervasive and blatant repetition, and the habit continues throughout the poem. To compare stanzas VII and VIII, for instance, is almost like reading alternative versions of the same passage (which, given Wordsworth's self-conscious attitude to revision and the context of the 'Note', can hardly be accidental). The narrator repeats himself before we first hear of Martha Ray, but the fierce multiple reiterations of her pain ('"Oh misery! oh misery! Oh woe is me! oh misery!"') dominate the poem to such an extent that it appears the narrator has learnt to repeat from her. Stanza VIII sees the interjection of the listener/interlocutor in the poem; just as the narrator seems constrained always to repeat, and obsessively to repeat Martha's plaintive cry in particular, so the interlocutor also seems to be infected by the habit. He not only catches the tendency towards general repetition; he also mimics Martha's self-repetition, repeating the question form with which he opens his stanza in its last lines:

VII
At all times of the day and night
This wretched woman thither goes,
And she is known to every star,
And every wind that blows;
And there beside the thorn she sits
When the blue day-light's in the skies,
And when the whirlwind's on the hill,
Or frosty air is keen and still,
And to herself she cries,
'Oh misery! oh misery!
Oh woe is me! oh misery!'

VIII
'Now wherefore thus, by day and night,
'In rain, in tempest, and in snow,
'Thus to the dreary mountain-top
'Does this poor woman go?
'And why sits she beside the thorn
'When the blue day-light's in the sky,
'Or when the whirlwind's on the hill,
'Or frosty air is keen and still,
'And wherefore does she cry?—
'O wherefore? wherefore? tell me why
'Does she repeat that doleful cry?'

There are various repetitions evident here. Most obvious is the almost exact similarity of the 6th–8th lines of each stanza, with other, smaller examples of quotation also being in evidence ('day and night'; 'beside the thorn'). These, suggestively, are elements of the story which orientate it in time and space. But there are other echoes too: the interlocutor picks up to a great extent the structure of Martha's cry in his own questions at the end of the stanza; ideas are recapitulated ('wretched woman'/'poor woman') even where there is no exact verbal repetition; lines 2 and 4 of both stanzas utilize the same rhyme sounds. The interlocutor's vocabulary aims to establish certainty: his first three words, for example, 'Now wherefore thus', all indicate ideas of logical connection. Yet his frantic questions are fruitless, and replace Martha Ray's bleak ontological certainty with a sense of confusion. However, that does not affect the dogged self-contained continuance when the quotation of Martha recurs, later in the poem. For preeminent and most striking amongst all of these repetitions are Martha Ray's words, heard for the first time in stanza VI (so that when we hear them in stanza VII, above, they are themselves already a repetition).

The most arresting, and apparently empirically observed, fact about Martha Ray is that she repeats the cry of 'Oh misery! oh misery! | Oh woe is me! oh misery!' In its endlessly reporting what Martha Ray says, the poem clings on to the only repetition which can be accurately replicated *in* a poem. The poem can't really imitate the height of a bush, it can only describe it (however evocatively or suggestively it might do so). But it can, and does, literally give Martha voice. Crucially, hers is a voice we can either understand as emptied out by the repetition it enacts, a form of perpetual redundancy which is itself tragic in this sense, or as powerfully gesturing towards meaningfulness in the only way possible: by announcing the impossibility of adequate articulation, another conventionally tragic posture. The former is the response engendered by the interlocutor who questions the narrator without achieving a sense of closure. The latter is the response engendered in the reader who looks more closely at the effects Wordsworth exploits. Talking about *King Lear*, Bruce Kawain describes the way these different possible effects of repetition exist in a linear relationship, one turning into the next as the repetition continues: 'Up to a certain point, repetition emphasizes the sense of what is repeated—builds, as it does in *King Lear*. Beyond that point, the repeated word loses its original meaning: it becomes a routine or cliché...But repeated past this point, the word can become a force'.[21] Echoing closely the sentiments of the passage from Wordsworth's 'Note' cited above, Kawain concludes that 'emphasis is nearly always expressive of frustration at the inadequacy of the simple statement to convey experience...We can only hint at what we cannot say—can only emphasize until emphasis itself communicates.'[22] In his depiction of Martha Ray, Wordsworth is participating in this tradition of tragic writing.

Tragedy, Repetition, and Martha Ray

There is something inherently repetitious about tragedy. Ideas of repetition cling both to the mechanics of the revenge which infests the tragic tradition, and to the sense of futility which is part of its constitution. Wordsworth's *The Borderers*, for

[21] Kawain, p. 170. [22] Kawain, p. 50.

example, fully exploits this connection. The combination of passion and inadequacy thus implied inevitably gestures towards the discourse of the sublime, tragedy's bed-fellow. For Schopenhauer, in *The World as Will and Idea* (1819),

> Our pleasure in the *tragedy* belongs not to the feeling of the beautiful, but to that of the sublime... What gives to everything tragic, whatever the form in which it appears, the characteristic tendency to the sublime, is the dawning of the knowledge that the world and life can afford us no true satisfaction, and are therefore not worth our attachment to them. In this the tragic spirit consists; accordingly, it *leads to resignation*.[23]

Schopenhauer's resignation is both consequence and cause of repetition; the lack of will to try to go beyond is there in the realization of the tragic condition as well as the response to it. Wordsworth's 'cling[ing] to words of the same character' might be seen both as a form of resignation (which gives up, merely repeating the same again rather than attempting progress), and as an indicator of the 'impassioned feelings' whose communication inevitably results in 'consciousness of the inadequateness of our own powers'. This, the tragic suffering of Martha Ray, is what Wordsworth's poem understands.

Numerous theories (aesthetic, moral, psychological, and linguistic) since the Romantic Period have dwelt upon the connections between tragedy and repetition, most obviously Sigmund Freud's.[24] Wordsworth, of course, had not read Freud, but he had read Shakespeare; although he had something of a reputation amongst his contemporaries for being 'antipathetic' to the bard, he included him as one of the 'four English poets whom I must have continually before me as examples'.[25] Shakespearean tragic drama, which Romantic writers persistently assert to be the pinnacle of aesthetic achievement, also exhibits a vital concern with the relationship between tragedy and repetition. King Lear's response to the death of Cordelia is a case in point: his only possible response in his immediate shock is to 'Howl, howl, howl, howl!' (Act V, Sc 3, l. 258); his last speech, on the death of the Fool, is suffused with repeated words: 'No, no, no... never, never, never, never, never... Look... Look... Look there, look there!' (Act V, Sc 3, ll. 306–12): repetition here indicates a form of madness which is the only outlet

---

[23] Arthur Schopenhauer, 'On the Aesthetics of Poetry', in *The World as Will and Idea*, trans. E. F. J. Payne, 2 vols (New York: Dover, 1966), ii, 424–38 (pp. 433–4), my emphasis.

[24] Freud's interest in repetition is most obviously found in 'Beyond the Pleasure Principle', and in 'Remembering, Repeating and Working-Through', in *Further Recommendations on the Technique of Psycho-Analysis II*, in *The Standard Edition of the Complete Psychological Works of Sigmund Freud*, Vol. 12 (1911–1913), trans. and ed. James Strachey and others (London: Hogarth Press and the Institute of Psycho-Analysis, 1955; 1981), pp. 147–56.

[25] Christopher Wordsworth, *Memoirs of William Wordsworth* [1851], 2 vols (Cambridge: Cambridge University Press, 2014), ii, 470; on Wordsworth and Shakespeare see Jonathan Bate, *Shakespeare and the English Romantic Imagination* (Oxford: Clarendon Press, 1986).

of really tragic suffering. There is simply no other possible response to the tragic events; even the Gods remain silent except to thunder, in an indistinguishable blur of sound. To this extent, Shakespeare exhibits a keen awareness that rhetorical strategy (rather than a *particular* content or 'meaning') is at the heart of the Aristotelian idea of the tragic. Relatedly, Shakespeare's keen interest in the clash between impotence and desire is figured as a linguistic as well as a literal problem throughout *Macbeth*: the impasse in which Macbeth and his wife are trapped *is* a form of repetition which is appropriately reflected in the language struggles of its protagonists, culminating in Macbeth's infamous response to the news of the death of Lady Macbeth, where 'Life' is reduced to rhetoric, but to rhetoric that is meaningless: to 'sound and fury, | Signifying nothing' (Act V, Sc 5, ll. 23–7). In the inarticulate ravings and monosyllabic repetitions of Lady Macbeth's madness at Act V, Sc 2 (O! O! O!...To bed, to bed, to bed), words are battered and tortured out of their normal use because normal use is shown to be insufficient to create meaning: really tragic suffering is beyond expression. In *Macbeth's* hammering repetitions we can see the same conviction which is expressed in Wordsworth's 'Note' to 'The Thorn': this is a form of madness which is ironically the only possible (and, therefore, the only sane, articulate) response to tragedy. When Martha Ray repeats her cry, she stands in this line of tragic expression.

If Martha Ray's repetition draws us towards the tragic truth of the poem, why does Wordsworth need his loquacious narrator, and his interlocutor's interjections? Perhaps Martha Ray's debt to a specifically Shakespearean tradition is still greater. Much Shakespearean tragedy is interested in the fact that the worst pain may lie in being unable to make one's own complaint. Lear is not the only Shakespearean character for whom tragic pain is beyond words; 'The Rape of Lucrece' and *Titus Andronicus* both contain characters trying and failing adequately to articulate tragic experience. Lucrece and Lavinia ultimately must invoke the words and stories of others, must *repeat* others, in order to tell their tales, yet the stories of others are inadequate for full expression of their individual anguish, and inability to express their ordeals is unarguably part of their tragic condition. Their linguistic impotence mirrors Shakespeare's own, but with one suggestive difference: the poet can accommodate the whole problem within a skilfully crafted rhetorical form. However much Macbeth may protest that life is but 'A tale | Told by an idiot, full of sound and fury, | Signifying nothing', by drawing attention to the artifice and limitations of his own art, Shakespeare challenges perceived potentialities for representation, writing at ease and eloquently in order to represent the difficulties of representation. For Mary Jacobus, 'The Thorn' is 'a poem not just about suffering, but about the difficulty of comprehending it'.[26] Wordsworth must tread the fine line between recognition

---

[26] Jacobus, p. 244.

of, and the assumption that he can sincerely comprehend and thus represent, Martha's experience. Wordsworth's narrator in 'The Thorn' is a self-aware approach to this problem. He *is* Macbeth's idiot, telling the tale of Martha Ray's tragedy. His repetitions are linguistic markers of his own failings: this is clear in the response provoked in early nineteenth-century criticism of 'The Thorn'. But the same repetitions also give voice to Martha's tragedy.[27]

If we recognize the influence of this trope of Shakespearean tragic writing on Wordsworth, placing 'The Thorn' within a tradition of tragedy whose expression is associated with repetition, other tragic allusions in the poem immediately present themselves. There are clear parallels, for example, between the characters in 'The Thorn' and the Old Testament's iconic figure of tragic suffering, Job, who is himself a figure of repetition. John Kerrigan's exposition of the text of Job in the specific context of revenge tragedy and repetition is helpfully illustrative: 'Once God has allowed Satan, the antagonist, to destroy Job's children...the disputations which follow have a spiralling uncertainty which could never reach conclusion.' Additionally, God's answering '"out of the whirlwind"' (38: 1 ff.) mostly consists of questions. Indeed, it is Job's admission that, in arguing beyond his faith, he has "uttered that I understood not" which precipitates the divine denouement'.[28] These extracts suggest parallels with significant aspects of 'The Thorn': in both texts, infant death instigates greatest suffering; just as Job's God answers out of a whirlwind, only to ask more questions, so a whirlwind is figured by the narrator and then the interlocutor in 'The Thorn' as one aspect of the scene in which Martha Ray sits to cry, and the interlocutor's recapitulation of that scene similarly prompts a torrent of questions; Job's admission of his ignorance, the uttering 'that he understood not', is reflected in Wordsworth's narrator's lack of knowledge, and his constant reiteration of that lack, which is consequently shared by his interlocutor's questions; and 'spiralling uncertainty which could never reach conclusion' is certainly the effect of Martha's repeated action in combination with the narrator's amalgamation of possible explanations, based more-or-less in evidence. Yet if we look closely at the significance of repetition in the case of Job, we can see that Martha Ray's tragedy inheres in her compulsion to repeat being set alongside the impossibility of any different ending: her child cannot be returned to her, because she is not in dialogue with an omnipotent God, but with a not-even-omniscient narrator, who seems to have been affected by the repetition Martha enacts, and to infect in turn the interlocutor within the poem.

---

[27] Questions of gender press on this account, though a sample size of one poem problematizes the enquiry. But insofar as she seems to follow Lucrece, Lavinia, and Lady Macbeth, there is something suggestively gendered about Martha Ray's predicament of inarticulacy, and its perceived roots in her maternity specifically; the layered narrative perhaps also offers a way for Wordsworth to address the inability of a male voice to respond adequately to the gendered predicament of his heroine.

[28] John Kerrigan, *Revenge Tragedy: Aeschylus to Armageddon* (Oxford: Oxford University Press, 1996), pp. 274–5.

I am not suggesting at all that 'The Thorn' is a form of paraphrase. It is not the case that the interlocutor is God, the narrator an amalgam of Job's comforters, and Martha Ray a figuration of Job (not least because in her solipsism we can assume that *she* knows her own story—not being able to tell it is part of her pain; moreover, she speaks only to herself, and never back to God). Job's is specifically a trial of faith, and whilst 'The Thorn' is interested in evidence and doubt, it is not a meditation on religious conviction. But it is striking how many elements the two otherwise very different narratives share. What they most importantly have in common is an awareness of the complex role of repetition in tragic suffering and articulation. The main way in which their narratives differ, whose recognition is perhaps necessary for the impact of 'The Thorn' fully to register, is in the idea of an ending. Both Job and Martha remain faithful to their own personal vigil. The Book of Job comes to a conclusion, even if it is an 'uncertain' one.[29] But Martha is left on the hillside, and the poem is left with her cry, still repeating: 'Oh misery! oh misery! | Oh woe is me! oh misery'. Kerrigan invokes Nietzsche's refutation of Schopenhauer to conclude his discussion of Job: '"Tragedy does *not* teach "resignation"', Nietzsche writes in *The Will to Power*: "Art affirms. Job affirms."'[30] But art, and Job, do nothing for Martha Ray, who can only keep on keeping on. The poem offers no end point for her repetition. There is no relief for her tragic suffering. The interlocutor's frustrated questions acknowledge and perform the desire to *know*, to hold on to fact and the unsublime, but therefore also untragic, world of knowledge. Not reaching full knowledge is our tragic condition; here, understanding that is achieved through *recognizing* Martha Ray's tragedy.

And yet, from within her situation, Martha Ray unaffectedly achieves poetry. Alan Bewell argues that her limited repetitions represent what Hugh Blair termed 'the first elements or beginnings of Speech',[31] and that in returning to these expressions, 'she clings to the words that best approximate her pain. Strikingly, this clinging not only produces repetition but also generates a new phrase, "Oh woe is me!" as an assonantal variation of "Oh misery!" This movement... epitomizes, in miniature, the conventional eighteenth century understanding of the origin and progress of human language'. Thus, '*poetry* is born from this repetition'. Moreover, 'Her passion does not stand separate... from this progress in language' and, therefore, 'out of this chain of repetitions is built up the fabric of repetitions and gaps that constitute poetic language and human passion in their primal forms.'[32] Recording Martha, the narrator can thus represent this articulation in a sincere form unachievable by himself, which meets the demands of Wordsworth's 'Preface'. To understand that is to 'recognize' in the Aristotelian

---

[29] Kerrigan, p. 275.   [30] Kerrigan, p. 278.
[31] Bewell, p. 174, citing Hugh Blair, *Rhetoric and Belles Letters*, 2nd edn, 3 vols (London: W. Strahan, 1875), i, 102.
[32] Bewell, pp. 174–5.

sense; Wordsworth's poem thus shifts the experience of tragic *anagnorisis*, the transition from ignorance to knowledge, away from the protagonist and onto the reader.

Within the poem, Martha Ray cries only 'to herself', not demanding sympathy; she is not performing, but existing. The narrator and his interlocutor, on the other hand, perform to an audience made up variously of each other, the presiding figure of the note-writing poet, and the reader whose recognition must evolve from the playing-out of their dynamic. In his discussion of tragic recognition, Terence Cave points out that 'Anagnorisis links the recovery of knowledge with a disquieting sense, when the trap is sprung, that the commonly accepted co-ordinates of knowledge have gone awry.' Insofar as its recognition scenes are so obviously 'a contrivance', Cave argues that they 'draw attention to themselves—and to literary form as a whole—as an artifice'. Looked at similarly as a recognition scene, this formally contrived poem, loaded with repetitions as it is, also draws attention to its own artifice. More significantly still, the 'different aspects of the idiosyncrasy of recognition' result for Cave in 'a sense of a means of knowing which is different from rational cognition. It operates surreptitiously, randomly, elliptically and often perversely'.[33] The insistent if faltering empirical discourse of narrator and interlocutor in 'The Thorn' proves exactly the background against which the 'truth' or 'knowledge' of Martha Ray is thrown into relief, or at least made possible to infer: that hers is a tragic suffering which cannot be articulated through such pragmatic conversation. Cave turns to the reporting of the recognition in *The Winter's Tale* (a moment where tragedy turns to comedy, though without forgetting its generic roots), to demonstrate the pedigree of his point:

> Such a deal of wonder is broken out within this hour that ballad-makers cannot be able to express it... This news, which is call'd true, is so like an old tale, that the verity of it is in strong suspicion.[34]

This declaration, that truth or knowledge cannot survive in the ballad's narrative, lends a sense of confusion to the possibility of expression here, alert to the fact that the gentleman who speaks *is* communicating the very wonder whose communication he is arguing is impossible. Like the playwright, the gentleman can express his struggle to express in an artfully meaningful form. Yet even here, confusion arises because the old tale (which is actually a new tale) is touched with 'wonder': the gentleman can report that it is wonder; he can identify and label it. But he cannot so easily express what lies behind it to make it wonderful. The declared inability of balladeers to express *this* wonder, the resurrection of the king's daughter, is attributed to its excessive quantity and its quality in combination (it

---

[33] Cave, pp. 2–3.   [34] *The Winter's Tale*, Act V, Sc 2, ll. 23–9.

is '*such* a *deal*'). The gentleman cannot escape from the impasse which confronts those who try to articulate awe: who try to put the sublime into words.

Accepting Schopenhauer's account of tragedy as sublime (or simply registering that the impossibility of adequate articulation closely allies it to the sublime) means acknowledging with the gentleman of *The Winter's Tale* that the sublime is tricky to control in art. *The Winter's Tale* chooses to fall into a hybrid, tragicomic genre. The pathos of the sublime can more accidentally lapse into the bathos of the comic: it is easy when trying to hit the heights to plumb the depths. Exclamation is an acute microcosm of this: exclamation marks denote both agony and ecstasy; they indicate astonished wonder, but also suggest hyperbole, ridicule, and disgust. Martha Ray is restricted to exclamations which, understood as paradoxically articulate of her state, are tragic-sublime, but which can't ever be divorced from their alternative, potential significances. Hence the easy misreading of 'The Thorn' by Southey and Coleridge, even after the prompt to recognize the narrator as a device. Perhaps Wordsworth does misjudge the balance of the repetitions in 'The Thorn', facilitating rather than resisting such critical misrecognition. But it is important that we do not ignore the narrator's continual declaration of his own ignorance ('I cannot tell' is reiterated in various stanzas; even when he is narrating, he appends an apologetic 'No more I know').[35] If the poem generically aims at a form of recognition, like 'Stepping Westwards', then it fails, spectacularly. But that failure is deliberate: it is the narrator's, *not* Wordsworth's.

The narrator is thus a necessary device because through his inarticulacy the real tragedy of Martha Ray *can* be *almost* articulated, and moreover the situation of the poet can be intimated. In the 'Note', Wordsworth describes the narrator's type as 'credulous and talkative'; he is one who would 'cleave to the same ideas'.[36] We find his cleaving both in the repetitive style of the narration, but also in the way he constantly reverts to a small number of subjects (the thorn, Martha Ray, the moss, the pond, and the mountain dominate the content of the stanzas): specific, repeated linguistic traits, clearly intended to characterize a particular figure. This narrator is no poet; he cannot form the material he has to depict certain ideas about the scene or events, and his verse form, whilst strident, is unconventional and syntactically various (which is particularly striking in a poem in which regular rhythm and repetition are so marked). It is also the case that the narrator willingly admits his own lack of knowledge of the narrative at several points in the poem. Yet if the narrator is repetitious, so (in action and in speech) is Martha Ray; we are surely supposed to appreciate the relevance. Wordsworth represents the subject of the poem, Martha Ray's suffering, in this refracted way because it is the most sincere way in which he can negotiate the familiar irony of the poet artfully and

---

[35] For 'I cannot tell', see l. 89; l. 214; 243. For 'No more I know', see l. 155.
[36] 'Note' to 'The Thorn', p. 351.

expressively communicating the inability to express at all. Whilst the poet remains aware that he is ultimately unable to escape that impasse, to be too explicit would be to subvert the difficulty; the narrator-as-device draws attention to the struggle to avoid it, and thus demands attention to that struggle. Wordsworth the theorist of repetition ('the author's own person', as he styles himself in the 1798 'Advertisement' to *Lyrical Ballads*) is trapped in the same effects he aims to diagnose. He needs his 'loquacious' narrator,[37] because he knows that saying things over and over again is simply tedious. In this sense, the poet himself almost becomes a tragic figure, unable to escape from the need to repeat but compelled by his art to resist it. His poem quietly claims to be a repetition of the repetition within the narrative, which is ultimately itself only an echo (a warped repetition) of Martha Ray's repetitions, which beat out the passion that Wordsworth describes in the 'Note', and thus (even as they recognize it *as* impossible) approximate the impossible communication of her grief. Thus, the poet picks his way through the struggle to express sincere feeling. None of this, of course, is any comfort to Martha Ray who, we are to imagine, continues to repeat her cry and her pain, and who continues sincerely to feel, endlessly, repeatedly.

---

[37] 'Advertisement' to *Lyrical Ballads* [1798], in *Lyrical Ballads, and Other Poems, 1797–1800*, pp. 738–9 (p. 739).

9
Crafted Repetition

That Wordsworth was interested in repetition beyond the direct attention to it in the 'Note' to 'The Thorn', and that his exploitation of its effects was received as original and distinctive, is clear from the critical response it engendered. Even Coleridge detected 'occasional prolixity, repetition, and an eddying instead of progression of thought' amongst the 'classes of defects' he discovered in Wordsworth's poetry.[1] Wordsworth's contemporaries attacked the literal word repetitions within his work as one of the characteristics which rendered it (to them) facile, and they also responded to his more direct declarations about the possibilities of crafted repetition. Repetition provided particularly rich material for Wordsworth's parodists: so apparently characteristic were the features mimicked by J. H. Reynolds's *Peter Bell* (a work much less seriously angry than Shelley's infamous response to the same poem), the parody was actually written in response to an advertisement, published before Wordsworth's *Peter Bell* had even appeared in print. A poem at which Coleridge rather treacherously 'laughed heartily,'[2] from the declaration in its mocking 'Preface' to 'have persevered with a perseverance truly astonishing, in persons of not the most pursy purses',[3] to the end of his poem, Reynolds sustains his attack on Wordsworthian repetition, even (as Gerald J. Pyle has noted) unashamedly stealing someone else's joke about the grave of one William Williams: 'Here lieth W.W. | Who never more will trouble you, trouble you'.[4] Despite the levity, such commentary always affected Wordsworth, and he responded to Reynolds and his fellow critics with a sonnet 'On the Detraction Which Followed the Publication of a Certain Poem' (1820).[5] Arguing that Reynolds's parody may ironically have helped to make Wordsworth's *Peter Bell* his biggest-selling title to date when it was finally published, Brian Bates has unpacked the well-poised appeal to Milton with which Wordsworth faced his

---

[1] *Biographia Literaria*, ii, 136.
[2] Coleridge to Taylor and Hessey, 23 April 1819, in *The Collected Letters of Samuel Taylor Coleridge*, ed. E. L. Griggs, 6 vols (Oxford: Oxford University Press, 1956–71), iv, 938.
[3] J. H. Reynolds, 'Peter Bell: A Lyrical Ballad', in *Romantic Parodies, 1797–1831*, ed. by David Kent and D. R. Ewen (Rutherford, NJ: Fairleigh Dickinson University Press; London: Associated University Presses, 1992), p. 174.
[4] See Reynolds, 'Peter Bell', p. 183, and Gerald J. Pyle, 'J. H. Reynolds' "Peter Bell"', *Notes and Queries*, 24 (1977), 323–4.
[5] In William Wordsworth, *Shorter Poems, 1807–1820*, ed. Carl H. Ketcham (Ithaca: Cornell University Press, 1989), p. 282.

detractors in this response.[6] Through its Miltonic allusion, and its clever reflection of the language of his critics, Wordsworth's sonnet enters into the discourse of parodic repetition in the very attempt to fight back against those who would criticize his dependence upon repetition. 'Wordsworth too', as Bates puts it, 'can imitate parodically another's work as well as any parodist can imitate him.'[7]

However delicious, Reynolds's sort of attention-seeking parody, and the attention it draws to literary imitation of various types (parody, echo, allusion) as forms of repetition, reflects the far deeper resonances of repetition in Wordsworth's writing. Wordsworth understands repetition not as an effect so much as the enabling condition of sincere verse. In the 1805 *Prelude*, he traces his early 'Gleams' of 'Remembrable things' (I.615–7) to a time when:

> The scenes which were a witness of that joy
> Remained, in their substantial lineaments
> Depicted on the brain, and to the eye
> Were visible, a daily sight: and thus,
> By the impressive discipline of fear,
> By pleasure, and repeated happiness,
> So frequently repeated, and by force
> Of obscure feelings representative
> Of joys that were forgotten, these same scenes,
> So beauteous and majestic in themselves,
> Though yet the day was distant, did at length
> Become habitually dear; and all
> Their hues and forms were by invisible links
> Allied to the affections.
>
> (ll. 628–41)

Implicitly and explicitly, in content and form, this passage cites the power of repetition as the basis of the possibility of *The Prelude* itself. Criticism has pursued this attachment to repetition in various directions. It has followed the many deliberate revisions of Wordsworth's works; traced an interest in memory (Christopher Salvesen going so far as to assert that 'memory is the great force in Wordsworth's poetry'[8]), and, relatedly, his preoccupation with childhood; it has charted the effects of his going back (imaginatively) to past events and (imaginatively or physically) to formerly visited places; it has examined his self-conscious positioning within a canon of previous poets and his persistent allusion to and

---

[6] Brian Bates, 'J. H. Reynolds Re-Echoes the Wordsworthian Reputation: "Peter Bell," Remaking the Work and Mocking the Man', *Studies in Romanticism*, 47.3 (Fall 2008), pp. 273–97 (p. 290).

[7] Bates, 'J. H. Reynolds', p. 292.

[8] Christopher Salvesen, *The Landscape of Memory: A Study of Wordsworth's Poetry* (Lincoln: University of Nebraska Press, 1965), p. 200.

echoing of poetic precursors in his writing, and it has explored his fascination with the mechanisms of consanguinity, heredity, and succession. Scholarship has also gone beyond textual analysis: Lucy Newlyn points out that 'for members of the Wordsworth family, the importance of rhythm to physical and mental health was intuitively understood'; part of that understanding is manifest in the way that repeating poetry by reading it aloud was a vital way of communicating with Dorothy Wordsworth when she was caught in the grip of dementia, but it was also 'a lifelong household ritual.'[9]

All of these paths point in an obvious and fundamental way to a fascination with repeating or trying to repeat experience (of life, of place, of verse) in the mind or on the page, and with trying to understand the nature of such repetition. Stephen Gill's *Wordsworth's Revisitings* demonstrates the centrality of revisiting, revising, and of resituating lines to Wordsworth's poetry. In Gill's elegant account, such repetition is unambiguously essential to Wordsworth's craft, as well as to the matter, of his work:

> [R]evisitings of various kinds are at the heart of Wordsworth's creativity. They might issue in published poems which directly or indirectly allude to earlier work in his evolving corpus. They might be acts of self-borrowing, or of self-reference, hidden from the world in manuscript... Revisiting was also literal... repeatedly Wordsworth went back to places that had mattered to him as man and as poet and tested his sense of the present and the intervening years in fresh acts of creation.[10]

Within the texts which depict such varied forms of re-encounter, critics have also noticed Wordsworth's extensive verbal repetitions. Often, following the attention the 'Note' to 'The Thorn' invites, commentary has focused on examples of tautology, which are inherently recapitulative (and are sometimes understood as problematically so, and thus in need of defending). For instance, Corinna Russell identifies one example of Wordsworthian recapitulation in what she calls the 'Belt and braces' tautology of formulations like 'rock or stone', which present terms as equivalents, whilst 'simultaneously hinting at their desynonymization'.[11] As part of his argument that *Home at Grasmere* establishes a scale of values in which tautology replaces logic as a means of expressing the truth of the self-contained landscape, Kenneth Johnston convincingly demonstrates the way in which 'unsubtle repetition of words from the same root draws attention to the faulty logic of the statement only to flaunt the irrelevance of logic to the rhetoric of the situation.'[12] Elsewhere, Christopher Ricks's discussion of Wordsworth's circular line, 'But in the very world which is the world [of all of us]', insists that the

---

[9] *All in Each Other*, p. 303.   [10] *Wordsworth's Revisitings*, pp. 8–9.   [11] Russell, p. 108.
[12] 'Reclusive Song', p. 17.

recapitulative formulation 'suggests the utter intransigence...of a tautology' (though his point is that the run-on into the next line 'of all of us' moves such a reading on, in a different direction).[13] All three thus draw attention to examples of a fundamentally teasing, though potentially also profoundly moving, tautological effect.

Several of Wordsworth's works explore experiences of repetition: repeated sounds, repeated sights, and repeated emotions, but also of analogous episodes. Wordsworth's fascination with revolution, be it political, social, or even geological, constitutes another thematically crucial aspect of his verse, with obvious connections to ideas of repetition. And the 'Note' to 'The Thorn', the 'Preface' to *Lyrical Ballads*, and the poet's 'Essays upon Epitaphs' all exhibit an explicit interest in the possibilities and limitations of textual repetition, from conventional forms and diction to actual instances of repeated words or phrases, with the 'Preface' citing *recollection* in tranquillity as the necessary condition of poetic composition. Wordsworth displays this obsession with recapitulation throughout his poetry, and this study cannot chart exhaustively each of Wordsworth's innumerable textual repetitions. My intention in this chapter is rather to survey, dwelling briefly on some representative examples of verbal repetition, in order to consider some of the ways in which repetition distinguishes Wordsworth's craft as a poet.

As already discussed, form, metre, and rhyme all depend upon a sense of repetition and the successful manipulation of it, and Wordsworth's pronouncements on his adoption of wildly various forms (from the experimentation of *Lyrical Ballads* to the blank verse homage of *The Prelude*) have provoked rich critical debate. But more microcosmically, Wordsworth frequently repeats words and combinations of words, not simply in the way that concordances reveal to critics interested in the valence of particular vocabularies, but often in close proximity, outside of any of the demands of versification or explicit theme. Wordsworth's style, that is, incorporates a heavy tendency towards repetition in its use of a specific, repeated lexis. Significant emotive power has been attributed to such literal repetitions; Howard Erskine-Hill concludes a discussion of the duplication of a line from Book 2 of *The Prelude* (l. 144), 'We beat with thundering hoofs the level sand,' in Book 10 (l. 566), by describing it as 'perhaps the most breathtaking *coup* of *The Prelude*'; Stephen Gill attends to the same repetition as a key moment for the appreciation of 'Wordsworthian revisiting' in his study of such repair.[14] Not all repetitions lift entire lines, of course. Hugh Sykes Davies's criticism of the numerical study of Wordsworth's work by Franklin Bliss Snyder is again relevant here. As Sykes Davies points out, there are various limitations relating to the way Snyder conducted his research, but it nonetheless highlights

---

[13] *Force of Poetry*, p. 108.
[14] Howard Erskine-Hill, *Poetry of Opposition and Revolution: Dryden to Wordsworth* (Oxford: Clarendon Press, 1996), p. 250; *Wordsworth's Revisitings*, pp. 6–8.

incontrovertibly that there are words which were 'favourites' of Wordsworth (and which are therefore repeated across his works with higher frequency than might be expected, compared with the more general usage of the same words[15]). On top of this, as Sykes Davies illustrates at some length, there are *clusters* of words which repeatedly appear close to one another in Wordsworth's writing.[16] On top of this again are the revivals of particular details which the attentive reader can trace across Wordsworth's career, so that, according to Sykes Davies, 'the only way of determining the meaning of any word in [Wordsworth's] poetry is to take all its context together; and to ensure that the closest attention is indeed given to those words which, by the process of repetition and tautology' (a process Sykes Davies has already explained as taking place 'from poem to poem, over the whole range of his writing—even to his prose') 'had come to bear in it a weight, a power, greater than they usually carry.'[17] For Sykes Davies, this poetic process mimics the growth of the poet's mind as Wordsworth describes it, as all of these 'apparent tautologies... with repetition [gather] force and clarity, as memories grow in strength when they recur in active meditation.'[18]

Beyond the sort of linguistic repetition which can be demonstrated numerically, which impacts primarily in Sykes Davies's account upon the semantic reception of his work, Wordsworth's writing persistently exploits the various rhetorical effects repetition can engender. In countless instances, these effects sit between or across the 'natural' language Wordsworth sets out to reclaim in the *Lyrical Ballads*, and the poems 'upon which general approbation is at present bestowed':[19] the many types of formal repetition outlined by Cicero and Aristotle as techniques of classical oratory are also dominant aspects of conversational spoken language (aspects of 'the real language of men'), *and* the 'phrases and figures of speech which from father to son have long been regarded as the common inheritance of Poets.'[20] We might see such effects as particularly attractive to a poet who seeks to distance himself from conventional poetic language in the 'Preface' to *Lyrical Ballads*, yet operates quite deliberately within certain poetic traditions, and is anxious about his perception as a poet by others.[21] Formally and informally, repetition in language is undeniably powerful at establishing conviction and reassurance, at lending a sense of incremental build up (positive or negative), and at creating dramatic fervency, suggestive of deep feeling. Repetition also is enabling for Wordsworth, because its use tends to preserve its rhetorical purpose of furthering rational argument, *along with* its powerfully (strictly non-rhetorical) emotional effects.

---

[15] See Sykes Davies, 'Wordsworthian Words' (pp. 25–118).   [16] See Sykes Davies, pp. 79–80.
[17] Sykes Davies, pp. 46–7.   [18] Sykes Davies, pp. 95–6.
[19] 'Preface' to *Lyrical Ballads*, p. 130; p. 120.   [20] 'Preface' to *Lyrical Ballads*, p. 118; p. 132.
[21] For one account of Wordsworth's 'anxieties about whether poetic labour was a properly accountable pursuit', see David Simpson, *Wordsworth's Historical Imagination*, pp. 30–9 (p. 38).

In 'Goody Blake, and Harry Gill', words and structures cluster thickly. The poem's opening lines establish this pattern:

> Oh! what's the matter? what's the matter?
> What is't that ails young Harry Gill?
> That evermore his teeth they chatter,
> Chatter, chatter, chatter still.[22]

and the narrative sustains it. Such 'jigging rhythms and jangling onomatopoeia'[23] might be explained as fundamental aspects of the ballad tradition, which is, formally, inherently repetitious. If the *Lyrical Ballads* did not launch Wordsworth's career, they certainly cemented his reputation in a particular direction upon their publication; Wordsworth directly recognizes his debt to Percy's *Reliques of Ancient Poetry* (and the ballad revival Percy represents) in the 1815 'Essay, Supplementary to the Preface',[24] and the title of his collection is an obvious signposting of his participation (albeit one aiming to challenge or extend) in those conventions. It is to this collection that Wordsworth adds his 'Note' to 'The Thorn', creating a composite piece which explicitly and then implicitly explores the possibility of repetition and tautology. Yet, it is a critical truism that 'the traditional ballad seems to have had little direct influence on Wordsworth's experiment',[25] and in any case, examples of the types of repetition associated with balladry are spread across all of Wordsworth's works. It would therefore be entirely wrong to dismiss the repetitions of the *Lyrical Ballads* as simply or merely responding to the demands of a particular form; rather, their effects are rhetorically, semantically, and affectively complex, as attention to 'The Thorn' already has demonstrated.

Often, Wordsworth's use of repetition clusters within texts; a passage containing one particularly marked example will frequently contain others in close proximity. And even within apparently single examples of repetition, different repetitious rhetorical effects often gather and thicken one another. To take an example from *Home at Grasmere*,

> not betrayed by tenderness of mind
> ...Did we come hither, with romantic hope
> To find in midst of so much loveliness
> Love, perfect love; of so much majesty

---

[22] 'Goody Blake, and Harry Gill, a True Story', repr. in *Lyrical Ballads, and Other Poems, 1797–1800*, pp. 59–62 (ll. 1–4).
[23] Jacobus, p. 236.
[24] See 'Essay, Supplementary to the Preface', pp. 75–6. On Wordsworth's debt to Percy, see Sutherland, 'The Native Poet'.
[25] Jacobus, p. 211.

> A like majestic frame of mind in those
> Who here abide, the persons like the place.
> Not from such hope or aught of such belief
> Hath issued any portion of the joy
> Which I have felt this day.[26]

Despite the intensity of feeling suggested here, generated partly by the fervent repetitions in the passage, to find love 'in the midst of...loveliness' plays with the apprehension of affective response, teasingly half-glancing, almost, at an etymological game: is the 'love' in 'loveliness' the same as the love implied in 'romantic hope'? What is the relationship between them? The internal rhyme of mind/find also hints that we are supposed to be searching out a puzzle here. But then, the emphatic reoccurrence of 'love' (which again seems playful in its being lexically and declaredly a 'perfect' repetition of 'love') reasserts its rightfulness in this emphasis, especially falling as it does before the pause of the semi colon. As an example of ploce,[27] this 'love' looks back and modifies itself, tugging away from 'loveliness' as it associates itself more exactly with [just] 'love'. But as 'perfect love' echoes 1 John 4.18, divine rather than romantic love is pushed forwards as another possibility. The multiple meanings contained within a single word proliferate as that word moves through the forms of repetition in the passage. The doubling of the polyptoton[28] as 'majestic' and 'majesty' are introduced, is reinforced by the shared structure, 'of so much...'. This draws loveliness and majesty together, suggesting their relationship, too. The majesty further indicates a love which is divine, rather than 'romantic', and in turn majesty is allowed to share in the intensity of 'love perfect love'; as the poem tends in this way towards a sense of the sublime, the 'loveliness' of the poet's surroundings re-emerges as the source of 'love', rather than vice versa. The intensity of the meaning implied here, a meaning so powerful because it strains and bursts out despite being compressed into a single word, 'love', pulls the poem towards a form of sublime feeling. But suddenly the reader is corrected. The poem loops back to the start of the passage as Wordsworth reveals that the feeling underpinning the previous lines has been inspired 'Not from such hope': it was the 'hope', and not the 'romantic', which we should have been attending to all along; we should have been thinking about the *effect* of the loveliness, rather than dwelling on the complicated interrelations of the 'love'. The structural and lexical repetitions which loop and link within and across lines and sentences exploiting various classical rhetorical devices

---

[26] *Home at Grasmere: Part First, Book First, of The Recluse*, ed. Beth Darlington (Ithaca: Cornell University Press, 1977), 'MS D Reading Text', ll. 309–18. All references to *Home at Grasmere* in this book will be to this Reading Text unless otherwise stated.

[27] Ploce: 'repetition of a word in an altered or more expressive sense, or for the sake of emphasis', *OED*.

[28] Polyptoton: 'repetition of a word in different cases or inflections', *OED*.

simultaneously in the passage lend a thickness to the texture of repetition which is far from uncommon in Wordsworth's writing. His depiction of the two vanished swans in *Home at Grasmere*, for example, a moment of intense personal identification and feeling, appears shortly before these lines, and speaks of 'They strangers, and we strangers; they a pair, | And we a solitary pair like them' (*Home at Grasmere*, ll. 254–5), brilliantly enacting the binding of community Wordsworth describes in the poem, through minute lexical and structural forms of repetition which again allow subtle modifications, thus avoiding overly simplistic forms of identification or metaphor.

Pure epizeuxis[29] is rarely found in Wordsworth's writing (it more frequently appears across a line break in what is strictly speaking anadiplosis[30]), so when it does appear, it stands out. Two striking examples lie in *Home at Grasmere*, and both of them palpably play with the way that repetition sustains competing tendencies towards reinforcement and redundancy. At line 439, Wordsworth invokes a light 'Mortal though bright, a dying, dying flame.' Here, the innate redundancy of perfect repetitions like this sounds out the fading it describes, as the flame dies away; simultaneously, though, the very same repetition inevitably refuses to let it die. This line sits in a context in which Wordsworth is asserting the communal nature of existence and affective response: the appreciation of the Lakeland surroundings does not belong solely to the poet and his sister ('We do not tend a lamp | Whose lustre we alone participate, | Which shines dependent upon us alone', *Home at Grasmere*, ll. 436–8). Rather, in a good example of the tendency for lines containing forms of repetition to come in clusters, the poem continues: 'Look where we will, some human heart has been | Before us with its offering;... | Joy spreads and sorrow spreads' (*Home at Grasmere*, ll. 440–5). The last repetition here allows joy and sorrow both independent and conjoined existence, the awareness of which in various forms animates the poem. 'Spreads', that is, literally broadens out to encompass both joy and sorrow. But the repetition also gathers it back together, because it stalls on the same idea of spreading. Like watching wine spill across a table, and momentarily waiting to see which runnel needs attention first, for a moment, both poet and reader are arrested in the fact of the spreading emotions which seem to be contradictory, and going in opposite directions, but which are also (though the repetition) tied together. In this example, *and* is also at work, to amplify the effect of addition which supplements the same thing, and, conterminously, attaches an alternative, without requiring contradiction.

In the same poem, in another example of thick repetition, Wordsworth contemplates the birds which soar above him, tracing their movements even as

---

[29] Epizeuxis: the emphatic repetition of a single word.
[30] Anadiplosis: a device in which the last word of a line, sentence, or clause is repeated at the beginning of the next line, sentence, or clause.

he recognizes his own experiential exclusion from it. The birds' actions are remarkable to him precisely for their many repetitions, which are themselves both fascinatingly the same, and different:

> On tracing and retracing that large round,
> Their jubilant activity evolves
> Hundreds of curves and circlets, to and fro,
> Upwards and downwards
> *(Home at Grasmere*, ll. 211–14)

Just as the revisit is different to the visit, so tracing is different to retracing, and so the birds' movements are an evolution rather than a straightforward replication: the observer's recognition of them *as* repetitions, indicates their subtle difference; repetition contains this variation within it. The passage then enacts a shift in attention to the sound rather than the sight:

> Faint, faint at first, and then an eager sound,
> Passed in a moment, and as faint again!
> *(Home at Grasmere*, ll. 220–1)

As in the 'dying, dying' light, discussed above, 'faint' here gets both weaker (through its redundancy) and stronger (in its reiteration) through the repetition; in its meaningfulness it thus becomes both fainter and less faint. In this second example, epizeuxis leads into ploce, as 'faint' resurges in the following line to amplify the same effect of fuller sense. Thus, we are prepared for the stanza to conclude as it does with a further resistance to ending: the passage cannot satisfactorily end, because the poem argues for experience as a non-linear phenomenon which resists conclusion, 'spreading' out rather than boxing in. Again exemplifying the way that instances of repetitious effects tend to cluster, and in lines describing repeated action, Wordsworth's poem can find 'rest' only ironically, by denying the possibility of completed rest, through repeated-but-different words (here, the shift from noun to verb):

> then up again aloft,
> Up with a sally and a flash of speed,
> As if they scorned both resting-place and rest.
> *(Home at Grasmere*, ll. 227–9)

If epizeuxis is relatively rarely to be found in his writing, Wordsworth frequently turns to forms of diacope[31] to draw in the minor modifications it allows, whether

---

[31] Diacope: repetition of a word or words with other words added between.

in the fervency of his praise of the eloquence of Burke, 'Now mute, for ever mute', in the 1850 *Prelude* (VII.518), or to exploit the sense of passionate balance implied in 'I gazed—and gazed', which reaches with the poet's eye and his recollecting mind across the mass of golden daffodils in 'I wandered lonely as a cloud'.[32] In 'The Thorn', 'from vale to vale' (l. 26) suggests a stretching expansiveness in a more exclusively geographical sense, and a similar but extended effect is discovered through the passage from *Home at Grasmere* which swells with the 'unfettered liberty' of the roving schoolboy, felt as the capacity

> To flit from field to rock, from rock to field,
> From shore to island, and from isle to shore,
> ...
> From high to low, from low to high
> (*Home at Grasmere*, ll. 39–43)

The clustered antimetabole here[33] mimics the constant sense of expansion of the world, which belongs to the boy (and is also known by the poet) as he moves between different landmarks. But its inherent repetition also contains the contraction which ultimately pulls the boy back into 'the bound of this huge Concave', though it is only the poet, and *not* the boy, who is aware that 'here | Must be his Home, this Valley be his World.' (ll. 44–5). The stanza break after 'both resting-place and rest', mentioned above, thus mimics the experience of the boy in the poem, who believes in an expansiveness to the landscape which the poet knows is an illusion. Both stanzaic and topographical features provide an illusory but necessary limit, which textual repetition functions brilliantly to perform.

It is striking that both of the examples of epizeuxis mentioned above imply a fading away, and thus seem alert to their own irony. Elsewhere in *Home at Grasmere*, Wordsworth's sensitivity to the effects of repetition similarly spills over into self-enactment. The anadiplotic lines, 'At sight of this seclusion, he forgot | His haste—for hasty had his footsteps been,' (ll. 9–10) for example, convey a highly self-conscious sense of catching at the very haste Wordsworth is describing, in order to arrest it. And indeed, this, the MS D reading text, expands this sense from the MS B version, 'At sight of this seclusion, I forgot | My Haste—for hasty had my footsteps been', MS B, ll. 6–7. This is more personal, of course; but the pronouns mean that the lines lack the more extensive, aurally breathless 'h' repetition found in the MS D text. As well as being naturally emphatic (as, for instance, in 'I loved whate'er I saw: nor lightly loved, | But most intensely; never dreamt of aught | More grand, more fair, more exquisitely framed', *The Prelude*, 1850, XII.176–8), repotia[34] can operate in a similarly performative manner. In

---

[32] See *Poems, in Two Volumes, and Other Poems, 1800–1807*, pp. 207–8.
[33] Antimetabole: 'A figure in which the same words or ideas are repeated in inverse order', OED.
[34] Repotia: repetition of a phrase with a slight difference.

'Aye, think on that, my Heart, and cease to stir; | Pause upon that, and let the breathing frame | No longer breathe' (*Home at Grasmere*, ll. 80–2), as we move from 'think'ing to 'paus[e]'ing, 'that' provokes the very 'pause' being commanded, holding us up just long enough to slow reading down, allowing (as another example of repetition emerges) 'breathing' to exhale into 'No longer breathe'. Elsewhere in the same poem, such linguistic self-enacting is given up in favour of a purer form of insistence in an example which refuses interrogation. Kenneth Johnston finds that 'plain denomination passes as a kind of definition by means of sheer repetition: "I would call thee beautiful, for... beautiful thou art." Weak writing, on one scale of values, but entirely appropriate to the scale established by the structure of "Home at Grasmere" [... in which o]rdinary ways of interpreting meaning are blocked or skewed.'[35] As is entirely appropriate to the rhetorical environment the poem has established according to Johnston's reading of it, repetition is left to carry the weight of a truth function, and so to be an index of sincerity.[36]

Often, examples of repetitious effects in Wordsworth's work employ more than one device of classical rhetoric: in 'I loved whate'er I saw: nor lightly loved' in the lines quoted above, the epanalepsis[37] of 'loved... loved' coexists with the anaphoric self-assertion of 'I loved... I saw', as well as with the fervent, fittingly accumulative emphasis of the triple repetition of 'more' which follows. Wordsworth frequently employs anaphoric and tricolonic structures: whether in *The Prelude*, concluding that 'we love, not knowing that we love, | And feel, not knowing whence our feeling comes' (VIII.171–2), or declaring in the heavily Miltonic 'Prospectus' to *The Recluse* (as it appeared in the 'Preface' to the *Excursion* in 1814) that the poem is to be 'On Man, on Nature, and on Human Life'; an eye cast down the left margin of the same page further encounters three 'And's, two 'Or's, six 'Of's and two 'To's before we reach the climactic epic verb, 'I sing'.[38] Book 1 of the 1805 *Prelude* opens with a focus on a breeze which 'blows from the green fields and from the clouds | And from the sky'; a few lines later, Wordsworth surpasses himself, repeating the rhetorical questioning structure 'what X shall Y?' four times in quick succession (I.11–14). It is not uncommon

---

[35] 'Reclusive Song', p. 10.

[36] See Johnston: 'Wordsworth's language shifts from linear metaphor ("termination"/"last retreat") to circular forms ("Centre," "Whole," and the idea of being "happy in itself")... The conclusion here is simply that Grasmere is unconditioned. It does not depend on anything other than itself: Grasmere is Grasmere; beautiful is beautiful. The last two words in the paragraph, "Unity Entire," are entirely and effectively characteristic. Adjective and noun add so little to each other that they approach self-contained tautology... summing up the quality of embracedness, of being-closed-in, with which he began, and which he wants and needs in order to feel himself as one person intact.' ('Reclusive Song', p. 12.)

[37] Epanalepsis: 'A figure by which the same word or clause is repeated after intervening matter' (*OED*), more specifically used to denote repetition at the end of a line, sentence, or clause of a word or words from the beginning of the same line, sentence, or clause.

[38] See *The Excursion*, p. 39.

to find Wordsworth introducing a double negative into his accounts (in Book 1 of *The Prelude* he is 'not unwilling' (l. 68); the sound the hills offer back to the joyful children playing on the ice in the same section of the poem is 'not unnoticed' (l. 472); in Book 2 we find domestic love mingled 'not unwillingly' with sneers (l. 455); in Book 3, a track 'not untrod before' is pursued (l. 121), and so on). The double negative is a particularly interesting form of repetition because it is fundamentally emphatic, but it accumulates backwards, rather than building up in a more positive sense though repeated ideas or sounds. In this sense, it is very like rhyme itself as Gillian Beer describes it, and it is absolutely recapitulative in nature. Polyptoton is another fascinating form of repetition. Its derivation from the Greek 'many' and 'to fall' (it is also translated occasionally as 'to fail' in biblical translation) implies a weakening of force at least, and possibly even a cascade, which might be in some sense moral. Yet often in Wordsworth's use of it, polyptoton reaches to redeem the poet who 'did not judge, | I never thought of judging' (*The Prelude* XI.238-8). Polyptoton is especially generous at allowing a sense of slippage between noun and verb, which in turn allows language productively to hover between the concrete and the abstract (just as Donald Davie finds other aspects of Wordsworth's language meaningfully to do[39]). Polyptotonic repetition can enhance superlatives: Simon Lee is 'weak | —The weakest in the village'; he is 'poorest of the poor'.[40] The modified repetition found in diacope can go still further, surpassing superlatives, in 'the intense tranquillity | Of silent hills, and more than silent sky'.[41]

Wordsworth clearly delights in the parallelism which asks 'With what strange utterance...|...and with what motion' (*The Prelude* I.349-51), or describes Martha Ray's being 'known to every star, | And every wind that blows' ('The Thorn', ll. 69-70). A similar chiasmic play is at work at the start of the passage from Book 8 of *The Prelude* which delineates Wordsworth's immediate response on his first entry to London, where the ability to discriminate collapses, and sheer overwhelming quantity can only be figured through the redundancy repetition contains:

> I sate
> With vulgar men about me, vulgar forms
> Of houses, pavements, streets, of men and things,
> Mean shapes on every side
>
> (VIII.694-7)

---

[39] See Donald Davie, *Articulate Energy*, p. 295.
[40] 'Simon Lee, the Old Huntsman', repr. in *Lyrical Ballads, and Other Poems, 1797-1800*, pp. 64-70 (ll. 39-40; l. 60).
[41] In *Last Poems, 1821-1850*, ed. Jared Curtis, Apryl Lea Denny-Curtis, and Jillian Heydt-Stevenson (Ithaca: Cornell University Press, 1999), p. 24 (ll. 13-14).

The repetition of 'vulgar' initially diminishes the inhabitants of the city into an undifferentiable mass (in which one set of vulgar forms are indistinguishable from another), but the line break is characteristically teasing: the second instance of the word refers really to 'forms' not of more men, but of houses. Thus, the sense of amalgamation is reduced (introducing a new noun distinguishes new aspects of the scene, albeit in a limited way) and increased (forms of men are not only lumped in with forms of other men, but with other types of forms). Yet the bland features of the city (houses, pavements, streets) lead back, through the repetition of 'of', to 'men'; again, humanity is just part of the heaving mass of *things* of which Wordsworth is blurrily aware. By the next line, apprehension is reduced to 'mean shapes': as he realizes he has entered the city, discrimination collapses; the *idea* of having done so induces a moment of such powerful, overwhelming feeling that Wordsworth can only 'Remember that it was a thing divine' (l. 710):

> A weight of Ages did at once descend
> Upon my heart, no thought embodied, no
> Distinct remembrances; but weight and power,
> Power, growing with the weight
>
> (ll. 703–6)

The powerfully weighty repetitions of 'weight' and 'power' attempt but fail to communicate the magnificence aroused in Wordsworth by the *idea* that he is entering the city,[42] but also the realization of the impossibility of these words to communicate anything other than 'trifling' things: their repetition is both emphatic and redundant. By the end of the passage, repetition has resolved into conjunction: London is 'Chronicle at once | And Burial-place of passions and their home | Imperial, and chief living residence' (ll. 749–51). In doing so, it renounces the attempt to communicate the content of the idea of the city, instead resting on the equivocality the conjunction, *and*, inaugurates: 'The concluding lines of the passage, with their breathless conjunctive linking of opposites, indicate this equivocality... Burial-place *and* living residence... The city's living-dead character is awesome. It is for the poet to feel that awe, but also to look steadily through and beyond it.'[43] The poem resists giving in to the illusion of adequate description, but in doing so asserts the 'steadiness' of the revising poet who in this resistance approaches sincerity.

Thickly clustered repetition with difference animates 'Peele Castle'.[44] This poem describes a form of 'revisit', to use Gill's term, in that a picture of the castle reminds Wordsworth of his erstwhile 'Neighbour' (l. 1), and it bursts with forms of repetition:

---

[42] See Jarvis, *Wordsworth's Philosophic* Song, p. 144.
[43] *Wordsworth's Philosophic* Song, p. 147.
[44] In *Poems, in Two Volumes, and Other Poems 1800–1807*, pp. 266–8.

> So pure the sky, so quiet was the air!
> So like, so very like, was day to day!
>
> (ll. 5–6)

The likeness insisted on is enacted by the lines, even as they allow for the accommodation of difference which a retrospect must by definition acknowledge. Wordsworth's response in the poem is mediated through his grief for Beaumont, the painting's artist, and the poem declares its own inflection with the intermediary distress that Beaumont's death has caused: 'Not for a moment could I now behold | A smiling sea, and be what I have been.' (ll. 37–8). Yet the lines give way to a blurring of the picture of the castle and its reality ('*this* huge Castle, standing *here* sublime', for example (l. 49, my emphases)), and of Wordsworth's past experience, and his picture-inspired memory, which is nonetheless figured through the present tense ('I love to see the look with which it braves...| The light'ning', ll. 50–2). The elision draws together past and present experience. In another level of complication, the castle with which Wordsworth claims intimacy is one which was experienced through its reflection in a 'glassy sea' (l. 4), whereas the picture is one of 'trampling waves' (l. 52); the original reality of the castle is displaced so that Wordsworth recognizes its significance only ever exists insofar as it is a reflection or image. This leaves it vulnerable, but also allows for both versions to be 'right', sincere, because the poem is really the 'Poet's dream' (l. 16).

The work that repetition does in Wordsworth's poems is often complex. Travelling along the Simplon Pass, the longevity of the forests Wordsworth witnesses is mirrored in the repetitions of a line which actually undoes the very possibility of the decay the trees suggest: 'The immeasurable height | Of woods decaying, never to be decay'd, |...Winds thwarting winds' (*The Prelude* VI.556–60). In his 1850 revision of the poem, Wordsworth made extensive additions to his recollections of the Alps. He returned to and augmented the idea of immortality suggested here by the Alpine forests and 'Nature's' voice (1850, VI.431), in lines even more densely packed with repetitious effects:

> These forests unapproachable by death,
> That shall endure as long as man endures
> To think, to hope, to worship, and to feel,
> To struggle, to be lost within himself
> In trepidation; from the blank abyss
> To look with bodily eyes, and be consoled
>
> (1850, VI.467–71)

The 'consolation' offered to Wordsworth here by the voice of Nature is the ultimate solace offered by the suggestion of immortality. These lines are exemplary of the work to which Wordsworth puts repetition: most obvious is the self-enacting reduplication of 'endure'/'endures', and the anaphoric listing of infinitives which begins in the third of these lines and persists to their grand conclusion (there is an innate timelessness to infinitive verb forms, particularly as their listing is largely asyndetic here, which adds to this feeling of repetition), all of which lean towards the sense of perpetuity Wordsworth fosters. But there are more subtle effects at play too, which perhaps wait for a second reading to become obvious: structurally, the lines tend to fall into balanced halves (apart from line 469, which neatly divides each half in half again); even when the self-loss described is performed by the *sentence* run-on to 'In trepidation', the structural balance in the *line* is preserved. This subtle, repeated structure is entirely fitting to the endurance Wordsworth is invoking. Moreover, the infinitives which dominate the passage seem powerfully to be resolved and to climax in the strident, existential 'be' of 'be consoled'; but 'be' has already appeared, in quieter and more pessimistic form, two lines previously, in 'to be lost within himself'. Occupying as both clauses do the second half of their respective lines, the two instances of 'be' recall one another, themselves forming another balanced pair (be lost/be consoled) which participates in the general sense of equilibrium, repeated throughout the passage, moderating what might otherwise become merely excessive.

Towards the end of the 'Prospectus' to *The Recluse*, Wordsworth declares,

> if with this
> I mix more lowly matter; with the thing
> Contemplated, describe the Mind and Man
> Contemplating; and who, and what he was,
> The transitory Being that beheld
> This Vision;—when and where, and how he lived;—
> Be not this labour useless.[45]

The repetition of 'Contemplated' in 'Contemplating' is immediately striking (not least for the witty play which causes us to trip upon it, and thus to pause and contemplate). Such contemplation is figured here through the way repetitions implicitly describe the act of contemplating, even as we read explicitly about it: 'and who, and what' is a very simple anaphoric structure which seems to have resolved and to have moved on in the following line, only to return as 'and where, and how' in the line below, confirming the significance of the sort of turning over of thought that Coleridge describes in the *Biographia* as 'the pleasurable activity of mind... Like the motion of a serpent... at every step he pauses and half recedes'.[46] All of this is conducted in a passage which simultaneously sings with repeated sounds: the stridently alliterative 'Mind and Man' has its way prepared via the

---

[45] *The Excursion*, p. 41.   [46] *Biographia Literaria*, ii, 14.

previous line's 'mix', 'more', and 'matter'; 'with this' sets up a precedent through which its [ɪ] and [θ] sounds find echoes in the following line's 'with the thing' (and the [ɪ] finds further assonance in 'mix'), so that 'contemplated' stands out as both syllabically and rhymingly surprising, or odd, only to be confirmed as in fact quite right in the following line's polyptotonic 'contemplating'.

Given its indisputable interest in revisiting, it is unsurprising that Wordsworth should have opened 'Tintern Abbey' similarly engaged in the contemplation of his own mind, or that he does so in a passage whose repetitions adopt exactly the motion of return evoked by Coleridge's serpent:

> Five years have passed; five summers, with the length
> Of five long winters! and again I hear
> These waters, rolling from their mountain-springs
> With a sweet inland murmur.—Once again
> Do I behold these steep and lofty cliffs,
> That on a wild secluded scene impress
> Thoughts of more deep seclusion; and connect
> The landscape with the quiet of the sky.
>
> ('Tintern Abbey', ll. 1–8)

The triple repetition of the first word, 'five'; the structural repetition (with a degree of modification) of 'five [+ season]'; the way 'again' (itself semantically engaged in a discourse of repetition) in line 2 creeps to the end of line 4 so that the repetition is heard, but we have to look more closely to find the first instance hidden back within the line when it does sound (blank verse encourages us to tune our ears to rhymes beyond line endings); the way the modification of 'length' (l. 1) to 'long' (l. 2) invokes repetition with difference, and of course the way the 'secluded' scene leads to the 'more deep seclusion' of the mind (another instance of the way repetition accommodates change): despite all of this, the 'connect'ion Wordsworth makes in the final line here is not, as we might suppose, between the scene and himself, but the purely physical meeting of land and sky. The habitual repetition, that is, lulls us to follow the pattern the poem creates up until line 8, when we are jolted from our complacency in a way that forces us to recognize our misdirection. This is another example of Wordsworth's prompting of recapitulation, which acknowledges a first and a second sense we have made of the lines. This is the logical, necessary consequence of the types of revisiting Gill documents, and that Prynne notes: a revisit recognizes something previously known, *and* understands itself as a new occasion. Such recapitulation is where conjunction supports repetition in the mind of the poet: what matters is the connection between events, experiences, and versions, not simply their difference from one another. But before the connections can be established, the difference within the repetition must be recognized.

Beyond local effects of repetition, and apart from Wordsworth's conception of the relationship between his works, critical understanding of the structure of Wordsworth's longer poems has long involved an appreciation of their internal repetitions. Johnston argues that the structure of *Home at Grasmere* 'is reflected in the basic semantics and syntax of the sentences in the poem, which are characterized by redundancy, repetition, and a subtle eliding of predication that makes subjects and objects collapse in upon each other' (Johnston recognizes that this 'is also generally characteristic of Wordsworth's verse'). In Johnston's account, the 'proofs' Wordsworth arrives at 'are more rhetorical than logical, circling round to an identification with their point of origin rather than moving from a cause to an effect'.[47] According to this understanding, the very structure of *Home at Grasmere* is characterized by 'a rubric of circularity' which ultimately arrests the possibility of poetic progression: 'Wordsworth's experience writing the poem seems to have been a recurrent confrontation with his own image, as in a hall of mirrors—which may help to explain why "Home at Grasmere" was the only part of the first part of *The Recluse* to be written; a hall of mirrors will not do for the narthex of a cathedral'.[48] But if London is 'An undistinguishable world to men, |...melted and reduced | To one identity, by differences | That have no law, no meaning, and no end' (*The Prelude*, VII.700–5), *Home at Grasmere*, insofar as it supplies a sense of interconnection, obviates the need for the cathedral. Grasmere offers unity formed through an ongoing but circular relationship, a structure reminiscent of a protective, woven nest, rather than the disturbingly infinite onward projection of the city. The vale allows poetic rest because Wordsworth finds within it (and has achieved in his writing *about* it) a form of general unity which accommodates specific distinction; he can only find that *here*, because only *this* life allows it. Going on thus becomes going round; still attentive and thoughtful, but no longer isolated. The community (in its widest sense) of Grasmere demonstrates the 'Humble and rustic life', and the language associated by Wordsworth with those who live it; it is thus the social environment in and for which it is appropriate to use 'language arising out of repeated experience and regular feelings, [which] is a more permanent and a far more philosophical language than that which is frequently substituted for it by Poets'.[49] *Home at Grasmere* suggests the achievement of poetic contentment.

In attempts to establish its position in the contested history of epic and the eighteenth-century long poem, *The Prelude* has provoked substantial attention to its form, and here too the pull of various types of repetition has been noted. Herbert Lindenberger finds repetition to be one of the principles of organization in the poem, understanding that 'To repeat means also to accumulate', and that 'The repetitive method [involves] the constant alternation of sharply opposed

---

[47] 'Reclusive Song', p. 8; p. 9.   [48] 'Reclusive Song', p. 13; p. 4.
[49] 'Preface' to *Lyrical Ballads*, p. 124.

levels of intensity—these are central to Romantic art'.[50] He argues that this alternation is 'more than a method of literary composition. Basically, it is something rooted in the Romantic sensibility...of the poet's or, indeed, life's divided nature.'[51] Lindenberger therefore proposes to 'look at each spot of time throughout *The Prelude* as a repetition of the last, in fact, to the look at the poem as saying essentially the same thing again and again. From beginning to end Wordsworth is constantly at work finding new ways to invoke the inexpressible.'[52] Wordsworth introduces 'spots of time' specifically as moments which are powerful because of their place in the memory, and because their recollection can restore the poet. Lucy Newlyn finds them to be as momentous as 'the climaxes in conversion-narratives',[53] and she cites such narratives as a deep influence upon *The Prelude*, noting affinities with Bunyan's *Grace Abounding*, and pointing out that Bunyan's epiphanic moment 'led to a process of obsessional revisiting.'[54] 'Spots of time', then, participate fully in a mode of repetition: without imaginative and intellectual repetition in the mind, they lack meaning. Though shocking or disorientating when experienced, these moments possess a 'renovating Virtue', by which 'our minds | Are nourish'd, and invisibly repair'd'; they are stored up from experiences 'in which | We have had deepest feeling that the mind | Is lord and master' (XI.260–72): these are affirmations of intellectual, imaginative pre-eminence; moments in which the self is affirmed. Renovation implies restoration and repair, though its original meaning associates it more specifically with spiritual rebirth. The weight Wordsworth lends to these moments is undoubtedly great, and widely acknowledged. Even when they possess a magnificent sublimity, there is no doubt that they are associated, to a greater or lesser degree, with psychological trauma, and a great deal of critical attention has been caught throughout the twentieth century on the thorns of a discourse of repetition-compulsion. However, it is not necessary to resituate Wordsworth's traumatic memories in a post-Freudian context which explains their repetition. Those repetitions declare themselves, and in doing so they attest to the possibilities of verse: because the texts of poems proceed through repetitious effects, they face and (frequently) manage the dilemma that Wordsworth attaches to experience. Textual repetitions demonstrate the innate character of repetition with difference, or recapitulation, which Wordsworth understands to be inherent in the apprehension of the world and its translation into verse. In performing this recapitulation, poems thus encompass the nature of experience, in a way which is supplementary to their semantic content.

As soon as one begins to survey examples, multiple instances of Wordsworth's exploitation of repetition's effects jostle and compete for attention, often from

---

[50] *On Wordsworth's Prelude*, pp. 193–4.   [51] *On Wordsworth's Prelude*, pp. 192–3.
[52] *On Wordsworth's Prelude*, p. 188.   [53] 'The noble living and the noble dead', p. 63.
[54] 'The noble living and the noble dead', p. 63.

amongst his best-known passages. So, in *The Prelude*, we find Wordsworth writing of 'the very world which is the world | Of all of us' (X.725–6), declaring that 'The sky seemed not a sky' (I.350); recollecting that 'It was a Summer's night, a close warm night' when he set out to watch the sun rise over Snowdon (XIII.10); insisting that 'I made no vows, but vows | Were then made for me' to be 'a dedicated Spirit' (VI.341–4), and remembering 'Oh! when I have hung | ... Oh! at that time, | While on the perilous ridge I hung' (I.342–8; this last is another example of how recapitulative effects often cluster as, on top of the obvious word-repetitions in 'Oh!' and 'hung', which gesture to emotion and experience, Wordsworth reiterates the significance of the particularity of that moment, as 'when' is recapitulated as 'at that time'). Expounding the creative process in Book VIII, Wordsworth describes 'a ferment quiet, and sublime; | Which, after a short space, works less and less' (VIII.723–4), where the almost oxymoronic tautology ('less' is *more* lessness, when we encounter it for the second time in the line) brilliantly mimics the extraordinary juxtaposition of 'quiet' with 'ferment' and sublimity in the previous line. A typically Wordsworthian play with lines of sight and vision is at work in the Arabian dream in Book V (a dream which Wordsworth gives to 'a friend' in 1805, but claims as his own in 1850), which ends: 'His countenance, meanwhile, grew more disturb'd, | And, looking backwards when he look'd, I saw | A glittering light' (V.127–9). We are led to misread the first 'look' here as belonging to the figure, and thus need to modify our reading to attribute it to the dreamer; but then the figure does look too, and the mutual looking simultaneously connects the pair, so that the dreamer is in as much peril from 'the fleet waters of the drowning world' (l. 136) as the figure from the dream, despite the former's awaking just a few lines later. Wordsworth enjoys the richness of proximate lines which contain subtle rearrangements of the same words ('Remembering how she felt, but what she felt | Remembering not', II.335–6) or different forms of the same word: the 'sheltered and the sheltering grove' in the 1850 *Prelude*, for example (I.69), or the polyptotonic layering of 'thinking'/ 'thought' which crowns the duplicate 'a' and triplicate 'all' in 'A motion and a spirit, that impels | All thinking things, all objects of all thought' in lines 101–2 of 'Tintern Abbey' (a poem appropriately dense with repetition more generally, given its explicit preoccupation with going back). All of these repetitions probe the very possibility of repeating exactly, even as they describe, or remember, or suggest, or judge: they operate on another level to the semantic content of the poem, even as the poem makes its meaning. This is the work poetry can perform.

Whether focused on form, or on minute textual details within poems, offering examples of textual repetition in Wordsworth's work is fundamentally an arbitrary and almost superfluous task, so commonly are they to be found. Affirming that this pervasive tendency is more than just an exhibition of rhetorical flair, and in fact is indicative of a conceptual fascination with repetition, my next two chapters will dwell on two particular types of recapitulation. In thinking about the relationship between repeated sound, and experience itself, I hope to extend my argument that to Wordsworth, the appreciation of similarity with difference, related as it is to an idea of repetition which accommodates change within itself, is vital to his apprehension of the world. Only by attempting to reflect that characteristic in his verse can he achieve the sincerity he defines and demands.

10
Resounding Voices, Habitual Haunts
Recapitulation, Specifics, and Generals

Strains That Never Die

In 1884, W. A. Heard observed that Wordsworth had 'a peculiarly sensitive ear', which 'seems never to sleep', and attributed to Wordsworth an especial 'sensibility to the sounds of nature'.[1] This attention to natural sounds recurs in subsequent scholarship: John Hollander, for example, has argued that English Romantics privilege 'sounds heard out of doors' as more 'worthy of imaginative concern' than formal music.[2] Deliberate reflection upon the *repetition* of specific sounds marks 'Stepping Westward', 'The Solitary Reaper', and 'There was a Boy'. All three are interested in the return of voiced sounds specifically: the turning over of a lilting question; a caught melody; familiar birdsong. Wordsworth famously pays conventional music little attention.[3] Yet, as Hollander makes clear, 'the non-linguistic but otherwise nonmusical sounds of wind, water, bird song, and the effects of these in trees, rocks and open spaces, are continually treated in a language of musical description' by the poet,[4] and the line between verse and song is notoriously fine. David Perkins memorably explicates the way Wordsworth and Coleridge 'chaunted' verse, their recitation occupying a kind of middle ground between speaking and singing.[5]

Wordsworth's solitary reaper also chaunts, at least by implication ('No Nightingale did ever chaunt | So sweetly', ll. 9–10) in a poem whose rhyme and measure Susan Wolfson invokes as types of repetition which counter the Arnoldian dictum, that Wordsworth 'has no style'.[6] The reaper's song is profoundly moving to Wordsworth, and the power it exerts stems from its capacity to repeat itself: 'the Maiden sang | As if her song could have no ending | . . . The music in my heart I bore, | Long after it was heard no more.' (ll. 25–32). The rhythmic motion of the poem transfers to the action of the reaper ('reap' even sounds like

---

[1] W. A. Heard, 'A few thoughts upon on Wordsworth's treatment of sound', *Transactions of the Wordsworth Society* (1884), pp. 40–57 (pp. 41–2).
[2] John Hollander, *Images of Voice: Music and Sound in Romantic Poetry* (Cambridge: Heffer, 1970), p. 7.
[3] On Wordsworth's lack of enthusiasm for conventional music see Brian Morris, 'Mr Wordsworth's Ear', *Wordsworth Circle*, 10.1 (Winter 1979), 113–21.
[4] *Images of Voice*, p. 26.   [5] 'How the Romantics Recited Poetry', p. 657.
[6] Wolfson, 'Wordsworth's Craft', pp. 110–12.

'repeat'), leaving us with a sense of repetition, without ever disclosing the detail of the song actually being rehearsed. The poem is about this sense, this *affectiveness*, rather than the narrative or musical content of the music Wordsworth hears; indeed, the 'melancholy strain' (l. 6) is more powerful in the poem because of its fundamental silence for the reader, remaining fascinatingly beyond earshot, resisting irritating readerly earworminess. Yet this fundamental silence is paradoxically enforced by the refusal of the poem to *be* silent: an earworm is precisely what Wordsworth declares he is left with. When Margulis discusses the phenomenon of the earworm, she argues that repetition 'makes it possible for us to experience a sense of expanded present characterized...by a heightened sense of orientation and involvement.'[7] Margulis argues that 'music's distinct phenomenology consists of its merging of the objective and subjective stance.'[8] Read in the lyric context of 'The Solitary Reaper', Margulis's assertion gains an enriched significance, particularly as she goes on to suggest that 'Part of the aesthetic orientation is a perceptual openness, a willingness to notice and believe in connections and meanings that may not be instantly apparent.'[9] The return of Wordsworth's reaper's song, both within the 'scene' described by the poem and within the mind of the poet reflecting upon it, seems to exhibit exactly this. The effect extends further in Dorothy Wordsworth's commentary on 'the sound of those two Lines "Oh listen! for the Vale profound | Is overflowing with the sound—" I often catch myself repeating them in disconnection with any thought, or even, I may say, recollection of the Poem.'[10] Here is the earworm, which Margulis asserts is conjured only by music, wriggling into life through the profound aural effect of Wordsworth's verse *about* a repeating song.

The paradoxical effect of being unable to relinquish a sound we cannot really hear gains a supplementary inflection in the light of Garrett Stewart's discussion of examples of 'transegmental drift' in 'The Solitary Reaper'. Stewart argues that our ability to orientate ourselves within the scene described is interrupted by aural ambiguity. Such an effect, in a poem adamantly interested in a sound (the song of the reaper) which is nonetheless never fully realized in the text, is surely self-aware. Listening to the poem's opening words, 'Behold her', Stewart points out that we might register a simple imperative, or an address to a *beholder*; for Stewart, Romanticism's 'entire aesthetic of imaginative manifestation comes into focus in this arguable ambiguity on "behold=(h)er"—as involving both subject and object, both rhetorical addressee and paragrammatical denomination.'[11] The process of reading the poem fully in this account is one of continual readerly revision, without any ambition for resolution in 'a' reading. Indeed, the more it is read, the more the poem gives up: particularly after a preliminary reading has disclosed

---

[7] Margulis, p. 9.   [8] Margulis, p. 12.   [9] Margulis, p. 13.
[10] D[orothy] W[ordsworth] to Lady Beaumont, 29 November 1805, in *Letters*, i, 648–52 (p. 650).
[11] Stewart, pp. 155–6.

the stirring activity of the reaper to be her singing, it is striking that in the same line that interests Stewart, her being solitary, her 'single'ness in the field, literally contains the idea of voicing her song: the metrical stress combines with the fact that the first syllable here is its own word (a word which might well follow an imperative to look at someone performing a remarkable action). Is this an injunction to behold her *sing*? No; we are almost instantly corrected. And yet the poem proves the first hearing true: from the opening line, we do hear the reaper singing, even though the nature of her song remains concealed.

Through repeated readings, these delicate, subtle effects surrender themselves, as the minute revisions of sense that Wordsworth's words and lines demand are revealed. Such readings create a climate of revision through recapitulation (the repeated reading, but also the revision to sense which goes on within and between the words themselves at a finer level). This revision exacts no decision from the reader, but allows more than one reading to exist, without competition: as Wittgenstein puts it, 'one does not annul a shake of the head by shaking it again'.[12] In a different context, Sharon Cameron identifies a similar effect in Emily Dickinson's fascicles: 'Poems are *variants* that revise, but not consequentially so, what has preceded them. And the effect of the equivocation—of all, even opposites, being entertained—is that we do not know whether something is chosen, or whether it is declined'.[13] We do not need to know; it does not matter. And yet the poem, through forms of repetition, keeps in play a sense that our apprehension of the reaper is inadequate: the movement through 'her' (a grammatically singular pronoun), 'single', 'solitary', 'by herself', and 'Alone' in the first stanza insists on 'her' singularity, but the apparently necessary reduplication of her singular status suggests the failure to communicate it *sufficiently*. We are forced to keep asking for more information, even though the whole of the poem asserts the necessity of letting go the desire for a single meaning. As the 'Note' to 'The Thorn' argues, direct repetition (here, the *idea* of repetition located in the reverberating song of the reaper, and the repetition which is enacted in constant readerly micro-recapitulations) is more meaningful than any sense created through synonymic expansion. Here, the 'deficiencies of language' which are discovered, according to the 'Note', in the attempt to communicate 'impassioned feeling' are represented by the reader's continuing ignorance of the song being written about, in a context dominated by the idea of the song's repetition.[14] 'The Solitary Reaper' is an amalgam of all its potential, different soundings-out, and so it *must* echo, repeat and revise itself in different ways, in order to exist in its fullest form. Thus, although its neatly rhymed verse and measured returns suggest

---

[12] Ludwig Wittgenstein, *Philosophical Investigations*, trans. G. E. M. Anscombe (Oxford: Basil Blackwell, 1958), p. 149
[13] *Choosing Not Choosing*, pp. 151-2.   [14] 'Note' to 'The Thorn', p. 351.

completion, the poem remains resistant to ending, echoing on with the reaper's echoing song. In this way, it reaches for the sublime.

In the passage from the Alfoxden Notebook beginning 'There was a spot', Wordsworth recollects his 'favourite station when the winds were up'. Initially attending to the spatial arrangement of 'Three knots of fir-trees', skirting close to picturesque analysis in their being 'Too formally arranged', he appeals to the dictates of 'the delicate eye of Taste', and recounts his own position relative to the 'group', a revision from the even more picturesque 'clump' of his draft text.[15] Soon, however, the poet's visual attention gives way to an aural figure, the aeolian harp, suggested as Wordsworth observes the wind moving through the trees:

> Right opposite
> The central group I loved to stand and hear
> The wind come on and touch these several groves
> Each after each, and thence in the dark night
> Elicit soft proportions of sweet sounds
> As from an instrument. 'The strains are passed,'
> Thus often to myself I said, 'the sounds
> Even while they are approaching are gone by,
> And now they are more distant, more and more.
> O listen, listen, how they wind away;
> Still heard they wind away, heard yet and yet,
> While the last touch they leave upon the sense
> Is sweeter than whate'er was heard before,
> And seems to say, that they can never die.'
>
> (ll. 6–19)

Wordsworth's self-quotation here is structured by verbal reiterations which strain to evoke the idea of, and response to, a frequently repeated sound. His speech announces its own redundancy: strains that 'can never die' should not need a speech about their dying away to be made 'often'; their going 'by' lingers on in the rare end-rhyme 'never die', to reinforce the irony. Relatedly, Wordsworth's repeating here is a present act (of remembering) which necessarily looks back to a past action, but which asserts its continuing existence in the present through the hanging word, 'passed': the page confirms that it is *not* 'past', though the ear might assume that it is. Then and now are both equally present, and equally necessary for a full, 'sincere' appreciation of the episode.[16] The 'pass'ing of the wind here shares

---

[15] Repr. in *Lyrical Ballads, and Other Poems, 1797–1800*, pp. 286–8 (ll. 1–7).

[16] Guinn Batten recognizes this phenomenon when in *The Orphaned Imagination: Melancholy and Commodity Culture in English Romanticism* (Durham and London: Duke University Press, 1998) she points out that *The Prelude* 'possesses many moments that are breathlessly suspended between the "it

the peculiar temporality of 'now', and its subtlety is perhaps best appreciated through an understanding of the changes to the English language which were crystallizing in Wordsworth's lifetime. Adamson explains that, by 1776,

> grammarians of the period recognise a distinction in the present tense between the simple present (e.g. *he walks*) as the appropriate form of 'gnomologic' propositions or habitual events and the progressive present (e.g. *he is walking*) as the form oriented to the 'real now' of current experience... Poets of the generation immediately preceding the Romantics make very little use of this contrast... Romantic poets, by contrast, embraced both colloquial diction and immediate personal experience and there was a corresponding leap in the incidence of present progressives.[17]

But what Wordsworth achieves with words like 'now' and 'still', and here, 'passed', is not a choice of *either* general *or* immediate, personal experience. Rather, their juxtaposition and the rich possibility that both exist at once allow Wordsworth to include the specific *and* the general within the same rendered moment.

There is further verbal play in 'There was a spot' with the word 'wind', which appears early in the poem as the meteorological phenomenon around which the description is based, but by line 15 occurs in its verbal form, meaning 'to bend around'.[18] This is again a distinctly complex and multiple experience. Through Wordsworth's self-quotation, an event already multifaceted in character (both passed, and still approaching; both remembered, and re-experienced presently, in the act of remembering) is represented as itself a repetition of the verbal self-quotation the poem includes, and the experiential repetitions to which it alludes. As a self-declared, frequently repeated repetition ('Thus often to myself I said'), articulated through unashamed, hyper-extended use of pairs of words ('more and more'; 'listen, listen'; 'yet, and yet'), the passage might appear almost clumsy, its self-enactment of the effects it relates over-deliberate, and destined to fail: if the final effect is as sublime as Wordsworth's lines suggest, it surely cannot be replicated so easily? Here, perhaps, the recapitulative effect of Wordsworth's lines function not unlike the self-consuming artifact of Stanley Fish, which 'signifies most successfully when it fails, when it points *away* from itself to something its forms cannot capture.' Fish argues that some writing 'disallows to its productions the claims usually made for verbal art—that they reflect, or contain

---

was" of a past that has been lost and the "this" of the present' (p. 165), though the argument of her study is rather different to mine; Weiskel's *Romantic Sublime* is also interested in the potential sublimity of this effect.

[17] Adamson, *Cambridge History of English Language Vol. IV*, p. 666.

[18] John Hollander finds also 'almost "wend" (as of "way")'; see 'Wordsworth and the Music of Sound', in Geoffrey H. Hartman, ed., *New Perspectives on Wordsworth and Coleridge* (New York: Columbia University Press, 1972), pp. 41–84 (p. 66).

or express Truth—and transfers the pressure and attention from the work to its effects, from what is happening on the page to what is happening in the reader.'[19] 'Truth' to Wordsworth here *is* the 'progressive decertainizing' Fish identifies;[20] the poet's articulated insistence upon the active role the reader must play reinforces the sense that only through the reader's willing acceptance of the different possibilities dwelling within the text simultaneously, can the poem achieve Fish's 'Truth', or what Wordsworth calls sincerity. Here, those possibilities (and the resistance to choosing a single, concrete one) are indicated by the play of recapitulative effects. This sophisticated form of Fish's self-consuming artifact 'points *away* from itself' by artfully pointing *to* itself, repeating its own sense of repetition in order to render the sense of multiple experiences of the same thing.

Far from being clumsy, the passage thus remains delicate, as Wordsworth develops his interest in the possibility of an aural equivalent to the visionary. Vital to this is the subtlety with which repetition's effects operate. Kenneth Johnston urges us to resist paying attention too closely: for him, such 'habits of language are too small and awkward to be other than personal, organic habits of Wordsworth's poetic speech; to interpret them as conscious literary devices induces vertigo, not admiration. By their unobtrusive, really invisible operation, we are prepared to be swayed'.[21] Yet that the minute sonic properties of repetitions are vitally important to Wordsworth, and that he is highly sensitive to their possibilities, is clear from the moment in 'Nutting' when he lays his cheek against mossy stones and 'heard the murmur and that murmuring sound' of the water.[22] As Hollander remarks, 'It is the listening itself we are on the brink of hearing here.'[23] Angela Leighton agrees that 'the move from "murmur" to "murmuring sound" draws out of that apparent tautology an anatomization of, or disjunction between, hearing and listening to hearing'.[24] The reader is offered an insight into the sophisticated aural splitting Wordsworth performs, of the *idea* of murmuring from the literal sound it makes. His expression of this separation is paradoxically dependent upon the repetition of the same word: a synonym might simply imply distinctions within the sound, but the repeated word demands that we fracture its sense. This is the resistance Wordsworth's repetitions perform towards tautology, cultivated by their context and the reader's trained disposition to recapitulate. It is there again in *The Prelude*'s 'roar of waters, torrents, streams | Innumerable, roaring with one voice' (XIII.58-9), and perhaps also in his excited claim, 'I hear, I hear, with joy I hear!' ('Ode: Intimations of Immortality'[25]). Hollander's interest in Wordsworth and sound proceeds from the fact that, whilst the

---

[19] Fish, *Self-Consuming Artifacts*, pp. 3-4. [20] Fish, *Self-Consuming Artifacts*, p. 384.
[21] 'Reclusive Song', p 12.
[22] 'Nutting', repr. in *Lyrical Ballads, and Other Poems, 1797–1800*, pp. 218-20 (l. 36).
[23] 'Wordsworth and the Music of Sound', p. 59. [24] *Hearing Things*, p. 69.
[25] 'Ode: Intimations of Immortality from Recollections of Early Childhood', in *Poems, in Two Volumes, and Other Poems, 1800–1807*, pp. 269-77 (l. 50).

visual and the visionary are at play together in Wordsworth's writing, the aural has no equivalent vocabulary of transcendence. Whilst we may lack the technical terminology, however, these exquisite moments of recapitulation beautifully hint towards the intangible transcendence which an equivalent term might denote, if only it existed.

Thus, in 'There was a spot', in lines loaded with the vocabulary of non-visual sensation, Wordsworth declares that 'the last touch they leave upon the sense' is 'sweeter than whate'er was heard before, | And seems to say that they can never die.' That the sounds in these lines are 'still heard', even 'while' the 'sweeter' sound (which, importantly, is not actually a sound here) reverberates in the memory, indicates the noetic *with* the literal sound. That there is no literal sound remaining in the memory is negotiated through a kind of necessary synaesthesia in a context where sound lacks a vocabulary, as Wordsworth falls back on 'touch'. The idea returns in the way strains of music are given a physical form, and made to 'wander', in Wordsworth's 'Inside of King's College Chapel Cambridge'. Wordsworth declares the glorious roof of the chapel to be a space 'where music dwells | Lingering—and wandering on as loth to die; | Like thoughts whose very sweetness yieldeth proof | That they were born for immortality.'[26] Simile and metaphor replace the reality of experienced sound, whose 'wandering' reflects Wordsworth's inability to capture it adequately on the page. Poetry, a series of inscribed sounds, fails to express the effect of protracted, lingering sound, except in its artful ability beautifully to communicate its failure.

This sweetness and perpetuity of sound strikingly remembers the same features in the lines from the Alfoxden Notebook, where the invocation 'O listen, listen' is complex, demonstrating Wordsworth's interest in the possibility of articulating the effect of sound on the ear: insofar as Wordsworth adopts the posture of talking to himself here, the ironic echo (a voiced invocation is a self-created sound to which he cannot help but listen, especially when he says it twice) is a more strident version of the powerful imperative in 'The Solitary Reaper', 'O listen',[27] which similarly ends with an imaginative echo: 'The music in my heart I bore, | Long after it was heard no more.' (ll. 31–2). Jeremy Prynne has written on the latter poem's imperative, noting that:

> This impassioned expression of strong wish or command (perhaps invitation) is full of paradox, with its entwined homophonic etymologies (*list*, v.) of desire and inclination. There is also a distinct if refined lexical nuance, as set out in *OED* 2: *listen*, v., is divided into sense 1a (transitive)...and sense 2a (intransitive)... These sense allocations are set very close; but the first bears towards 'pay

---

[26] Repr. in *Sonnet Series and Itinerary Poems, 1820–1845*, ed. Geoffrey Jackson (Ithaca: Cornell University Press, 2004), pp. 201–2.
[27] 'The Solitary Reaper', ll. 7–8.

attention with the ear strongly and intently, so as to receive the full import of what (someone or something) is to be heard'...whereas the second bears towards 'make an effort to hear what may be faint or indistinct, so as not to miss the sound of someone or something'.[28]

As we fall into the gaps that paradox and refined sense open up, we perhaps come closer to the type of aural sublimity Wordsworth explores here (and in 'On the Power of Sound', where he resorts to visual simile to suggest the possibility less suggestively: 'As if within thee dwelt a glancing Mind, | Organ of Vision'[29]). The Alfoxden Notebook lines also strain to communicate an aurally induced sublimity, hinting that there can be no aural equivalent of the visionary without the aural equivalent of a first sight (real or imaginative); that to listen in the transcendent sense Wordsworth wants to be able to articulate must be via an *implied* form of echo, or recapitulation, even if the implication is made through *actual* echoes and repetitions. In resting on implication, Wordsworth's lines begin to manage the challenge of expressing inexpressibility.

In 'There was a spot', 'And now' (l. 14) exploits the characteristic usage in which *and* is both supplement and alternative, and *now* suggests an immediate moment, and a narrative, diachronic movement within the description. This enhances the sense of tremendous fullness of experience which characterizes sublimity, which is also the real experience of visiting this familiar place, as far as Wordsworth is concerned. It is always this visit, and an amalgamation of all previous visits (and further, imaginative revisits). In a complementary way, through these double senses, 'And now' suggests both unique instance and habitual repetition, allowing Wordsworth to contain both specific and general experience in the poem simultaneously. Making sense of things, for Wordsworth, depends on an awareness and assessment of their relation to other things and experiences, as here, where he undergoes different experiences—recapitulations— of essentially the same phenomenon and place. The double conjunction 'And now' explicitly declares the centrality of connection, the relationship between different instances of the same thing, *to* the totality of the experience. If we replace Hegel's 'philosophy' with 'experience', it might be said that Wordsworth's accounts of remembered experience embrace the Hegelian sense that 'philosophy moves essentially in the element of universality, which includes within itself the particular'.[30] The compound sense of particular and general, intimately connected, characterizes experience of the world for Wordsworth. The capturing of it convincingly in verse thus results in 'sincere' poetry.

---

[28] J. H. Prynne, *Field Notes: 'The Solitary Reaper' and Others* (n.pub: Cambridge, 2007), p. 37.
[29] In *Last Poems* [1835 text], pp. 113–24 (ll. 2–3).
[30] Hegel, 'On Scientific Knowledge', p. 1 [para 1].

Recapitulation and the Unification of Specific and General

Wordsworth explicitly engages with the idea that recapitulation recognizes both similarity and difference in the 'Preface' to *Lyrical Ballads* which, despite its rejection of standard poetic conventions, identifies repetition as a fundamental part of poetic experience. The language really spoken by men of 'Low and rustic life' is 'a more permanent and a far more philosophical language than that which is frequently substituted for it by Poets', *because* it is 'a language arising out of repeated experience'.[31] The familiar words bear reiteration:

> For all good poetry is the spontaneous overflow of powerful feelings; but...our continued influxes of feeling are modified and directed by our thoughts, which are indeed the representatives of all our past feelings; and as by contemplating the relation of these general representatives to each other, we discover what is really important to men, so by the repetition and continuance of this act feelings connected with important subjects will be nourished...[32]

A process of continual return and rehearsal is here vital to poetry. Such repeated intellectual activity reveals a truth which is general, rather than particular: Wordsworth's footstamping, adamant insistence is that 'Poetry is the most philosophic of all writing: it is so: its object is truth, not individual and local, but general, and operative'.[33] Through the reference to an authoritative if slightly skewed Aristotelianism (Aristotle actually says that poetry is *more* philosophical than history, because it articulates the universal rather than the particular[34]), Wordsworth's attention to descriptive poetry's navigation between specificity and generality is brought to the fore. Hugh Sykes Davies finds the tension between specific and general to lie at the epicentre of Wordsworth's impulse to write, and to be the source of his originality:

> What distinguishes Wordsworth...is an intensity of personal experience, localised, individualised. And his problems as a writer...rise from the need to render not merely the general theme [i.e. the relation between Man and Nature], but also this personal intensity and individuality.[35]

Thomas De Quincey was engaging with this idea when, discussing Wordsworth's attention to 'an effect of *iteration*' in the context of species and individuals, and the significance of man's 'active' connection to those individuals, he observed that 'Most men look at nature in the hurry of a confusion that distinguishes nothing',

---

[31] 'Preface' to *Lyrical Ballads* [1800], p. 124.   [32] 'Preface' to *Lyrical Ballads* [1800], p. 126.
[33] 'Preface' to *Lyrical Ballads* [1850], p. 139.
[34] The relevant extract is from Chapter 9 of *Poetics*; see p. 16.   [35] Sykes Davies, p. 3.

whereas Wordsworth provides glimpses of 'novelty' which reveal 'truth'.[36] Both accounts suggest the vital importance of the *relationship* between specific and general, which renders repetition and conjunction some of the most powerful poetic tools Wordsworth employs.

Quite aside from the taunting of his contemporaries, Wordsworth's repetitions have not always been appreciated. Geoffrey Hartman, for instance, suggests that the 'sheltered and the sheltering grove' in the 1850 *Prelude* (I.69) might be read as an example of 'typical Wordsworthian verbosity'. Yet the power of repetition asserts itself despite Hartman's critical instincts, as he goes on to point out that 'The redundance, however, does suggest that whatever is happening here happens in more than one place...The locus doubles, redoubles: that two-fold agency which seems to center on the poet is active all around to the same incremental effect...The poet, in a sense, is only a single focus to something universally active.'[37] Even as he is sceptical of its value, Hartman's 'single' and 'universal' recognize that repetition calls into play the dynamic between specific and general. In his attitude towards the balance of the two, Wordsworth is strikingly close to Hegel, whose 'Preface' to *The Phenomenology of Spirit* criticizes the tendency of 'conventional opinion' to adhere to 'the antithesis of truth and falsity':

> It does not comprehend the diversity of philosophical systems as the progressive unfolding of truth, rather sees in it simple disagreements. The bud disappears in the bursting-forth of the blossom, and one might say that the former is refuted by the latter; similarly, when the fruit appears, the blossom is shown up in its turn as a false manifestation of the plant, and the fruit now emerges as the truth of it instead. These forms are not merely distinguished from one another, they also supplant one another as mutually incompatible. Yet at the same time their fluid nature makes them moments of an organic unity in which they not only do not conflict, but in which each is as necessary as the other; and this mutual necessity alone constitutes the life of the whole.[38]

For Wordsworth, different perceptions of events and experiences, altering over time (sometimes manifest in textual revisions) constitute 'the life of the whole', the entire body of his work, imagined as the complex cathedral. The poet's challenge is to represent, or at least acknowledge, differentiated versions of experience within the single text. Forms of repetition and recapitulation allow him to do exactly this.

---

[36] Thomas De Quincey, 'On Wordsworth's Poetry', in *The Works of Thomas De Quincey, Vol. 15: Articles from Blackwood's Edinburgh Magazine and Tait's Edinburgh Magazine, 1844–1846*, ed. Frederick Burwick (London: Pickering & Chatto 2003), pp. 223–42 (pp. 240–1).
[37] Geoffrey H. Hartman, *Wordsworth's Poetry 1787–1814* (New Haven: Yale University Press, 1964), p. 37.
[38] Hegel, 'On Scientific Knowledge', p. 2.

The lines in *The Prelude* beginning 'There was a Boy' are exemplary here, and have sustained multiple readings, focused on the complex connections made between nature, mind, and poetry; on the anxious self-consciousness revealed (it is argued) by Wordsworth as he re-works the passage, and on ideas about language acquisition and about education in its broadest sense. The putative identify of the halloing child (who might, but might not, be based on Wordsworth's owl-mimicking childhood acquaintance, William Raincock) has disrupted the smooth biographical placing of the text (though Wordsworth clearly encourages identification of poet with boy in the earliest version of the lines, a 1798 draft whose pronouns slip from third to first person[39]). Abstracted from *The Prelude*, in its original place in *Lyrical Ballads*, or in its re-situation as the first of the 1815 'Poems of the Imagination', it has been read variously as lyric, elegy, and quasi-epitaphic. Erica McAlpine has addressed the poem's revision as part of her interest in Wordsworth's mistakes.[40] Many of the key preoccupations of the episode as they have been identified by critics are reflected at least in part in Wordsworth's unsettled reworking and repositioning of the poem. As Susan Wolfson puts it,

> the process of revision is a compelling activity for Wordsworth, one whose several operations in his imagination produce an extended conversation among the various voices and versions of the self. His revisions, in effect, perpetuate the recollective activity in which the autobiography originates[.][41]

Alongside its participation in processes of revision, the Boy of Winander passage self-consciously evokes echoing, imitation, and repeated action:

> There was a Boy, ye knew him well, ye Cliffs
> And Islands of Winander! many a time
> At evening, when the stars had just begun
> To move along the edges of the hills,
> Rising or setting, would he stand alone
> Beneath the trees, or by the glimmering Lake
>
> (V.389–94)

---

[39] See the transcription of MSS JJ, in *The Prelude, 1798–1799*, ed. Parrish, pp. 86–7.

[40] See Erica McAlpine, 'Wordsworth's Imperfect Perfect', in *The Poet's Mistake* (Princeton, NJ: Princeton University Press, 2020), pp. 28–46. For one survey of twentieth-century approaches to the lines, see Steven Lukits, 'Wordsworth Unawares: The Boy of Winander, the Poet, and the Mariner', *Wordsworth Circle*, 19.3 (Summer 1988), 156–60 (p. 160, n. 3); Lukit's list predates significant accounts, including those in David Bromwich's *Disowned by Memory*, Wolfson's *Formal Charges*, and Pieter Vermeulen's 'The Suspension of Reading: Wordsworth's "Boy of Winander" and Trauma Theory', *Orbis Litterarum*, 62.6 (2007), 459–82.

[41] Wolfson, 'The Illusion of Mastery', p. 918.

As in 'There was a spot', opening 'There was' declares a strident moment of existence, a measurable, identifiable place in space and time; it is an instance of Cartesian confidence complicated but also confirmed by its position in the past. John Jones notes that '"To be", in Wordsworth, is the agent of primary meaning, not pointing forward in argument towards *ex post facto* synthesis, but bending back, like the growing child in the Immortality Ode, upon an entire experience';[42] to be is always both to be now, and to have become. Repetition through retellings and 'revisitings' in this account constitute present being. Such existential certainty is mirrored in the lines on the Boy of Winander, in the geographical particularity established by the topographical features which follow hard upon his heels: the boy was right *there*. But it also claims a far less fixed sense of existence in a fairy-tale dimension: 'There was' begins the stories which swirl in a vaguer past, wholly appropriate to the mythical world of 'Fortunatus' and 'Jack the Giant-Killer', both invoked as blessings which allow the 'precious gain' of self-forgetting in the lines preceding the boy's appearance (V.364–9). The passage opens with both versions of the boy present to its unfolding. The description begins by portraying his solitary 'standing' in this place, an apparently static posture, as already an act of repetition, performed 'many a time'. As the past tense of 'will', 'would' here claims this is something he routinely has been drawn (and *chosen*) to do; however, as the subjunctive of 'will', 'would' also introduces a sense of conditionality or mental indecision: memory, or other, imagined forms of experience are already subtly implicated in the record of the actual experience, through a touch of indecision which leaves the repetition of the scene open for variation.

As record of an actual, an imagined, or a memorial visit, the dominant idea lent by the lines is one of customary action, though the passage sustains a sense of the particular along with this suggestion of the general: 'at evening' lends some precision to the time of day, yet is simultaneously a vague and unfixed moment (evening's active 'ing' suffix implies passage and movement, rather than a particular point in time); the scene happens on 'many', therefore different, evenings. Similarly, that the 'stars had just begun | To move' (ll. 391–2) seems to root the description in a minutely observed moment, *just now*; but again, we quickly discover that this is a general and shifting celestial scene which, Wordsworth knows, moves laterally and vertically: the stars are 'Rising or setting' (l. 393), *or* fully exploiting its complex character to suggest individual stars in their extended motion, as well as multiple stars at different stages of their calculable astronomic journeys. Wordsworth is attentive to the passing of time; the specific not only accommodates, but also depends upon, different and other occasions. Charted, familiar, predictable: this is a specific, single moment in which the observing poet is comfortably aware of what always happens.

---

[42] Jones, p. 64.

Relatedly, the boy is 'Beneath the trees, or by the glimmering Lake': the careful conjunction here draws attention to different instances, whilst suggesting that a precise image is not really the aim, even though details matter (just as it matters what is going on in the London of Book VII, though the specifics are not the *point* of the description). Wordsworth is explicit that he is not a natural historian, bent on recording empirical fact: in one of the Fenwick notes, he refers to the works inspired in some part by his schoolmaster at Hawkshead (loosely transformed in Wordsworth's writings to 'Matthew'):

> poems connected with Matthew would not gain by a literal detail of facts. Like the Wanderer in the Excursion, this Schoolmaster was made up of several both of his class & men of other occupations. I do not ask for pardon for what there is of untruth in such verses, considered strictly as matters of fact. It is enough, if, being true & consistent in spirit, they move & teach in a manner not unworthy of a poet's calling.[43]

This assertion obliquely recognizes repetition which accommodates variation: Wordsworth's survey must ascertain the similarities between men, even as it acknowledges difference. In the Fenwick note, such a form of repetition is necessary to the making of biography and to the understanding of the growth of the poet's mind. It testifies to Wordsworth's sensitivity to that fact that repetition need not imply identical replication. It is an understanding of the mind dependent upon the forging of repeated synaptic pathways, which are then replicated both in compulsive 'revisitings', in Gill's sense, but also in the meticulous close texture of Wordsworth's verse. So, to return to the Boy of Winander, it is not possible or necessary to be sure whether the lake at one particular moment glimmers, or whether it always glimmers, or whether 'the trees' are so far from the lake that a visit to one cannot also be a visit to the other. *Or* here proposes that to wonder is not worthless, yet is not of central significance. The poem evokes a place which is also several places, depending on how we look, just as it is a particular moment, and several repeated moments, depending on when we look. It is a real memory, and also a constructed one. It is all of these things without contradiction; in this way the complex, layered apprehension which constitutes reality can best, or most *sincerely*, be translated into verse.

The next word in the Boy of Winander passage is another conjunction, as we see the boy move:

> And there, with fingers interwoven, both hands
> Press'd closely, palm to palm, and to his mouth

---

[43] *Fenwick Notes of William Wordsworth*, p. 38.

> Uplifted, he, as through an instrument,
> Blew mimic hootings to the silent owls
>
> (ll. 395–8)

'And there...' calls back to the introductory 'There was a boy', sharing the uncertainty of that opening deictic. *And* purports to introduce a particularized observation, apparently at odds with the optionality of *or* in the preceding line. Yet through the particular valency of *and*, it allows this also to be a conglomerate moment, piling on top of the detail of the forgoing passage. Such is exactly the effect Wordsworth requires: enabled by these different forms of repetition and conjunction, he delineates specific events which nonetheless articulate generalities.

To take the famous example from Johnson's *Rasselas*, it might seem that one cannot simultaneously be precise about the number of streaks on an individual tulip, *and* obliterate the particular in favour of the species. Yet repetition thus allows Wordsworth to accommodate specific and general in his writing, because his understanding of it allows, even encourages, the accommodation of difference within similitude; his appreciation of the operation of connection allows those differences to maintain a significant degree of unity. In the 'Preface' to *Lyrical Ballads*, Wordsworth adverts to 'the pleasure which the mind derives from the perception of similitude in dissimilitude', and argues that 'upon the accuracy with which similitude in dissimilitude, and dissimilitude in similitude are perceived, depend our taste and our moral feelings.'[44] This alertness to the possibilities held within forms of repetition with difference was ridiculed by contemporaries. Brian Bates finds one example of such mockery in Reynolds's 'disparaging of Wordsworth's idea of similitude in dissimilitude' when he 'portrays Wordsworth asserting the "value" of...repetition not as self-plagiarism but as original labor; in fact, the mock Wordsworth suggests that their value only increases.'[45] Reynolds's play with Wordsworth's attitudes is clever and funny, but its mockery misunderstands the serious grounds of Wordsworth's contention. Understood properly, the holding together of similarity and difference within repetition is vital to Wordsworth's struggle to articulate 'sincerely'. The 'Ode: Intimations of Immortality' is exactly preoccupied with the knowledge of repetition and change.[46] In his expression of a refined and particular form of nostalgia, Wordsworth is aware that his perception of the nature of things (rather than the things themselves) has undergone transformation: 'It is not now as it has been of yore' (l. 6). This realization is something which itself strikes with a repetitive motion. Wordsworth's interest is in the loss of affective experience: 'there hath pass'd away a glory from the earth' (l. 18). But it is figured through attention to a

---

[44] 'Preface' to *Lyrical Ballads* [1800], p. 148.   [45] Bates, 'J. H. Reynolds', p. 283.
[46] Repr. In *Poems, in Two Volumes, and Other Poems, 1800–1807*, pp. 269–77.

real world which *nonetheless* continues to repeat both itself (lambs still bound; birds still sing) and its own story of loss: 'The Pansy at my feet | Doth the same tale repeat' (ll. 54–5). The formal properties of the Ode require the repetitions (structural, rhythmic, and rhymic) which demonstrate on the page the type of memory and forgetting which consumes the poet: the satisfaction of 'embers' in 'remembers' for example (ll. 132–4) is a perfect representation of the idea of a repetition which glows back into life, yet does not flame, in its recapitulation. The 'Child of Joy' of the poem's third stanza recalls the Boy of Winander as his jubilant voice is redoubled. Yet Wordsworth entreats an encircling in sound which is less a reply to his imperative call, than a recapitulative echo, travelling round rather than to the poet, mimicked by the line's densely clustered phonics: 'Shout round me, let me hear thy shouts, thou happy Shepherd Boy' (ll. 33–4). Where the Boy of Winander hoots 'to' the owls, and they are 'Responsive' to him (ll. 398–401), in the 'Ode', Wordsworth seems preserved from full, immediate participation in the acoustic and visual scene which surrounds him. And yet the poem ends defiantly, with the proclamation that there is no 'severing of our loves' (l. 191); the 'remember[ing]' (l. 134) and the 'recollections' (l. 152) of prior experience inform and constitute part of present experience. In combination, past and present can inspire 'love' (l. 195), and profundity: 'Thoughts that do often lie too deep for tears' (l. 206).

Whilst, then, it might intuitively seem that one cannot be precise about particularities, *and* obliterate the particular in favour of the general, what allows both to co-exist (and for their coexistence to constitute the reality of experience), is the appreciation of their relationship to, and connection with, one another. Because its preoccupation is with the organization and effect of words, poetry can perform the experience of repetition which is central to lived experience, whether or not it actually depicts it in a semantic sense. Repetition alone might simply be clumsy or dull; ideas of conjunction are thus intimately necessary to articulate relationships between instances. John Jones argues that critical interest in the way in which Romantic poets aimed to express unity has 'obscured the structure of distinct but related things' in Wordsworth's verse.[47] Looking back in *The Prelude*, Wordsworth finds the sublime inspiration of his childhood in

> gentle agitations of the mind
> From manifold distinctions, difference
> Perceived in things where to the common eye
> No difference is
>
> (II.317–20)

---

[47] Jones, p. 33.

Rehearsing ideas contained within the 'Preface', the lines establish a vital role for the poet in perceiving and communicating the 'structure' Jones identifies. The same sentiment is found in lines which eventually found a place in *The Excursion*:

> While yet a Child...
> He had perceived the presence and the power
> Of greatness; and deep feelings had impress'd
> Great objects on his mind, with portraiture
> And colour so distinct...
> Even in their fix'd and steady lineaments
> He traced an ebbing and a flowing mind,
> Expression ever varying![48]

'I look'd for universal things', Wordsworth declared in 1805, 'perused | The common countenance of earth and heaven' (III.110-11). In a letter to Lady Beaumont of 1806, he insisted that 'the mind can have no rest among a multitude of objects, of which it either cannot make one whole, or from which it cannot single out one individual, whereupon may be concentrated the attention divided among or distracted by a multitude'.[49] Eight years later, in the 'Essay, Supplementary to the Preface', he declared that 'In nature, everything is distinct, but nothing defined into absolute independent singleness'.[50] For Wordsworth, the subtle negotiation between the specific and the general is the pivot on which poetic perception rests.

In his depictions of his relationship with his sister, and the anxiety he experienced in London, Wordsworth understands the ability to grasp connection as central to the possibility of being 'steadied'. I have suggested that the handling of repetition and conjunction, both conceptually and literally, is important to his capacity to manage those experiences into verse. In *Home at Grasmere*, Wordsworth contrasts the community of his retirement with the 'vast Metropolis', 'Where numbers overwhelm humanity, | And neighbourhood serves rather to divide | Than to unite' (*Home at Grasmere*, ll. 597-601): urban difference is profoundly problematic. Grasmere is, by contrast, 'A Whole without dependence or defect, | Made for itself and happy in itself, | Perfect Contentment, Unity entire.' (*Home at Grasmere*, ll. 149-51). This assertion of unity is enhanced as it is enacted by the effects of poetic language: in this new Eden, Wordsworth asks,

> What want we? Have we not perpetual streams,
> Warm woods and sunny hills, and fresh green fields,

---

[48] *The Excursion*, I.150-79.
[49] W[illiam] W[ordsworth] to Lady Beaumont, 21 May 1807, in *Letters*, ii, 145-51 (p. 148).
[50] *Prose*, i, 77.

> And mountains not less green, and flocks and herds,
> And thickets full of songsters, and the voice
> Of lordly birds—an unexpected sound
> Heard now and then from morn till latest eve
>
> (*Home at Grasmere*, ll. 126–31)

As they co-exist with 'herds' amongst green fields and mountains, the initial assumption is that Wordsworth's 'flocks' (l. 128) are of sheep. But through the repetition of the 'erd' sound, they begin to transform into fowl, as 'songsters' are introduced in the following line, fully to emerge *as* 'birds' (the rhyme with 'herds' now realized, albeit displaced from the line-ending) in the next. Blank verse encourages such play with rhyme sounds because the ear cannot fully relinquish the expectation of repeated sound, despite the ostensible renunciation of it in conventional terms. Wordsworth winks at this formally displaced moment of rhyme as he notes the presence of 'an unexpected sound', just at the moment in which we hear the herds/birds rhyme formally satisfied. The 'unexpected sound' is therefore also one which is (as the enjambment describes) literally 'Heard now' ('Heard' repeating 'herd' from earlier in the poem), definitively refigured as pertaining to the avian life of the Lakes, *and* the poet's perception of that life. Such aural repetitions work actively through the rhyming words, not 'just' rhyming, but also challenging the reader to pay attention to make sense, and they are complemented by other moments of repetition in the lines: the alliterative binding of the opening question which is re-established in the line immediately below, and the polysyndetic itemization of the natural features which issue forth in the poem, which themselves are woven together through the repetition which marks their description. The full repetition of 'green' is reinforced by the rhyme of the words which characterize the greenness, 'fresh' and 'less', and even at the moment of gentle surprise in the poem (the 'unexpected sound'), the poem's structure preserves a sense of control though the balance of its ideas: the sound is 'Heard **now** and **then** from **morn** till latest **eve**', a pair of oppositions which lends a sense of reassuring enclosure, and which in microcosmic form mimics the encompassing safety offered by the circumscribed space of the vale. Repetitions like this create in the text the connections the vale's real unity requires and exhibits.

Beyond the minute texture of his verse, Wordsworth's work is full of repeated action. Repetition itself lends events significance, whether it occurs through the strikingly similar aspects of shocking or misfortunate circumstances in which Wordsworth recalls finding himself, or through affection formed by simple habit (by 'pleasure and repeated happiness, | So frequently repeated', 1850, I.633–4). *The Prelude* asserts that 'each man is a memory to himself' (III.189), finding meaning in the revisiting of and dwelling upon significant moments. Newlyn asserts that, 'Repeated throughout childhood, Wordsworthian memories make up a private associative language whose significance is realized only in retrospect...our sense of the narrator's empathy and responsibility is intensified by this awareness of the passage of time, and the reflective distance it brings.'[51] (And, we might add, intensified still further by the repeated reflection upon them *as* that time passes.) This for Wordsworth offers evidence of the possibility of 'human progress'.[52] To read across a range of Wordsworth's critics is to find numerous subtle connections between different poems, and different extracts of the same poem, being drawn. Wordsworth habitually returns to the same specific events not only at different times, but also in different poems: one might point most obviously to way that various aspects of Wordsworth's early life, including the profoundly significant 'spot of time' in which he waits for the horses in Book XI of the 1805 *Prelude* (ll. 345 ff.), had already been explored in 'The Vale of Esthwaite' (1787), itself a poem which suggestively exploits repetition in order to draw parallels between the imagination of the generic minstrel of the text, and Wordsworth's own.[53] Duncan Wu discusses the significance of the way that the 'rough and stony moor' in the 'visionary dreariness' passage within the two-part *Prelude* (I.296 ff.) 'closely parallels the "heap of garments" in the preceding episode' (in which the dead man shockingly rises from the water of the lake).[54] Isobel Armstrong demonstrates that the boat-stealing episode in *The Prelude* adapts and reorders the vocabulary of the woodcock-springing:

> The 'eternity of thought' reorders, conflates and abstracts these earlier passages and gives them breath and motion as new forms and images of themselves ... The echoes of the horror of the earlier passages are 'not unnoticed', assimilated but alien (the double negative suggests their subliminal presence), constantly present in the joy of the redeveloped moment which contains their histories within itself.[55]

Hugh Sykes Davies devotes a whole section of *Wordsworth and the Worth of Words* to chasing down clusters of ideas which recall one another across different texts. Examples proliferate, and we might find a quasi-biblical typology in the connections between different episodes which are thus asserted (a way of reading cultivated by the same *Lectures* in which Lowth had asserted the vital significance of verbal repetition to Hebrew poetry).

The effect is intimately related to the notion of 'spots of time' expounded in Book 11 of *The Prelude*. A 'spot' is an isolated, independent point, 'distinct', in Wordsworth's terms (XI.258–9). Yet in formulating them 'of time', and in

---

[51] 'The noble living and the noble dead', pp. 64–5.
[52] 'The noble living and the noble dead', p. 67.
[53] See for example Jack Vespa, 'Veiled Movements in "The Vale of Esthwaite"', *Wordsworth Circle*, 45.1 (Winter 2014), 62–5, *passim,* https://www.jstor.org/stable/24044362, accessed 2 June 2022.
[54] Wu, 'Tautology and Imaginative Vision' (not paginated).
[55] *Language as Living Form*, pp. 40–1.

attributing to them a 'renovating virtue' (l. 260) when 'memory' operates to recall moments 'in which | We have had deepest feeling that the mind | Is lord and master, and that outward sense | Is but the obedient servant of her will' (l. 278; ll. 270–3), Wordsworth identifies the specific significance of each 'moment' *within* a larger compilation of 'passages of life', 'scatter'd everywhere' in the past (ll. 270–5). The specific spot only gains full significance within the general context of such spots in their multiplicity. In the 1815 'Preface' to Wordsworth's *Poems*, Wordsworth wrote:

> The Imagination also shapes and *creates*; and how? By innumerable processes; and in none does it more delight than in that of consolidating numbers into unity, and dissolving and separating unity into number.

In the same year, in the 'Essay, Supplementary to the Preface', he declared as we have already seen that 'In nature every thing is distinct, yet nothing defined into absolute independent singleness.'[56] In these examples, Wordsworth is theorizing the relationship between the particular and the general, but he stops short of *explaining* the mechanics of the dynamic. In his reading of the Boy of Winander passage, Paul de Man finds 'the transformation of an echo language into a language of the imagination by way of the mediation of a poetic understanding of mutability'.[57] Perhaps in a '*poetic* understanding of mutability', the effects of the text, rather than the straightforward assertions of its content, articulate both change and difference, specific and general, and indicate their relationship. Certainly, poetic repetition involves and enacts a process of change which can function in exactly this way.

But beside the grander-scale repetition of episodes, events *perceived as* repetitions, and more explicitly totemic moments, Wordsworth's body of verse also demonstrates the assembly of memory through more mundane activity and feeling. The poet's work is shot through with the evocation of habit, and the necessary repetitions of quotidian life and favoured pastimes: of visiting a particular place, taking a particular walk, playing a particular game, or going back to familiar books:

> Returning at the holidays, I found
> That golden store of books which I had left,
> Open to my enjoyment once again
> ...Full often through the course
> Of those glad respites in the summer time
> ...I have lain

---

[56] *Prose*, i, 77.   [57] De Man, *The Rhetoric of Romanticism*, p. 54.

> Down by thy side, O Derwent! murmuring Stream,
> On the hot stones and in the glaring sun,
> And there have read...
> Till, with a sudden bound of smart reproach...
> I to my sport betook myself again.
>
> (V.502 ff.)

Opening in the continuous present (and thus immediately resisting the impression of a single, fixed event), and beginning with 'Returning', itself part of the verbal field of recapitulation, this passage is exemplary of the way in which the elements of the past which Wordsworth selects as significant and necessary to the text of *The Prelude* dramatize routine and return. In describing the competing pull between two customary sources of boyish delight, reading and fishing, the resumption of both is described as happening 'again'; this in turn is something which happens 'full often'; the effect is not only of repeated pursuits but also of a vacillation between them which is itself so habitual that the final verb here, 'betook', referring to the resumption of the sport, almost hastens over itself to sound as the 'book' Wordsworth must put down in order to resume. The oscillation between two repeated activities elides them into one singular repeated event which encapsulates 'that time' (l. 482), the past. Specific and general acts retain separateness: Wordsworth remembers both fishing and reading by the river. Yet they merge together through assertion and through the operation (both in the text and the life it describes) of repetition. The repetition portrayed and enacted in the passage performs the unifying action Wordsworth attributes elsewhere to the perfection of the Vale of Grasmere: the specific and the general are both simultaneously present in the verse. Detail is cherished because of this capacity.

Wordsworth frequently reverts to memories such as his reading and fishing: to those 'delights' which 'were sought insatiably' in younger days, which were 'a transport of the outward sense, | Not of the mind, vivid but not profound' (XI.186–9). Book 11 of *The Prelude*, for instance, exploits a repetitious structure (itself borrowed from elsewhere within his own corpus of work[58]), depicting a time when he was 'greedy in the chace, | And roam'd from hill to hill, from rock to rock', to introduce his own 'craving' for 'combinations of new forms' (ll. 190–2). Even here, that is, in recalling these apparently more trivial episodes, he retains a strong awareness that individual moments or pleasures ultimately make sense as aspects of a more general and organized amalgamation (in the same way that we are to understand the individual 'hill's and 'rock's as specific and particular, even whilst in this context of memorialization, the repetition of the nouns makes them inevitably general). A similar effect is engendered when Wordsworth outlines his

---

[58] See the Norton edition, ed. Wordsworth, Abrams, and Gill, p. 426, n. 9.

response to 'those few nooks to which my happy feet | Were limited', being 'with the gift | Of all this glory fill'd and satisfied', in the very next lines finding space for an experience both identical and translated: 'And afterwards, when through the gorgeous Alps | Roaming, I carried with me the same heart' (XI.229–42): the affective response, the 'heart', remains constant, despite the bodily movement of the person (also figured most potently by 'heart' here: the word does a typically double job) to a different landscape and a different set of experiences, a translation heightened for the reader by the metrical wrench on 'Roaming'. Such connections mimic the structural relationship (figured through the image of the cathedral) which Wordsworth claims for the entire corpus of his works.

In all of these examples, memory is a crucial part of immediate experience. Yet as well as being aware of the changes in his own perspective which necessitate revisions of his works, Wordsworth is attentive to the fact that his remembrances are personal, and that others might remember differently. He faces the consequential effect of encountering the (mis)remembering (or misrepresenting) of others, when he is confronted with the theatrical version of the 'Maid of Buttermere' in Book VII of *The Prelude*. But he openly admits his own deliberate construction of fake memories when he addresses the place of Coleridge, his addressee, in his biographical poem:

> O Friend! we had not seen thee at that time;
> And yet a power is on me and a strong
> Confusion, and I seem to plant Thee there.
>
> (VI.246–8)

Through a passage sticky with repetition, Wordsworth writes Coleridge into a past he was never really part of:

> But Thou are with us, with us in the past,
> The present, with us in the times to come...
>
> (ll. 251–2)

Such syntactic repetition insists; it enacts the deliberateness with which Wordsworth wants to believe he is convinced of Coleridge's place in his life. If straightforwardly part of a list, we might expect a precedent 'and' before 'The present'; or, in the interests of balance, we might expect 'with us in' to be repeated there, just as it is before 'the past' and 'the times to come'. The slight awkwardness here thus derives from the refusal of repetition, but it is engaging: it sounds as if the present is to offer something different, when in fact it is the only time Wordsworth can be certain of Coleridge's real accompaniment. Sitting outside the structure of repetition which marks the rest of the sentiment, it offers a kind of misdirection, or *almost* mis-stepping, similar in nature to the kind Ricks identifies in Wordsworth's manipulation of line-endings. Wordsworth makes us imagine an alternative, whose correction enforces Coleridge's presence even more strongly. Here, where the repetition is of something imaginary (Coleridge's presence), textual effects go so far as to make it real. Memory bears an important role in this context of recapitulation, but it turns out that memory can be created by the poetic imagination. And indeed, to an extent, Wordsworth's lines here recall his friend's work on the secondary imagination, which 'dissolves, diffuses, dissipates... yet still at all events it struggles to idealize and to unify',[59] and his earlier claim that 'The dim intellect sees an absolute oneness, the perfectly clear intellect *knowingly perceives* it. Distinction and plurality lie in the betwixt.'[60] The negotiation between specific and general echoes the situation of the poet, swimming in 'the betwixt', and charting a path through it which is as sincere as possible to that experience in order to reach the unity of 'oneness'. In their capacity to contain difference within similarity the repetitions within Wordsworth's poetry facilitate the expression of the specific and the general in the same moment, allowing the articulation of 'truth', or truth to experience, which always encompasses and includes both, and whose poetic representation therefore *requires* both, simultaneously.

---

[59] *Biographia Literaria*, i, 304.
[60] Note dated 1803, in *Anima Poetæ: From the Unpublished Note-books of Samuel Taylor Coleridge*, ed. Ernest Hartley Coleridge (London: William Heinemann, 1895), p. 53.

11
Echo and Response

Echo

Echo is a form of repetition to which Wordsworth has 'an exceptional alertness'.[1] Rhyme and many other poetic devices depend on echoes being heard in the reader's ear or mind: sound must come back, albeit transferred, for such effects to function. To echo in a text might equally be to make a literary allusion. But Wordsworth's imagination is frequently caught by more literal echoes: the question which is the impetus of 'Stepping Westward'; the 'mountain echoes' of the boat-stealing passage, the resounding soundscape of the ice skating episode, and the lines on the Boy of Winander and the owls, dense with call and response, in *The Prelude*. Wordsworth's evocations of the distorted reflection and return of echo remind us that 'far from being a fixed given, emitted from an object and correspondingly heard, sound depends on a carrying medium which can deflect and change it.'[2] In straightforward terms, echo keeps repeating the same content; it has nothing new to say. In this regard, it is like Socrates's words, which seem to 'understand what they are saying, but if you ask them what they mean by anything they simply return the same answer over and over again.'[3] Francis Bacon assures us that Echo

> is the true philosophy which echoes most faithfully the voices of the world itself, and is written as it were at the world's own dictation, being nothing else than the image and reflection thereof, to which it adds nothing of its own, but only iterates and gives it back.[4]

Bacon's Echo is a philosopher-poet, almost a reiterative 'witness' in the Wordsworthian sense, through her mimetic artistry. Absent here, though, is the Romantic requirement for the mind or will of the poet to inflect what is returned. And echo does contain change within it, both in that it shares the character of repetition more generally (the fact of its being an echo makes the sound inherently *different* to the original), but also as it scatters sound spatially, detaching it from its

---

[1] McDonald, p. 90. On echo and literature generally, see Hollander, *The Figure of Echo*.
[2] *Hearing Things*, p. 4.
[3] See Plato, *Phaedrus & Letters VII and VIII*, trans. Walter Hamilton (Harmondsworth: Penguin, 1973), p. 97.
[4] Francis Bacon, *De Dignitate et augmentis scientarum*, cited in Hollander, *The Figure of Echo*, p. 10.

origin in order to suggest another source, or multiple sources. Insofar as it degrades as it proceeds, echo also ultimately enacts depletion, fading to nothing, thus offering the opposite of the strident reinforcement repetition elsewhere declares: reiterated injunction, for example, might tend to rouse rather than to die away.[5] Echo's reflection back is, moreover, inflected by the surfaces which act as acoustic mirrors, so, in a very literal way it can populate an empty landscape with multiple unembodied voices (like the 'Answers and we know not whence' heard in Wordsworth's 'Yes! full surely 'twas the Echo'[6]). Caught up mythologically with an idea of frustration, Echo is not only unable to control the content of her responses; she cannot *not* reply: the idea of will is thus complicated, and Wordsworth's fascination with echo often raises the complex questions of originality which inhere within it. In the pursuit of self-reflection, Wordsworth's desire for sincerity leads him to try to avoid becoming merely an echo chamber (though the poet remains aware that, as Hollander puts it, if he 'demythologises or at any rate degothicises his mountain echo, it is to reconstruct the world of aerial spirits inhabiting concavities, "correspondent breezes", in some inner psychic space.'[7]) The combination of repetition with variation which constitutes echo and the various characteristics which attach to it find parallels in Wordsworth's wider preoccupation with recapitulation and change.

When we first encounter the Boy of Winander in *The Prelude*, his behaviour seems to exhibit simple delight, until the failure of the soundscape to offer an anticipated repetition renders it far more meaningful, and the reader is forced to recognize that he was always partly a symbol:

> There was a Boy, ye knew him well, ye Cliffs
> And Islands of Winander! many a time
> At evening, when the stars had just begun
> To move along the edges of the hills,
> Rising or setting, would he stand alone,
> Beneath the trees, or by the glimmering Lake,
> And there, with fingers interwoven, both hands
> Press'd closely, palm to palm, and to his mouth
> Uplifted, he, as through an instrument,
> Blew mimic hootings to the silent owls
> That they might answer him.
>
> (V.389–99)

---

[5] See for example Wolfson's reading of Blake: following a repetitive verbal and syntactic form, 'Blake turns the couplet charge of the final lines in this slightly expanded sonnet into a repetition that exceeds the semantic linkage of a couplet.' (*Formal Charges*, p. 61.)

[6] In *Poems, in Two Volumes, and Other Poems, 1800–1807*, pp. 255–6.

[7] *Images of Voice*, p. 27.

The boy has a solipsistic existence beyond the penetration of the poem, hinted at here in the suggestion of his will (through 'would'), and the inferences towards this being just one of many actions (which inevitably fall outside the frame of the passage); but, naturally, he exists for the reader only through the perception of him by the poet, and we see him only through the text of the poem which reflects him, standing there. The lines thus achieve descriptively even as they betray the fiction of mimesis, and consequently light the 'lamp' of Abrams's simile (itself borrowed from Yeats);[8] a repetition in a mirror shows us something exact, and complete in that exactness, but it only shows one plane. Wordsworth's poem is self-aware in its attitude to this. In the ways these lines exploit ideas of repetition and conjunction, they demonstrate sensitivity to this predicament of artistic partiality, and begin to transcend it. The interest in repetition is epitomized in the boy's posture. As he stands with 'hands | Press'd closely, palm to palm' (V.395–6), his position performs a self-mirroring which imitates the poem's technique. We might here find Wordsworth seeing himself in the boy, *and* knowing that the original boy was not him, *and* recognizing that even if the boy was him then, he is not the same person now, and thus conflicted over whether or not the descriptive passage is directly autobiographical, or only so in its contribution to the formation of his mind. The attention in the passage to ideas of reflection refuses to allow the boy ever simply to 'be', or to be Wordsworth, but this is the opposite of failure: it is entirely appropriate to the nature of experience as Wordsworth understands it.

Despite his declared solitude (emphasized, like other instances of solitariness in the poem, by its place at the end of the line[9]), the Boy of Winander is not the lonely Wordsworthian figure of A. C. Bradley's construal.[10] Another example of literal repetition breaks down his solitude into community with the owls he repeats, and who repeat him, in an instinct of 'Responsive' (l. 401) and joyous intimacy. The child's physical motion, his lifting of his hands to his mouth in order to make a hooting noise, leads Wordsworth to begin line 397 'Uplifted'; with this word, the poem registers simultaneously the rising mood of the observing poet and the sense of joy Wordsworth injects into an already glittering scene. Such asserted delight colours the subsequent experience of the hooting boy, in an episode marked by multiple repetitions:

>   —And they would shout
> Across the watry Vale, and shout again,
> Responsive to his call, with quivering peals,

---

[8] See W. B. Yeats, 'Introduction' to the *Oxford Book of Modern Verse* (Oxford: Oxford University Press, 1936), v–xlii (p. xxxiii).
[9] See for example Bk I, l. 300; l. 322; l. 347; l. 379; see also l. 373.
[10] See A. C. Bradley, *Oxford Lectures on Poetry* (London: Macmillan, 1909), p. 142.

> And long halloos, and screams, and echoes loud
> Redoubled and redoubled; concourse wild
> Of mirth and jocund din! And when it chanced
> That pauses of deep silence mock'd his skill,
> Then sometimes in that silence, while he hung
> Listening, a gentle shock of mild surprize
> Has carried far into his heart the voice
> Of mountain torrents, or the visible scene
> Would enter unawares into his mind
> With all its solemn imagery, its rocks,
> Its woods, and that uncertain Heaven, receiv'd
> Into the bosom of the steady Lake.
>
> (V.398–413)

This is the diagnosis Wordsworth makes in the 'Note' to 'The Thorn', the response of the mind which 'luxuriates in the repetition of words which appear successfully to communicate its feelings'.[11] As Alan Bewell argues, the pleasure which 'incites the old sailor to repeat his tale' in 'The Thorn' is cognate with the pleasure of the boy here, as each echo sets up 'a pattern of anticipation and response'.[12] The frustration of redundant repetition is totally absent. Instead, the acute condition of paying attention as the boy waits for the expected answer initiates a state of mind conducive to intense experience. Crucially, there is no real beginning to the pattern of expectation and reply; obviously, the lines must begin somewhere, but the poem escapes the impasse that the idea of originality inflicts on mutual relationship through its claims to Platonic privilege. The boy's primary sound is introduced as already a repetition of the owls' own call; his are 'mimic hootings'. Yet the owls are expressly 'silent' when they are first introduced: their hoots are thus copies of the boy's sound in the poem (*if* they do come: 'might' and 'would' nod to the possibility of non-appearance later to be dwelt upon as the poem again charts and sustains by implication multiple possibilities at once, though of course, in the poem, the ear is subsequently struck by the volley of their calls). A chicken-and-egg puzzle, an echo-which-refuses-to-be-an-echo, their community reaches back beyond the known time of the poem: 'There was a boy', and also always other, previous boys, other shared experiences. Repetition and echo here are indistinguishable to the reader: did the owls shout with 'echoes loud' which they themselves 'Redoubled and redoubled', or were the echoes given back independently from the landscape? Perhaps both are true.

---

[11] See 'Note' to 'The Thorn', p. 351.
[12] Bewell, p. 209. For Bewell, through the attention of the passage to the hooting boy's repetitive attempts 'to articulate sounds ... this episode also contributes to a hypothetical history of the process by which the child is ushered into language' (Bewell, p. 209).

The visual apprehension of the landscape here is also ultimately one of reflection, though we are not aware of this until we have already imagined it: only after its description is 'the visible scene' given to us as received 'Into the bosom of the steady Lake', that is, reflected back from the surface of the water which provides a metaphor for the 'mind' of line 410. Thus, this highly specific moment in the poem is in layered ways mapped onto multiple general moments, and the response onto different *types* of response; the particular instance must be aware of prior instances in order to understand and explain the relationship of echo or reflection alluded to. Repetition accommodates variation, both particularly (in each hoot, in each instance of the boy's calling to the owls) and in the general truth that the boy goes and calls to the owls often, and that they might or might not respond to him. But the idea, the event, the story, the singular sense that 'There was a boy', combines all of these possibilities (real or imagined) into a cohesive unity. The boy's, the poet's, and the reader's grasp of the 'gentle shock of mild surprize', the central affective content of the poem, depends on the familiar *and* the variation from it. For the poem to be written, it is for Wordsworth to choose the lineaments of *this* occurrence of it. Declaring that the boy 'might' elicit a response of music, the poem recognizes that he might not; as in the previous use of 'would', the element of the poem which is unsure pushes up against a suggestion of godlike poetic power (of might and will). Yet to be sincere, the poem must remain attentive to these multiple levels of experience and the complexity of combining them into a unified moment which communicates the 'gentle shock', even as it performs that unification, and only in doing so may it remain both specifically and generally 'true'. As the poems bursts into its exhilarated owl song, the *and*s in the passage further contribute to this effect: they certainly add more detail, being suggestive of increasing specificity, but they are always also open to the possibility that the scene being described is actually a composite of different occasions which are connected. In Wordsworth's looking back upon it, the scene is rendered both as a specific and a general recollection, in which repetitions and conjunctions assist the communication of the sense of 'many at the same time'.

For all its noisiness, this passage is interested in listening as much as in sound: the boy listens for the birds; the owls listen for the boy, who has previously listened to them; the sounds almost listen to themselves in the idea of echo, and then of the 'mock'ing silence; the boy listens to silence, and then to the landscape (his first sensory response after the shock is to *hear* the mountain torrents). Significance is thus lent to the posture of listening. As the reader hears imaginatively (even read aloud in the most dramatic or expressive way possible, a faithful reading does not mimic the 'concourse'; it can only describe it), he or she shares the posture of the boy. It is therefore entirely appropriate that the *and*s in this passage begin both sentences and lines, so that the two become blurred; the reader must listen *harder*, and pay attention, and is rewarded for doing so: '[A]nd long halloos', for example, *is* 'surprizing', because we might have assumed they had stopped. Moreover, as

McDonald suggests, the literal repetitions in the poem 'facilitate a degree of attention in which the reader, like the poet, hears things twice, as both "influx" and "reflux".'[13] The poem mimics the experience of the boy and of the poet as it describes it, and the reader shares that experience with each reading. (Relatedly, the second sonnet 'On the Inside of King's College Chapel, Cambridge' implores: 'from the arms of silence—list! O list! | The music bursteth into second life— | The notes luxuriate—every stone is kiss'd | By sound, or ghost of sound, in mazy strife'.[14] This suggests the difficulty of discriminating 'sound' from 'the ghost of sound' which the chapel's acoustic provokes; in this way, it is always already echoic. Instead, it is really the listener who becomes the source of repetition through the repeated imperative, 'list! O list!': straining to catch the sound, they become in one sense its origin.)

Upon the boy's call, the owls reply. He adopts their hooting language; they in turn repeat him/themselves in notably human tones: they shout, 'and shout again'. These 'echoes' are 'Redoubled and redoubled': this is an intense repetition within the poem itself which precedes a moment of true community through the vocal concert, a 'concourse wild | Of mirth and jocund din'. The explicit depiction of repeated sound is figured through a playful passage: in an unrhymed poem, the word 'loud' on the end of the line calls stridently back as it discovers the same vowel sound in the line-ending three lines above ('shout'), which in turn calls back to the line-ending three lines above that ('mouth'). The rebellious rhyme in a blank verse setting is reinforced by the semantic connection it declares (mouth-shout-loud). 'Loud' registers loudest, as the rhyming sequence is buttressed en route; 'shout' has been reinforced by its repetition (in the explicitly repetitive context of 'shout again') in the interim. This emphasis of the [aʊ] sounds is co-opted, as the soundscape builds in intensity through the polysyndeton of the sentence, which through the utility of *and* suggests both accumulation and sequence. It also invokes the idea of echo's repetition with variation, as following its emphasis in 'mouth-shout-shout-loud', the [aʊ] is tugged in multiple directions in a single line: 'redoubled' (itself reiterated) contains the visual echo of 'loud', but does not rhyme with it; the next word, 'concourse' also rhymes visually but not aurally.

These strata of repetitious effects operate similarly to the way in which, Stephen Booth and Jonathan Culler have argued, nonsense poems can appear meaningful: such effects confer an 'ability to let us understand something that does not make sense as if it *did* make sense.'[15] Noticing Wordsworth's minute repetitions and dissonances and assimilating them as if they were reconciled into the perfect rhyme we might on some deep level expect, as if there were no disruption,

---

[13] McDonald, p. 91.   [14] Repr. in *Sonnet Series and Itinerary Poems, 1820–1845*, pp. 202–3.
[15] Culler, p. 184.

operates like the rhyme of nursery poems, which mutes the illogicality of semantic content. Culler asserts the profound potential of such effects:

> The poem, in giving us an impression of the rightness of what we don't understand, the sense that we control what we don't understand, has 'the ability,' [Booth] writes, 'to free us from the limits of the human mind,' in, I would add, a miniature version of the sublime, to which rhythm, along with other forms of repetition, energetically ministers.[16]

A kind of unintelligible collocation of difference (nonsense in the nursery rhyme; different sounds in Wordsworth's poem) is reconciled through its simultaneous similarity (in Wordsworth's poem, the eye-rhymes which sit amongst a multi-layered reflection on repetition itself). Wordsworth's manipulation of repetition with variation perhaps achieves just the form of sublimity Culler here identifies, as it appeals to the mind's sense of exact repetition, refuses it (and even highlights that refusal), and yet moves on, in a moment of microcosmic sublimity which mimics the boy's delight just as it mimics his 'mimic hootings'. On top of these subtle but powerful textual effects, in the Boy of Winander passage, repetition, which intuitively might suggest dull predictability, does not preclude the possibility of the astonishment necessary for the experience of the sublime; indeed, in this passage, it is perfectly conducive to it. The significance of the recollection pivots on the oxymoronic sublimity of the 'gentle shock of mild surprise' which the boy experiences when the owls do *not* respond. This typically has been read as an example of when 'an anxiously desired event takes an abrupt...turn into the unexpected', characteristic of the spots of time through *The Prelude*.[17] But here, the silence *is* expected by the poet, and by the waiting boy; it is one aspect of a known and familiar repetition of a familiar scene whose central interest is precisely layered acts of repetition. This in turn is reflected as the poem moves on to contain its other repetitions.

As Book V of *The Prelude* turns away from the vitality of the lakeside concert to incorporate the death of the Boy, its attention to repetition, and particularly its relationship to connection, continues. The taphophilic pilgrimage to the churchyard where 'oftentimes | A full half-hour together I have stood | Mute—looking at the Grave in which he lies' (V.420–2) is a record of *repeated* visits. Repetition functions also at the textual level in the way the lines catch up words and images from earlier in the passage: the 'watry vale' comes back in 'The Vale where he was born' (l. 417); the powerful image of the boy who 'hung | Listening' by the lake returns in the churchyard which 'hangs | Upon a Slope' (ll. 417–8). For Bewell,

---

[16] Culler, p. 185, citing Stephen Booth, *Precious Nonsense* (Berkeley: University of California Press, 1998).
[17] See Lukits, 'Wordsworth Unawares', p. 156.

such direct repetition 'reinforces the structural parallelism between the two parts of the narrative':[18] to an extent, one is a recapitulative echo of the other. Wordsworth's ideas of social connection begin with the 'infant babe', and extend to incorporate and to depend upon the dead. This conviction is deeply involved in ideas of repetition through the nature of a broad, communal heredity, the bonds of community and society which press on every reading. With the change of location, the attention of the poem shifts also from the boy's singleness, his being representative of the solipsistic lakeside experience, to the wider human community of which he is a part; the 'silent neighbourhood of graves' (l. 428) which represents 'a visible centre of a community of the living and the dead',[19] and whose proximity to the school allows Wordsworth to move seamlessly from the past to a future generation, the 'race' of real children he hopes will be beheld in time to come, as the cycle turns again (l. 432). Through its many recapitulations, the episode incorporates the specific moment of lakeside joy within an idea of a whole social reality; that whole is simultaneously enfolded within the specific memory. Like the plant-stages of Hegel's analogy, one is not possible without the other.

Wordsworth describes being at the centre of an echo again, in *Poems on the Naming of Places*. Describing a walk taken with Joanna Hutchinson, Wordsworth recalls being lost in visual entrancement. He remarks particularly on the blending of the specific and the general in 'That intermixture of delicious hues, | Along so vast a surface, all at once, | In one impression, by connecting force | Of their own beauty, imag'd in the heart.'[20] Here is acknowledgement of relationship, and the vital role of 'connection' in appreciating both the distinct 'hues' and their 'intermixture', in lines which recall Newton's *Opticks*. The act of connection here is given to the colours themselves, yet also depends upon the poet, on whom the impression is registered and in whose heart the connection is made. But Wordsworth is startled to find that, observing the 'ravishment' in the poet's eyes, Joanna's response is to laugh (l. 53). Wordsworth charts the echoes which issue forth thus:

> The rock, like something starting from a sleep,
> Took up the Lady's voice, and laugh'd again:
> That ancient Woman seated on Helm-crag
> Was ready with her cavern; Hammar-Scar,
> And the tall Steep of Silver-How sent forth
> A noise of laughter; southern Loughrigg heard,
> And Fairfield answer'd with a mountain tone:
> Helvellyn far into the clear blue sky

---

[18] Bewell, p. 211.   [19] *Essays upon Epitaphs*, p. 56.
[20] 'To Joanna', repr. in *Lyrical Ballads, and Other Poems, 1797–1800*, pp. 244–6 (ll. 47–50).

> Carried the Lady's voice;—old Skiddaw blew
> His speaking-trumpet;—back out of the clouds
> Of Glaramara southward came the voice;
> And Kirkstone toss'd it from his misty head.
>
> (ll. 54–65)

This ability to trace the sound precludes the more affecting disorientation Wordsworth achieves in the Winander passage. The balance between description and suggestion is inverted, even as Wordsworth wonders whether

> this were in simple truth
> A work accomplish'd by the brotherhood
> Of ancient mountains, or my ear was touch'd
> With dreams and visionary impulses,
> Is not for me to tell; but sure I am
> That there was a loud uproar in the hills.
>
> (ll. 68–73)

In its delineation of a particular visit, its display of exact geographical knowledge, in Wordsworth's certainty of his own experience, and his concurrent wondering whether he is hearing things he himself imagines (highlighted in the 1827 variant of line 67: 'To me alone imparted, sure I am'), this poem depicts an unquestionably specific experience of echoing sound. Despite the fact that Joanna is laughing at him, what echoes back to Wordsworth here is his own self-confidence. The Boy of Winander passage resists this kind of certainty *through* its recollection of echo, and the instability this lends to any singular sense of occasion, or 'truth'. The containment and exploitation of repetition there, the indication that multiple specific instances can form a general 'truth' which includes variation, and the gestures the poem makes towards the significance of connection, combine to render it a far more affective and profound work.

Sing, Cuckoo

Early in 'On the Power of Sound', the cuckoo appears: 'Shout, Cuckoo! let the vernal soul | Go with thee to the frozen zone; | Toll from thy loftiest perch, lone Bell-bird, toll!' As he commands the scene and performs the echo himself ('Toll...toll!'),[21] Wordsworth's poem again loses the suggestive wonder of the Boy

---

[21] In *Last Poems* [1835 text], pp. 113–24 (ll. 25–7).

of Winander passage, where the affect arises from the predictable unpredictability of the owl's response. Further echoes appear in the lines which follow:

> Ye Voices, and ye Shadows,
> And Images of voice—to hound and horn
> From rocky steep and rock-bestudded meadows
> Flung back, and, in the sky's blue caves, reborn,
> On with your pastime!
>
> (ll. 33–7)

These lines are dense with slightly altered repetitions: voices/voice, and rocky/rock (amplified by the accompanying alliteration of 'steep' and 'bestudded'); the position in the line of the 'Ye–' construction; the alliteration of 'hound and horn', combined with their different subsequent vowel sound; the attention-drawing rhymes (both shadows/meadows and horn/reborn are slightly off, the slant-rhyme of the former matched by the shift from monosyllable to disyllable in the latter): all of these meet in the casual vigour of sound 'flung back'. Yet the ode overall remains unconvincing in its attempt adequately to express its subject, and in the end Wordsworth can repeat only a version of the biblical description of origin and eternity as circular, in his resolving on 'the WORD, that shall not pass away.' (l. 224) When he tries to seize it too directly, sound slips from Wordsworth's grasp: Echo here carries with it, ironically, the disappointment of Narcissus, returning only Wordsworth's own voice. The echoes in the passage beginning 'There was a boy' manage to transcend this (or at least, to suggest the possibility of such transcendence); listening for birdcall, the boy gets back a more complicated repetitive sound, which initiates a more complex, profound affect. The texture of the verse allows the reader to share in this experience.

Lacking the quality of the passage on the echoing owls, 'On the Power of Sound' is far from the only place in Wordsworth's writing that we find a cuckoo: the bird's famous call provides Wordsworth with other opportunities further to suggest the capacities of poetic repetition. 'To the Cuckoo'[22] participates in the genre of Romantic poetry which celebrates a bird as a symbolic marker. Wordsworth does not choose a skylark, or a nightingale for his subject, both birds which might (and in Keats's and Shelley's writing, do) more naturally lend themselves to such symbolism. The cuckoo is famous for his double note, but also as a cheat and imposter; for not being what it might at first seem.[23] Here, his 'twofold shout' (a description of the call Wordsworth adds to later revisions) is figured as a

---

[22] In *Poems, in Two Volumes, and Other Poems, 1800–1807*, pp. 213–15.
[23] This desirable ambivalence is the source of the comedy inherent in Housman's ironic addendum: to Wordsworth's 'Shall I call thee bird, | Or but a wandering voice?', Housman apparently appended: 'State alternative preferred | With reasons for your choice.' The rumour is source-less, but it is a good story with the ring of truth about it.

deliberate trick of the voice, the poet disorientated as the bird 'made me look a thousand ways; | In bush, and tree, and sky.' (ll. 19–20) The depiction of a sound which echoes around the landscape but cannot be pinned down, and the mystery which attaches to the *idea* of the cuckoo, feed the deceptiveness of repetition: the echo which haunts its song reflects the complexity of recapitulation. Wordsworth's interest in the 'twofold shout' of the bird embodies well the duality established within the poem, figured through the central question: 'shall I call thee Bird, | Or but a wandering Voice?' The bird transcends the passage of time: it is 'The same whom in my School-boy days | I listen'd to'. Yet these past days exist in a continuous present, in which Wordsworth 'can listen to [the bird] yet'; the bird is both 'blithe New-comer', and an old familiar, habitually encountered, the subject therefore of past experience also ('I have heard...'). Like the spring it is commonly held to herald, the cuckoo marks the start of a new year, as well as functioning as a symbol of return. Wordsworth's bird represents repetition *with* novelty, just as the boy beside Winander performs at once a specific and a general action. However, the evocation of the cuckoo lacks profundity. Whilst his precarious identification with the Boy of Winander is intensely affective, Wordsworth cannot locate the source of the cuckoo's sound: lines which enact its echo through repeated words assert that 'From hill to hill it seems to pass | About, and all about!', and the overall effect of the poem, despite his veneration of the *idea* of the bird, is one of disorientation. The irregularity of the ricocheting voice meets with the unevenness of the repetitions in Wordsworth's lines to depict a cuckoo singing to and for itself, perennially elusive, and decisively separate from the poet who strains his ears to hear it. Ultimately, this functions to rehabilitate 'the earth we pace', and thus to reassure the poet, but its effect is less complex, less moving, for the reader than that of the lines on the Boy of Winander.

In 'Yes! Full surely',[24] the doubleness of the cuckoo's call reappears, as Wordsworth again appraises the ideas of echo the bird invokes. This more complex poem both refers to and includes echoes, and it explicitly claims an interest in the idea of being 'Like—but oh how different!' (l. 12) which echoes (and recapitulation generally) represent. Composed in 1806, published in 1807, republished in 1815 and then again (revised) in 1827, the poem is a good example of the way Wordsworth's revisionary habits themselves participate in a discourse of textual echoing and repetition, and in this poem, the content also lends itself to deliberate reflection on such themes. James Castell points out that, through its rhyme scheme, 'Yes! Full surely' 'rings with the sonic material that Wordsworth is both describing and encountering...Natural sound...and metaphysical sounding-out...are themselves voiced and sounded out by the echo-chamber of

---

[24] Repr. in *Poems, in Two Volumes, and Other Poems, 1800–1807*, pp. 255–6.

lyric—the recurring echoes, rhymes and silences of the poem and its form'.[25] Tracing these echoes in the text, Castell argues that the exchanges in the poem 'turn out to be nothing more than repetitions where, in fact, nothing is exchanged at all.'[26] Discussing 'The repetition (and internal rhyme) of "Sound for Sound"', he insists that

> the very success of this answering—its responsiveness to itself—creates a sonic and logical tautology that coincides with but also exceeds the rhetorical one. The repetition of 'Sound' risks redundancy as well as communication; the echo... skirts the edge of being nothing more than a meaningless return[.][27]

Yet there is an element here again of the ability of the nonsense poem to assert sense; an ability for repetition itself to be meaningful whilst transcending meaning, which might hover on the edge of sublime experience. And Castell must acknowledge that, placed in the context of the 'Note' to 'The Thorn', 'the repetition could be a sign of effusive passion in the face of metaphysical sublimity'. He rejects this interpretation, because 'the repetition needed to fulfil the metrical requirement of the form is as in the dark as the poet or the cuckoo'. But this rejection depends on a reading of the 'Note' in which the 'impassioned feeling' invoked in it is unambiguously positive; the text of 'The Thorn' itself suggests this is only a partial understanding of Wordsworth's claims:

> Like the voice through earth and sky
> By the restless Cuckoo sent;
> Like her ordinary cry,
> Like—but oh how different!
>
> (ll. 9–12)

While 'Like' here is obviously a rhetorical device, articulating a struggle to express *better*, it is also important thematically because in its repeated likeness it suggests repetition and difference at the same time. Ironically, the more times 'like' is employed, the less 'like' seems to means 'like', and the more it seems to acknowledge its own failure, and it is here that the poem surrenders to this implication: 'Like—but oh how different!' Once more we find Wordsworth focusing on a subject which allows him to articulate or at least to expose the complexities of the idea of repetition, casting its character as fundamentally different in each act of apparent identity. This effect is reduced by the changes Wordsworth made to the poem in 1815 (and it is hard not to suspect that the extensive contemporary

---

[25] James Castell, 'Wordsworth, Silence and the Nonhuman', *Wordsworth Circle*, 45.1 (2014), 58–61 (p. 58; p. 60), http://www.jstor.org/stable/24044360, accessed 2 June 2022.
[26] Castell, p. 58.   [27] Castell, p. 59.

criticism of his attachment to repetition played a part in these alterations). Nonetheless, even the revision retained a doubling of the word 'like', in which 'the degree of stress the word carries in a given context is important to its meaning in repetition: a fully stressed 'Like' carries a note of caution, where an unstressed 'Like' issues no such *caveat*.'[28] In his perceptive account of the poem's repetitions, McDonald concludes that the poem's echo 'resembles closely the nature of rhyme in Wordsworth's most self-aware poetry: a transformed repetition that offers meaning in its accommodation of the poet's calling voice.'[29] Escaping the blank parroting of Plato's *Phaedrus*, here, words given back are fully meaningful *in their being given back*.

Both 'To the Cuckoo' and 'Yes! full surely' are fundamentally optimistic poems, offering a sense of confidence to the poet, but both are haunted in turn by an echo of their own lack of knowledge; their inability to pin the cuckoo's voice down. This is reflected in the particular revisions Wordsworth made to the final stanza of 'Yes! full surely'.[30] The variants display a lack of decision relating to the possession of the 'ear' ('thy'? 'our'?) they invoke, as well as a lack of assurance about the precise source of the sound, its relative frequency of encounter, and the active agency of the 'inward ear'. Such vacillation is evident also within the poem's texture; indecision is part of the theme and the effect of its uncertain, questioning manner of proceeding: the triumphant and emphatic confidence heard in the 'Yes!' of the first word is short-lived. The lines on the Boy of Winander and the owls refuse to nominate an original cause of the sound they transcribe, but whatever Wordsworth's uncertainty in the cuckoo poems, he knows that the cuckoo sings by and for itself. Yet the double note of the cuckoo is an echo with an untrustworthy source: both cuckoo poems are on edge, containing within themselves the possibility of failure (to hear; to understand; to follow), along with the unsettling awareness of the duplicitous reputation of the bird: what you think you hear is not necessarily what you get. Castell notes that the 'affirmative atmosphere' of the ending of 'Yes! full surely' does not 'erase the preceding uncertainties', leaving the reader with a series of 'non-syntheses' which 'rest on the unstable terrain of echoes that have preceded them.'[31] Wordsworth's achievement is to depict this in language which itself intimates to the attentive reader exactly the same effect of confident uncertainty, to relate a sense of the contentment available in not knowing, in the giving in to the acceptance of the 'unsubstantial' articulated in the closing stanza of the poem.

In a letter to Lady Beaumont of January 1810, Coleridge directly associated reputation and echo, defining 'Reputation' as 'the opinions of those who *re-suppose* the *suppositions* of others'; as it 're-echoes an echo', Coleridge's is a

---

[28] McDonald, p. 45.　　[29] McDonald, p. 44.
[30] See *Poems, in Two Volumes, and Other Poems, 1800–1807*, p. 256 n.　　[31] Castell, p. 60.

degraded sound, problematically detached from its original source.[32] But Wordsworth's echo in places begins to attain the transcendence of the visionary. Both Hollander and McDonald find the 'rebounds' caught by Wordsworth's 'inward ear' in 'Yes! full surely' to be an aural parallel of 'that inward eye | Which is the bliss of solitude'.[33] In different ways, those of Wordsworth's poems which contain evocations of echoes simultaneously exploit techniques of recapitulation in their texture, in order to suggest such rebounds, independently of his writing *about* them explicitly (though naturally, the context of his writing about them leaves the reader especially open to the reception of the poems' sonic effects). To some extent, this is a form of recording sounds to complement the content of the verse, even if it can't perfectly replicate them, and our inability *exactly* to catch the sound is pertinent to the sublime experience of echo Wordsworth reaches to communicate. In the 'Descriptive Sketches', sounds' echoic qualities render their Alpine origins harmonious:

> An idle voice the sabbath region fills
> Of Deep that calls to Deep across the hills,
> Broke only by the melancholy sound
> Of drowsy bells for ever tinkling round;
> Faint wail of eagle melting into blue
> Beneath the cliffs, and pine-woods steady sugh[34]

The first line here perhaps alludes to lines from Isaiah 58:13; either way, an interest in echo, in various senses, is obvious. The idleness of the 'voice' might suggest echo (which needs only a single active source; there is a laziness to the way it bounces from surface to surface with no apparent input), but the passage also depicts literal echoes (deep calling to deep; bells 'for ever tinkling round'; the 'melting' call of the eagle—in this established context, 'melting' suggests the slow fading away encountered in echoed sound). It also partly enacts them, in the literal repetition of 'deep', and the uncomplicated rhyme scheme which climbs along increasingly protracted vowel sounds. This is emphasized in the note to the final line: Wordsworth felt the need to gloss 'sugh', as 'a Scotch word expressive of the sound of the wind through the trees.'[35] He further emphasized its strangeness by italicizing it in the 1836 edition of the poem.[36] *Sugh* is thus a word which asks the reader to pay particular attention to it, and it describes the sighing out of sound, like the end of an echo. Yet almost immediately, Wordsworth notes a qualification to this soundscape 'where no trace of man the spot profanes': a 'boy' appears, who

---

[32] *The Collected Letters of Samuel Taylor Coleridge*, iii, 277.
[33] See McDonald, p. 46; 'Wordsworth and the Music of Sound', p. 46.
[34] In *Descriptive Sketches* [1793 edn], ed. Eric Birdsall (Ithaca: Cornell University Press, 1984), ll. 432–7.
[35] See *Descriptive Sketches*, p. 80.   [36] See *Descriptive Sketches* [1836 edn], ll. 376.

'Shouts from the echoing hills with savage joy' (1793, ll. 440–1; 1836, ll. 379–80). The line is beautifully poised so that we can't really know if the hills are echoing *him*, or everything else; it is appropriately impossible for the reader quite to catch the echo. The echo Wordsworth hears in the Alps is seemingly (not literally) infinite, and it is seemingly (not necessarily) a non-deliberative effect generated in idleness; it slips from his grasp and apprehension, just as it slips from ours in reading about it. In these ways, echo in the poem is able to gesture towards the sublime, and thus to offer a 'sincere' record of experience, as Wordsworth understands it. Echo is a self-contained, graspable example of the far broader nature and effects of recapitulation which intimate sublimity in Wordsworth's writing.

12
Coleridge and Repetition
A Comparative Case

Coleridge adopts a different attitude towards verbal repetition to that of Wordsworth, and it would be a mistake to over-emphasize the relationship between the two poets, yet it would seem perverse to ignore Coleridge here. Coleridge's account of the imagination offers an insight into the intellectual context in which Wordsworth wrote, allowing a fuller appreciation of the significance attached to the role and possibilities of repetition within Wordsworth's circle. The repetitions in Coleridge's poetry offer illustrative comparison with Wordsworth's; moreover, Coleridge engaged critically with Wordsworth's statement on, and creative use of, repetition, his commentary offering an opportunity for useful clarification. This chapter therefore offers an overview of the significance of repetition to Coleridge, in order to enrich the background to Wordsworth's attitude towards, and his poetic exploitation of, recapitulation.

Coleridge, Repetition, and the Mind

Turning his attention to 'The Thorn' in his *Biographia Literaria*, Coleridge echoed the many other criticisms which had been levelled at Wordsworth's poem; these are the lines in which Coleridge maintains that, in a lyric poem, 'it is not possible to imitate truly a dull and garrulous discourser, without repeating the effects of dullness and garrulity'. But he went further:

> the passages exclusively appropriate to the supposed narrator ... are felt by many unprejudiced and unsophisticated hearts, as sudden and unpleasant sinkings from the height to which the poet had previously lifted them, and to which he again re-elevates both himself and his reader.[1]

Although Coleridge tempered the attack with reference to passages 'which have given, and which will continue to give universal delight', the description of reading the poem as a kind of big dipper, lurching between bathos and pleasure, is hardly

---

[1] *Biographia Literaria*, ii, 49–52.

redeemed by the concession: the impression of the passage is one of uncomfortable critical wriggling under the imagined gaze of its subject. Yet the regressive-progressive movement Coleridge describes here is not so very far from that he attaches elsewhere to 'The best part of human language, properly so called', which is 'is derived from reflection on the acts of the mind itself'.[2] The idea of reflection naturally calls attention to itself in this context of repetition, but Coleridge's fuller engagement with ideas of repetition in his accounts of mental activity, and in particular his account of 'the mind's self-experience in the act of thinking',[3] are more pertinent still. Without ignoring the fact that, discussing the *Biographia Literaria*, we are constantly 'forced to explain schemes that never quite work,[4] its expositions of the imagination and of 'desynonymy' indicate the importance of ideas of repetition to Coleridge's philosophical thought.

By 1818, Coleridge was finding experience itself to be essentially based in repetition: 'To have had a sight of a Thing does not justify us in saying, that we had *experience* of it. It must have had antecedents, from which we might anticipate it.—*Ex*-perior. Omne ex-pertum est *re*-pertum.'[5] Debra Channick translates this as 'I *ex*perience. Everything ex-perienced is *re*-experienced.'[6] According to Coleridge, however, these repetitions of experience are not exact in character (the previous things experienced are not necessarily identical to the current thing), and they therefore incorporate variation. Moreover, clearly influenced by Hartley's development of Lockean thought,[7] Coleridge argues that it is through moments of difference, recognized as such, that language and therefore thought can progress. Desynonymy emerges in this context as a way of showing how apparently synonymous words in fact mean differently, but it has more than a straightforward, linguistic purpose: as Paul Hamilton argues, desynonymy actually 'furnishes Coleridge with a model of the workings of human understanding', and illustrates 'the progressive character of human knowledge'.[8] Coleridge describes the impulse towards desynonymy as 'an instinct of growth, a certain collective, unconscious good sense working progressively' in societies:[9]

> let them recollect that the whole process of human intellect is gradually to desynonymize terms, that words, the instruments of communication, are the only signs that a finite being can have of its own thoughts, that in proportion as

---

[2] *Biographia Literaria*, ii, 54.   [3] *Biographia Literaria*, i, 124.
[4] Paul Hamilton, *Coleridge's Poetics* (Oxford: Basil Blackwell, 1983), p. 1.
[5] Entry from October 1818, in *The Notebooks of Samuel Taylor Coleridge Volume 3: 1808–1819*, ed. Kathleen Coburn (London: Routledge, 1973), p. 4453.
[6] Debra Channick, '"A Logic of Its Own": Repetition in Coleridge's "Christabel"', *Romanticism and Victorianism on the Net*, 50 (May 2008) (not paginated), https://doi-org.ezp.lib.cam.ac.uk/10.7202/018144ar, accessed 2 June 2022.
[7] See David Hartley, *Observations on Man, His Frame, His Duty, and His Expectations* (London and Bath: James Leake and William Frederick, 1749); and Locke's *Essay Concerning Human Understanding*.
[8] *Coleridge's Poetics*, p. 65.   [9] *Biographia Literaria*, i, 82.

what was conceived as one and identical becomes several, there will necessarily arise a term striving to represent that distinction.[10]

For Coleridge, thought is codified and therefore limited by the language which can express it. Through the atomizing effect of desynonymy, the linguistic resources of the mind are increased, originality is enabled, and dull repetition is avoided. In the *Biographia*, Coleridge explains his belief that desynonymy is necessary in order for knowledge to progress: 'In order to obtain adequate notions of any truth, we must intellectually separate its distinguishable parts'; this is 'the technical *process* of philosophy',[11] and desynonymization is posited as one of its tools: 'The first and most important point to be proved is, that two conceptions perfectly distinct are confused under one and the same word, and (this done) to appropriate that word exclusively to one meaning, and the synonyme [sic] (should there be one) to the other.' Coleridge continues: if 'no synonyme exists, we must either invent or borrow a word.'[12] Progress thus depends on distinction and originality; pure repetition can only impede this proliferation of divergent paths which, like a network of branching tributaries, increase the flow of advancing knowledge.

As it is defined in the *Biographia*, however, 'truth' is not disparate, but unified. Therefore, having separated the 'distinguishable parts' of truth, we 'must then restore them in our conceptions to the unity in which they actually co-exist; and this is the *result* of philosophy.'[13] Instead of the image of tributaries stretching *away* from the source, knowledge tends towards the single locus. Plato is for Coleridge a true philosopher who 'wrote the greater part of his published works, to strike at the root of sophistry in the ambiguity of words',[14] because, Coleridge maintains, as far as possible, philosophical language must approach a purity dependent upon distinction for absolute clarity of meaning. Poetic language on the other hand strives for a form of unity at odds with such a model. It is poetry which can therefore perform the reunification of language necessary to truth, because, like primitive language, it 'seeks to return us to our mythic origins, in which the world is present in the word, not as an idea but as a reality'.[15]

If art is to represent the world as its subject, it must in some sense be mimetic. Coleridge develops his theory of the imagination in such a way as to account for the potential of originality and difference *within* mimesis, in order to release it

---

[10] *The Philosophical Lectures of Samuel Taylor Coleridge*, ed. Kathleen Coburn (London: Pilot Press, 1949), p. 173.
[11] *Biographia Literaria*, ii, 11.   [12] *Biographia Literaria*, i, 83–4.
[13] *Biographia Literaria*, ii, 11.
[14] This quotation is cited in Michael Kent Havens, 'Coleridge on the Evolution of Language', *Studies in Romanticism*, 20.2 (Summer 1981), 163–83, who notes that it is taken from W. G. T. Shedd's edition of *The Complete Works of Samuel Taylor Coleridge* (New York: Harper Brothers, 1864), iv, 405 ff., but that 'Shedd gives neither date nor addressee for this letter, and I have not been able to find it in Griggs's *Collected Letters*' (Kent Havens, p. 175, n. 26); I have similarly failed to locate it.
[15] Gerald L. Bruns, *Modern Poetry and the Idea of Language: A Critical and Historical Study* (New Haven: Yale University Press, 1974), p. 58.

from the shackles of mere copying (the dull form of repetition), and allow for the divine creativity which might be manifest within it. Frederick Burwick notes that, along with the distinction Coleridge draws between fancy and imagination, 'the distinction between copy and imitation is essential to Coleridge's theory [...of] the creative process.'[16] In order to clarify Coleridge's position, Burwick teases out his relationship with Schellingian theory: according to Schelling, 'perfect mimicry...misdirects the purposes of art into mechanical redundancy', whereas 'True imitation seeks the essence, "the indwelling spirit of nature."...As long as the similarity is not a deliberate copy but the result of "the same striving towards the same means," the imitation will involve the revelation of vital essence. Although the shift from copy to imitation is thus attained, the artist has not yet reached the ultimate goal of art.'[17] This is a legacy, then, which attributes problematic redundancy to precise repetition (the notion that Wordsworth differently attempts to break down in the 'Note' to 'The Thorn'). For Coleridge, Burwick establishes,

> only an imitation, not a copy, can produce 'the great total effect'. A copy reflects only the accidents of the moment. An imitation reveals the informing presence of the mind. When Schelling describes the union of mind and matter in the work of art, there is simply a merging of the conscious with the unconscious...Coleridge insists on the controlling presence of the artist's imagination. The distinction between *copy* and *imitation* thus has a non-Schellingian emphasis. It is 'not the mere copy of things, but the contemplation of mind upon things.'[18]

Expanding in this way his account of the imagination, Coleridge engages with ideas of repetition in the mind of the artist so that the 'contemplation' of that mind inflects each repetition, thus rendering it inherently *different*.

Coleridge applies a process of desynonymization to the term 'imagination' itself (along with 'fancy'):

> 'fancy' and 'imagination' had both come, Coleridge felt, to denote a faculty capriciously or arbitrarily associating words and images. Coleridge assigns this meaning to 'fancy,' reserving 'imagination' for the faculty that actually unifies words and images, intuiting their common ground in Reason. The superfluous synonym, 'imagination,' thus finds a happy use as vehicle of a 'new' meaning.[19]

Paul Hamilton points out that 'Coleridge sometimes describes language as dividing and multiplying its meanings in the way that a basic organism separates and

---

[16] See Frederick Burwick, 'Coleridge and Schelling on Mimesis', in Richard Gravil and Molly Lefebure, eds, *The Coleridge Connection: Essays for Thomas McFarland* (London: Macmillan, 1990), pp. 167–85 (p. 167). Burwick's essay also includes a survey of critics who have been interested in Coleridge and copying and imitation. See p. 167, n. 2.
[17] Burwick, p. 171.   [18] Burwick, p. 179.   [19] Kent Havens, p. 177.

becomes two distinct organisms.'[20] For Coleridge, this is an act of 'polypizing', which is expanded in a footnote to Chapter 4 of the *Biographia*:

> There is a sort of *minim immortal* among the animalcula infusoria, which has not naturally either birth, or death, absolute beginning, or absolute end: for at a certain period a small point appears on its back, which deepens and lengthens till the creature divides into two, and the same process recommences in each of the halves now become integral. This may be a fanciful, but it is by no means a bad emblem of the formation of words, and may facilitate the conception, how immense a nomenclature may be organized from a few simple sounds by rational beings in a social state. For each new application, or excitement of the same sound, will call forth a different sensation, which cannot but affect the pronunciation. The after recollection of the sound, without the same vivid sensation, will modify it still further; till at length all trace of the original likeness is worn away.[21]

As Hamilton recognizes, Coleridge confuses individuation and evolution here,[22] but Coleridge's self-declaredly 'fanciful' metaphor is helpfully illustrative, and significant because it implies that the repetition of the same word can be a refined form of desynonymy, rather than the opposite of it. In this light, Coleridge's objection to 'The Thorn' appears more complex than has sometimes been asserted, not rooted straightforwardly in the poem's repetitions, or in the claims Wordsworth makes about repetition and tautology in his 'Note' to the poem.

Whereas Southey's attack on 'The Thorn' complained about the 'tiresome loquacity' of its narrator, Coleridge's fundamental problem is with the *character* of its 'dull and garrulous discourser', which is not quite the same thing; Coleridge is focused on the figure rather than the loquacity itself.[23] His criticism is really, as his discussion of poetic language more generally goes on to imply, of Wordsworth's neglect (as Coleridge sees it) of language which is derived from the self-reflective mind, language 'formed by a voluntary appropriation of fixed symbols to internal acts, to processes and results of imagination.'[24] Wordsworth's narrator is a problem because his speech suggests no such reflection. Coleridge holds up as flawed 'the passages exclusively appropriate to the supposed narrator'. He cites the (extensive) relevant lines in the notes to his text, but even in the case of his first (and most obviously pedantically bathetic) example, 'I've measured it from side to side; | 'Tis three feet long, and two feet wide', he never spells out *explicitly* what his objections to the lines themselves are.[25] This lack of precision avoids a flat criticism of all repetition; such a blanket dismissal would conflict with his claim for the potential inherent in repetition as a form of desynonymy.

---

[20] *Coleridge's Poetics*, p. 82.   [21] *Biographia Literaria*, i, 83.   [22] *Coleridge's Poetics*, p. 82.
[23] *Biographia Literaria*, i, 49–50.   [24] *Biographia Literaria*, ii, 54.
[25] *Biographia Literaria*, ii, 49–52.

And Coleridge concludes his chapter with a defence of repetition, and a partial agreement with Wordsworth:

> It is indeed very possible to adopt in a poem the unmeaning repetitions, habitual phrases, and other blank counters, which an unfurnished or confused understanding interposes at short intervals, in order to keep hold of his subject which is still slipping from him, and to give him time for recollection... Nothing assuredly can differ either in origin or in mode more widely from the *apparent* tautologies of intense and turbulent feeling, in which the passion is greater and of longer endurance, than to be exhausted or satisfied by a single representation of the image or incident exciting it. Such repetitions I admit to be a beauty of the highest kind; as illustrated by Mr. Wordsworth himself from the song of Deborah.[26]

Invoking Wordsworth's discussion of a passage from Judges, and just as surely influenced by Lowth, Coleridge's chapter ends here, without clarifying how the reader might distinguish 'blank counters' from 'tautologies of intense and turbulent feeling'. We are left to fall back upon the previous statement, that the distinguishing aspect of the language of the poem depends upon the 'character' from which the repetitions proceed. In this sense, 'The Thorn' defends itself from Coleridge's criticism: as I have suggested, it exhibits a strident self-consciousness about the possibility of expression, exploring the possibility of articulating tragedy through layered voices which are all ultimately and inevitably the products of the poet's 'feeling', even when they are articulated by the character of the 'Captain of a small trading vessel'.[27] Coleridge instead works backwards, focusing on rhetorical effects he refuses to define absolutely, in order to attribute an independent character which drags the poem down.

As Coleridge defines it, 'fancy' is 'no other than a mode of Memory...blended with and modified by...CHOICE.'[28] Eighteenth-century Humean philosophy advanced a model of the imagination which offered merely a lowly repetition of real experience. Coleridge above any other English poet in the period transformed this understanding, initiating a revolution in literary thought which crowned the imagination as the creative power. His clearest explication of his theory is found in his evocation of a water-insect as 'emblem' of the mind's action; in this description we find the operation of the imagination dependent upon a particular form of recapitulation:

> In every voluntary movement we first counteract gravitation, in order to avail ourselves of it. It must exist, that there may be a something to be counteracted,

---

[26] *Biographia Literaria*, ii, 57.   [27] 'Note' to 'The Thorn', p. 350.
[28] *Biographia Literaria*, i, 305.

and which, by its re-action, aids the force that is exerted to resist it. Let us consider, what we do when we leap. We first resist the gravitating power by an act purely voluntary, and then by another act, voluntary in part, we yield to it in order to alight on the spot, which we had previously proposed to ourselves. Now let a man watch his mind while he is composing; or, to take a still more common case, while he is trying to recollect a name; and he will find the process completely analogous.[29]

Composition and recollection are here similar processes, involving forceful resistance, followed by yielding. The reference to deliberate, active recollection recalls Wordsworth, and the idea of poetic composition as 'powerful feelings... recollected in tranquillity',[30] though the dynamic is obviously and importantly different in Coleridge's description. But for both writers, poetry is rooted in an active gathering back of thought, a deliberate bringing to mind. In Coleridge's account, despite his repetition of its 'voluntary' nature, this process is not subject wholly to the will: the 'yield'ing itself may be voluntary, but it nonetheless involves a temporary renunciation or relaxation of will. The imagination provides the means by which this active-passive distinction is reconciled. Coleridge continues:

> Most of my readers will have observed a small water-insect on the surface of rivulets, which throws a cinque-spotted shadow fringed with prismatic colours on the sunny bottom of the brook; and will have noticed, how the little animal *wins* its way up against the stream, by alternate pulses of active and passive motion, now resisting the current, and now yielding to it in order to gather strength and a momentary *fulcrum* for a further propulsion. This is no unapt emblem of the mind's self-experience in the act of thinking. There are evidently two powers at work, which relatively to each other are active and passive; and this is not possible without an intermediate faculty, which is at once both active and passive. (In philosophical language, we must denominate this intermediate faculty in all its degrees and determinations, the IMAGINATION. But in common language, and especially on the subject of poetry, we appropriate the name to a superior degree of the faculty, joined to a superior voluntary controul over it.)[31]

According to Coleridge's description, the quasi-peristaltic motion of the insect allows it to advance *through* a struggle with the current, to which it must at moments surrender only to surge again. This is an image of recapitulative motion which, as the insect is carried backwards, tips almost into futility, but which is redeemed by the 'fulcrum' in the mind. Like the insect, the mind must struggle

[29] *Biographia Literaria*, i, 124. [30] *Prose*, i, 148. [31] *Biographia Literaria*, i, 124–5.

against a current moment (watery for the insect, temporal for the thinking mind) when it remembers or creates. In her description of the evolution of English stylistics, Sylvia Adamson finds the Romantic model diverging from an eighteenth-century periodic style which had left 'no room for the interruptions, digressions and new directions of spontaneous speech'.[32] In a passage which finds close echoes in Adamson's account, Paul Curtis points out that

> Coleridge's analogy of the water-beetle demonstrates how the iconography of the mind had changed by his time from a linear configuration to one that acknowledges discontinuity, indirection and alternating sequence... Progress is gained, lost, retraced... As a complex image of contrary motions, the insect seems static on the surface of the brook since he must 'move' at least as fast as the water to stay 'still'. As an image of progress, mere stasis signifies considerable movement. Coleridge's insect suggests how rich a static moment is, and how each is hard-won instead of following automatically in succession.[33]

Coleridge's water-insect passage is 'about' the imagination, understood as, in part, an act of re-membering ('composing'; 'trying to recollect a name'). But repetitions here, in the insect's motion, are *both* 'dead', *and* living and productive. Here, this resolves into a passive/active distinction, but it also reflects on the nature of recapitulation (including repetition in poetry) as *both* a redundant tautology, or even worse, a negative effect, slipping backwards, *and* a positive gain. Just as we 'rhyme backwards', here, the image allows us to recognize 'backwards' as positively necessary to forward momentum (the 'win upstream'). This is how Coleridge's imagination encounters and processes repetition. His 'alternate pulses of active and passive motion' illuminate repetition's push and pull: at once towards a distillation of experience or thought, and simultaneously the diffusion caused by the same thing in inevitably different contexts (within a text, and/or within the scene the text describes).

Coleridge's beetle is in dynamic relationship with the current of the brook; if the effect of the water on the insect is one of compulsion to be resisted and yielded to in turn, the effect of the insect on the water is reciprocally significant. The insect casts a shadow, not in an image of dark insubstantiality, but of vibrant creativity: the shadow is 'cinque-spotted', 'fringed with prismatic colours', a detailed image of generative artistry which seems entirely out of proportion with its insignificance against the water's thrust. As the insect beats time, its shadow indicates depth, the static moment thus pregnant with potential sublimity. If the collapse of the attempt to provide an account of the imagination in Chapter 13 of the *Biographia* enacts the impossibility of capturing the operation of the sublime on

---

[32] Adamson, *Cambridge History of English Language Vol. IV*, p. 632.   [33] Curtis, pp. 7–8.

the page, it does so on a point which infers sublimity in the model of the mind it strains to express: 'The IMAGINATION then I consider either as primary, or secondary. The primary IMAGINATION I hold to be the living Power and prime Agent of all human Perception, and as a repetition in the finite mind of the eternal act of creation in the infinite I AM.'[34] Repetition is explicitly privileged as *necessary*. This type of repetition is what, Coleridge elsewhere explains, redeems the shadow the water-insect casts from insubstantiality, lifting it into an aspect of primary imaginative activity: 'That, which we find in ourselves, is (gradu mutato) the substance and the life of *all* our knowledge. Without this latent presence of the "I am," all modes of existence in the external world would flit before us as colored shadows'.[35] Just as Wordsworth seeks to reclaim repetition from mere tautology, arguing instead for its capacity to indicate 'impassioned feelings',[36] so the quasi-mechanical repetition of the insect's movements here, apparently the opposite of sublimity, proves able to escape from the same impasse Wordsworth faced, and instead indicates the operation of the sublime imagination.

Coleridge is not content to leave the imaginative burden entirely on the shoulders of the poet-artist. Elsewhere in the *Biographia* he sketches a strikingly similar motion as he outlines readerly experience: 'The reader should be carried forward, not merely or chiefly by the mechanical impulse of curiosity, or by a restless desire to arrive at the final solution' (that is, the reader should not be motivated by the desire simply to make semantic sense);

> but by the pleasurable activity of mind excited by the attractions of the journey itself. Like the motion of a serpent, which the Egyptians made the emblem of intellectual power; or like the path of sound through the air; at every step he pauses and half recedes, and from the retrogressive movement collects the force which again carries him onward.[37]

The propulsion and relaxation of the water-insect's progress is here transformed into the similar movement of a serpentine wave; in both cases, the carrying forward retraces the previous journey at each step and the reader is led to perform a remarkably similar motion to the creative imagination. Both serpent and insect provide an image of gathering up and going over (to alter or to supplement the sense already made); they assert the motion which good writing demands of the reader as a movement of recapitulation. In terms of the conjunctions discussed earlier in this book, this is a process which involves *or* as well as *and*. As far as the act of imagining is concerned, in this model power accrues through the

---

[34] *Biographia Literaria*, i, 304.
[35] S. T. Coleridge, *The Statesman's Manual; or, The Bible the Best Guide to Political Skill and Foresight [...]* (London: Gale and Fenner, 1816), xviii.
[36] 'Note' to 'The Thorn', p. 351.   [37] *Biographia Literaria*, ii, 14.

combination of a letting go, of a dwelling in the current moment, and a forward thrust: a repetitious, circular combination of activity and passivity which allow or even enable one another. Stewart uses this image of the serpent's motion to exemplify the 'hovering aural dispersion' which renders lines of verse ambiguous or multiply meaningful: Stewart's argument is that even a single word might bear repeated, revisionary readings as we are forced to confront the need to modify the sense we initially make of a word or line.[38] Ricks draws on the same passage in the context of his essay on line endings and their matching of sound and sense in the 'relationship of eye to ear': this relationship complicates the sense of simple semantic meaning in order to enrich our experience of the poem, by requiring a form of recapitulation—of going over again what we thought we had read, however transitorily and perhaps even thoughtlessly, 'protected, say enlightened, by our ears.'[39] Such a process functions both micro- and macrocosmically for Coleridge: seeking in the *Biographia* for a 'solid foundation, on which permanently to ground' his literary opinions, Coleridge concludes that 'Not the poem which we have *read*, but that to which we *return*, with the greatest pleasure, possesses the genuine power, and claims the name of *essential poetry*'.[40] Forms of recapitulation are essential in these accounts both to the composing and the reading mind in the encounter with verse.

The cynic might note the particular pertinence of repetition to Coleridge's philosophy, which famously dances along a fine line between plagiarism and influence. As James Engell summarizes, 'In forming his concept of the imagination, Coleridge draws on nearly every other writer who discussed the subject.'[41] In Engell's exposition of Coleridge, 'Sense, reason, and understanding' operate to 'receive and give their own immediate apprehensions as modified by all faculties. The synthetic process is constant...continuous feedback':[42] here again, in the idea of 'feedback', is the implication that a form of repetition is central to the operation of the Coleridgean imagination; this is also patently the case in his infamous attempt to put down that understanding on the page. In Chapter 13's attempt to describe the 'Imagination, or esemplastic power', the 'Primary Imagination' is specifically an 'Echo', a repetition of the divine (a copying back of the world as it has been created by 'the infinite I AM'[43]). The secondary imagination (secondary not in rank but rather in sequence[44]) is dependent upon the conscious will; once that will operates, the secondary imagination 'dissolves, diffuses, dissipates in order to re-create.'[45] Here Coleridge's description sounds surprisingly similar to

---

[38] Stewart, p. 1; p. 5.   [39] *Force of Poetry*, p. 104.   [40] *Biographia Literaria*, i, 22–3.
[41] James Engell, *The Creative Imagination: Enlightenment to Romanticism* (Cambridge, MA: Harvard University Press, 1981), p. 328.
[42] Engell, p. 339.   [43] *Biographia Literaria*, i, 304.
[44] As Engell puts it, '"secondary" does not imply a lesser power but signifies that "superior degree of the faculty," much in the way a secondary school advances over but builds on the primary grades' (Engell, p. 344).
[45] *Biographia Literaria*, i, 304.

Hume's *'liberty of the imagination to transpose and change its ideas'*,[46] the double sense of 'dissipate' tilting us momentarily towards a very Humean sense of the squandering wastefulness of imaginative activity. But of course, Coleridge is looking in an entirely different direction, just as when he had asserted in 1801 that 'any system built on the passiveness of the mind must be false, as a system.'[47] What Coleridge is really describing in the *Biographia* is a harnessed form of repetition with difference, a theorized way of accommodating the competing pull of repetition towards tedium on the one hand; towards pleasing mimetic and aesthetic effects and intellectual advancement on the other. Coleridge depicts the will as the means of the imagination's redemption from passivity, allowing variation to inflect its repetitions. Locke's theory of language and of mind doesn't allow for an *or*; empirical philosophy seeks a transparent and absolute correspondence between word and idea or thing. But like a magnificent *or*, in Coleridge's secondary imagination, mere copying is resisted by the preservation of the possibility of choice. It is

> an echo of the [primary imagination], co-existing with the conscious will, yet still as identical with the primary in the *kind* of its agency, and differing only in *degree*, and in the *mode* of its operation. It dissolves, diffuses, dissipates, in order to re-create; or where this process is rendered impossible, yet still at all events it struggles to idealize and to unify. It is essentially *vital*, even as all objects (*as* objects) are essentially fixed and dead.[48]

Daniel Stempel describes Coleridge's awareness that 'his own intellectual quest had been paralleled (and anticipated) by the movement of ideas from Tetens through Kant to Fichte:

> Creativity, Tetens insisted, is not dependent on the capacity of the memory; it does not merely reproduce images. It is *self*-creative imagination... which, as in the works of Klopstock and Milton, molds the raw material of images into new and original wholes.[49]

These ideas were vigorously circulating in Coleridge's mind before the publication of the *Biographia Literaria*. In a letter to Joseph Cottle of 1815, for example, we find him insisting that:

---

[46] Hume, p. 12.
[47] Coleridge to Thomas Poole, 23 March 1801, in *The Collected Letters of Samuel Taylor Coleridge*, ii, 710.
[48] *Biographia Literaria*, i, 304.
[49] Daniel Stempel, 'Revelation on Mount Snowdon: Wordsworth, Coleridge, and the Fichtean Imagination', *The Journal of Aesthetics and Art Criticism*, 29.3 (Spring 1971), 371–84 (p. 372).

> The common end of all *narrative*, nay, of *all*, Poems is to convert a *series* into a *Whole*: to make those events, which in real or imagined History move on in a *strait* Line, assume to our Understandings a *circular* motion—the snake with it's Tail in it's Mouth. Hence indeed the almost flattering and yet appropriate Term, Poesy—i.e. poiēsis = *making*. Doubtless, to *his* eye, which alone comprehends all Past and all Future in one eternal Present, what to our short sight appears strait is but a part of the great Cycle—just as the calm Sea to us *appears* level, tho' it be indeed only a part of a *globe*. Now what the Globe is in Geography, *miniaturing* in order to *manifest* the Truth, such is a Poem to that Image of God, which we were created into, and which still seeks that Unity, or Revelation of the *One* in and by the *Many*[.][50]

Thus incorporating variation within repetition in another image of circular motion, appealing to a relationship between specificity and generality, Coleridge's accounts sustain a conviction that the imagination *thereby* remains specifically divine. The mind, and the poem it imagines into life, allow the multiple mini-repetitions in which the imagination's work consists to function collectively as a transcendent repetition of divine creativity. The many small parts form a whole, or 'truth'. Whilst we cannot grasp them all at the same time, God can, and thus witnesses their unification into the whole of 'truth'. But in their individual existences, each mini-repetition in its turn functions as a miniature version of the same thing, exhibiting the sameness-with-difference which underpins desynonymy, in the power of 'the apparent tautologies of intense and turbulent feeling', the '*vital*' operation of the imagination.[51] Just as there is power in the apparent stasis of the water-insect, so the mind tips towards sublimity as it apprehends the gaps these samenesses-with-difference reveal.

Lowth's significant legacy to Wordsworth's experimentation with repetition in the 'Note' to 'The Thorn' is refracted in Coleridge's commentary on the poem, but whilst Coleridge's dialogue with Lowthian theological traditions was important to his emergent theories of mind and of versification, German writers were still more significant to his philosophical writing and poetic praxis. Coleridge's letters from Germany at the end of the 1790s frequently revert to a preoccupation with the inadequacy of language.[52] In the same period, he was intellectually stimulated by the general German revolt against rhyme, associated with Friedrich Gottlieb Klopstock's biblical epic *Der Messias* (1748–73), 'hailed as Germany's answer to Milton, even to Homer'.[53] By the late 1790s, interest had spread to English

---

[50] Coleridge to Joseph Cottle, 7 March 1815, in *The Collected Letters of Samuel Taylor Coleridge*, iv, 545.
[51] *Biographia Literaria*, ii, 57; i, 304.
[52] See for example Miller, 'Coleridge and the Scene of Lyric Description', esp. p. 522.
[53] See Ernest Bernhardt-Kabisch, '"When Klopstock England Defied": Coleridge, Southey, and the German/English Hexameter', *Comparative Literature*, 55.2 (Spring 2003), 130–63 (p. 131).

journals, including the *Monthly Magazine*. Coleridge encountered Klopstock's work both in print and through the reports of friends; encouraged by the Wordsworths, he engaged vigorously in the critical discussion.[54] When Coleridge and the Wordsworths travelled to Germany in 1798, they met with Klopstock in Hamburg, though communication was a stilted affair, filtered through a bit of Latin, some French interpreted for Coleridge by Wordsworth, and the few English words Klopstock possessed.[55] Because of its interest in scansion (the adoption of hexameter verse was fundamental to the movement), Klopstock's influence is most obviously relevant to Coleridge's unconventional syllabic prosody in 'Christabel', and his attempts at hexameter verse written during his stay in Germany. Ernest Bernhardt-Kabisch outlines the considerable broader influence that these intellectual and literal encounters with Klopstock had on Coleridge, understanding Coleridge's attempt to 'naturalise the classical hexameter' as part of a wider Romantic desire to 'throw off the tyranny of... strictly syllabic prosody... in favor of a freer, more varied and organic rhythm, one produced by a cadential (rather than syllabic) and tonal, or musical, prosody closer to actual speech.'[56] But in his 1779 treatise 'Vom deutschen hexameter', Klopstock's discussion of repetition is congruent with a Lowthian understanding of Hebrew poetry (though it is unclear whether Klopstock was directly aware of Lowth's work). According to Katrin Kohl, Klopstock 'emphasises the importance of repetition as a central constituent of poetry, and sharply distinguishes between uniform repetition ('Wiederholerey') and repetition which embraces meaningful variation. The early hymns have no metrical repetition, but repetition of words and syntactic patterns is rife.'[57] Kohl finds Klopstock moulding his use of repetition according to biblical parallelism, exploiting repetition for intensification, utilizing 'various forms of repetition for emotive effect',[58] but also employing it hermeneutically, to make connections between different elements of the hymns. In Klopstock's hands, 'repetition in words and syntax becomes an effective means of achieving his paramount aim: das Herz ganz zu rühren' ['To stir the heart

---

[54] In December 1798, Wordsworth was complaining that Coleridge had made 'no mention of Klopstock' in his correspondence (W[illiam] W[ordsworth] and D[orothy] W[ordsworth] to S. T. Coleridge, 14 or 21 December 1798, in *Letters*, i, 235–43), though Wordsworth's own account of Klopstock in a letter to Thomas Poole reported 'nothing remarkable either in his conversation or appearance, except his extreme gaiety with legs swelled as thick as your thigh', a preoccupation with the German's lower limbs repeated in his private notes on the meeting. See W[illiam] W[ordsworth] to Thomas Poole, 3 October 1798, in *Letters*, i, 229–31, and *Prose*, i, 91, on Klopstock's 'much swelled' legs.

[55] For an account of Wordsworth's 'Conversations with Klopstock', see *Prose*, i, 89–98, and see also James Engell, 'Coleridge and German Idealism: First Postulates, Final Causes', in *The Coleridge Connection*, pp. 144–66 (p. 146).

[56] Bernhardt-Kabisch, p. 140; p. 159.

[57] Katrin Kohl, *Rhetoric, the Bible, and the Origins of Free Verse* (Berlin and New York: de Gruyter, 1990), pp. 188–9. Kohl suggests that Klopstock's abandonment of metrical repetition is directly connected to his desire to emulate the Psalms; see Kohl, p. 189.

[58] See Kohl, pp. 190–4.

completely'].[59] As an influence upon Wordsworth and Coleridge, Klopstock has probably been underestimated; his specific importance here, however, is in the ways he thus negotiates a particular way of thinking about repetition: Klopstock allows repetition to incorporate variation, and to articulate passion.

Explicit and implicit reflections on the value of repetition are scattered across Coleridge's writings. For example, near the beginning of the *Biographia*, he complains about Pope's heroic couplets because 'a *point* [is] looked for at the end of each second line', resulting in a problematic 'sorites' in which the consequent relentlessness of the verse form requires an absolute repetition, regardless of any other consideration. Variation is not admitted, so that 'the matter and diction seemed to me characterized not so much by poetic thoughts, as by thoughts *translated* into the language of poetry.'[60] Coleridge's poetic praxis fully exploits the rhetorical effects of repetition: we have already seen an example of this in Susan Wolfson's reading of 'To Asra', where we surely find the 'tautologies of intense and turbulent feeling' of which Coleridge writes in the *Biographia*.[61] Coleridge obsessively revised his own writing: as Robert Brinkley and Keith Hanley have suggested, editors of Coleridge 'cannot avoid the pervasive quality of their author's revisions',[62] indicating a form of poetic craft in which repetition (the constant return to the same lines), accompanied by an assumption that difference might be introduced, is fundamental. Brinkley and Hanley draw attention to one editor of Coleridge's work, whose response to the 'revisionary nature' of Coleridge's poetry was to issue a variorum edition which refuses to authorize one single copy text, as the only way adequately of representing the intensity of his revision: 'From an aesthetic perspective this means that *the* poem has been displaced by its many versions.'[63] Here again, we find an idea of repetition *with* variation to lie at the heart of Coleridge's work, both as he conceived of it, and as it has been received by his readers.

Repetition in Coleridge's Poetry

As Norman Fruman concedes, 'Poets, like other human beings, are not incapable of deliberately falsifying the past, and an endless number of motives, conscious and unconscious, can enter into the process of "counterfeiting the memory."'[64] This goes further than a simple interest in memory: Coleridge is famously a borrower at best, a plagiarist at worst, and (somewhere in between) worries that

---

[59] Kohl, p. 205. [60] *Biographia Literaria*, i, 18–19.
[61] See *Formal Charges*, p. 176; *Biographia Literaria*, ii, 57.
[62] Robert Brinkley and Keith Hanley, 'Introduction' to *Romantic Revisions*, pp. 1–17 (p. 5).
[63] Robert Brinkley and Keith Hanley, 'Introduction', pp. 4–5.
[64] Norman Fruman, 'Creative Process and Concealment in Coleridge's Poetry', in *Romantic Revisions*, pp. 154–68 (p. 154).

he might be 'an involuntary Imposter'.[65] Such anxieties reflect a desire about originality, but in 'Frost at Midnight', poetic revision draws attention to the related idea of memory more specifically. According to Michael O'Neill, one virtue of the revision of 'Frost at Midnight' is 'the greater fluidity of the relation between [Coleridge's] present and past selves' which is introduced. For O'Neill, repetitions of *quietness* in 'Frost at Midnight' demonstrate self-consciousness about the act of poetic creation:

> The icicles which begem the end of 'Frost at Midnight', 'Quietly shining to the quiet Moon' (74), may seem to satisfy yet redefine the restless search for harmony between mind and nature, language and reality undertaken by the poet's 'idling spirit' (20). Yet earlier in the poem the film which lay on the fire was 'the sole unquiet thing' (16), its restlessness giving it 'dim sympathies with me who live' (18). The echo points up the self-conscious yet subliminal and even disquieting way unquietness is erased by the final line.[66]

The self-consciousness the reader is compelled to recognize means that 'The poem watches itself progress from stage to stage, yet its progressions are surprising to itself and its readers; as a result the poet's role in shaping a pattern is conceded, but the possibility that the linguistic pattern corresponds to a larger design is held open'.[67] Self-consciousness about repetition in verse articulates anxieties about fundamental experience (the dynamic between copying and imitation noted above): for O'Neill, the poem 'is at once ingenious and haunted in the way it represents consciousness and nature becoming "Echo or mirror" (22) of each other'.[68] But neither echoes nor mirror-images are identical. Echoes degrade sound as they progress; mirrors invert the image they reflect. The restlessness to which these ideas of repetition-with-difference draw attention is a key attribute of the 'film' which lies on the fire in 'Frost at Midnight', 'the sole unquiet thing' whose lack of tranquillity gives it 'dim sympathies with me who live'.[69]

Coleridge's wider engagement with repetition in his poetry has attracted critical attention in various places. Theologian critics have been particularly drawn to the 'Rime of the Ancient Mariner', and specifically to issues of repetition and difference in theological and liturgical contexts. A subset of this work has been essentially formal: both Catherine Pickstock and John Milbank, for instance, identify an interest in repetition with difference which is understood to be partly

---

[65] Coleridge to Robert Southey, 5 August 1803, in *The Collected Letters of Samuel Taylor Coleridge*, ii, 959, cited in Fruman, p. 165.
[66] O'Neill, p. 70; p. 67.   [67] O'Neill, pp. 68–9.   [68] O'Neill, p. 69.
[69] Samuel Taylor Coleridge, 'Frost at Midnight', in *S. T. Coleridge's Collected Works Vol 16: Poetical Works I; Poems (Reading Texts) Part I*, ed. J. C. C. Mays (Princeton, NJ: Princeton University Press, 2001), 452–6, ll. 15–18. All further references to Coleridge's poems will be to this volume of this edition.

indebted to the Lowthian tradition.[70] Several twentieth-century literary theorists predictably interpreted the Mariner's predisposition to repeat his tale by bringing to bear psychoanalytic understandings of repetition compulsion, for instance, or post-structuralist anxieties about incompletion, on their readings.[71] Drawing literary and theological traditions together, Peter Larkin concludes that 'In the *Opus Maximum* it is only the fullness of the divine self which is "wholly and adequately repeated" and it is that "very repetition [which] contains the distinction from the primary act." Only in aspiring toward the liturgical can the Mariner rediscover his own lostness, and from within a repetition echoing divine distinction and difference cease to centre that loss obsessively on his own self-narration.'[72]

Linguistic analysis has also found Coleridgean repetition to be bound up with distinction, true to his insistence on the value of desynonymy: Lane Cooper highlights Coleridge's 'pleaonastic compounds', pointing out that 'In Coleridge and other romantic poets one sign of their release from tradition is the free use and coinage of hyphenated adjectives and nouns... Coleridge possesses a set of tautological compounds whose general nature is traceable, so far as I am aware, to no external source.' Listing many examples, Cooper argues that, far from inducing a sense of redundancy, these 'add their grateful flavor to the numerous devices of echo and repetition with which the poet increases his general epic effect.'[73] More recently, Stewart has noted that Coleridge shares a 'Romantic instinct for phonetic iteration'.[74] Stewart offers Coleridgean examples of the 'transegmental drift' he anatomizes, in which competing sounds and meanings latent within lines of writing force a form of mental repetition which revises our sense of the poem: the 'sibilant juncture' of 'delicious surges' means we also hear entirely appropriate *urges* in 'The Eolian Harp'; in the phrase 'A Light in sound', Stewart points out that the 'transegmental drift'

> erodes, in particular, the readerly threshold between eye and ear—between a written sequence and a malleable phonic sequacity—to produce the transegmental or esemplastic reassemblage 'alight'. In this sense, the poem's titular symbol itself,

---

[70] See Catherine Pickstock, *After Writing: On the Liturgical Consummation of Philosophy* (Oxford: Blackwell, 1998), pp. 181–2, and John Milbank, *Theology and Social Theory: Beyond Secular Reason* (Oxford: Blackwell, 1993), p. 291. Both are cited in Larkin, p. 147.

[71] See for example David Bunyan, 'Compulsive Repetition and "The Ancient Mariner": Coleridge's Romantic "Uncanny"', *Journal of Literary Studies*, 6 (1990), 115–25 (esp. pp. 110–11); and Homer Obed Brown, 'The Art of Theology and the Theology of Art: Robert Penn Warren's Reading of Coleridge's "The Rime of the Ancient Mariner"', *Boundary*, 2.8 (1979), 237–60. Peter Larkin discusses these and other texts in their relevance to ideas of the Mariner's anxious compulsion (see Larkin, pp. 146–59).

[72] Larkin, p. 157.

[73] Lane Cooper, 'Pleonastic Compounds in Coleridge', *Modern Language Notes*, 19.7 (November 1904), 223–4 (pp. 223–4; p. 224), https://www-jstor-org.ezp.lib.cam.ac.uk/stable/pdf/2917138.pdf, accessed 2 June 2022.

[74] Stewart, p. 150.

the wind harp—a structure of taut lines waiting the breath (or inspiration) of the wind, a material symbol of a latency whose music is potentiated only by the breath of 'vocal' performance—is therefore a 'meet emblem' (to borrow Coleridge's phrase from this same poem) of the poem itself, this and any poem.[75]

Of all Coleridge's poems, 'Christabel' is most obviously preoccupied with recapitulation. Coleridge prefaces the poem with a note setting out the dates of its composition. Incidentally demonstrating that the timing of Coleridge's metrical experiment coincides with his interest in Klopstock, the dates are included, Coleridge insists, 'for the exclusive purpose of precluding charges of plagiarism or servile imitation from myself': the note is explicitly intended to exorcize the possibility that Coleridge might be accused of copying—repeating—the work of others, and he nervously maintains that, had the poem been published when it was composed, 'the impression of its originality would have been much greater than I dare at present expect.'[76] Coleridge moves on from these questions of imitation to pre-empt criticism of his experimental, accentual metrical form. 'Christabel' was intended for (though it was not included in) the *Lyrical Ballads*, and in that sense, it originates as part of a project whose title invokes certain kinds of formal repetition, even if it does not cleave to those expected patterns. But Coleridge's use of formal repetition was to be entirely new, playing with preconceived ideas of regularity and irregularity. As his preface asserts,

> the metre of the Christabel is not, properly speaking, irregular, though it may seem so from its being founded on a new principle: namely, that of counting in each line the accents, not the syllables. Though the latter may vary from seven to twelve, yet in each line the accents will be found to be only four.[77]

Here, metre is a source of repetition whose disruption—whose variation, that is— is meaningful *because* such regularity throws it into relief: 'this occasional variation in number of syllables is not introduced wantonly, or for the mere ends of convenience, but in correspondence with some transition, in the nature of the imagery or passion.'[78]

Beyond the experiment with accentual versification, the most perfunctory reading of 'Christabel' cannot overlook its interest in repeated words, ideas and sounds:

> Tis the middle of Night by the Castle Clock,
> And the Owls have awaken'd the crowing Cock:
> Tu-u-whoo!—Tu-u-whoo!

---

[75] Stewart, pp. 151–4 (pp. 153–5).
[76] 'Preface' to 'Christabel', in *Coleridge's Collected Works*, p. 481.
[77] 'Preface' to 'Christabel', pp. 482–3.   [78] 'Preface' to 'Christabel', p. 483.

> And hark, again! the crowing Cock,
> How drowsily it crew.
>
> Sir Leoline, the Baron rich,
> Hath a toothless mastiff Bitch:
> From her Kennel beneath the Rock
> She maketh Answer to the Clock,
> Four for the Quarters, and twelve for the Hour,
> Ever and aye, by Shine and Shower,
> Sixteen short Howls, not overloud;
> Some say, she sees my Lady's Shroud.
>
> Is the Night chilly and dark?
> The Night is chilly, but not dark.[79]

The strident end-rhymes often depend on identical words, within and across stanzas, and the number of different rhyme sounds is limited (AABABCCAADDDD, etc.), forcing lines to reach back, and making progress slow. But in these opening lines, the repeated words are always challenged, so that they simultaneously become *different*. This is partly because their status as repetitious and secondary declares their difference from their first iteration. But secondariness here is overt: 'the crowing Cock' is explicitly crowing 'again'; the clock also chimes repeatedly, but understood via the dog's response to it, the clock chimes *differently* at each repetition. In most published versions of the poem (including the original 1816 edition), the cry of the owl modifies itself ('tu-whitt' becomes 'tu-whoo'[80]). The nature of the cock's crow is unexpectedly developed as it is revealed to have been drowsy (we might equally be surprised that 'again' in line 4 refers to the cock, and not the bell or the owl). The question at the start of the second stanza is answered with a correction. Small, individual points; but cumulatively these recapitulations reveal that *nothing* is as the reader is first led to think. The lines also force a redirection of attention: despite implicitly and explicitly being told to listen to the cock, we actually hear the owl transliterated on the page, so when we are directed to listen 'again', we must overwrite what we have literally heard. And there is a wider interest in disruption here: if the preface declares a new attention to metrical time, so clock time seems to be out of sorts. The poem's opening invokes the time of day, but despite the declared unending sameness (the clock's chiming for 'Ever and aye'), things are disjointed: chanticleer has been awoken in an untimely manner which leaves him uncharacteristically sleepy, and we are confronted

---

[79] 'Christabel', in *Coleridge's Collected Works*, pp. 477–504, ll. 1–15.
[80] J. C. C. Mays, editor of the Princeton edition, explains his reasons for reinstating the MS version of the line in his reading text of the poem, though notes that this departs from the norm of his edition (p. 318), and the amendment seems a curious deviation from the original version published in *Christabel: Kubla Khan, A Vision; The Pains of Sleep* (London: John Murray, 1816), p. 3.

almost immediately with the repeated stories of rumour in the assertion that 'Some say...'.[81] This rumour insinuates the haunting (itself a form of disturbing repetition) explicitly invoked elsewhere in the lines.

Forms of repetition are also thematically significant in 'Christabel' insofar as they are associated with ideas of copied sources, and through the idea of the poem as an inadequate repetition of a dream. Debra Channick argues that 'Christabel' illustrates 'the complications that excessive repetition can cause when it impedes meaning'. Yet she concludes that Coleridge identifies repetition as integral to poetic experience, and necessary to poetry creativity, and that he negotiates these insights through the inclusion of Bracy the Bard. Sir Leoline is merely and detrimentally haunted, but the bard is more complex: in Channick's account, for the poet-figure inside the poem, 'uncontrollable repetition becomes a site of inventiveness' as the bard embraces the way in which repetition accommodates difference in order to manage its potentials.[82] All of this is very much consonant with Coleridge's comments on repetition explored above, and yet, despite its rehabilitation by Bracy, Coleridge's failure to finish 'Christabel' indicates his struggle fully to master the complexities of repetition within his own poetry.

Coleridge's experimentation with the capacity of recapitulation to meet the demands of expression persistently marks his verse. 'The Rime of the Ancient Mariner', for example, struggles to reach an end because it is caught in a cycle of narrative repetition.[83] Peter Larkin argues that 'The restless self-repetition of the Mariner's story, together with his more marginal but equally unaccomplished procession to the kirk... are not innocent forms of open-endedness so much as fraught modes of incompletion.'[84] Here, repetitions speak to the Romantic interest in fragments found in Shelley's 'Ozymandias', and Keats's 'Ode on a Grecian Urn'. In 'The Rime', even as repetition is apparently focused towards a form of liturgical participation, it induces tormenting anxiety and simultaneously promises escape from the impasse of adequate expression. Likewise facing up to the challenge and seductions of the fragment, 'Kubla Kahn' is dominated by clamorous aural repetitions.[85] Its reiteration of specific words hardly needs listing. Just as arresting on first encounter is the poem's strident metrical repetition, and close on its heels is the rhyme scheme, which progresses somewhat in the manner of Coleridge's water-beetle, frequently pulling back and repeating previous rhyme-sounds just once or twice more than we might anticipate. On top of these features are the alliterative pairs which end each of the first five lines ('Kubla Khan'/'dome decree'/ 'river, ran'/'measureless to man'/'sunless sea'), all of which force extra stress onto already stressed beats. The 'measureless'ness of line 4 is already punning in a

---

[81] See 'The Thorn', l. 216.　　[82] Channick (not paginated).
[83] Coleridge, 'The Rime of the Ancient Mariner', in *Coleridge's Collected Works*, pp. 365–419.
[84] Larkin, p. 146.
[85] 'Kubla Khan; or, A Vision in A Dream', in *Coleridge's Collected Works*, pp. 509–14.

poem so aware of its own poetic measure (and is revived later in the poem as a specifically musical 'mingled measure', following a direct repetition of the 'caverns measureless to man'). But measurelessness is immediately modified by the spatial measuring of line 6, itself enclosed within an idea of repetition: of 'twice five miles'. The ambiguity of the description, 'So twice five miles of fertile ground | With walls and towers were girdled round', moreover, demands a kind of repetitious reading comparable to that described by Ricks's attention to line endings: it contains within itself the necessity for revision, in order for the reader to be able to settle upon 'a' sense, or to register the impossibility of doing so. Coleridge's fertile ground might be girdled round for ten miles, but it might also be a five-mile perimeter girdled twice. We don't need to decide which is topographically correct (to do so would destroy something fundamental to the poem), but the imaginative flicker which turns over the lines in order to gather in the different potential meanings presses Coleridge's serpentine readerly mind into action.

Repetition is also present thematically, in the poem's interest in heredity and prophecy. The 'Ancestral voices prophesying war!' (l. 30) call back to a past which was looking to the future, positing lineage as a form of authority. The poem also self-consciously declares and contains the frustration of repeated song, in its image of the damsel with a dulcimer: the plea within the lines is not simply to hear the song again, but to 'revive within me | Her symphony and song' (ll. 42–3). The series of conditionals ('Could I'/ ''twould win'/'would build'/'should see'/ 'should cry', ll. 42–9) suggest only potential. Yet at the end of the poem, the potentials become real:

> And all should cry, Beware! Beware!
> His flashing eyes, his floating hair!
> Weave a circle round him thrice,
> And close your eyes with holy dread:
> For he on honey-dew hath fed,
> And drank the milk of Paradise.
>
> (ll. 49–54)

The repeated imperative, the warning to 'Beware!', cannot but act as a vocalized cry (even if vocalized only in the reader's head). Through it, Coleridge is able to land on the incantatory repetition of a circle, woven 'thrice' around Kubla Khan himself. All the attention to repetition in the poem has led to this, and the result is the final lines, where even whilst we imagine that we close our eyes, as instructed, enough has been done for the imagination to see the now-concrete, literally physical(ized) image of one who 'hath fed, | And drank'. We are led to envisage not a conditional but a concrete form, so that we *do* repeat the experience, with Coleridge, as he attempts to repeat the dream on the page. And yet, of course, the overriding impression is one of loss; of even the best approximation as insufficient. After all, the poem is also significant in terms of Coleridge's interest in repetition in its self-declared status as a transcription. It is given to us as an unsuccessful attempt to repeat a dream (and a dream state) which itself is a translated repetition of the reading in Purchas which Coleridge declares to be inspirational.[86] In this layering, the source of the imagery is displaced, so that the lines between copying and imagining are blurred. We are left with the impossibility of true repetition, both in the poem ('*could* I revive...', l. 42) and also in the fiction of the person from Porlock who disrupts the dream (and yet who through his role in the wider narrative remains in some sense a part of it).

Other poems by Coleridge also engage with the layering of imagination involved in repetitions of experience. M. H. Abrams insists that each of Coleridge's greater Romantic lyrics 'rounds itself to end where it began, at the outer scene, but with an altered mood and deepened understanding which is the result of the intervening meditation.'[87] For Coleridge, then, this sense of return, the idea that something might be superficially the same yet fundamentally altered, is part of the effect of the poem, as well as a characteristic of its structure. But more than this, insofar as the much-revised 'This Lime-tree Bower' extends Coleridge's interest in the idea of 'one life within us and abroad',[88] a unity between the human and the divine in nature, it speaks directly to the idea of the 'One' as a 'repetition in the finite mind' articulated in the *Biographia*.[89] It engenders a degree of progression through stagnation which mimics the preoccupation of the water-insect, and in this way is perhaps the closest that Coleridge comes to achieving in verse what he theorized about imagination and repetition in the *Biographia*.

To some extent, the repetitions in 'This Lime-tree Bower' are straightforward, particularly in the opening section of the poem.[90] Often, a word or phrase (the 'roaring dell' of ll. 9–10, for instance) is emphasized by its reiteration; 'view again' suggests the nature of poetic, imaginative experience as inherently a repetition of lived experience, which Coleridge conceptualizes elsewhere. But even these examples are complicated. On its first mention, the dell is 'still roaring'. The idea of *still*ness is always a particular one in the context of repetition and natural description, where it hangs between adverb and adjective; here, the word reaches back to a pre-history of stable existence and continuity. Yet the initial impression of the dell must be revised as it is augmented: a line later, it reappears and is given greater detail and specificity. We *now* know more. This process of revision as we read is not dissimilar to Coleridge's description of his own process of composition:

---

[86] See *Coleridge's Collected Works*, p. 511.
[87] M. H. Abrams, 'Structure and Style in the Greater Romantic Lyric', in Frederick W. Hilles and Harold Bloom, eds, *From Sensibility to Romanticism: Essays Presented to Frederick A. Pottle* (New York: Oxford University Press, 1965), pp. 527–60 (p. 530).
[88] The phrase is from Coleridge's 'The Eolian Harp', in *Coleridge's Collected Works*, pp. 231–5, l. 26.
[89] *Biographia Literaria*, i, 304.
[90] 'This Lime-tree Bower my Prison', in *Coleridge's Collected Works*, pp. 349–54.

like the water-insect, we go back, in order to move slightly further forward. We must relax, give up our own imaginative construction, in order to gain from the addition of material, which we may then add into our re-composition of the scene. But it remains peculiar in character in Coleridge's lines, in that more detail is persistently gained alongside direct repetition, which would seem simultaneously to resist specificity, by giving us more of the same.

Words like 'still' and 'told' (l. 9) might purport to deny imaginative activity in the moment of composition. Yet as Kelvin Everest has pointed out, the conflicting meanings of 'still' 'underpin the development in Coleridge's mood from static, barren introspection, to the dynamic growth in consciousness that is effected in the description of an imagined experience.'[91] 'Still' is an example of the many ambiguous words Coleridge presses into service, which entail a sense of return as the reader qualifies their meaning. Here, 'still' often appears with an oxymoronic sense of movement ('Still roaring'; 'tremble still'; 'still nod'). But any ambiguity involves a kind of re-reading on the part of the reader when it becomes clear that the sense might be different to that which we first assumed. The word 'again' is likewise favoured by Coleridge, inherently involved in experience itself as a form of repetition. 'Now' also exerts its subtle effect, as the last rook swoops out of the end of the poem, 'Now a dim speck, now vanishing in light' (l. 72): these and other instances of repeated 'now's in the poem compress the different meanings of the word (one to do with the present instance, the other a marker of diachronic progression), without pretending to reconcile them. All of this indicates a self-conscious interest in the special possibilities of repetition, and its importance to the poem.

'Still' and 'now' are particular because of the tense contradiction between time and space they both contain, but there are other examples of word repetition-with-revision even in the first stanza of 'This Lime-tree Bower': Coleridge includes the 'Ash ... that branchless Ash', leaves which 'ne'er tremble ... yet tremble still', and weeds which 'Still nod and drip beneath the dripping edge' (the latter two examples notably re-employing the idea of stillness). The same attachment to repetition with revision is found at the opening of 'Frost at Midnight': 'The owlet's cry | Came loud—and hark, again! loud as before' (ll. 203); 'that film, which fluttered on the grate, | Still flutters there' (ll. 15-16; here again, 'still' introduces a sense of spatial and temporal expansion). These examples seem self-consciously to be playing with the idea of what a repetition might be; we are surely to take them as 'the apparent tautologies of intense and turbulent feeling',

---

[91] Kelvin Everest, *Coleridge's Secret Ministry* (Hassocks: Harvester, 1979), p. 250. Miller has criticized Everest for neglecting the link between the two senses of 'still', and thereby misrepresenting 'Coleridge's poetic attachment to stillness', arguing that 'the deepest poetic resonance' of the word 'still' 'renders the sense of simultaneity that haunted him' (Miller, pp. 536-7n. and p. 522); relatedly, McDonald has also discussed Coleridge's (and other poets') use of the word 'like' (see McDonald, pp. 44-5).

rather than the frustrating 'blank counters' of the *Biographia*, as almost inverted echoes, in which intensity builds rather than fading away. And indeed, the second cry of the owlet in 'Frost at Midnight' *is* more significant because it is a repetition of the first. We are only implored to listen when it comes for a second time; the repeated word is 'loud', and it seems as if we are about to gain some clarification of the volume (as loud as...what?): we reach for more meaning, and when it turns out only to be as loud as itself, we are made aware of our own imaginative engagement. As we listen for repetition, we are not alone: according to Christopher Miller, 'In many repeated words, we hear the poet listening to the sound of his own words'.[92]

'This Lime-tree Bower' uses various standard poetic devices to force the reader into a continual process of revision. Verbs are often delayed, and clauses are persistently added to qualify the scene, in terms of time, place, and action. Linear verse is necessarily sequential, but Coleridge seems to draw attention to continual, often imperfect revisions: in lines 9–10, for example, 'of which I told' implies a hitherto unmentioned prior recitation, as well as the occurrence of the event itself which has been recounted; the more obvious repetition of the 'dell', and the playfulness of the idea of 'still' is half-echoed in the way that dell and still half rhyme; and all of this cumulative sense of scene is preceded after all by 'perchance' (a resistance to a claim to total knowledge of the scene which is sustained through a similar vocabulary of 'perhaps' and 'may'). Even as it builds, the poem thus reveals Coleridge's uncertainty about its accuracy. This augments the tendency of the poem to vacillate between control and impotence (found in, for instance, the suggestive words which teeter between passive description and imperative command: 'and there my friends | Behold the dark green file of long lank Weeds', ll. 16–17; 'Now, my friends emerge...', l. 20). It thus reflects Coleridge's own position as speaker-poet, describing through the recapitulation of his own past experience a present scene not immediately visible to him, containing different participants, and thus different perspectives, at a different point in time, and which is thus inevitably *different*.

In lines themselves framed by the repetition of the address, 'My gentle-hearted Charles',[93] *or* functions in the poem in a similar way:

> My gentle-hearted Charles! when the last Rook
> Beat its straight path along the dusky air
> Homewards, I blest it! deeming, its black wing
> (Now a dim speck, now vanishing in light)
> Had cross'd the mighty Orb's dilated glory,

---

[92] Miller, p. 529.   [93] The phrase appears at l. 28, l. 69, and l. 76.

> While thou stood'st gazing; or, when all was still,
> Flew creeking o'er thy head, and had a charm
> For thee, my gentle-hearted Charles...
>
> (ll. 69–76)

The *or* at line 74 is an 'inclusive' one: because the poem originates in Coleridge's imagination (and surpasses any *actual* experience in value, as the end of the poem makes clear), both possibilities exist equally within it. Both of these things have happened, and yet either or both might not have done. It is even possible to find, as 'deeming' sounds again in 'creeking', a sense in which Coleridge writes himself into the experience of his friends: as 'deeming' is explicitly Coleridge's authorial prerogative, when the bird (perhaps) flies over Charles's head, the aural association of 'creeking' with 'deeming' momentarily renders Coleridge *as* the bird, sharing its ability to transcend and witness the experience of the walkers. Within the blank verse, the repetitious effect of rhyme thus contributes to Coleridge's simultaneous sharing in and exclusion from the company of his friends, through the writing of the poem, augmenting the vacillation which would seem intuitively to sit at odds with the reinforcing certainty of repetition.

Repetitions in the lines successfully create scenic effects, but they also hint at the frustrations which provide the impetus for the poem. This is especially apparent in the repetitions of words from early lines at the very end of the text. So, whilst through the poem Coleridge ostensibly writes himself out of his mood, and what is lost in the early stanzas is found by the end, the progress suggested is less obviously resisted by the texture of the verse itself, which continually hints that the imagination might be modified by the effects of repetition in the process of writing the poem. To dwell further on line 9 ('To that still roaring dell, of which I told;'), for example, 'still' and 'of which I told' might seem to deny imagination in the current moment in favour precisely of a repetition of something prior. The whole poem asks, similarly, for the scene to be 'view[ed] again'. Such repetitions purport to add more of the same, even as they really add more detail, both because the reader is neither 'gentle-hearted Charles' nor Coleridge (and is therefore unaware of these previous experiences or recollections), and by virtue of their status *as* repetitions to those who might have heard them before: taken out of context, the line might even teeter towards the tedium of the oft-repeated anecdote. Miller concludes that 'The fundamental realization of the poem is that one cannot recall and register simultaneously; there is a tension between remembering and noticing, and between words and vision.'[94] Coleridge is also aware, though, that repetition negotiates the here and now *with* the there and then; repetition is

---

[94] Miller, p. 533.

thus the means by which this situation or posture can be intimated in the text of the poem itself.

Coleridge's description in the poem is alive with texture, perspective and shade, but the actual colours he mentions are simple: a palette of yellow, green, blue, purple, and black. The use of 'blue' exemplifies well the way in which a colour might be reduced *and* enhanced by repetition. Coleridge invokes

> the dark green file of long lank Weeds,
> That all at once (a most fantastic sight!)
> Still nod and drip beneath the dripping edge
> Of the blue clay-stone.
>
> (ll. 17–20)

As the dripping green weeds are finally put into place, they are found out beneath a 'blue clay-stone' which itself repeats their dripping. It does so, moreover, in a complex way, as its suddenness and the shock of its 'fantastic'ness resist a sense of prior awareness, recalling Wordsworth's record of surprised encounter with his infamous daffodils (who toss their heads in a similar movement to the weeds' nodding). When the word 'blue' returns six lines later as 'The slip of smooth clear blue' of the sea (l. 25), it is, we intuit, a totally different colour, texture, *thing*. Similarly, 'purple shadow' (l. 26) returns as 'purple heath-flowers' (l. 35); 'poor yellow leaves' (l. 14) are remembered in the 'yellow light' (l. 36) of distant groves; the 'blackest mass' (l. 55) of elm branches returns in the last rook's 'black wing' (l. 71). Repetition intensifies and purifies each colour (blue is really, really blue; yellow is really, really yellow, etc.), yet it also fractures it prismatically into shades inflected by different associations. Such effects recall Coleridge's acknowledgement in the *Biographia* of the potential of repeated words to communicate intensity, they illustrate simultaneously the process of desynonymization, and they thus expand and demonstrate the importance of an understanding of repetition which accommodates, even as it apparently resists, difference.

In a straightforward way, 'This Lime-tree Bower' seems to fit neatly within Wordsworth's definition of poetry in the 'Preface' to *Lyrical Ballads*, as derived from contemplation of a previous emotional experience. It is a deliberate re-experiencing, or repetition, until 'an emotion, similar to that which was before the subject of contemplation, is gradually produced, and does itself actually exist in the mind.'[95] The repetition in this account is not exact; it is only ever *similar*: repetition is conceived of as allowing variation. 'This Lime-tree Bower' is declaredly a recollection, as Coleridge imagines for his friends a walk he has taken before. At the same time, it is an imaginative creation; insofar as Coleridge can only imagine

---

[95] *Prose*, i, 148.

what it would be to accompany his friends, it can only be *similar* to any previous experience. The imagination involves a process of repetition which is both positive and negative, surrendering active presence yet achieving imaginative success through this very passivity. As in the description of the water-insect, the richness of the experience of being left behind can be articulated only through the recollection of an occasion which registers its own status as a repetition which is not quite the same as the current event: the 'win upstream' depends on the giving up, relaxing back into a sense of loss. Yet at the end of the poem, the shift in perception allows for the experience of 'radiance' (l. 53) where previously had been only imprisonment. This is a form of revision which transcends by incorporating all others. John Jones argues that the fundamental difference between Wordsworth and Coleridge is that 'the theme of the one [Coleridge] was unity and the other [Wordsworth] significant relation'.[96] The desire for unity pervades Coleridge's thought. Disagreeing with Wordsworth on the qualities of poetic diction, for instance, he insists that 'educated man chiefly seeks to discover and express those *connections* of things, or those relative *bearings* of fact to fact, from which some more or less general law is deducible. For *facts* are valuable to a wise man, chiefly as they lead to the discovery of the indwelling *law*, which is the true *being* of things'.[97] Elsewhere he recasts his understanding of the dynamic between specifics and generals (central to Wordsworth's understanding of repetition and conjunction) thus: 'The difference between an organic and an inorganic body lies in this:—in the first—a sheaf of corn—the *Whole* is nothing more than a collection of the individual phænomena; in the second—a man—the whole is the effect of, or results from, the parts—is in fact everything, and the parts nothing.'[98] This idea of the part remaining partial or particular, and yet allowing the apprehension of a whole, is important. Coleridge is not Wordsworth, but there are similar preoccupations here to how to produce the history of 'a' mind, which can only be understood as the sum of the parts which have made it, which in turn can only be understood in the context of that whole. For Wordsworth, negotiating the line between specific and general or representative is the very role of the poet. For Coleridge, the line itself is the potential source of the sublime, as the part gestures towards the absent whole. He isn't concerned with repetition's calling on the mind to develop a structure of connection and relationship, but more with an echo which in its very insistence on the difference between one repetition and another alludes to the gaps which always exist, to the knowledge that things and apprehensions are only ever parts of the 'All', indeed only gain their own meaning by virtue of that participation, and can always be received differently even though they are the same thing (a thing which *is* the whole, the unified, the one). In this glance at their stretching capacity to mean, and

---

[96] Jones, p. 84. [97] *Biographia Literaria*, ii, 53.
[98] *The Collected Works of Samuel Taylor Coleridge, Vol. 14, Part I: 'Table Talk'*, ed. Carl Woodring (Princeton, NJ: Princeton University Press and Routledge, for the Bollingen Foundation, 1990), p. 258.

the inevitability of a partial apprehension, the theory nods at a *potential* source of sublimity, but Coleridge's own verse struggles actually to achieve it.

In one sense, the revising, restless imagination undoubtedly at work in Coleridge's poems, perennially attracted to devices and moments of repetition, meets well his own criteria for the imagination. But in general, the examples here suggest a rather less successful engagement with repetition in verse. Coleridge couldn't finish 'Christabel', or (for other reasons, perhaps), 'Kubla Khan'. Repetition resists ending, and Coleridge struggles to manage this fact, whereas Wordsworth turns it to meaningful advantage. Despite significant explicit attention to its operation in poetic texts and as part of his model of the mind, and whilst he seems to be aware of its potentials, Coleridge never quite achieves the poetic subtlety Wordsworth comes to command through repetition. As Peter McDonald argues in his comparison of Wordsworth's 'There was a boy' with Coleridge's 'The Nightingale', for example, through repetition Coleridge 'engineers a straightforward moment of anticipation', whereas Wordsworth 'allows repetition to become his medium as well as his subject', to the extent that he brings about 'a state of "Listening" in which repetition seems to fill with an intent that resists overt statement or verbal formulation'.[99] Nonetheless, this attention further suggests the extent to which ideas of repetition, revision, and recapitulation, both as devices which might enrich literary texts and as wider ideas connected to the possibilities of the imagination, were circulating amongst Wordsworth's community, from the 1790s onwards. In this sense, it is Coleridge's model which is the more convincing: in terms of sociability and influence, 'Not only is the Whole greater than a Part; but when it is a Whole, and not a mere All or Aggregate, it makes each part that which it is.'[100]

---

[99] McDonald, pp. 89–90.

[100] Coleridge makes this statement in a note, addressing the question of whether men are made for the state, or the state for men; the editors of his *Collected Works* draw attention to it in their annotations of *Table Talk* from December 1831 (see *The Collected Works of Samuel Taylor Coleridge, Vol. 14, Part I*, p. 259, n. 8).

13
Conclusion

Recapitulation and Sincerity

In August 1817, Hazlitt published a review of the *Biographia* in the *Edinburgh Review*, which lamented that 'Mr. Coleridge bewilders himself sadly':

> There is no natural harmony in the ordinary combinations of significant sounds: the language of prose is not the language of music, or of *passion*: and it is to supply this inherent defect in the mechanism of language—to make the sound an echo to the sense, when the sense becomes a sort of echo to itself . . . —that poetry was invented.[1]

Making the sound an echo of the sense implies the possibility of a direct correlation between the articulated poem, and that which the poet desires to communicate. Paul Hamilton points out that 'passion is the fundamental category in Coleridge's definition of poetry'.[2] If the sound is really to be an echo to the sense, then according to this definition, it must echo passion: it must communicate *feeling*. This is fundamentally a criterion of sincerity. Echo, as Wordsworth's poetry has demonstrated, is a type of repetition which is wholly constituted by its source, but which exists as a subtly different form of that source as it bounces, returns, and fades. Hazlitt's 'echo' depends on two key ideas: firstly, that sound *might* echo sense (where 'sense' refers to 'passion', or feeling); and secondly, that that 'sense' *might* be comprehended, and articulated. Importantly, Hazlitt goes on to allow space for the comprehension he is invoking *not* to be of a single and entirely stable thing: as 'the sense becomes a sort of echo to itself', Hazlitt offers an image of flexible reflection, in which poetry is 'to take the imagination off its feet, and spread its wings where it may indulge its own impulses'. Just as the mountains give back to Wordsworth (and thence to the reader) echoes which are shaped by their reflection and direction, and thus are *different* from the articulated sound, so here poetry prompts not identical feeling, but rather offers inspiration, and a more personal response. In their recapitulation, the words of poetry thus offer capacious

---

[1] William Hazlitt, 'Coleridge's Literary Life', *The Edinburgh Review*, 28.56 (August 1817), 488–515 (p. 514).
[2] *Coleridge's Poetics*, p. 147.

scope for difference, but insofar as they are shared, this difference is experienced as vital connection.

In its discussion of Adamson's linguistic 'index of feeling and truth'; in the comparison of different versions of the same episode, or its attention to Barrell's and Davie's teasing out the possibility of communicating 'fixed meanings'; in Wordsworth's own ponderings upon the 'truth' of his accounts, and in various other places, this book has introduced the idea that recapitulation, including the specialized repetition enacted through the employment of conjunctions *and* and *or*, bears significantly on the discourse of 'Romantic sincerity', and suggested that this is a crucial aspect of its value to Wordsworth. An idea of Romantic sincerity has been a persistent preoccupation of Wordsworth's readers. As David Perkins has described it,

> In the transformation of poetry throughout the eighteenth century, nothing is more remarkable than the emergence of sincerity as a major poetic value... The vocabulary of criticism in the Renaissance included neither 'sincerity' nor synonyms that come near our modern concept. The subsequent elevation of sincerity accompanied the profound changes that led us to think of poetry as something close to self-expression.[3]

At the beginning of the 1970s, Lionel Trilling declared that 'before authenticity had come along to suggest the deficiencies of sincerity and to usurp its place in our esteem, sincerity stood high in the cultural firmament'.[4] Kerry Sinanan and Tim Milnes more recently have written of a Romantic 'concern that focused on the authenticity of the selves who wrote such works as well as the sincerity of the feelings they expressed. Allied to this concern was a desire to discover a holistic self at the heart of writing, a hub at which the *meaning* of a word might be connected with the *truth* of an intention. Thus, it is in Romantic literature and thought that "sincerity" and "authenticity" are fused—and thereby transformed—for the first time.'[5] In these accounts, 'sincerity' is associated with an idea of truth to oneself; of perfect transparency between experience and record, of what Trilling describes as 'congruence between avowal and actual feeling'.[6] The association of this ideal with Wordsworth is already entrenched in 1879 when Arnold writes of 'the profound sincereness with which Wordsworth feels his subject, and... the

---

[3] *Wordsworth and the Poetry of Sincerity*, pp. 1–2.
[4] Trilling, *Sincerity and Authenticity*, p. 12.
[5] Tim Milnes and Kerry Sinanan, 'Introduction' to Tim Milnes and Kerry Sinanan, eds, *Romanticism, Sincerity and Authenticity* (Basingstoke: Palgrave Macmillan, 2010), pp. 1–28 (p. 2).
[6] Trilling, *Sincerity and Authenticity*, p. 2. On the significance of sincerity to the Romantic Period more generally, see also Perkins, *Wordsworth and the Poetry of Sincerity*; Milnes and Sinanan, eds, *Romanticism, Sincerity and Authenticity*; Abrams, *The Mirror and the Lamp*, pp. 317–20; Deborah Forbes, *Sincerity's Shadow* (Cambridge, MA: Harvard University Press, 2004), and Rosenbaum, *Professing Sincerity*.

profoundly sincere and natural character of his subject';[7] by 1902, Arthur Symons was claiming that 'Sincerity was at the root of all Wordsworth's merits and defects'. Perkins attributes the particular focus on Wordsworth to the 'Preface' to *Lyrical Ballads*: 'The older view', Perkins points out, 'had been that a poet is a "maker,"' but 'Wordsworth would have a poet speak not from the traditions of a craft, but from his full experience and concern as a man.'[8]

Inevitably, the idea of 'sincerity' raised very obvious questions in the mid-twentieth century, an era in which the death of the author was proclaimed (and rejected, and re-proclaimed), and the notion of 'intention' was interrogated, and dismissed (and re-asserted, and re-dismissed). As Angela Esterhammer concisely puts it, in such a climate, '"Sincerity", as a critical concept, did not do very well'.[9] In 1949, René Wellek and Austin Warren declared '"Sincerity" in a poem' to be a term 'almost meaningless':

> A sincere expression of what? Of the supposed emotional state out of which it came? Or of the state in which the poem was written? Or a sincere expression of the poem, i.e. the linguistic construct shaping in the author's mind as he writes? Surely it will have to be the last: the poem is a sincere expression of the poem.[10]

Yet by 1968, critics including Donald Davie had taken the ideals of the New Criticism to task. Davie recognized that 'until a few years ago...the question "Is the poet sincere?"—though it would continue to be asked by naïve readers—was always an impertinent and illegitimate question.'[11] His article asserted a nonetheless persistent sense that, as it was vital to author's (including to Wordsworth's) own understanding of their 'confessional' poetry (or 'the poetry of witness'), so it was the reader's responsibility to take the sincerity of that poetry into account. Even as he acknowledged 'the untidy, embarrassing, and disconcerting consequences' of doing so,[12] Davie remained adamant that readers 'must welcome the change from poetry seen as the extant body of achieved poems, to poetry seen as a way of behaving, a habit of feeling deeply and truly and responsibly'.[13]

Despite this confident reinstatement of the relevance of sincerity to the discipline of literary studies, and beyond the well-rehearsed suspicions of the possibility or utility of any idea of 'intention' behind texts, there are obvious ways in which achieving the Romantic ideal of 'sincerity' in poetry is problematic. As far back as

---

[7] Matthew Arnold, 'Preface', p. xxiv.   [8] *Wordsworth and the Poetry of Sincerity*, p. 13.
[9] Angela Esterhammer, 'The Scandal of Sincerity: Wordsworth, Byron, Landon', in *Romanticism, Sincerity and Authenticity*, pp. 101–19 (p. 101).
[10] René Wellek and Austin Warren, *Theory of Literature*, 3rd edn (New York: Harcourt, Brace & World, 1956), p. 208.
[11] Donald Davie, 'On Sincerity: From Wordsworth to Ginsberg', *Encounter* 31.4 (1968), 61–6, pp. 61–2.
[12] 'On Sincerity: From Wordsworth to Ginsberg', p. 64.
[13] 'On Sincerity: From Wordsworth to Ginsberg', p. 64.

1765, Richard Hurd was already convinced that 'sincerity, or a scrupulous regard to truth in all our conversation and behaviours, how specious so ever it may be in theory, is a thing impossible in practice.'[14] First amongst the difficulties is the ancient dilemma: poetry is figured in language which is generally inadequate for perfect expression of feeling. Drawing on lines from Tennyson to argue that words inevitably 'half reveal | And half conceal the Soul within',[15] Perkins notes,

> There is also the desire to exploit or recognize in the language of poetry devices that allow words to sustain multiple meanings. At the same time, we require that everything said or implied in a poem somehow hang together, making up a unified expression; yet an over-all integration may become more difficult to achieve to the extent that each part or element has been packed with many implications.[16]

Moreover, thoughts and feelings change all the time, but poems insist on fixing things down: 'In order to write at all, a poet must commit himself, at least temporarily, to some dominant concepts or feelings.'[17] How can a poem in its written form thus ever be 'sincere'? On top of such considerations, the existence of sincerity as an ideal inevitably introduces an awkward level of self-consciousness which suggests insincerity (relatedly, Trilling acknowledges that the emergence of psychoanalysis as a discourse problematizes the possibility of sincerity). There is also the fact that poets generally write within received traditions and conventions which inherently proclaim an external, arbitrary influence on one or more elements of the form of the poem created, whereas a properly sincere response might be understood as such only if it were free from that sort of external influence. Rhyme, for example, would seem to impede or resist true sincerity of response: it cannot represent sincere feeling, because feeling must adapt to fit its scheme. Jonathan Culler reminds us that 'The suspicion of rhyme persists in what, since Alexander Pope, has been the reigning critical conception: to avoid being mere bauble, rhyme should be thematically productive, suggesting an unexpected connection between the meanings of the two words that rhyme...It is as though "good rhyme has to be serious rhyme, which does work; it must not be evasive; it must not jingle and tinkle."'[18] Yet, just as Milton labels rhyme the 'modern bondage', the suspicion that even 'good' rhyme necessarily distracts from something more purely sincere or accurate powerfully persists. Furthermore, the same

---

[14] Richard Hurd, *Moral and Political Dialogues*, 3 vols (London: A. Millar, 1765), i, 5, cited in Rosenbaum, p. 3.
[15] See Tennyson, *In Memoriam*, ed. by Erik Gray (New York and London: Norton, 1973; 2004), p. 9, cited in *Wordsworth and the Poetry of Sincerity*, p. 5.
[16] *Wordsworth and the Poetry of Sincerity*, p. 7.
[17] *Wordsworth and the Poetry of Sincerity*, p. 5.
[18] Culler, p. 181, quoting Simon Jarvis, 'Why Rhyme Pleases', *Thinking Verse*, 1 (2011), 30.

devices of poetry which allow refined expression might themselves distract from the very possibility of sincerity: symbols, metaphors, and similes all might be said to replace the 'real' which can be its only true site. And further again, as Yeats famously recognized, to be truly sincere, the text would somehow have to include everything of any particular moment, so in the very action of selection which constitutes poetry, it might be said that sincerity is abandoned. Looking in another direction, Susan Rosenbaum has suggested that the status of poetry as a commodity renders sincerity problematic: 'Sincerity stands at the center of a persistent crisis in reading the lyric, a crisis that stems from the blurring of the moral ideals and commercial practices of authorship'.[19] For all of these and many other reasons which have borne sustained and intricate commentary by poets and by critics, it is easy to see why the possibility of Romantic sincerity continues to be treated sceptically.[20] Yet the contention of this book remains that the feature Perkins notes, in recognizing that poetry allows 'words to sustain multiple meanings', is less of a problem and more of an enabling facet of the achievement of sincerity than has been allowed; that Wordsworth deliberately harnesses forms of recapitulation and the difference they imply and contain, to facilitate sincere verse.

Much has been said about Wordsworth and sincerity specifically, not least in the analysis of his contention that 'Poetry is the spontaneous overflow of powerful feelings: it takes its origin from emotion recollected in tranquillity'.[21] It is clear that Wordsworth does not want to pretend that a poem could ever be an actual, perfect, and immediate response to a particular moment. We might think about the idea and nature of the overflowing, powerful feelings themselves, which inevitably seem to overspill the possibilities of representation in the first place, and also about the difficulties and the possibilities of that 'recollection' at a different time and in a different frame of mind; we could ponder the fact that the sincere poetic record must always reflect the poet at the moment of writing as well as at the moment of perceiving, and wonder if that can ever really be possible. Yet as earlier chapters of this book have suggested, it is indeed possible, through the ways in which types of repetition open up spaces for 'the same but different' to be present simultaneously. Particularly in the revisions to the *Prelude*, a work

---

[19] Rosenbaum, p. 5.
[20] See for one survey of recent attitudes Angela Esterhammer's 'The Scandal of Sincerity'. Esterhammer identifies a 'first wave of "sincerity studies" in the 1960s and 1970s', which 'focused on Wordsworth and recognized him, against an eighteenth-century background, as the first poet to cultivate sincerity as a poetic value': this is epitomized by Guilhamet's describing the 'Preface' to *Lyrical Ballads* as 'a revolutionary presentation of the first elaborate theory of sincerity'. Esterhammer continues: a more recent, 'second wave, which is much more likely to adopt Byron as its model, interprets sincerity as a code or convention'; Esterhammer explains that this wave followed Jerome McGann's assertion that 'the famous "true voice of feeling" is an artful construction' (Esterhammer, pp. 104–5, citing Guilhamet, *The Sincere Ideal*, and McGann, *The Poetics of Sensibility*). Esterhammer in turn advances 'a paradoxical notion of performative sincerity that is at least latent in Wordsworth', which 'probes the limits of expressibility and interpretability.' ('The Scandal of Sincerity', p. 105.)
[21] 'Preface' to *Lyrical Ballads*, p. 148.

explicitly cast as an account of the growth of the poet's mind, Wordsworth's work exemplifies the way in which changes to the mind in the light of further experience affect perceptions of previous events. In this case, *not* to revise might be less sincere than constant revision, and revisions to poems might alter the representations of those events in a sincere and serious way. The idea of recapitulation thus becomes central to sincerity, rather than distracting from it, because it faces and contains this idea of 'sameness with difference', macrocosmically. On a microcosmic level, the way in which the texture of Wordsworth's verse includes and encourages recapitulation functions similarly to indicate a stretching possibility of meaning, incorporating difference within similarity, which paradoxically reaches towards the achievement of sincerity. Additionally, the flexibility of the conjunctions *and* and *or* frequently serves to signal the *accommodation* of revisions of mind, or different possibilities, without necessarily implying the direct elimination of other experiences or feelings. These examples of recapitulation's ability to contain difference within it are vitally important to the way that Wordsworth's writing negotiates the problems of sincerity and change, and careful attention to its various forms illuminates his achievement.

To echo Wellek and Warren, though, we might legitimately ask: sincerity to *what*? If some form of revision must be constant in order to accommodate the kind of changes happening all the time to the poetic self representing the idea or event or scene, and thus to retain sincerity in the representation of that idea or event or scene, we must assume the possibility of a stable self, susceptible to change, in the first place. For Wordsworth, that does not seem to be in question. Wordsworth addresses issues of sincerity directly in his 'Essays upon Epitaphs' of 1810. In the second essay, he engages explicitly with the idea of 'a criterion of sincerity, by which a Writer may be judged':[22]

> no faults have such a killing power as those which prove that he is not in earnest, that he is acting a part, has leisure for affectation, and feels that without it he could do nothing. This is one of the most odious of faults; because it shocks the moral sense: and is worse in a sepulchral inscription, precisely in the same degree as that mode of composition calls for sincerity more urgently than any other.[23]

This displayed sincerity is especially urgent in memorials, because its absence 'shocks the moral sense' of those who can discern it. Sincerity here by direct implication marks writing which is in earnest, is *not* acting a part (i.e. which is 'sincere' to the attitude of the person doing the writing), and is not 'affected'. Wordsworth here participates in a long tradition of privileging the sincerity of

---

[22] *Essay upon Epitaphs, II*, in *Prose*, ii, 70.   [23] *Essay upon Epitaphs, II*, in *Prose*, ii, 70.

epitaphic text, and associating its obverse with acting.[24] Significantly, he does not problematize the possibility of earnestness, which is taken for granted. In this again, he is entirely in line with a tradition which had understood sincerity as the opposite of hypocrisy or dissimulation since its introduction into English discourse in the sixteenth century, and which understood sincere enunciation as 'unity and identity between the heart and tongue'.[25]

If with critics like Davie we therefore accept that Wordsworth's own insistence on a 'criterion of sincerity' deserves a faithful, accepting response from his readers, then how exactly is such sincerity manifest? The second 'Essay upon Epitaphs' attempts to delineate criteria which demonstrate that an inscription is the work of a 'sincere mourner'.[26] However, as Esterhammer remarks,

> The 'Essays on Epitaphs' already point towards the scandal of sincerity, by defining sincerity as the correspondence between the external signs on the grave-stone and the writer's inner feeling, while eliding the fact that the only evidence for the writer's feeling is the external signs or words.[27]

According to Esterhammer, 'Wordsworth goes on to develop his primary criterion for sincerity in epitaphs, namely, the absence of performance or affectation... A more consistent criterion than diction and imagery, it turns out, is spontaneity'. Yet through a reading of Wordsworth's 1835 'Extempore Effusion upon the Death of James Hogg' she demonstrates that 'The poem's presentation as a spontaneous utterance... contrasts with its formal symmetries and reflective tone', which are 'more redolent of "long and deep thought" than of "the spontaneous overflow of powerful feelings"'. Ultimately, Esterhammer concludes that 'Regardless of the intensity of Wordsworth's personal feeling, the very criterion of sincerity that he evokes—that is, spontaneity—at the same time imbues his poem with the performative... connotations of the nineteenth-century extempore effusion.'[28] The poet is caught on the horns of a dilemma here, in which to *appear* sincere, indeed to *appear* anything, is to be the very opposite; but to be literally spontaneous would risk condemnation of the work as unpoetic, uncrafted, chaotic, and simply bad verse.

---

[24] In an essay whose title fully exploits its pun on 'lie', for example, Scott L. Newstok demonstrates that, 'in the English Renaissance, epitaphs are associated with sincerity, more so than any other type of speech', whereas sincerity's obverse was associated with the stage: epitaphic writing and dramatic writing 'are two genres considered to stand at roughly opposite ends of a continuum of perceived sincerity.' See Newstok, '"Here Lies": Sincerity and Insincerity in Early Modern Epitaphs Onstage', *Christianity & Literature*, 67.1 (2017), 50–68.

[25] Nicholas Lokyer, *A Divine Discovery of Sincerity* (London: John Rothwell, 1659), p. 7. Lokyer is discussed by Newstok, in 'Here Lies'. See also Jane Taylor, '"Why do you tear me from Myself?": Torture, Truth, and the Arts of the Counter-reformation', in Ernst van Alphen, Mieke Bal, and Carel Smith, eds, *The Rhetoric of Sincerity* (Stanford: Stanford University Press, 2009), pp. 19–43.

[26] *Essay upon Epitaphs, II*, in *Prose*, ii, 66.   [27] Esterhammer, p. 105.

[28] Esterhammer, pp. 106–9.

In the first of the 'Essays upon Epitaphs', Wordsworth had already emphasized the wide accessibility and applicability of epitaphic writing: 'it is concerning all, and for all.'[29] In this reaching for 'the general language of humanity',[30] the content of the epitaph is figured as a sort of lowest common denominator which, because it is shared between all of us and available to everyone, highlights what we share: in the contemplation of death and grief, we recognize 'our common nature'.[31] Connection in the end trumps all difference, 'all-uniting and equalizing'[32] in a positive sense, at odds with the horrifying lack of connection Wordsworth experiences in the London of *The Prelude*. This connection is as vital to literary choices as it is to human and other relationships in the world. Perkins points to this as one of the impediments of sincerity: 'even in writing a long poem, one must impose an order; one must relate things to each other in some particular way, to the exclusion of other possible relations that may seem equally true... What is needed, then, is a poetic form that provides space without petrifying or stratifying the poet's experience, or his interpretation of it.'[33] This book has tried to demonstrate that insofar as the conjunctions *and* and *or* are inherently recapitulative, Wordsworth both literally and conceptually exploits their tendencies and effects in order to 'impose order' whilst not only allowing for but even encouraging the recognition of other possible orders, or other potential relations, at the same time. His exploitation of repetition in literal textual ways and, more conceptually, in the subjects of his poetry, similarly encourages a constant sense of potential recapitulation which resists fixed order.

Wordsworth goes on to refine his definition of 'sincerity' still further: 'where the internal evidence proves that the Writer was moved, in other words where this charm of sincerity lurks in the language of a Tombstone and secretly pervades it, there are no errors in style or manner for which it will not be, in some degree, a recompence':[34] despite the confusing diction of concealment here (why must it 'lurk', 'secretly'? These ideas perhaps betray an awareness of the tensions Esterhammer's argument finds), language which reflects the real feeling of the poet is the language of sincerity. But the anxieties motivating the institution of such a criterion and the real questions it raised for Wordsworth are articulated within his poetic output. Most obviously, they animate the revisions made to his works; but they resurface elsewhere, also: 'Tintern Abbey', for example, offers itself to the reader as a meditation or discussion between Wordsworth's present and past selves, pondering the ways in which he has changed since he was last at the same place: it is explicitly a poem of *and*s and *or*s. James Butler claims that:

> Present-day criticism of 'Tintern Abbey' has made the poem controversial... not particularly to determine what Wordsworth claims in the poem but to judge how

---

[29] *Prose*, ii, 59.   [30] *Prose*, ii, 57.   [31] *Prose*, ii, 59.   [32] *Prose*, ii, 57.
[33] *Wordsworth and the Poetry of Sincerity*, pp. 8–9.   [34] *Prose*, ii, 70.

much of his past selves, particularly of his past political and revolutionary selves, he has concealed or abandoned to make those affirmations.[35]

Concealment and abandonment suggest insincerity. This book has tried to demonstrate, however, that the possibilities of conjunction (the potentials discovered in *and* and *or*) and the operation of recapitulation within Wordsworth's poetry mean that we don't need to decide whether the poem is, in Butler's words, 'a confident Wordsworthian re-assertion of why he is still a "worshiper of nature" or a disingenuous masking of his doubt-riddled withdrawal from political radicalism';[36] it can be both. Wordsworth has changed and is always changing; had changed between the moment of experience and the moment of first writing, and between revisions. In this sense, the facts continually change, too, even though in a more empirical sense the facts remain the same. This change which is attached conceptually to the poet encompasses also the reader, who is at liberty to discover sincere meaning which might differ from anything we attribute to 'the poet', and yet still be just as sincere. All of this might be placed in the nineteenth-century intellectual environment in which Schleiermacher argued for perpetual revision in the activity of reading, because a single 'meaning' is impossible; and in which Hegel insisted that the different elements of the 'progressive unfolding of truth' actually together form 'an organic unity'.[37] Alertness to, and where possible self-conscious awareness of, the multiple nature of experience and thus 'meaning' is the closest that the poet can come to sincerity. Recapitulation denies total flexibility of interpretation, and an attendant mere ambiguity. This is important: recapitulation retains a firm hold on the first and other iterations. However, it can bend *enough* for sincerity to be preserved in the light of changed minds or different experiences, and imply other possibilities even as one particular reading is construed. By sustaining these different possibilities, poetry sustains specific moments or experiences *coterminous with* more general moments or experiences; more general 'truths'. Wordsworth's interest extends to an idea of the conjunction of or connections between these separate but similar versions of moments and experiences, which find their greatest significance *through* their relationship. When Tim Milnes examines the relationship between sincerity and sense in Wordsworth's writing, finding in The Prelude an 'understanding of the self as open, plural and socially embedded',[38] he is identifying exactly this characteristic; it is an effect enabled by the multiple recapitulations Wordsworth incorporates within his texts.

---

[35] James Butler, 'Poetry 1798–1807: *Lyrical Ballads* and *Poems, in Two Volumes*', in *The Cambridge Companion to Wordsworth*, pp. 38–54 (pp. 42–3).
[36] Butler, p. 43.
[37] Schleiermacher, *Hermeneutics*, p. 110; p. 41 (discussed in Chapter 3); Hegel, 'On Scientific Knowledge', p. 2.
[38] Tim Milnes, 'Making Sense of Sincerity in *The Prelude*', in *Romanticism, Sincerity and Authenticity*, pp. 120–36 (p. 133).

Alan Liu argues that *The Prelude* inaugurates 'a new, transcendental authority of history: Wordsworth's "I."'.[39] In the case of Wordsworth's account of the French Revolution as a historical event, for example, this history is one of events and times, though sincerity can be 'to' a range of forms, and different types of 'truth'. But the idea of sincerity is different to the need for flexible meanings and a more fluid understanding of truth which might be independent of an author, because it is rooted in an idea that context (of the writer or the reader) continually shifts and changes. Wordsworth is aware that a repeated visit or experience is both the same and different, and he manifests this tension in his verse, through reflection on the nature of repeated experience, and through the repetitions within the text that enact the reflection. At its best, Wordsworth's poetry thus skilfully and faithfully represents the experience of repetition with difference which inheres in the looking again at something, from a different standpoint: 'Poetry is the most philosophic of all writing: it is so: its object is truth, not individual and local, but general, and operative'.[40]

The anxieties about authenticity and sincerity which have dogged Wordsworth Studies pertain to the sincere representation of events and their effects on the mind, and they bear on descriptive poetry more generally. Poems which inherently declare their own need for revision might suggest wrongness in previous iterations, but change is not the same as error, and Wordsworth's attention to repetition, like his use of conjunction, allows his work to maintain a sense of accurate or sincere generality *through* divergent accounts, drawing attention to the necessity of remembering previous iterations or versions. Gill's *Wordsworth's Revisiting* is explicitly 'about the poet's continual return not to his past but to his past in his past writing...New creation is generated from earlier; our understanding and enjoyment of both are enhanced by perceiving the relationship.'[41] Gill expands on this when he points out that the full title of 'Tintern Abbey' 'emphasizes that this is a poem of the present, the result of a visit *now*, only to reverse the emphasis in what follows, where retrospect is the keynote: "Five years have passed...Once again", familiar locutions in quintessential Wordsworth territory—the present in relation to the past.'[42] Gill's appreciation of 'relationship' again attests to the importance of conjunction, in the way in which ideas are put together, and to the value which continues to attach to each various version of a particular event, as those versions are conjoined. Both from the point of view of the creating poet aiming at something which might be labelled sincerity, and from the point of view of the different insights that subsequent critics bring to bear on the words on the page, the objects of 'truth' and accuracy are continually shifting even when they lie quietly within the pages of an unopened book. Different forms of revision and repetition along with the conjunctions *and* and *or* allow us to

---

[39] Liu, p. 384.   [40] 'Preface' to *Lyrical Ballads* [1850], p. 139.
[41] *Wordsworth's Revisitings*, p. 10.   [42] *Wordsworth's Revisitings*, pp. 9–10.

witness the reconciliation, or at least the sincere co-existence, of the apparent contradictions that changes of perspective (authorial and/or critical) might assert: conceptually as well as literally, that is, recapitulation allows sincerity to exist within poetic works. This is the subtle work poems can do. As Wordsworth wrote in 1815, imagination 'recoils from every thing but the plastic, the pliant, and the indefinite':[43] suitable material for poems, that is, *must* always be *and*-ish and *or*-ish, and fundamentally recapitulative, to allow flexibility of comprehension even in the moment of the textual encounter. Insofar as recapitulation thus both conceptually and literally makes Romantic sincerity achievable, these common effects and overlooked little words together enable what we understand as great Romantic poetry.

[43] 'Preface' to the 1815 *Poems*, in *Prose*, III, 36.

Bibliography of Works Cited

Wordsworth's Works

The Poetical Works of William Wordsworth, ed. E. de Selincourt and H. Darbishire, 2nd edn, 5 vols (Oxford: Oxford University Press, 1952)

Wordsworth, William, *The Prelude: The 1805 Text*, ed. E. de Selincourt (Oxford: Oxford University Press, 1933), rev. edn, ed. Stephen Gill (Oxford: Oxford University Press, 1970)

The Prose Works of William Wordsworth, ed. W. J. B. Owen and J. W. Smyser, 3 vols (Oxford: Clarendon Press, 1974)

Wordsworth, William, *Home at Grasmere: Part First, Book First, of The Recluse*, ed. Beth Darlington (Ithaca: Cornell University Press, 1977)

Wordsworth, William, *The Prelude, 1798–1799*, ed. Stephen Parrish (Ithaca: Cornell University Press and Harvester, 1977)

Wordsworth, William, *The Prelude 1799, 1805, 1850: Authoritative Texts, Context and Reception*, ed. Jonathan Wordsworth, M. H. Abrams, and Stephen Gill (London: W. W. Norton, 1979)

Wordsworth, William, *The Borderers*, ed. Robert Osborn (Ithaca: Cornell University Press, 1982)

Wordsworth, William, *Poems, in Two Volumes, and Other Poems, 1800–1807*, ed. Jared Curtis (Ithaca: Cornell University Press, 1983)

Wordsworth, William, *Descriptive Sketches*, ed. Eric Birdsall (Ithaca: Cornell University Press, 1984)

Wordsworth, William, *The Fourteen-Book 'Prelude'*, ed. W. J. B. Owen (Ithaca: Cornell University Press, 1985)

Wordsworth, William, *Shorter Poems, 1807–1820*, ed. Carl H. Ketcham (Ithaca: Cornell University Press, 1989)

Wordsworth, William, *The Thirteen-Book 'Prelude'*, ed. Mark L. Reed, 2 vols (Ithaca: Cornell University Press, 1991)

Wordsworth, William, *Lyrical Ballads, and Other Poems, 1797–1800*, ed. James Butler and Karen Green (Ithaca: Cornell University Press, 1992)

Wordsworth, William, *The Prelude* (London: Edward Moxon, 1850; facs. edn, Oxford: Woodstock Books, 1993)

The Letters of William and Dorothy Wordsworth, ed. Ernest de Selincourt, 8 vols, 2nd edn, rev. Mary Moorman, Alan G. Hill, and Chester L. Shaver (Oxford: Clarendon Press, 1967–93)

The Fenwick Notes of William Wordsworth, ed. Jared Curtis (London: Bristol Classical Press, 1993)

Wordsworth, William, *The Prelude: The Four Texts (1798, 1799, 1805, 1850)*, ed. Jonathan Wordsworth (London: Penguin, 1995)

Wordsworth, William, *Translations of Chaucer and Virgil*, ed. Bruce E. Graver (Ithaca: Cornell University Press, 1998)

Wordsworth, William, *Last Poems, 1821–1850*, ed. Jared Curtis, Apryl Lea Denny-Curtis, and Jillian Heydt-Stevenson (Ithaca: Cornell University Press, 1999)

Wordsworth, William, *Sonnet Series and Itinerary Poems, 1820-1845*, ed. Geoffrey Jackson (Ithaca: Cornell University Press, 2004)
Wordsworth, William, *The Excursion*, ed. Sally Bushell, James A. Butler, and Michael C. Jaye (Ithaca: Cornell University Press, 2007)

Other Works

[Anon.], review of *Lyrical Ballads*, in *Critical Review*, 2nd ser., 24 (October 1798), 197-204
Abrams, M. H., 'Structure and Style in the Greater Romantic Lyric', in Frederick W. Hilles and Harold Bloom, eds, *From Sensibility to Romanticism: Essays Presented to Frederick A. Pottle* (New York: Oxford University Press, 1965), 527-60
Abrams, M. H., *The Mirror and the Lamp: Romantic Theory and the Critical Tradition* (Oxford: Oxford University Press, 1953; 1971)
Adamson, Sylvia, 'Literary Language', in Suzanne Romaine, ed., *The Cambridge History of English Language Vol. IV: 1776-1997* (Cambridge: Cambridge University Press, 1998), 589-692
Adamson, Sylvia, 'Literary Language', in Roger Lass, ed., *The Cambridge History of English Language Vol. III: 1476-1776* (Cambridge: Cambridge University Press, 1999), 539-653
Aristotle, *Poetics*, trans. Malcolm Heath (Harmondsworth: Penguin, 1996)
Armstrong, Isobel, *Language as Living Form in Nineteenth-Century Poetry* (Brighton: Harvester, 1982)
Armstrong, Isobel, *The Radical Aesthetic* (Oxford: Blackwell, 2000)
Armstrong, Kate, *Crisis and Repetition: Essays on Art and Culture* (Michigan: Michigan State University Press, 2001)
Arnold, Matthew, 'Preface' to *Poems of Wordsworth* (London: Macmillan 1879), v-xxvi
Asendorf, Christoph, *Batteries of Life: On the History of Things and their Perception in Modernity*, trans. Don Reneau (Berkeley and Los Angeles: University of California Press, 1993)
Attridge, Derek, *The Rhythms of English Poetry* (London: Longman, 1982)
Attridge, Derek, *Moving Words: Forms of English Poetry* (Oxford: Oxford University Press, 2013; 2015)
Auden, W. H., *The Dyers Hand* (New York: Vintage, 1989)
Auerbach, Eric, *Mimesis: The Representation of Reality in Western Literature*, trans. Willard R. Trask (Princeton, NJ: Princeton University Press, 1953; 2003)
Babbage, Charles, *On the Economy of Machinery and Manufactures* (London: Charles Knight, 1832)
Barker, Stephen, *The Elements of Logic*, 4th rev. edn (New York: McGraw Hill, 1985)
Baron, Michael, *Language and Relationship in Wordsworth's Writing* (Harlow: Longman, 1995)
Barrell, John, *Poetry, Language, and Politics* (Manchester: Manchester University Press, 1988)
Barton, Anne, 'Byron and Shakespeare', in Drummond Bone, ed., *The Cambridge Companion to Byron* (Cambridge: Cambridge University Press, 2004), 224-35
Bate, Jonathan, *Shakespeare and the English Romantic Imagination* (Oxford: Clarendon, 1986)
Bate, W. Jackson, *The Burden of the Past and the English Poet* (London: Chatto & Windus, 1971)
Bates, Brian, 'J. H. Reynolds Re-Echoes the Wordsworthian Reputation: "Peter Bell," Remaking the Work and Mocking the Man', *Studies in Romanticism*, 47.3 (Fall 2008), 273-97

Bates, Brian, *Wordsworth's Poetic Collections, Supplementary Writing and Parodic Reception* (London: Pickering and Chatto, 2012)
Batten, Guinn, *The Orphaned Imagination: Melancholy and Commodity Culture in English Romanticism* (Durham and London: Duke University Press, 1998)
Baxendall, Michael, *Patterns of Intention: On the Historical Explanation of Pictures* (New Haven and London: Yale University Press, 1985)
Beattie, James, *The Theory of Language*, new edn (London: A. Strahan, 1788)
Beer, Gillian, 'Rhyming as comedy: body, ghost and banquet', in Michael Cordner, Peter Holland, and John Kerrigan, eds, *English Comedy* (Cambridge: Cambridge University Press, 1994), 180–96
Beer, Gillian, '"Another Music": Rhyming and Transformation', for the George Herbert in Bemerton Group (2006), pp. 1–8, https://www.georgeherbert.org.uk/docs/Another%20Music%20-%20Rhyming%20and%20Transformation.pdf, accessed 2 June 2022
Benjamin, Walter, 'The Image of Proust', in *Illuminations*, ed. Hannah Arendt, trans. Harry Zohn (London: Fontana, 1973), 203–18
Benjamin, Walter, 'The Work of Art in the Age of Mechanical Reproduction', in *Illuminations*, ed. Hannah Arendt, trans. Harry Zohn (London: Fontana, 1973), 219–53
Bennett, Andrew, *Keats, Narrative and Audience: The Posthumous Life of Writing* (Cambridge: Cambridge University Press, 1994)
Berger, John, *Ways of Seeing* (London: The British Broadcasting Corporation and Penguin Books, 1972)
Bernhardt-Kabisch, Ernest, '"When Klopstock England Defied": Coleridge, Southey, and the German/English Hexameter', *Comparative Literature*, 55.2 (Spring, 2003), 130–63
Bewell, Alan, *Wordsworth and the Enlightenment: Nature, Man and Society in the Experimental Poetry* (New Haven and London: Yale University Press, 1989)
Bloom, Harold, *The Anxiety of Influence: A Theory of Poetry* (Oxford: Oxford University Press, 1973; 1997)
Booth, Stephen, *Precious Nonsense* (Berkeley: University of California Press, 1998)
Bradley, A. C., *Oxford Lectures on Poetry* (London: Macmillan, 1909)
Breithaupt, Fritz, 'The Invention of Trauma in German Romanticism', *Critical Inquiry*, 32.1 (Autumn 2005), 77–101
Brennan, Thomas J., *Trauma, Transcendence and Trust: Wordsworth, Tennyson, and Eliot Thinking Loss* (New York: Palgrave Macmillan, 2010)
Brigham, Linda C., 'Frail Memorials: "Essays Upon Epitaphs" and Wordsworth's Economy of Reference', *Philosophy and Literature*, 16.1 (April 1992), 15–31
Brinkley, Robert, and Keith Hanley, 'Introduction' to Robert Brinkley and Keith Hanley, eds, *Romantic Revisions* (Cambridge: Cambridge University Press, 1992), 1–17
Brogan, T. V. F., *English Versification, 1570–1980* (Baltimore and London: Johns Hopkins University Press, 1981)
Bromwich, David, *Disowned by Memory: Wordsworth's Poetry of the 1790s* (Chicago: University of Chicago Press, 1988)
Brown, Homer Obed, 'The Art of Theology and the Theology of Art: Robert Penn Warren's Reading of Coleridge's "The Rime of the Ancient Mariner"', *Boundary*, 2.8 (1979), 237–60
Bruns, Gerald L., *Modern Poetry and the Idea of Language: A Critical and Historical Study* (New Haven: Yale University Press, 1974)
Bunyan, David, 'Compulsive Repetition and "The Ancient Mariner": Coleridge's Romantic "Uncanny"', *Journal of Literary Studies*, 6 (1990), 115–25

Burwick, Frederick, 'Coleridge and Schelling on Mimesis', in Richard Gravil and Molly Lefebure, eds, *The Coleridge Connection: Essays for Thomas McFarland* (London: Macmillan, 1990), 167–85

Butler, James, 'Poetry 1798–1807: *Lyrical Ballads* and *Poems, in Two Volumes*', in Stephen Gill, ed., *The Cambridge Companion to Wordsworth* (Cambridge: Cambridge University Press, 2003), 38–54

Cameron, Sharon, *Choosing Not Choosing: Dickinson's Fascicles* (Chicago: University of Chicago Press, 1992)

Castell, James, 'Wordsworth, Silence and the Nonhuman', *Wordsworth Circle*, 45.1 (2014), 58–61, http://www.jstor.org/stable/24044360, accessed 2 June 2022

Cave, Terence, *Recognitions: A Study in Poetics* (Oxford: Oxford University Press, 1990)

Channick, Debra, '"A Logic of Its Own": Repetition in Coleridge's "Christabel"', *Romanticism and Victorianism on the Net*, 50 (May 2008), not paginated, https://doi-org.ezp.lib.cam.ac.uk/10.7202/018144ar, accessed 2 June 2022

Clare, John, *Poems Descriptive of Rural Life and Scenery* (London and Stamford: Taylor, Hessey and Drury, 1820)

Clare: The Critical Heritage, ed. Mark Storey (London and Boston: Routledge & Kegan Paul, 1973), 359–64

John Clare: A Critical Edition of the Major Works, ed. Eric Robinson and David Powell (Oxford: Oxford University Press, 1984)

The Early Poems of John Clare, 1804–1822, ed. Eric Robinson, David Powell, and Margaret Grainger, 2 vols (Oxford: Clarendon Press, 1989)

Clymer, Laura, 'Graved in Tropes: The Figural Logic of Epitaphs and Elegies in Blair, Gray, Cowper, and Wordsworth', *ELH*, 62 (1995), 347–86

Cobbett, William, *Rural Rides* [1830], ed. Ian Dyck (London: Penguin, 2001)

Cohen, Ralph, *The Art of Discrimination: Thomson's Seasons and the Language of Criticism* (London: Routledge & Kegan Paul, 1964)

Coleridge, *Christabel: Kubla Khan, A Vision; The Pains of Sleep* (London: John Murray, 1816)

Coleridge, S. T., *The Statesman's Manual; or, The Bible the Best Guide to Political Skill and Foresight [...]* (London: Gale and Fenner and others, 1816)

Anima Poetæ: From the Unpublished Note-books of Samuel Taylor Coleridge, ed. Ernest Hartley Coleridge (London: William Heinemann, 1895)

The Philosophical Lectures of Samuel Taylor Coleridge, ed. Kathleen Coburn (London: Pilot Press, 1949)

Collected Letters of Samuel Taylor Coleridge, ed. E. L. Griggs, 6 vols (Oxford: Oxford University Press, 1956–71)

The Notebooks of Samuel Taylor Coleridge Volume 3: 1808–1819, ed. Kathleen Coburn (London: Routledge, 1973)

Coleridge, Samuel Taylor, *Biographia Literaria*, ed. James Engell and W. Jackson Bate, 2 vols (London and Princeton, NJ: Routledge & Kegan Paul and Princeton University Press, 1983)

The Collected Works of Samuel Taylor Coleridge, Vol. 14, Part I: 'Table Talk', ed. Carl Woodring (Princeton, NJ: Princeton University Press and Routledge, for the Bollingen Foundation, 1990)

The Collected Works of Samuel Taylor Coleridge, Vol 16: Poetical Works I; Poems (Reading Texts) Part I, ed. J. C. C. Mays (Princeton, NJ: Princeton University Press, 2001)

Cooper, Lane, 'Pleonastic Compounds in Coleridge', *Modern Language Notes*, 19.7 (November 1904), 223–4, https://www-jstor-org.ezp.lib.cam.ac.uk/stable/pdf/2917138.pdf, accessed 2 June 2022

Henry Crabb Robinson on Books and Their Writers, ed. Edith J. Morley, 3 vols (London: J. M. Dent & Sons, 1938)
Culler, Jonathan, *Theory of the Lyric* (Cambridge, MA: Harvard University Press, 2015)
Curran, Stuart, *Poetic Form and British Romanticism* (New York and Oxford: Oxford University Press, 1986; 1989)
Curtis, Paul M., 'Romantic Indirection', in Alan Rawes, ed., *Romanticism and Form* (Houndsmills: Palgrave Macmillan, 2007), 1–22
David, Philip, 'Johnson: Sanity and Syntax', in Freya Johnston and Lynda Mugglestone, eds, *Samuel Johnson: The Arc of the Pendulum* (Oxford: Oxford University Press, 2012), 49–61
Davie, Donald, 'On Sincerity: From Wordsworth to Ginsberg', *Encounter* 31.4 (1968), 61–6
Davie, Donald, *Articulate Energy* [1965], repr. in *Purity of Diction in English Verse* and *Articulate Energy* (Manchester: Carcanet, 2006)
De Bolla, Peter, and Andrew Ashfield, eds, *The Sublime: A Reader in Eighteenth-Century Aesthetic Theory* (Cambridge: Cambridge University Press, 1996)
De Man, Paul, *The Rhetoric of Romanticism* (New York: Columbia University Press, 1984)
De Quincey, Thomas, 'On Wordsworth's Poetry', in Frederick Burwick, ed., *The Works of Thomas De Quincey, Vol. 15: Articles from Blackwood's Edinburgh Magazine and Tait's Edinburgh Magazine, 1844–1846* (London: Pickering & Chatto 2003), 223–42
De Quincey, Thomas, 'The Nation of London', in *Autobiographic Sketches, Vol. I* [1853], repr. in Daniel Sanjiv Roberts, ed., *The Works of Thomas De Quincey, Vol. 19: Autobiographical Sketches* (London: Pickering & Chatto, 2003), 109–31
De Selincourt, E., 'Wordsworth's Preface to "The Borderers"', in *Oxford Lectures on Poetry* (London: Oxford University Press, 1934), 157–79
De Vere, Aubrey, 'Recollections of Wordsworth', in *Essays Chiefly on Poetry*, 2 vols (London: Macmillan, 1887), ii, 275–95
De Vries, Jan, *The Industrious Revolution: Consumer Behaviour and the Household Economy, 1650 to the Present* (Cambridge: Cambridge University Press, 2008)
Deleuze, Gilles, *Difference and Repetition* [1968], trans. Paul Patton (London and New York: Continuum, 2004; 2007)
Deleuze, Gilles, and Félix Guattari, 'Introduction: Rhizome', in *A Thousand Plateaus: Capitalism and Schizophrenia* [1987], trans. Brian Massumi (London and New York: Bloomsbury, 2015), 1–27
Dewey, Godfrey, *Relativ [sic] Frequency of English Speech Sounds* (Cambridge, MA: Harvard University Press, 1923), https://doi-org.ezp.lib.cam.ac.uk/10.4159/harvard. 9780674419193, accessed 2 June 2022
Douglas-Fairhurst, Robert, *Victorian Afterlives: The Shaping of Influence in Nineteenth-Century Literature* (Oxford: Oxford University Press, 2002)
Douglas-Fairhurst, Robert, 'Alexander Pope: "renown'd in Rhyme"', in David Womersley and Richard McCabe, eds, *Literary Milieux: Essays in Text and Context Presented to Howard Erskine-Hill* (Newark, NJ: University of Delaware Press, 2008), 230–57
Empson, William, 'Rhythm and Imagery in English Poetry', *British Journal of Aesthetics*, 2.1 (January 1962), 36–54
Engell, James, *The Creative Imagination: Enlightenment to Romanticism* (Cambridge, MA: Harvard University Press, 1981)
Engell, James, 'Coleridge and German Idealism: First Postulates, Final Causes', in Richard Gravil and Molly Lefebure, eds, *The Coleridge Connection* (London: Macmillan, 1990), 144–66
Erskine-Hill, Howard, *Poetry of Opposition and Revolution: Dryden to Wordsworth* (Oxford: Clarendon Press, 1996)

Espie, Jeff, 'Wordsworth's Chaucer: Mediation and Transformation in English Literary History', *Philological Quarterly*, 94.4 (Fall 2015), 377–403
Esterhammer, Angela, 'The Scandal of Sincerity: Wordsworth, Byron, Landon', in Tim Milnes and Kerry Sinanan, eds, *Romanticism, Sincerity and Authenticity* (Basingstoke: Palgrave Macmillan, 2010), 101–19
Everest, Kelvin, *Coleridge's Secret Ministry* (Hassocks: Harvester, 1979)
Fish, Stanley E., *Self-Consuming Artifacts: The Experience of Seventeenth Century Literature* (Berkeley and Los Angeles: University of California Press, 1972)
Forbes, Deborah, *Sincerity's Shadow* (Cambridge, MA: Harvard University Press, 2004)
Fosso, Kurt, *Buried Communities: Wordsworth and the Bonds of Mourning* (Albany: State University of New York Press, 2004)
Freud, Sigmund, 'Remembering, Repeating and Working-Through', in *Further Recommendations on the Technique of Psycho-Analysis II*, in *The Standard Edition of the Complete Psychological Works of Sigmund Freud, Vol. 12 (1911–1913)*, trans. and ed. James Strachey and others (London: Hogarth Press and the Institute of Psycho-Analysis, 1955; 1981), 147–56
Freud, Sigmund, 'Beyond the Pleasure Principle' [1920], in *The Standard Edition of the Complete Psychological Works of Sigmund Freud, Volume 18 (1920–1922): Beyond the Pleasure Principle, Group Psychology and Other Works*, trans. and ed. James Strachey and others (London: Hogarth Press and the Institute of Psycho-Analysis, 1955; 1981), 7–64
Fruman, Norman, 'Creative Process and Concealment in Coleridge's Poetry', in Robert Brinkley and Keith Hanley, eds, *Romantic Revisions* (Cambridge: Cambridge University Press, 1992), 154–68
Gadamer, Hans-Georg, *Truth and Method*, 2nd edn, rev. trans. Joel Weinsheimer and Donald G. Marshall (London: Continuum, 2004)
Garrett, James M., *Wordsworth and the Writing of the Nation* (Aldershot: Ashgate, 2008)
Genette, Gérard, *Palimpsests: Literature in the Second Degree*, trans. Channa Newman and Claude Doubinsky (Lincoln: University of Nebraska Press, 1997)
Gill, Stephen, 'Introduction' to Stephen Gill, ed., *The Prelude: A Casebook* (Oxford: Oxford University Press, 2006), 3–41
Gill, Stephen, *Wordsworth's Revisitings* (Oxford: Oxford University Press, 2011)
Glauser, Richard, and Anthony Savile, 'Aesthetic Experience in Shaftesbury', *Proceedings of the Aristotelian Society: Supplementary Volumes*, 76 (2002), 25–74
Graver, Bruce, 'The Reception of Chaucer from Dryden to Wordsworth', in Ian Johnson, ed., *Geoffrey Chaucer in Context* (Cambridge: Cambridge University Press, 2019), 419–28
Griffin, Emma, *Liberty's Dawn: A People's History of the Industrial Revolution* (New Haven and London: Yale University Press, 2014)
Griffiths, Eric, 'Blanks, misgivings, fallings from us', in Katy Price, ed., *The Salt Companion to Peter Robinson* (Cambridge: Salt, 2007), 55–82
Griffiths, Eric, *The Printed Voice of Victorian Poetry*, 2nd edn (Oxford: Oxford University Press, 2018)
Guilhamet, Leon, *The Sincere Ideal: Studies on Sincerity in Eighteenth-Century English Literature* (Montreal: McGill-Queen's University Press, 1974)
Hamilton, Paul, *Coleridge's Poetics* (Oxford: Basil Blackwell, 1983)
Hanninen, D. A., 'A Theory of Recontextualization in Music: Analyzing Phenomenal Transformations of Repetition', *Music Theory Spectrum*, 25 (2003), 59–97
Hardison, Jr., O. B., *Prosody and Purpose in the English Renaissance* (Baltimore: Johns Hopkins University Press, 1989)

BIBLIOGRAPHY OF WORKS CITED 271

Harris, James, *Hermes; or, A Philosophical Inquiry concerning Universal Grammar*, 3rd rev. edn (London: John Nourse and Paul Vaillant, 1771)

Hartley, David, *Observations on Man, His Frame, His Duty, and His Expectations* (London and Bath: James Leake and William Frederick, 1749)

Hartman, Geoffrey H., *Wordsworth's Poetry 1787-1814* (New Haven: Yale University Press, 1964)

Hauser, Arnold, *The Social History of Art Vol. 2: Renaissance Mannerism, Baroque*, trans. Stanley Godman (New York: Vintage, 1985)

Havens, Michael Kent, 'Coleridge on the Evolution of Language', *Studies in Romanticism*, 20.2 (Summer 1981), 163-83

Hawkes, Terrence, *Meaning by Shakespeare* (London and New York: Routledge, 1992)

Hazlitt, William, 'Coleridge's Literary Life', *The Edinburgh Review*, 28.56 (August 1817), 488-515

Hazlitt, William, 'On the Living Poets', in *Lectures on the English Poets: Delivered at the Surrey Institution* (London: Taylor and Hessey, 1818), 283-331

Heard, W. A., 'A few thoughts upon on Wordsworth's treatment of sound', *Transactions of the Wordsworth Society* (1884), 40-57

Hegel, G. W. F., *Jenenser Realphilosophie II: Die Vorlesungen von 1805/06*, ed. Johannes Hoffmeister (Leipzig: Meiner, 1931)

Hegel, G. W. F., *Hegel's Aesthetics: Lectures on Fine Art*, trans. T. M. Knox, 2 vols (Oxford: Clarendon Press, 1975)

Hegel, Georg W. F., *The Phenomenology of Spirit* [1807], trans. A. V. Miller (Oxford: Clarendon Press, 1977)

Hess, Scott, 'Wordsworth's "System," the Critical Reviews, and the Reconstruction of Literary Authority', *European Romantic Review*, 16.4 (2005), 471-97, https://doi.org/10.1080/10509580500303991, accessed 2 June 2022

The English Works of Thomas Hobbes of Malmesbury, ed. William Molesworth (London: John Bohn, 1839-45)

Hobsbawm, E. J., *The Age of Revolution 1789-1848* (New York: Mentor, 1962)

Hogle, Jerrold E., 'Language and Form', in Timothy Morton, ed., *The Cambridge Companion to Shelley* (Cambridge: Cambridge University Press, 2006), 145-65

Hollander, John, *Images of Voice: Music and Sound in Romantic Poetry* (Cambridge: Heffer, 1970)

Hollander, John, 'Wordsworth and the Music of Sound', in Geoffrey H. Hartman, ed., *New Perspectives on Wordsworth and Coleridge* (New York: Columbia University Press, 1972), 41-84

Hollander, John, *The Figure of Echo: A Mode of Allusion in Milton and After* (Berkeley and Los Angeles: University of California Press, 1981)

Hollander, John, *Vision and Resonance: Two Senses of Poetic Form*, 2nd edn (New Haven: Yale University Press, 1985)

Houghton, Sarah, '"Some little thing of other days / Saved from the wreck of time": John Clare and Festivity', *John Clare Society Journal*, 23 (2004), 21-43

Houghton, Sarah, 'The "Community" of John Clare's Helpston', *Studies in English Literature, 1500-1900*, 46.4 (Autumn 2006), 781-802

Houghton-Walker, Sarah, *Representations of the Gypsy in the Romantic Period* (Oxford: Oxford University Press, 2014)

Houghton-Walker, Sarah, 'Forms of Repetition in "The Robins Nest"', *Romanticism*, 26.2 (2020), 139-52

The Clarendon Edition of the Works of David Hume: A Treatise of Human Nature, Vol. 1: Texts, ed. David Fate Norton and Mary J. Norton (Oxford: Oxford University Press, 2007)
Hurd, Richard, *Moral and Political Dialogues*, 3 vols (London: A. Millar, 1765)
Huron, David, *Sweet Anticipation: Music and the Psychology of Expectation* (Cambridge, MA: MIT Press, 2006)
Jacobus, Mary, *Tradition and Experiment in Wordsworth's Lyrical Ballads (1798)* (Oxford: Clarendon Press, 1976)
Jakobsen, Roman, 'Closing Statement: Linguistics and Poetics', in Thomas Sebeok, ed., *Style in Language* (New York and London: The Technology Press of Massachusetts Institute of Technology and John Wiley and Sons, 1960), 350-88
Janowitz, Anne, *Lyric and Labour in the Romantic Tradition* (Cambridge: Cambridge University Press, 1998)
Jarvis, Robin, *Wordsworth, Milton and the Theory of Poetic Relations* (New York: Palgrave Macmillan, 1991)
Jarvis, Simon, *Wordsworth's Philosophic Song* (Cambridge: Cambridge University Press, 2007)
Jarvis, Simon, 'Why Rhyme Pleases', *Thinking Verse*, 1 (2011), 3
Jeffrey, Francis, review of *The Excursion*, in the *Edinburgh Review* (November, 1814), [1]-30, repr. in Robert Woof, ed., *William Wordsworth: The Critical Heritage, Volume I 1793-1820* (New York: Routledge, 2001), 381-404
Jennings, Richard, *The Genealogy of Disjunction* (New York and Oxford: Oxford University Press, 1994)
Samuel Johnson: A Critical Edition of the Major Works, ed. Donald Greene (Oxford: Oxford University Press, 1984)
Johnston, Kenneth R., '"Home at Grasmere": Reclusive Song', *Studies in Romanticism*, 14.1 (Winter 1975), 1-28
Jones, John, *The Egotistical Sublime: A History of Wordsworth's Imagination* (London: Chatto & Windus, 1964)
The English Grammar: made by Ben Johnson [sic] for the benefit of all strangers out of his observation of the English language now spoken and in use (n.pub, 1640)
Kawain, Bruce, *Telling It Again and Again: Repetition in Literature and Film* (Ithaca: Cornell University Press, 1972)
The Letters of John Keats, ed. Maurice Buxton Forman, 4th edn (London: Oxford University Press, 1952)
John Keats: the Complete Poems, ed. Miriam Allott (New York: Longman, 1970)
Keats: The Critical Heritage, ed. G. M. Matthews (London: Routledge & Kegan Paul, 1971)
Kelley, Theresa M., 'Keats and "ekphrasis": Poetry and the Description of Art', in Susan J. Wolfson, ed., *The Cambridge Companion to Keats* (Cambridge: Cambridge University Press, 2001), 170-85
Kenner, Hugh, 'Further Thoughts: Little Words', in Christopher Ricks and Leonard Michaels, eds, *The State of the Language: 1990 Edition* (London: Faber and Faber, 1990), 62-5
Kerrigan, John, *Revenge Tragedy: Aeschylus to Armageddon* (Oxford: Oxford University Press, 1996)
Kidd, Stephen E., *Nonsense and Meaning in Ancient Greek Comedy* (Cambridge: Cambridge University Press, 2014)
[Kierkegaard, S.] 'Constantine Constantius', 'Repetition: An Essay in Experimental Psychology' [1843], in *Repetition and Philosophical Crumbs*, trans. M. G. Piety (Oxford: Oxford University Press, 2009), 1-81

King, E. H., 'James Beattie's *The Minstrel* (1771, 1774): Its Influence on Wordsworth', *Studies in Scottish Literature*, 8.4 (1970), 3–29
Kivy, Peter, *The Fine Art of Repetition: Essays in the Philosophy of Music* (Cambridge: Cambridge University Press, 1993)
Knox, Laurie, 'Repetition and Relevance: Self-repetition as a Strategy for Initiating Cooperation in Nonnative/Native Speaker Conversations', in *Repetition in Discourse: Interdisciplinary Perspectives*, ed. B. Johnstone (Norwood, NJ: Ablex, 1994)
Kohl, Katrin, *Rhetoric, the Bible, and the Origins of Free Verse* (Berlin and New York: de Gruyter, 1990)
Kort, Wesley A., *"Take, Read": Scripture, Textuality and Cultural Practice* (University Park: Pennsylvania State University Press, 1996)
Kracauer, Siegfried, *The Mass Ornament: Weimar Essays*, trans. and ed. Thomas Y. Levin (Cambridge, MA: Harvard University Press, 1995)
Krieger, Murray, *Ekphrasis: The Illusion of the Natural Sign* (Baltimore: Johns Hopkins University Press, 1992; 2019)
Lakoff, George and Mark Johnson, *Metaphors We Live By* (Chicago: University of Chicago Press, 1980; 2003)
The Letters of Charles and Mary Lamb, 1796–1801, ed. Edwin W. Marrs (Ithaca: Cornell University Press, 1975)
Landes, David, *The Unbound Prometheus: Technological Change and Industrial Development in Western Europe from 1750 to the Present* (Cambridge: Cambridge University Press, 2003)
Langford, Paul, *A Polite and Commercial People: England 1727–1783* (Oxford: Oxford University Press, 1989)
Larkin, Peter, 'Repetition, Difference and Liturgical Participation in Coleridge's "The Ancient Mariner"', *Literature & Theology*, 21.2 (June 2007), 146–59
Legaspi, Michael, *The Death of Scripture and the Rise of Biblical Studies* (Oxford: Oxford University Press, 2010)
Leighton, Angela, *Hearing Things: The Work of Sound in Literature* (Cambridge, MA: Belknap Press, 2018)
Lindenberger, Herbert, *On Wordsworth's Prelude* (Princeton, NJ: Princeton University Press, 1964)
Liu, Alan, *Wordsworth: The Sense of History* (Stanford: Stanford University Press, 1989)
Locke, John, *An Essay Concerning Human Understanding*, ed. P. H. Nidditch (Oxford: Clarendon Press, 1979)
Lokyer, Nicholas, *A Divine Discovery of Sincerity* (London: John Rothwell, 1659)
Lowth, Robert, *A Short Introduction to English Grammar: with Critical Notes*, 2nd edn (London: Millar and Dodsley, 1763)
Lowth, Robert, *Isaiah* (London: J. Dodsley and T. Cadell, 1778)
Lowth, Robert, *Lectures on the Sacred Poetry of the Hebrews*, trans. G. Gregory, 2 vols (London: J. Johnson, 1787)
Lukits, Steven, 'Wordsworth Unawares: The Boy of Winander, the Poet, and the Mariner', *Wordsworth Circle*, 19.3 (Summer 1988), 156–60
Lynch, Diedre, 'Matters of Memory: Response', *Victorian Studies*, 49.2 (Winter 2007), 228–40
Macfarlane, Robert, *Original Copy: Plagiarism and Originality in Nineteenth-Century Literature* (Oxford: Oxford University Press, 2007)
Manning, Peter J., *Reading Romantics: Texts and Context* (Oxford: Oxford University Press, 1990)
Margulis, Elizabeth Hellmuth, *On Repeat: How Music Plays the Mind* (Oxford: Oxford University Press, 2014)

Marshall, David, 'The Eye-Witnesses of "The Borderers"', *Studies in Romanticism*, 27.3 (Fall 1988), 391–8
Matthews, David, 'Periodization', in Marion Turner, ed., *A Handbook of Middle English Studies* (Chichester: Wiley-Blackwell, 2013), 253–66
McAllister, David, *Imagining the Dead in British Literature and Culture, 1790–1848* (London: Palgrave Macmillan, 2018)
McAlpine, Erica, *The Poet's Mistake* (Princeton, NJ: Princeton University Press, 2020)
McCauley, Lawrence H., 'Milton's Missing Rhymes', *Style*, 28.2 (Summer 1994), 242–59
McDonald, Peter, *Sound Intentions: The Workings of Rhyme in Nineteenth-Century Poetry* (Oxford: Oxford University Press, 2012)
McGann, Jerome, *The Poetics of Sensibility: A Revolution in Literary Style* (Oxford: Oxford University Press, 1996)
Mennighaus, Winnifred, *In Praise of Nonsense* [1995], trans. Henry Pickford (Stanford: Stanford University Press, 1999)
Mennighaus, Winnifred, Valentin Wagner, Eugen Wassiliwizky, Thomas Jacobsen, and Christine A. Knoopa, 'The emotional and aesthetic powers of parallelistic diction', *Poetics*, 63 (August 2017), 47–59, https://doi.org/10.1016/j.poetic.2016.12.001, accessed 2 June 2022
Menninghaus, Winnifred, and Sebastian Wallot, 'What the eyes reveal about (reading) poetry', *Poetics*, 85 (April 2021), 1–15, https://doi.org/10.1016/j.poetic.2020.101526, accessed 2 June 2022
Michael, Ian, *English Grammatical Categories and the Tradition to 1800* (London: Cambridge University Press, 1970)
Milbank, John, *Theology and Social Theory: Beyond Secular Reason* (Oxford: Blackwell, 1993)
Miller, Christopher R., 'Coleridge and the Scene of Lyric Description', *Journal of English and Germanic Philology*, 101.4 (October 2002), 520–39
Miller, J. Hillis, *Fiction and Repetition: Seven English Novels* (Oxford: Basil Blackwell, 1982)
Milnes, Tim, 'Making Sense of Sincerity in *The Prelude*', in Tim Milnes and Kerry Sinanan, eds, *Romanticism, Sincerity and Authenticity* (Basingstoke: Palgrave Macmillan, 2010), 120–36
Milnes, Tim, and Kerry Sinanan, 'Introduction' to Tim Milnes and Kerry Sinanan, eds, *Romanticism, Sincerity and Authenticity* (Basingstoke: Palgrave Macmillan, 2010), 1–28
Milton, John, *Paradise Lost*, ed. Alastair Fowler (London and New York: Longman, 1971; 1992)
The Complete Works of John Milton, Volume 2: The 1671 Poems: Paradise Regain'd and Samson Agonistes, ed. Laura Lunger Knoppers (Oxford: Oxford University Press, 2008)
Morris, Brian, 'Mr Wordsworth's Ear', *Wordsworth Circle*, 10.1 (Winter 1979), 113–21
Newlyn, Lucy, *Coleridge, Wordsworth, and the Language of Allusion* (Oxford: Oxford University Press, 2001)
Newlyn, Lucy, '"The noble living and the noble dead": Community in *The Prelude*', in Stephen Gill, ed., *The Cambridge Companion to Wordsworth* (Cambridge: Cambridge University Press, 2003), 55–69
Newlyn, Lucy, *William & Dorothy Wordsworth: All in Each Other* (Oxford: Oxford University Press, 2013)
Newstok, Scott L., '"Here Lies": Sincerity and Insincerity in Early Modern Epitaphs Onstage', *Christianity & Literature*, 67.1 (2017), 50–68
Nord, Deborah Epstein, 'The City as Theater: From Georgian to Early Victorian London', *Victorian Studies*, 31.2 (Winter 1988), 159–88

Nuss, Melynda, '"Look in My Face": The Dramatic Ethics of the Borderers', *Studies in Romanticism*, 43.4 (Winter 2004), 599-621

Nuttall, A. D., *Two Concepts of Allegory* (New Haven and London: Yale University Press, 2007)

O'Neill, Michael, *Romanticism and the Self-Conscious Poem* (Oxford: Clarendon Press, 1997)

Ong, Walter J., *Rhetoric, Romance, and Technology: Studies in the Interaction of Expression and Culture* (Ithaca: Cornell University Press, 1971; 1990)

Owen, Robert, *An Outline of the System of Education at New Lanark* (Glasgow: University Press, 1824)

Owen, Robert, *A New View of Society and Other Writings* [1816], ed. Gregory Claeys (London: Penguin, 1991)

Pacey, Arnold, *Meaning in Technology* (Cambridge, MA: MIT Press, 1999)

Pepper, W. Thomas, 'The Ideology of Wordsworth's "Michael: A Pastoral Poem"', *Criticism*, 31.4 (Fall 1989), 367-82

Perkins, David, *Wordsworth and the Poetry of Sincerity* (Cambridge, MA: Harvard University Press, 1964)

Perkins, David, 'How the Romantics Recited Poetry', *Studies in English Literature, 1500-1900*, 31.4 (Autumn 1991), 655-71

Peterson, Richard S., 'The Influence of Anxiety: Spenser and Wordsworth', *Studies in Romanticism*, 51.1 (Spring 2012), 77-88

Pfau, Thomas, *Romantic Moods: Paranoia, Trauma, Melancholy, 1790-1840* (Baltimore: Johns Hopkins University Press, 2005)

Pickstock, Catherine, *After Writing: On the Liturgical Consummation of Philosophy* (Oxford: Blackwell, 1998)

Pinker, Stephen, *The Language Instinct: How the Mind Creates Language* (London: Penguin, 1994)

Plato, *Phaedrus & Letters VII and VIII*, trans. Walter Hamilton (Harmondsworth: Penguin, 1973)

Pope: Complete Poetical Works, ed. Herbert Davis (Oxford: Oxford University Press, 1978)

Porter, Roy, 'Consumption: Disease of the Consumer Society?', in John Brewer and Roy Porter, eds, *Consumption and the World of Goods* (Abingdon: Routledge, 1993), 58-84

Porter, Roy, *The Making of Geology: Earth Science in Britain, 1660-1815* (Cambridge: Cambridge University Press, 1997)

Praeger, F., 'On the Fallacy of the Repetition of Parts in the Classical Form', *Proceedings of the Royal Musical Association* (1882-3), 1-16

Prickett, Stephen, *Romanticism and Religion: The Tradition of Coleridge and Wordsworth in the Victorian Church* (Cambridge: Cambridge University Press, 1976)

Prickett, Stephen, *Words and 'The Word': Language, Poetics and Biblical Interpretation* (Cambridge: Cambridge University Press, 1986; 1989)

Prickett, Stephen, *Origins of Narrative: The Romantic Appropriation of the Bible* (Cambridge: Cambridge University Press, 1996)

Prickett, Stephen, 'Biblical and Literary Criticism: A History of Interaction', in David Jasper and Stephen Prickett, eds, *The Bible and Literature: A Reader* (Oxford: Blackwell, 1999), 12-43

Prynne, J. H., *Field Notes: 'The Solitary Reaper' and Others* (n.pub: Cambridge, 2007)

Prynne, J. H., 'Tintern Abbey, Once Again', *Glossator*, 1 (2009), 81-7

Puttenham, George, *The Arte of English Poesie*, ed. Edward Arber (Westminster: A. Constable, 1895)

Pyle, Gerald J., 'J. H. Reynolds' "Peter Bell"', *Notes and Queries*, 24 (1977), 323–4
Quentin R. Skrabec, Jr., *The Metallurgic Age: The Victorian Flowering of Invention and Industrial Science* (Jefferson: McFarland, 2006)
Quirk, Randolf, Sidney Greenbaum, Geoffrey Leech, and Jan Svartvik, *A Grammar of Contemporary English* (London: Longman, 1972)
Rajan, Tilottama, and Julia M. Wright, eds, *Romanticism, History and the Possibility of Genre* (Cambridge: Cambridge University Press, 1998)
Rawes, Alan, ed., *Romanticism and Form* (Houndsmills: Palgrave Macmillan, 2007)
Raz, Yosefa, 'Robert Lowth's Bible: Between Seraphic Choirs and Prophetic Weakness', *Modern Language Quarterly*, 81.2 (June 2020), 139–67
Reiman, Donald H., ed., *The Romantics Reviewed: Contemporary Reviews of British Romantic Writers: Part A—The Lake Poets*, 2 vols (New York and London: Garland, 1972)
The Collected Letters of Sir Joshua Reynolds, ed. Frederick Whiley Hilles (Cambridge: Cambridge University Press, 1929)
Reynolds, Joshua, *Discourses on Art*, ed. Robert R. Wark (San Marino: The Huntingdon Library and Art Gallery, 1959)
Reynolds, J. H., 'Peter Bell: A Lyrical Ballad', in David Kent and D. R. Ewen, eds, *Romantic Parodies, 1797–1831* (Rutherford, NJ: Fairleigh Dickinson University Press; London: Associated University Presses, 1992), p. 174
Richards, I. A., *Principles of Literary Criticism* [1924] (London and New York: Routledge, 2002)
Richter, David H., ed., *Ideology and Form in Eighteenth-Century Literature* (Lubbock: Texas Tech University Press, 1999)
Ricks, Christopher, *The Force of Poetry* (Oxford: Oxford University Press 1984; 2002)
Ricks, Christopher, *Allusion to the Poets* (Oxford: Oxford University Press, 2002)
Risatti, Howard, *A Theory of Craft: Function and Aesthetic Expression* (Chapel Hill: University of North Carolina Press, 2007)
Roe, Nicholas, 'Wordsworth, Milton, and the Politics of Poetic Influence', *The Yearbook of English Studies*, 19 (1989), 112–26
Rosenbaum, Susan B., *Professing Sincerity: Modern Lyric Poetry, Commercial Culture, and the Crisis in Reading* (Charlottesville, VA: University of Virginia Press, 2007)
Russell, Corinna, 'A Defence of Tautology: Repetition and Difference in Wordsworth's Note to "The Thorn"', *Paragraph*, 28.2 (2005), 104–18
Sacks, Oliver, *Musicophilia: Tales of Music and the Brain* (London: Picador, 2008)
Said, Edward, 'On Repetition', in *The World, the Text, and the Critic* (Cambridge, MA: Harvard University Press, 1983), 111–35
Salvesen, Christopher, *The Landscape of Memory: A Study of Wordsworth's Poetry* (Lincoln: University of Nebraska Press, 1965)
Samuel, Raphael, 'The Workshop of the World: Steam Power and Hand Technology in Mid-Victorian Britain', *History Workshop*, 3.1 (Spring 1977), 6–72
Schleiermacher, Friedrich, *Hermeneutics: The Handwritten Manuscripts*, ed. Heinz Kimmerle, trans. James Duke and Jack Forstman (Atlanta, GA: Scholars Press, 1977)
Schmidgen, Wolfram, 'Undividing the Subject of Literary History: From James Thomson's Poetry to Daniel Defoe's Novels', in Kate Parker and Courtney Weiss Smith, eds, *Eighteenth-Century Poetry and the Rise of the Novel Reconsidered* (Lewisburg: Bucknell University Press, 2013), 85–99
Schopenhauer, Arthur, 'On the Aesthetics of Poetry', in *The World as Will and Idea*, trans. E. F. J. Payne, 2 vols (New York: Dover, 1966), ii, 424–38

Schor, Esther, *Bearing the Dead: The British Culture of Mourning from the Enlightenment to Victoria* (Princeton, NJ: Princeton University Press, 1994)
Scott, John, *Critical Essays on some of the Poems, of several English Poets* (London: James Phillips, 1785)
Shadwell, Arthur, *Industrial Efficiency* (London, 1906)
The Riverside Shakespeare, 2nd edn, ed. G. Blakemore Evans and others (Boston and New York: Houghton Mifflin, 1997)
Sharp, Michele Turner, 'The Churchyard among the Wordsworthian Mountains: Mapping the Common Ground of Death and the Refiguration of Romantic Community', *ELH*, 62 (1995), 387–407
Shedd, W. G. T., *The Complete Works of Samuel Taylor Coleridge* (New York: Harper Brothers, 1864)
Shelley's Poetry and Prose, ed. Donald H. Reiman and Sharon B. Powers (New York: W. W. Norton, 1977)
Shklovsky, Victor, 'Art as Technique' [1917], in *Russian Formalist Criticism*, trans. Lee T. Lemon and Marion J. Reis (1965), repr. in David Lodge, ed., *Modern Criticism and Theory: A Reader* (London: Longman, 1988)
Simpson, David, *Wordsworth and the Figurings of the Real* (Houndsmills: Macmillan, 1982)
Simpson, David, *Wordsworth's Historical Imagination: The Poetry of Displacement* (New York: Methuen, 1987)
Simpson, David, *Wordsworth, Commodification and Social Concern: The Poetics of Modernity* (Cambridge: Cambridge University Press, 2009)
Smith, Adam, 'Of the Nature of that Imitation which takes place in what are called The Imitative Arts' [1795], in *The Glasgow Edition of the Works and Correspondence of Adam Smith, Vol. 3: Essays on Philosophical Subjects with Dugald Stewart's Account of Adam Smith*, ed. W. P. D. Wightman, J. C. Bryce, and I. S. Ross (Oxford: Oxford University Press, 1980)
Smith, Adam, *The Wealth of Nations: Books I–III* [1776], ed. Andrew Skinner (London: Penguin, 1970; 1999)
Snyder, Franklin Bliss, 'Wordsworth's Favourite Words', *Journal of English and Germanic Philology*, 22 (1923), 253–6
Soderholm, James, 'Dorothy Wordsworth's Return to Tintern Abbey', *New Literary History*, 26.2 (Spring 1995), 309–22, https://www.jstor.org/stable/20057284, accessed 2 June 2022
Somervell, T., 'Mediating Vision: Wordsworth's Allusions to Thomson's *Seasons* in *The Prelude*', *Romanticism*, 22.1 (2016), 48–60
Stein, Edwin, *Wordsworth's Art of Allusion* (University Park: Pennsylvania State University Press, 1988)
Stempel, Daniel, 'Revelation on Mount Snowdon: Wordsworth, Coleridge, and the Fichtean Imagination', *The Journal of Aesthetics and Art Criticism*, 29.3 (Spring 1971), 371–84
Stephens, Leslie, 'Wordsworth's Ethics' [1876], in *Hours in a Library*, 3 vols (London: Smith, Elder, 1892), ii, 270–307
Stewart, Garrett, *Reading Voices: Literature and the Phonotext* (Berkeley and Los Angeles: University of California Press, 1990)
Stewart, Susan, *Poetry and the Fate of the Senses* (Chicago: University of Chicago Press, 2002)
Strang, Barbara, 'John Clare's Language', Appendix to *John Clare: The Rural Muse*, ed. R. K. R. Thornton (Ashington: Carcanet and the Mid Northumberland Arts Group, 1982), 159–73

Styles, John, 'Manufacturing, Consumption and Design in Eighteenth-Century England', in John Brewer and Roy Porter, eds, *Consumption and the World of Goods* (Abingdon: Routledge, 1993), 527–54

Sutherland, Kathryn, 'The Native Poet: The Influence of Percy's Minstrel from Beattie to Wordsworth', *Review of English Studies* (New Series), 33.132 (November 1982), 414–33

Swingle, L. J., 'The Romanic Emergence: Multiplication of Alternatives and the Problem of Systematic Entrapment', *Modern Language Quarterly*, 39.3 (September 1978), 264–83, https://doi.org/10.1215/00267929-39-3-264, accessed 1 June 2022

Sykes Davies, Hugh, *Wordsworth and the Worth of Words*, ed. John Kerrigan and Jonathan Wordsworth (Cambridge University Press: Cambridge, 1986)

Taylor, Jane, '"Why do you tear me from Myself?": Torture, Truth, and the Arts of the Counter-reformation', in Ernst van Alphen, Mieke Bal, and Carel Smith, eds, *The Rhetoric of Sincerity* (Stanford: Stanford University Press, 2009), 19–43

Tennyson, Alfred Lord, *In Memoriam*, ed. by Erik Gray (New York and London: Norton, 1973; 2004)

Terry, Richard, 'Transitions and Digressions in the Eighteenth-Century Long Poem', *Studies in English Literature, 1500-1900*, 32.3 (Summer 1992), 495–510

Thomas, Gordon K., '"The Thorn" in the Flesh of English Romanticism', *The Wordsworth Circle*, 14.4 (Autumn 1983), 237–42

Thompson, E. P., *The Making of the English Working Class* (London: Penguin, 1963; 1980)

Trentmann, Frank, *Empire of Things* (London: Penguin, 2017)

Trilling, Lionel, *Sincerity and Authenticity* (London: Oxford University Press, 1972)

Valéry, Paul, 'The Idea of Art' [1935], from *Aesthetics*, in *The Collected Works of Paul Valéry*, ed. Jackson Matthews, 15 vols [1958–75], xiii, trans. Ralph Manheim (London: Routledge & Kegan Paul, 1964), 70–9

Valéry, Paul, 'Letter about Mallarmé', from *Leonardo, Poe, Mallarmé* [1956], in *The Collected Works of Paul Valéry*, ed. Jackson Matthews, 15 vols [1958–75], viii, trans. Malcolm Cowley and James R. Lawler (Princeton, NJ: Princeton University Press, 1972), 240–53, https://doi.org/10.1515/9781400873104, accessed 7 June 2022

Vermeulen, Pieter, 'The Suspension of Reading: Wordsworth's "Boy of Winander" and Trauma Theory', *Orbis Litterarum*, 62.6 (2007), 459–82

Vernon, James, *Distant Strangers: How Britain Became Modern* (Berkeley and Los Angeles: University of California Press, 2014)

Vespa, Jack, 'Veiled Movements in "The Vale of Esthwaite"', *Wordsworth Circle*, 45.1 (Winter 2014), 62–5, https://www.jstor.org/stable/24044362, accessed 2 June 2022

Webb, Timothy, *The Violet in the Crucible: Shelley and Translation* (Oxford: Oxford University Press, 1976)

Weiskel, Thomas, *The Romantic Sublime: Studies in the Structure and Psychology of Transcendence* (Baltimore: Johns Hopkins University Press, 1976)

Wellek, René, and Austin Warren, *Theory of Literature*, 3rd edn (New York: Harcourt, Brace & World, 1956)

Wierzbika, Anna, *Lingua Mentalis: The Semantics of Natural Language* (Sydney and New York: Academic Press, 1980)

Wittgenstein, Ludwig, *Philosophical Investigations*, trans. G. E. M. Anscombe (Oxford: Basil Blackwell, 1958)

Wolfson, Susan J., 'The Illusion of Mastery: Wordsworth's Revisions of "The Drowned Man of Esthwaite," 1799, 1805, 1850', *PMLA*, 99.5 (October 1984), 917–35, https://doi.org/10.2307/462144, accessed 1 June 2022

Wolfson, Susan J., *Formal Charges: The Shaping of Poetry in British Romanticism* (Stanford: Stanford University Press, 1997)
Wolfson, Susan, 'Wordsworth's Craft', in Stephen Gill, ed., *The Cambridge Companion to Wordsworth* (Cambridge, Cambridge University Press, 2003), 108–24
Woodcock, George, *The Tyranny of the Clock* (The Anarchist's Library, 1944)
Wordsworth, Christopher, *Memoirs of William Wordsworth* [1851], 2 vols (Cambridge: Cambridge University Press, 2014)
Wordsworth, Dorothy, *Recollections of a Tour Made in Scotland, A.D. 1803*, ed. J. C. Shairp (Edinburgh: Edmonston and Douglas, 1874)
Wordsworth, Dorothy, *The Grasmere Journals, including the Alfoxden Journal*, ed. Pamela Woof (Oxford: Oxford University Press, 1991; 2002)
Wordsworth, Jonathan, *William Wordsworth: The Borders of Vision* (Oxford: Clarendon Press, 1982)
Wordsworth, Jonathan, 'Revision as Making: *The Prelude* and its Peers', in Robert Brinkley and Keith Hanley, eds, *Romantic Revisions* (Cambridge: Cambridge University Press, 1992), 18–42
Wrigley, E. A., *The Path to Sustained Growth: England's Transition from an Organic Economy to an Industrial Revolution* (Cambridge: Cambridge University Press, 2016)
Wu, Duncan, *Wordsworth's Reading 1770–1799* (Cambridge: Cambridge University Press, 1993)
Wu, Duncan, *Wordsworth's Reading 1800–1815* (Cambridge: Cambridge University Press, 1995)
Wu, Duncan, 'Tautology and Imaginative Vision in Wordsworth', *Romanticism on the Net*, 2 (May 1996), not paginated, https://doi-org.ezp.lib.cam.ac.uk/10.7202/005717ar, accessed 1 June 2022
Wu, Duncan, *Wordsworth: An Inner Life* (Oxford: Blackwell, 2003)
Wynter, Andrew, *Our Social Bees; or, Pictures of Town & Country Life, and other papers* (London: Robert Hardwicke, 1865)
Yeats, W. B., 'Introduction' to *The Oxford Book of Modern Verse* (Oxford: Oxford University Press, 1936), v–xlii
Zuckerkandl, Victor, *Sound and Symbol* (New York: Pantheon, 1956)

Index

Note: Footnote numbers are indicated by 'n.', following the page number.

For the benefit of digital users, indexed terms that span two pages (e.g., 52–3) may, on occasion, appear on only one of those pages.

Abrams, M. H. 42, 52–3, 247
Adamson, Sylvia 75–9, 96–7, 123, 193–4, 233–4, 255
aesthetics 5
　eighteenth-century 43–4
　'aesthetics of near-repetition', the 5
　Romantic poetry 14n.54, 191–2
Alfoxden Notebook 193, 196–7
anagnorisis/recognition 137–8, 166–7
Ancient Greeks 3n.3, 8–9, 13
Aristotle 174, 198
　anagnorisis/recognition 137–8, 166–7
　tragedy 163–4
Armstrong, Isobel 10, 30–1, 40, 117–18, 130, 206–7
Armstrong, Kate 30–1
Arnold, Matthew 25–6, 254–5
art 5–6
　Enlightenment, art, and repetition 42–3
　mimesis, art, and repetition 3–4, 40–2
　repetition vii, 3–5, 30–1
　repetition, art, and the mind 40–4
Asendorf, Christoph 60–1, 63–4, 126, 146–7
Attridge, Derek 24–5, 126
Auden, W. H. 11–12
Auerbach, Eric 117–18, 137–8
Augustine, St 38, 49–50
Austin, J. L. 27–8

Babbage, Charles 58–9
Bacon, Francis 212–13
ballads 13, 48, 54n.58, 72–3, 175
　see also *Lyrical Ballads*
Baron, Michael 114–15
Barrell, John 85–7, 255
Bate, Walter Jackson 31–2
Bates, Brian 170–1, 203–4
Baxendall, Michael 31–2
Beattie, James
　conjunctions, and 79–81, 111–12
　Minstrel, The 33–4
　Wordsworth, William, and 33–4, 79–80

Beer, Gillian 7–10, 180–1
'Beggars' (Wordsworth) 83–5, 87–8
Benjamin, Walter 43–4, 46, 53–5, 105–6, 146
　memory 110
Bennett, Andrew 83
Berger, John 43n.11
Bernhardt-Kabisch, Ernest 238–40
Bewell, Alan 48, 64n.107, 95–6, 137, 166–7, 215, 218–19
Bible, The
　Book of Isaiah 225–6
　Book of Job 165–6
　Ecclesiastes 4–5, 44–5
　Higher Criticism 44–9
　Psalms 46–7
　repetition in 4–5, 44–5, 158–9
　sublimity of 45
　translation of 48
　Wordsworth, William and 45, 165–6, 225–6
Blair, Hugh 45, 47, 166–7
Blake, William 56–7
　'To Summer' 27
Bloom, Harold 31–2
Boat-Stealing episode 98–106
　conjunctions in 99–106, 126–7
　echo 212
　memory 100, 102–6
　'now' 126–8
　recapitulation 102–3, 105
　repetition 100–6
　sublimity 100–3, 105, 206–7
　see also Book I under *Prelude, The*, specific books (Wordsworth)
Booth, Stephen 15, 217–18
Borderers, The (Wordsworth) 149–51
　tragedy 162–3
Boy of Winander, *see* 'There was a boy'/the Boy of Winander
Bradley, A. C. 214
Brigham, Linda 93–4, 140–1
Brinkley, Robert, and Keith Hanley 240
Bromwich, David 114

Bunyan, David 186-7
Burwick, Frederick 229-30
Butler, James 261-2
Byron, George Gordon, Lord 49-50, 258n.20

Cameron, Sharon 83, 192-3
Castell, James 222-4
Cave, Terence 137-8, 167
Channick, Debra 228, 245
Chaucer, Geoffrey 72-3, 115-16
  Wordsworth's translation of 'The Prioress's Tale' 72-3, 114-17
Cicero 174
Clare, John 27, 62-4
Clare, John, 'A Scene' 16-22
  ear-rhyme in 17-20
  eye-rhyme in 17-20
  language 20-2
  meaning/semantic issues 17-18, 20-2
  onomatopoeia 18-19
  repetition in 16-18, 21-2, 27
  repetition of sound in 17-22
  rhyme 17-21
  sonnet form 18, 20-1
  sublimity 21-2
  wideness 16-17
Cobbett, William 62-3
Coleridge, Samuel Taylor 63-4, 100
  conjunction or, the 249
  critiques of Wordsworth's work 33-4, 48-9, 94-5, 157-9, 168, 170-1, 227-8, 231-2
  definition of poetry 254-5
  desynonymy 228-32, 238, 242
  echo 224-5, 241-2, 248-9
  imagination 227, 229-38, 247, 251-3
  metre 24n.1, 243
  mimesis 229-30
  originality and repetition 229-30, 240-1
  plagiarism and influence 236-7, 240-1, 243
  recapitulation 235-6, 243, 245-6, 249
  repetition and the mind 227-40
  repetition with difference 236-8, 240-2, 251-3
  revision 240-1, 247-9, 251-3
  rhetorical effects of repetition 240
  rhyme 244-5
  specific and the general, the 238, 251-3
  sublimity 234-5, 251-3
  tautology 240, 242, 248-9
  thematic repetition 245-6
  translation 34-5
  truth, concept of 229
  Wordsworth/Coleridge comparison 227, 233-5, 251-3
  Wordsworth/Coleridge relationship 72-4, 190, 210-11, 227
  Wordsworth's *Prelude*, and 70-1, 100, 149-51, 210
Coleridge, Samuel Taylor, works
  Biographia Literaria 34-5, 157, 184-5, 227-37, 240, 247-9, 251, 254
  'Christabel' 243-5, 253
  'Eolian Harp, The' 242
  'Frost at Midnight' 240-1, 248-9
  'Kubla Khan' 245-7, 253
  Lyrical Ballads, shared authorship of 79
  'Nightingale, The' 253
  'Rime of the Ancient Mariner, The' 241-2, 245-6
  'This Lime-tree Bower' 247-53
  'To Asra' 27, 240
  see also *Lyrical Ballads*
community
  disjunction, and absence of community 139-55
  Dorothy/William Wordsworth relationship 136-9
  Essays upon Epitaphs 94-5
  Home at Grasmere 143-4, 176-7, 186, 205-6
  London, and 139-55
  Prelude, The 139-46, 151-2, 155, 261
  recognition, connection, and community 133-9
  'Stepping Westward' 138-9
  'There was a boy' 214
  'Thorn, The' 95-6
  'Tintern Abbey' 135-7
  'We are Seven' 94-6
conjunctions viii, 75-90, 123, 255, 263-4
  eighteenth century 74-5, 77-80
  ambiguity of 93
  Beattie, James, and 79-81, 111-12
  Chaucer, Geoffrey, and 72-3, 115-16
  Coleridge, Samuel Taylor, and 249
  complex conjunctions 79-85, 89-90
  'conjunction reduction' 81n.40
  connection and 70-4, 86-7, 112, 148
  coordinating conjunctions 69, 78-9, 109, 152-3
  Enlightenment 76-9
  functions of 69, 74, 86-9, 98, 100-1, 104
  Keats, John, and 83
  meaning/semantic issues 75, 79, 81-3, 86-8, 91, 104
  Pope, Alexander, and 78-9
  recapitulation and 69, 87-9, 123, 235-6, 255
  repetition and 79, 88-9, 98, 123
  revision and 111

specific and the general, and 70
sublimity and 97–8
supplement, as 78–9, 88–9, 100–1, 109, 177, 197
Thomson, James, and 74
see also Wordsworth and conjunctions
Cooper, Lane 75–6, 242
Croker, John Wilson 8–9, 22
cuckoo poems 220–6
  see also 'On the Power of Sound'; 'To the Cuckoo'; 'Yes! full surely'
Culler, Jonathan 15, 24–5, 136–7, 217–18, 257–8
Curran, Stuart 25–6
Curtis, Paul M. 46, 233–4

'Daffodils', *see* 'I wandered lonely as a cloud'
Davie, Donald 85–7, 180–1, 255–6, 259–60
Davis, Philip 76–7
Deleuze, Gilles 4–5, 11–12, 38–9, 49n.38, 124
Deleuze, Gilles, and Félix Guattari, *Thousand Plateaus, A* 119–20
De Man, Paul 42, 208
De Quincey, Thomas 146, 198–9
Derrida, Jacques 6, 49n.38
  itérabilité 33
'Descriptive Sketches' (Wordsworth) 33–4, 224–6
De Vere, Aubrey 148–9
DeVries, Jan 61–2, 61n.92
Dewey, Godfrey 89–90
Dickinson, Emily 192–3
Diderot, Denis 34–5
Douglas-Fairhurst, Robert 7, 31–2
Dryden, John 34–5, 115–16

earworms
  Margulis, Elizabeth Hellmuth 13, 190–1
  Romantic poetry, in 13
echo
  Bacon, Francis, on 212–13
  Boat-Stealing episode, in 212
  Coleridge, Samuel Taylor, and 224–5, 241–2, 248–9
  'Descriptive Sketches', in 224–6
  'On the Power of Sound', in 220–1
  recapitulation, and 27–8, 212–13, 224–6, 254–5
  repetition with difference, and 212–13, 254–5
  rhyme, and 8, 212
  sincerity, and 254–5
  'Solitary Reaper, The', in 192–3, 196
  sound as echo to sense 254–5
  'Stepping Westward', in 133–5, 137–8, 212
  sublimity and 225–6

'There was a boy', in 200, 203–4, 212, 215–16, 218–21
'Thorn, The', and 168–9, 223–4
'Tintern Abbey', and 136
'To Joanna', and 219–20
'To the Cuckoo' and 221–2, 224
Wordsworth, William, and 212–13, 224–5, 254–5
'Yes! Full surely', and 222–4
ekphrasis 36–8, 63–4, 114–15, 125
Engell, James 236–7
Enlightenment 137
  aesthetics 43–4
  art and repetition 42–3
  conjunctions 76–9
  science and repetition 43–5, 51
epitaphic writing 261
  sincerity 260
  see also Essays upon Epitaphs
Erskine-Hill, Howard 173–4
Espie, Jeff 116
'Essay, Supplementary to the Preface' (Wordsworth) 122–3, 175, 205, 208
Essays upon Epitaphs (Wordsworth) 149–52, 260
  First 'Essay upon Epitaphs' 93–5, 114, 261
  Second 'Essay upon Epitaphs' 95–6, 259–60
  Third 'Essay upon Epitaphs' 136, 140–1
  death and community 94–5
  repetition 173
  sincerity 259–60
Esterhammer, Angela 256, 258n.20, 260–1
Everest, Kelvin 248
Excursion, The (Wordsworth) 73–4, 205
  'Preface' to 113, 117–18, 180–1
experimental method, repetition, and 'truth' 43–5, 51
'Extempore Effusion upon the Death of James Hogg' (Wordsworth) 260
eye-rhyme 9–10, 17–20, 217–18

Fenwick Notes of William Wordsworth 202
Fish, Stanley 30, 194–5
form
  ballad 13, 48, 54n.58, 72–3, 175
  blank verse 72–3, 85–6, 155, 173–4, 185, 206, 217, 250
  epic 186–7
  hexameter verse 238–40
  linearity and 38
  lineation and 29, 148
  repetition, metre, and form 24–7, 173–4
  Romantic poetry 25–7
'For the Spot where the Hermitage Stood' (Wordsworth) 111

French Revolution, Wordsworth's account of 119–20, 263
Freud, Sigmund 3–5, 49n.38, 163–4
Fruman, Norman 240–1

Gadamer, Hans-Georg 43–5, 54–5
Genette, Gérard 33n.48
Gill, Stephen 73–4, 113–14, 263–4
  revisiting 43–4, 126–8, 172–4, 182, 185, 202
'Goody Blake, and Harry Gill' (Wordsworth) 158–9, 175
Grammar of Contemporary English 79
Graver, Bruce 115–16
Graveyard School 50–1
Griffin, Emma 57–8, 62–3
Griffiths, Eric 11–12, 30–1, 116
Guattari, Félix 4–5
  Thousand Plateaus, A 119

Hamilton, Paul 228, 230–1, 254–5
Hardison, O. B. 22
Harris, James 78–9
Hartley, David 228
Hartman, Geoffrey 199
Hawkes, Terence 88n.67
Hazlitt, William 25–6, 254–5
Heard, W. A. 190
Heath, Malcolm 137–8
Hebrew verse/poetry 45–8
  see also Lowth, Robert
Hegel, G. W. F. 108, 197, 218–19, 262
  Jenaer Realphilosophie 63–4, 126
  Phenomenology of Spirit, The 199
  recapitulation, and 108–9
  repetition, on 4–5
  rhyme, on 8
Hess, Scott 73–4
Higher Criticism 44–9
Hobbes, Thomas 54
Hobsbawm, Eric 55–7
Hogle, Jerold 36–7
Hollander, John 11–12, 14, 23n.76, 190, 194n.18, 195–6, 212–13, 224–5
Home at Grasmere (Wordsworth)
  community in 143–4, 176–7, 186, 205–6
  meaning/semantic issues in 129–30
  repetition in 156, 175–80, 186, 198, 206
  repetition with difference in 178–9
  rhyme in 176–7, 206
  sound in 206
  structure of 186, 206
  tautology in 156, 172–3
  see also *Recluse, The*

Homer 44–5, 98, 238–40
  Iliad, The 13
  Odyssey, The 13
Hume, David 4–5, 11–12, 38–9, 88–9, 121–2, 232, 236–7
  Treatise of Human Nature 41
Hunt, Leigh 115–16
Hurd, Richard 256–7
Huron, David 4n.7

imagination
  eighteenth-century ideas of 42
  Coleridge, Samuel Taylor, on 227, 229–38, 247, 251–3
  repetition and 42, 54n.58
  theory of mind, and 42
  Wordsworth, William, on 208, 212
Industrial Age, the 53–64
  consumer society in 61–2
  Industrial Revolution 55–60, 62–3
  mass production 61–2
  repetition in 57–61, 63–4
  standardization and 59–60
'Inside of King's College Chapel Cambridge' (Wordsworth) 196
Isocrates 3n.3
'I wandered lonely as a cloud' (Wordsworth)
  conjunctions in 120–2
  criticism of 122–3
  Dorothy Wordsworth's notes on 120–1
  meaning/semantic issues in 120–1
  repetition in vii, 121–2, 178–9

Jacobus, Mary 48, 164–5
Jakobsen, Roman 25
Janowitz, Anne 95–6
Jarvis, Simon 125, 154–5
Jeffrey, Francis 73–4, 122–3
Jennings, Richard 82
Johnson, Mark, and George Lakoff 6
Johnson, Samuel 49–50, 52–3
  Rasselas 51–2, 203–4
  syntax 76–7
Johnston, Kenneth R. 156, 172–3, 179–80, 186, 195–6
Jones, John 75, 113–14, 142–3, 201, 203–5, 251–3
Jonson, Ben, *The English Grammar* 82

Kawain, Bruce 4n.7, 5–6, 13, 44–5, 162
Keats, John 9–10
  conjunctions 83
  'day is gone, The' 27
  ekphrasis 63–4, 125
  Endymion 8–9
  'Ode on a Grecian Urn' 83, 245–6

'Ode to a Nightingale' 28-9
  rhyme 8-9, 22
Kelley, Theresa M. 125
Kenner, Hugh 89-90
Kerrigan, John 165-6
Kidd, Stephen 3n.3
Kierkegaard, Søren 4-5, 39, 49n.38
Kivy, Peter 147
Klopstock, Friedrich Gottlieb 238-40, 243
Knox, Laurie 12
Kohl, Katrin 238-40
Kort, Wesley 48-9
Kracauer, Siegfried 92
Krieger, Murray 36, 125-6

Lacan, Jacques 4-5
Lakoff, George, and Mark Johnson 6
Lamb, Charles 139-40
Landes, David 60-1
Langford, Paul 62-3
language
  English as 'mixed language' 85-6
  origin, theory of 166-7
  'poetic function' of (Jakobsen) 25
Larkin, Peter 241-2, 245-6
Legaspi, Michael 44-5
Leighton, Angela 11-12, 29-30, 195-6
Lindenberger, Herbert 73-4
  organisation principles in *The Prelude* 118-20, 186-7
'Lines Composed a Few Miles above Tintern Abbey', *see* 'Tintern Abbey'
Liu, Alan 114, 263
Locke, John 40-1, 75, 77n.26, 142-3, 228, 236-7
Longinus 96-8
Lowth, Robert 45-8, 238-40
  conjunctions and 75, 79-80
  Lectures on the Sacred Poetry of the Hebrews 37, 46-8, 123, 207
  metaphor 37
  parallelism 46-9
  Short Introduction to English Grammar, A 75, 79-80
  Wordsworth, William, and 46-8, 123, 158-9, 232, 238-40
Lynch, Deidre 53-4
Lyrical Ballads (Wordsworth and Coleridge) 72-3, 175
  'Advertisement' 158-9, 168-9
  'Christabel' (Coleridge) 243-5, 253
  co-authorship, nature of 79
  definition of poetry in 198, 251-3, 263
  'For the Spot where the Hermitage Stood' (Wordsworth) 111

'Goody Blake, and Harry Gill' (Wordsworth) 158-9, 175
  Industrial Revolution and 56-7
  memory in 109
  'Michael, A Pastoral Poem' (Wordsworth) 111
  'Nightingale, The' (Coleridge) 253
  'Note' to 'The Thorn' (Wordsworth) 48, 94-5, 105-6, 123-4, 156-9, 161-4, 168-73, 175, 192-3, 215, 223
  'Nutting' (Wordsworth) 195-6
  Poems on the Naming of Places (Wordsworth) 219-20
  'Preface' to vii, 25-6, 56-7, 73-4, 87-8, 94-5, 109, 115-17, 121, 132, 135, 139, 151-2, 166-7, 173-4, 203-4, 251-3
  Prelude, The, and 56-7, 72-3, 87-8, 109, 139, 151-2
  recapitulation in 198
  repetition in vii, 121, 173-5, 198
  repetition with difference in 131, 203-4
  'Rime of the Ancient Mariner, The' (Coleridge) 241-2, 245-6
  'similitude in dissimilitude' 131, 203-4
  'Simon Lee, the Old Huntsman' (Wordsworth) 180-1
  'Slumber did my spirit steal, A' (Wordsworth) 136
  'spontaneous overflow of powerful feelings... recollected in tranquillity' 25-6, 87-8, 121-2, 132, 198, 258-60
  tautology 175
  'There was a boy' (*Lyrical Ballads* version, Wordsworth) 200
  'To Joanna' (Wordsworth) 219-20
  see also 'Thorn, The'; 'Tintern Abbey'; 'We are Seven'

McAlpine, Erica 200
McCauley, Lawrence 23
McDonald, Peter 224-5
  on repetition 7, 10-12, 40, 130-1, 212, 216-17, 223-4, 253
  on rhyme 7-12, 223-4
Macfarlane, Robert 32-3
Manning, Peter 33-4
Margulis, Elizabeth Hellmuth 4n.7, 6
  earworms 13, 190-1
  music/poetry relationship 12-16
Marshall, David 149
Martha Ray 160-9, 181
  see also 'Thorn, The'
Marx, Karl 56-7
Maudslay, Henry 58-9

meaning/semantic issues
  aural and semantic properties of language as separable 9–10, 14–22, 14n.54, 34–5
  conjunctions and 75, 79, 81–3, 86–8, 91, 104, 120–1
  Home at Grasmere, in 129–30
  poetry and semantic content 14–16, 257–8
  Prelude, The, in 85–6, 117–20, 130–1
  repetition and 24, 30–1, 40, 129
  sincerity and 255–6
  'Tintern Abbey', in 85–7
  transegmental drift and 27–9
  Wordsworth, William, and 29, 87
memory 109–10, 240–1
  Benjamin, Walter, on 110
  Coleridge, Samuel Taylor, and 240–1
  influence as a form of 33–4
  'Ode: Intimations of Immortality', in 109, 203–4
  'Penelope work of' 105–6, 110
  'Preface' to *Lyrical Ballads*, and 109
  Prelude, The, in 99–100, 102–6, 109–10, 114, 117–19, 127–8, 202, 206–10
  repetition and vii, 40–2
  sincerity of 102–3
  textual vs actual 33–4
  'Tintern Abbey', in 135, 137
  Wordsworth, William, and 99, 109–10, 171–2, 206–8, 210–11
Menninghaus, Winnifred 14n.54
metaphor 6
  ekphrasis and 36
  Lowth, Robert, on 37
  Prelude, The, in 130
  Romantic poetry 36–7, 40
  Shelley, Percy Bysshe, on 36–7
metre vii, 24–7, 54n.58, 158–9, 173–4, 243
  Coleridge, Samuel Taylor, and 24n.1, 243
'Michael, A Pastoral Poem' (Wordsworth) 111
Michael, Ian 78–9
Michaelis, Johann David 44–5, 48
Milbank, John 241–2
Miller, Christopher 52–3, 53n.52, 248–51
Miller, J. Hillis 110, 124
Milnes, Tim 262
Milnes, Tim, and Kerry Sinanan 255–6
Milton, John 96–7
  Paradise Lost 8–9, 22–3, 134–5, 257–8
  Paradise Regained 134–5
  rhyme 8–9, 22–3, 257–8
  rhyme and poetic sincerity 22
  Thomson, James, and 74
  Wordsworth, William, and 23, 33–4, 45, 74, 100, 134–5, 137, 142, 170–1

mimesis 137–8
  art and repetition 3–4, 40–2
  Coleridge, Samuel Taylor, on 229–30
  repetition as 39
Murry, John Middleton 21–2
music
  industrialization and 58–9
  poetry, and 11–16, 190
  repetition 3–4, 4n.7, 6, 12, 14–15, 147
  song 11–13, 190–3

Newlyn, Lucy 33–4, 87–8, 137, 171–2, 186–7, 206–7
Newstok, Scott L. 260n.24
Newton, Isaac 51–3, 219
Nietzsche, Friedrich 4–5, 25, 49n.38, 124, 166
nonsense 3, 14n.54, 81
  nonsense poems 15–16, 217–18, 223
Nord, Deborah Epstein 139–40
'now' 124–9
'Nutting' (Wordsworth) 195–6

'Ode: Intimations of Immortality' (Wordsworth) 93, 201
  memory and 109, 203–4
  repetition in 203–4
  sound 195–6
O'Neill, Michael 128n.70, 130–1, 240–1
Ong, Walter 59–60
onomatopoeia 18–19, 175
'On the Detraction Which Followed the Publication of a Certain Poem' (Wordsworth) 170–1
'On the Inside of King's College Chapel, Cambridge' (Wordsworth) 216–17
'On the Power of Sound' (Wordsworth) 197, 221–2
  echo in 220–1
originality and repetition vii, 43–4, 54
  Coleridge, Samuel Taylor, on 229–30, 240–1
  poetry, and 33
Owen, Robert 59–60, 62–3
oxymoron 187–8, 218, 248

Pacey, Arnold 58–9
Parker, Reeve 149
'Peele Castle' (Wordsworth) 182–3
Pepper, W. Thomas 56–7
Percy, Thomas, *Reliques of Ancient Poetry* 175
  Wordsworth, William, and 175
Perkins, David 151–2, 190, 255–8, 261
Peter Bell (Wordsworth) 170–1
Pickstock, Catherine 241–2
Pinker, Stephen 29

plagiarism 32, 79–80, 236–7, 240–1, 243
  self-plagiarism 203–4
Plato 212, 215, 229
  allegory of the cave 4–5
  Phaedrus 223–4
  Platonic ideal 40–1
  repetition 4–5, 39–41
Plutarch 3n.3, 54
Poems [1815] (Wordsworth)
  'Preface' to 9–10, 45, 47–8, 73–4, 123n.55, 207–8
  reception of 73–4
Poems, in Two Volumes (Wordsworth), reception of 73–4, 122–3
Poems on the Naming of Places (Wordsworth) 219
poetry
  Coleridge's definition of 254–5
  compared to everyday speech 15–16
  compared to prose 48
  as 'most philosophic' writing 194–5, 263
  music and 11–16, 190
  semantic content 14–16, 257–8
  sincerity and 84–5, 255–9, 262–4
  sound and 11–12, 14
  see also Romanticism
poetry and repetition vii, 3–4, 6–7, 9–12, 24, 166–7
political revolution 64–5
Pope, Alexander 9–10, 25, 34–5, 78–9, 240, 257–8
Porter, Roy 61–2
Praeger, Ferdinand 12
Prelude, The (Wordsworth)
  as autobiography 43–4, 69, 88–9, 111–14, 119, 206, 214
  blank verse form 72–3, 85–6, 155, 173–4
  Coleridge, Samuel Taylor, and 70–1, 149–51, 210
  community in 139–46, 151–2, 155, 261
  conclusion of 128–9
  conjunctions in 70–4, 88–9, 98–9, 111–13, 119–20, 127–8, 139, 145–6, 148, 152–5, 202
  connection in 69–73, 98–9, 103, 105, 139–55, 200, 218–19
  criticism of 199
  formal organisation of 73–4, 111–12, 118–20, 186–7
  Industrial Revolution and 56–7
  lyric 'I' in 140
  meaning/semantic issues in 85–6, 117–20, 130–1
  memory in 99, 102–6, 109–10, 114, 117–19, 127–8, 202, 206–10

metaphor in 130
punctuation of 71–2, 71n.3, 100, 101n.32, 104, 142–3, 146
recapitulation in, effect of 155
repetition 69, 109, 117–18, 127–8, 139, 146–7, 155, 171–4, 178–83, 186–8, 208–10
revision 54, 69, 71n.3, 88–9, 98–9, 109, 111–12, 114, 117–18, 127–8, 130, 143–4, 258–9
self-awareness in 70, 103–4, 117–18, 139
sincerity and 102–3, 262
specific and the general in 70, 127–8
sublimity 100–3, 105–6, 186–8, 218
syntax 85–6
tautology 187–8
textual variants, discussion of 71–2, 98–9, 101n.32, 102–6, 117–18, 141–5, 147–8, 183–4, 187–8
theatre/spectacle in 139–40, 147–52
Prelude, The, specific books (Wordsworth)
  Book I 70, 99, 111, 117–18, 127–8, 140, 180–1; *see also* Boat-Stealing episode
  Book II 70, 119–20, 126–7, 151–2, 173–4, 180–1, 204
  Book III 153–4, 180–1
  Book V 56–7, 187–8, 208–9, 218–19; *see also* 'There was a boy'
  Book VI 183–4
  Book VII 139–55, 178–9, 186, 202, 210, 261
  Book VIII 70–1, 105, 107, 155, 180–2, 187–8
  Book IX 69
  Book, X 173–4
  Book XI 105, 117–18, 180–1, 206–10
  Book XII 179–80
Prickett, Stephen 47–9
print/print culture 42–3, 58–60, 73–4
Prynne, Jeremy 132, 185, 196–7
punctuation, *see* Wordsworth and punctuation
Puttenham, George, *The Arte of English Poesie* 7

reader
  'attentive' reader, Wordsworth's 87–8, 95–6, 116–17, 129–30, 173–4
  Coleridge's description of 235–6
  as reviser 129–31
  trust and the 85–6
reading 3–4, 21–2, 87–8
  aural dimension of 27–30
  linear reading 95–6
  pseudo-reading 87–8
  reading aloud 11–12, 28–9, 171–2, 216–17
  recapitulation in the act of reading 27–31, 130
  repetition 3–4, 24

reading (*cont.*)
  re-reading 30, 42–3, 55, 129–30, 156–7, 191–3, 248
  revised reading 130, 262
  silent reading 11–12, 28–9
realism vii, 3–4
recapitulation 24, 255
  Coleridge, Samuel Taylor, and 232, 234–6, 243, 245–6, 249
  conjunctions 69, 74, 87–9, 123, 235–6, 255
  echo 27–8, 212–13, 225–6, 254–5
  ekphrasis as 36
  Hegel, G. W. F., on 108–9
  metaphor and 6n.17, 37
  recapitulation of other writers' works 33–4
  recapitulation/revision in the act of reading 27–31, 130–1, 235–6
  Romantic poetry 27–31, 130, 255, 263–4
  sincerity, and 255, 262–4
  sound, and 27–30
  subtlety of 38–9
  translation 116–17
  truth 262
  see also Wordsworth and recapitulation
Recluse, The (Wordsworth) 73–4
  harmonious unity in 143–4
  'Prospectus' to 184
  Recluse, The/The Prelude relationship 72–3
  repetition in 180–1, 184–5
recognition 167
  Aristotelian *anagnorisis* 137–8, 166–7
  recognition, connection, and community 133–9
  as remembering 132
  repetitiveness, recognition of 38–9
  as revision 132
  'Stepping Westward' 138–9, 168
  'Thorn, The' 164–8
  'Tintern Abbey' 132
  tragedy and 167
  translation as 116
  Wordsworth, William, and 132, 138
religion 3, 149–51
  see also Bible, The
repetition 3–12
  art 3–5, 30–1; *see also* mimesis
  conjunctions and 123
  Deleuze's 'platonic repetition' and 'Nietzschean mode of repetition' 124
  Enlightenment, science and repetition 43–5, 51
  Hegel, G. W. F. 4–5
  Higher Criticism and 44–9
  imagination and 42, 54n.58
  impossibility of perfect repetition 4–5, 7, 33, 39, 158–9
  Industrial Age 57–61, 63–4
  itérabilité 33
  Klopstock, Friedrich Gottlieb, on 238–40
  life as repetitive 5
  Lowth, Robert, on 45
  meaning/semantic issues 24, 30–1, 40, 129
  memory and vii, 40–2
  metre, form and vii, 24–7, 173–4
  music 3–4, 4n.7, 6, 12, 14–15, 147
  negative effects of 5
  order, disorder, repetition, and variation 49–53
  paradoxes of 3, 6
  philosophical tradition and 4–5, 43–4
  Plato, on 4–5, 39–41
  psychoanalytic criticism vii, 3
  pure repetition 4–5, 229
  realism vii, 3–4
  redundancy and 6, 105–6, 123–4, 162, 177–8, 181, 193–4, 223, 229–30; *see also* 'Note' to 'The Thorn' *under* 'Thorn, The'; tautology
  repetitious/repetitive distinction 5
  rhyme vii, 6–8, 173–4
  rhythm 6–7
  Romantic period 55, 58–9, 63–4
  sincerity and 48–9
  sound, repetition of vii, 6–7, 17–18
  sublimity and 40, 45
  temporality 126
  tragedy and 162–4, 166
  translation 114–17
  truth and 17–18, 43–5, 51
  unobtrusiveness of 38–9
  word-repetition vii, 6–7, 158–9, 173–4, 185
  see also metre; poetry and repetition; repetition with difference; rhyme; rhythm; tautology; Wordsworth and repetition
repetition with difference 25, 39, 50–1
  Coleridge, Samuel Taylor, and 236–8, 240–2, 251–3
  echo as 212–13, 254–5
  influence and 32
  Lowth, Robert, and 45, 47n.29
  rhyme and 8
  see also Wordsworth and repetition with difference
revision
  Coleridge, Samuel Taylor, and 240–1, 247–9, 251–3
  conjunctions and 111

recognition as revision 132
revised reading 129–31, 262
sincerity and 259
translation and 35–6, 114–16
see also Wordsworth and revision
Reynolds, John Hamilton 171, 203–4
Peter Bell 170–1
Reynolds, Joshua 40–1, 47n.29, 51–3
rhetoric
  repetition and vii, 6–7
  rhetorical effects of repetition 174–7, 187–8, 240
  rhetorical redundancy 123–4, 177, 181
rhyme
  Clare, John, 'A Scene', and 17–21
  classical literature, in 8–9
  Coleridge, Samuel Taylor, and 244–5
  echo and 8, 212
  end-rhyme 9, 17–21, 27, 128–9, 157, 193–4, 244–5
  English poetry and 7–9
  German revolt against rhyme 238–40
  Hegel, G. W. F., on 8
  Milton, John, and 8–9, 22–3, 257–8
  monosyllabic rhyme vii, 19
  repetition vii, 6–8, 173–4
  repetition with difference and 8
  'rhyming backwards' 29, 234
  rhythm and 13
  Romantic poetry and 8–11
  sincerity and 22, 257–8
  sound and 7–9, 11–12, 16–22
  see also eye-rhyme; poetry; Wordsworth and rhyme
rhythm
  health and 171–2
  musical rhythm 13
  repetition and 6–7
  rhyme and 13
  'Solitary Reaper, The', in 190–1
  see also metre; poetry
Richards, I. A. 20–1, 25, 54n.58
Ricks, Christopher 23, 30–1, 87–8, 142–3, 172–3, 210–11, 235–6
  lineation, on 29, 129–30, 245–6
  prepositions and conjunctions, on 75–6, 101
Risatti, Howard 54–7, 54n.58
Robinson, Henry Crabb 85–6
Romantic Idealism 95–6
Romanticism 91
  ekphrasis and 36
  form 25–7
  grammar 194
  indirection 26–7

knowledge 59–60
metaphor and 36, 40
originality, individuality, and genius 35–6
periodic sentence 76–8
political revolution 64–5
repetition 3–12, 40, 55, 58–9, 63–4, 245–6
repetition, art, and the mind 40–4
repetition, metre, and form 24–7
repetition between and across works 31–9
rhyme 8–11
Romantic-period writing 76–9, 233–4
sincerity in viii, 255–8, 263–4
sound and repetition 12–23
sublimity 40, 96–7
syntax 77
translation 34–6, 114–15
truth 43–4, 91
Rosenbaum, Susan 56–7, 257–8
Russell, Corinna 48, 156–7, 172–3
Russian Formalism 5

Sacks, Oliver 13
Said, Edward 52–3, 88n.67
Salvesen, Christopher 171–2
Samuel, Raphael 60–1
'Scene, A' (John Clare), *see* Clare, John, 'A Scene'
Schleiermacher, Friedrich 34–5, 48–9, 262
Schmidgen, Wolfram 74, 98, 124–5
Schopenhauer, Arthur 163–4, 166, 168
Scott, John 50–1
self-awareness/self-consciousness 9, 27, 129–30, 139
  Prelude, The 103–4, 117–18
  sincerity and 257–8, 262
  'Thorn, The' 164–5
  Wordsworth, William, and 70, 72–3, 114, 200, 214, 223–4
self, sense of 70, 114
semantic issues, *see* meaning/semantic issues
Shakespeare, William
  as disorderly 50–1
  King Lear 162–5
  Macbeth 163–5
  Titus Andronicus 164–5
  tragedy 163–5
  Winter's Tale, The 167–8
  Wordsworth, William, and 33–4, 147, 163–4
Shelley, Percy Bysshe 28–9, 34–5, 170–1
  ekphrasis 63–4
  'Ozymandias' 36, 64–5, 245–6
  poetry as 'vitally metaphorical' 36–7
Shklovsky, Victor 5–6
Simmel, Georg 54–8

'Simon Lee, the Old Huntsman'
    (Wordsworth) 180–1
Simpson, David 56–7, 84–5, 87–8, 132
Sinanan, Kerry, and Tim Milnes 255–6
sincerity/sincere verse
    sixteenth century 259–60
    nineteenth century 262
    twentieth century 256–7
    distractions/challenges to 257–8, 261
    echo and 254–5
    insincerity 84–5, 257–8, 262
    meaning and truth 255–6
    poetry as self-expression 255
    recapitulation 255, 262–4
    repetition and 48–9
    revision and 259
    rhyme 22, 257–8
    Romantic sincerity viii, 255–8, 263–4
    self-consciousness 257–8, 262
    'trust' in *intention* to be sincere 87
    truth 77–8, 159–60, 194–5, 255–7, 263–4
    Wordsworth Studies, in 263–4
    see also Wordsworth and sincerity
'Slumber did my spirit steal, A'
    (Wordsworth) 136
Smith, Adam 14–15, 63–4
    Wealth of Nations, The 60–1
Snyder, Franklyn Bliss 75–6, 173–4
Soderholm, James 136–7
'Solitary Reaper, The' (Wordsworth) 190
    Dorothy Wordsworth's notes on 13, 190–1
    echo in 192–3, 196
    repetition in 190–3
    repetition of sounds 190
    rhyme in 192–3
    rhythm in 190–1
    silence in 190–1
    sublimity in 192–3, 197
    'transegmental drift' in 191–2
sound
    as echo to sense 254–5
    Home at Grasmere, in 206
    language, aural properties of 14–16, 34–5
    patterns of 24–5
    poetry and 11–12, 14, 20–1
    reading and 28–30
    recapitulation and 27–30, 195–6
    repetition of vii, 6–7, 17–18; *see also* 'Solitary Reaper, The'; 'Stepping Westward'; 'There was a boy'; There was a spot';
    rhyme and 7–9, 11–12, 16–22
    sound and repetition 12–23
    words 14–15, 34–5
    see also echo; music; Wordsworth and sound

Southey, Robert, criticism of Wordsworth's 'The Thorn' 48–9, 157–9, 161, 168, 231–2
specific and the general, the 148–9
    Coleridge, Samuel Taylor, and 238, 251–3
    conjunctions and 70
    Prelude, The, in 70, 127–8
    Wordsworth, William, and 70, 127–8, 194, 197–211, 251–3
    see also tautology; Wordsworth, William; Wordsworth and repetition
Stempel, Daniel 237
Stephen, Leslie 134–5
'Stepping Westward' (Wordsworth) 134–5
    connection and community in 138–9
    Dorothy Wordsworth's notes on 133, 138–9
    echo in 133–5, 137–8, 212
    recognition in 138–9, 168
    repetition in 133–5
    repetition of sounds 190
    return 138–9
    revisiting 133, 135, 137–8
    sublimity in 133–4
Stewart, Garrett 8, 11–12, 30–1, 235–6
    transegmental drift 27–9, 129–30, 191–2, 242–3
Stewart, Susan 29–30
'still' 124–9
Stillinger, Jack 112
Strang, Barbara 21–2
Styles, John 61–2
sublimity 15–16, 82
    Bible, The, and 45
    Boat-Stealing episode, and 100–3, 105, 206–7
    Clare, John, 'A Scene', and 21–2
    Coleridge, Samuel Taylor, and 234–5, 251–3
    conjunctions and 97–8
    echo and 225–6
    egotistical sublime 105
    Hebrew verse and 47–8
    'perspicuous sublimity' 96–7
    repetition and 40, 45
    Romantic sublimity 96–7
    'Solitary Reaper, The', in 192–3, 197
    'Stepping Westward', in 133–4
    'Thorn, The', in 223
    'Tintern Abbey', in 96–7
    tragedy and 162–3, 168
    Wordsworth, William, and 30–1, 84–5, 87, 96–7, 124
Swingle, L. J. 91
Sykes Davies, Hugh 72–3, 76, 109–10, 173–4, 198, 207
    Wordsworth and the Worth of Words 75–6
Symons, Arthur 255–6

syntax
  conjunctions 75–86
  hypotaxis 77–8
  Johnson, Samuel 76–7
  parataxis 77–8
  perspicuity 75
  Prelude, The 85–6
  Romantic-period writing 76–9, 233–4
  Wordsworth, William 87, 115–16
  see also conjunctions; Wordsworth and conjunctions
system, poetic 73–4

tautology
  Coleridge, Samuel Taylor, and 232, 234, 238, 240, 242, 248–9
  Home at Grasmere, in 156, 172–3, 180n.36
  Lyrical Ballads, in 175
  Prelude, The, in 105–6, 187–8
  'Thorn, The', in 123–4, 156–8, 172–3, 175, 231
  Wordsworth, William, and 63–4, 105–8, 123–4, 156, 173–4, 195–6, 223
  see also Wordsworth and repetition
Taylor, William Cooke 62–3
Terry, Richard 50–1
theatre
  Borderers, The (Wordsworth) 149
  London as theatre 139–40
  'Maid of Buttermere, The' 149–52, 210
  Prelude, The 139–40, 147–52, 210
  spectatorship 149–52
'There was a boy'/the Boy of Winander (Wordsworth) 114, 159–60, 200–4, 208, 213–19, 221–2, 253
  alternative readings of 200
  community in 214
  comparison to Coleridge's 'The Nightingale' 253
  conjunctions in 202–3, 214, 216–17
  death of the Boy of Winander 218–19
  echo and 200, 203–4, 212, 215–16, 218–21
  memory in 202
  place and time in 201–2
  recapitulation 203–4, 218–19
  repetition 200–1, 203, 214–16, 218–19
  repetition of sound 190, 203–4, 215–17, 224
  repetition with difference 216, 218, 220–2
  revision 200
  rhyme 217–18
  silence 214, 216–18
  sincerity/sincere verse 202
  see also Book V *under Prelude, The*, specific books (Wordsworth)

'There was a spot' (Wordsworth) 193–7, 201
  conjunctions in 197
  repetition 193–6
  sound 193–6
Thomas, Gordon K. 159–60
Thompson, E. P. 62–3
Thomson, James 50–1, 74, 124–5
'Thorn, The' (Wordsworth) 39
  Coleridge's response to 48–9, 94–5, 157–9, 168, 227–8, 231–2
  criticism of 48–9, 157, 164–5, 172–3
  death and community in 95–6
  echo and 168–9, 223–4
  gender in 165n.27
  Hebrew poetry and 48
  as introspective 159–60
  Job, Book of 165–6
  Martha Ray 160–9, 181
  Martha Ray's baby 160, 165
  narrator of 48–9, 159–61, 164–9, 231–2
  'Note' to 'The Thorn' 48, 94–5, 105–6, 123–4, 156–9, 161–4, 168–73, 175, 192–3, 215, 223
  recognition 164–8
  repetition 149, 156–69, 173, 175, 178–9, 192–3, 215, 223–4
  revision 159–60
  rhyme 161–2
  self-awareness 164–5
  sincerity/sincere verse 159–60, 168–9
  Southey's criticism of 48–9, 157–9, 161, 168, 231–2
  sublimity 223
  tautology 123–4, 156–7, 172–3; *see also* 'Note' to 'The Thorn'
  tragedy 162–9
  truth 159–60, 167
  variant editions of 158–9
'Tintern Abbey' (Wordsworth) 132–6
  apostrophic address 136–7
  conjunctions in 97–8, 261
  connection and community in 135–7
  Dorothy Wordsworth, significance of 136–7
  echo and 136
  meanings 85–7
  memory in 135, 137
  narrator 95–6
  prepositions 101
  recapitulation 185
  recognition 132
  repetition 97, 136, 185, 187–8
  repetition with difference 185
  return 132
  revisiting 135–6, 185, 263–4
  sublimity 96–7

'To A Sky-Lark' (Wordsworth) 128–9
'To Joanna' (Wordsworth) 219–20
'To the Cuckoo' (Wordsworth)
  conjunctions in 127–8
  echo 221–2, 224
  repetition 127–8
  repetition with difference 221–2
tragedy
  Aristotle 163–4
  Borderers, The 162–3
  recognition 167
  repetition 162–4, 166
  resignation 163, 166
  revenge tragedy 162–3, 165
  Shakespearean tragedy 163–5
  sublimity and 162–3, 168
  'Thorn, The', as 162–9
transegmental drift 27–9, 129–30, 191–2, 242–3
translation 37–8
  Bible, The 48
  Coleridge, Samuel Taylor 34–5
  as recapitulation 116–17
  as recognition 116
  repetition 114–17
  revision 35–6, 114–16
  Romantic-period 34–6, 114–15
  Wordsworth, William, and 35–6, 114–17
  Wordsworth's translation of Chaucer's 'The Prioress's Tale' 72–3, 114–17
  Wordsworth's translation of Virgil's *Georgics* 158–9
Trilling, Lionel 147, 255–8
truth
  Coleridge, Samuel Taylor, and 229
  conjunctions and 113
  experimental method, and 43–5, 51
  Hegel, G. W. F, and 108–9
  intention 255–6
  recapitulation and 262
  Romanticism 43–4, 91
  sincerity and 77–8, 159–60, 194–5, 255–7, 263–4
  'Thorn, The', and 159–60, 167
  transcendental truth 52
  'We are Seven', and 159–60
  Wordsworth, William, and 108–9, 113, 148–9, 194–5, 198–9, 210–11, 220, 263
Tytler, Alexander Fraser 34–5

Vale of Esthwaite, The (Wordsworth) 109–10, 206
Valéry, Paul 6, 32
Vernon, James 62–3
Virgil 44–5, 158–9

Wagner, Cosmia 14
Warhol, Andy 3–4
Warren, Austin, and René Wellek 256, 259
'We are Seven' (Wordsworth) 91
  conjunctions in 91–3, 95–6, 113
  death and community in 94–6
  narrator of 95–6, 159–60
  recapitulation 94–5
  repetition 92–3
  truth 159–60
  Wordsworth's note to 94–5
Weiskel, Thomas 97
Wellek, René, and Austin Warren 256, 259
Wesling, Donald 28–9
Wierzbika, Anna 81–2
Wilkinson, Thomas 33–4
Wittgenstein, Ludwig 4–5, 192–3
Wolfson, Susan 8–9, 23n.77, 27, 190–1, 240
  memory/memories 33–4, 112–13
  revision 112–13, 200
Woodcock, George 59–60
words
  aural properties of 14–15, 34–5
  meaning and nonsense 15
  musicality of 15–16
  word-repetition vii, 6–7, 158–9, 173–4, 185
Wordsworth, Catherine 95n.16
Wordsworth, Dorothy 72–3, 95n.16
  'Beggars' and 84–5
  Dorothy/William Wordsworth relationship 33–4, 136–9, 171–2, 205
  health issues 171–2
  notes on 'I wandered lonely as a cloud' 120–1
  notes on 'The Solitary Reaper' 13, 190–1
  notes on 'Stepping Westward' 133, 138–9
  'Thoughts on my sick bed' 137
Wordsworth, Jonathan 33–4, 112–13
Wordsworth, William
  ambiguity 71, 86–8, 93
  Bible, The, and 45, 165–6, 225–6
  diction 47–8, 115–16, 251–3
  echo 212–13, 224–5, 254–5
  imagination 208, 212
  industrialism and 56–7
  influences 33–4; *see also* Beattie, James; Bible, The; Lowth, Robert; Milton, John; Wordsworth, Dorothy
  interrelationship of works 72–4, 136, 206–10
  meaning/semantic issues 29, 87
  memory and 99, 109–10, 171–2, 206–8, 210–11
  modernization and 56–7
  poetic system of 73–4
  poetry as most philosophic writing 198, 263

prepositions 75–6
prose 156
recognition 132, 138
self-awareness 70, 72–3, 114, 200, 214, 223–4;
  see also self-awareness/self-consciousness
specific and the general, the 70, 127–8, 194,
  197–211, 251–3
'spontaneous overflow' of emotions 25–6, 121,
  132, 198, 258–60
sublimity 30–1, 84–5, 87, 96–7, 124
syntax 87, 115–16
translation 35–6, 72–3, 114–17, 158–9
truth 113, 148–9, 194–5, 198–9, 210–11,
  220, 263
vocabulary 87–8
see also Wordsworth, William, criticism of;
  Wordsworth and conjunctions;
  Wordsworth and punctuation of editions;
  Wordsworth and recapitulation;
  Wordsworth and repetition; Wordsworth
  and revision; Wordsworth and rhyme;
  Wordsworth and sincerity; Wordsworth
  and sound
Wordsworth, William, criticism of 25–6, 48–9,
  171–2
  'I wandered lonely as a cloud' 122–3
  Peter Bell 170–1
  Poems 122–3
  Prelude, The 199
  'Thorn, The' 48–9, 157, 164–5, 172–3
  'Thorn, The', Coleridge's criticism of 48–9,
    94–5, 157–9, 168, 227–8, 231–2
  'Thorn, The', Southey's criticism of 48–9,
    157–9, 161, 168, 231–2
  repetitiousness 170–2, 199, 223–4
Wordsworth and conjunctions 72–3, 75–9, 86–8,
  93–4, 113–14, 125, 205, 258–9, 261, 263–4
  'Beggars' 83–5, 87–8
  Boat-Stealing episode 99–106, 126–7
  Home at Grasmere 177
  'I wandered lonely as a cloud' 120–2
  Prelude, The 70–4, 88–9, 98–9, 111–13,
    119–20, 127–8, 139, 145–6, 148, 152–5, 202
  recapitulation 128–30, 261
  revision 111–12, 124
  sincerity 69, 79, 87, 262
  'There was a boy' 202–3, 214, 216–17
  'There was a spot' 197
  'Tintern Abbey' 97–8, 261
  'To the Cuckoo' 127–8
  'We are Seven' 91–3, 95–6, 113
  see also conjunctions
Wordsworth and punctuation of editions 71n.3
  comma 71–2

dash 143
Prelude, The 71–2, 71n.3, 100, 101n.32, 104,
  142–3, 146
semi colon 142–3
Wordsworth and recapitulation vii, 25, 35–6,
  39, 52–3, 64–5, 123–4, 172–3,
  255, 262–4
  Boat-Stealing episode 102–3, 105
  conjunctions viii, 128–9, 155, 261
  echo 197, 212–13, 221–2, 224–5
  experience 52–3, 199
  memory 203–4, 210–11
  'Preface' to Lyrical Ballads 198
  Prelude, The 102–3, 105, 155
  repetition 128–9, 192–3
  repetition with difference 25, 94–5, 123–4,
    155, 186–7, 218–19, 258–9
  revision 109, 116–17, 130–1, 192–3, 199
  similarity and difference 52–3, 83, 94–5, 131,
    198–9, 262
  sincerity viii, 37–9, 128–9, 255, 257–9, 261–2
  'Solitary Reaper, The' 192–3
  sound and 195–6
  specific and general, and 52–3, 198–211
  'Tintern Abbey' 185
  transcendence and 195–6
  translation and 35–6
  'We are Seven' 94–5
  witness, and 149–51
  see also recapitulation; tautology
Wordsworth and repetition vii–viii, 6, 43–4,
  64–5
  anadiplosis 177, 179–80
  anaphoric repetition 121–2, 180–1, 183–5
  antimetabole 179
  clustered repetition 173–7, 179, 182
  conjunctions 121–2, 124, 204
  criticism 170–2, 199, 223–4
  diacope 178–9
  double negative 180–1
  epanalepsis 180–1
  epizeuxis 177–80
  experience 52–3, 173, 198–9, 204–5, 208
  functions of repetition 39
  influences 33–4
  internal repetitions 186
  meaning/semantic issues 117–18
  parody 170–1
  ploce 176–8
  polyptoton 176–7, 180–1, 187–8
  recapitulation 128–9, 192–3
  repeated action 102–3, 165, 178, 200,
    206–7, 209
  repetitions as 'revisitings' 129

Wordsworth and repetition (*cont.*)
  repotia 179–80
  revision 107–8, 117–18
  revolution 173
  rhetorical effects of repetition 174–7, 187–8
  rhetorical redundancy 123–4, 177, 181
  sincerity/sincere verse 43–4, 50–3, 171, 179–80
  specific and the general 199, 208
  sublimity 30–1, 124
  tautology 63–4, 105–8, 123–4, 172–4
  textual repetition 43–4, 114–15, 173, 179, 186–8
  translation 116–17
  word-repetition 173–4, 185
  see also repetition; Wordsworth and repetition, specific works/passages; Wordsworth and repetition with difference
Wordsworth and repetition, specific works/passages
  Boat-Stealing episode 100–6
  Essays upon Epitaphs 173
  Home at Grasmere 156, 175–80, 186, 198, 206
  'I wandered lonely as a cloud' vii, 121–2, 178–9
  Lyrical Ballads vii, 121, 173–5, 198
  'Ode: Intimations of Immortality' 203–4
  Poems [1815], 'Preface' 9–10
  Prelude, The 69, 109, 117–18, 127–8, 139, 146–7, 155, 171–4, 178–83, 186–8, 208–10
  Recluse, The 180–1, 184–5
  'Solitary Reaper, The' 190–3
  'Stepping Westward' 133–5, 190
  'There was a boy' 200–1, 203, 214–16, 218–19
  'There was a spot' 193–6
  'Thorn, The' 149, 156–69, 173, 175, 178–9, 192–3, 215, 223–4
  'Tintern Abbey' 97, 136, 185, 187–8
  'To A Sky-Lark' 128–9
  'To the Cuckoo' 127–8
  'We are Seven' 92–3
Wordsworth and repetition with difference viii, 110, 129, 186–8, 263
  conjunctions 110, 113–14
  Fenwick Notes of William Wordsworth 202
  Home at Grasmere 178–9
  Lyrical Ballads 131, 203–4
  memory 110
  recapitulation 258–9
  sincerity/sincere verse 258–9, 263–4
  specific and the general 210–11
  tautology 156–7
  'There was a boy' 216, 218, 220–2
  'Tintern Abbey' 185

'To the Cuckoo' 221–2
truth 210–11
Vale of Esthwaite, The 109–10
see also repetition with difference; Wordsworth and repetition
Wordsworth and revision 73–4, 77–8, 87–8, 107–14, 132, 137–8, 253, 263–4
  conjunctions 111–12, 124
  past and present 126
  Prelude, The 69, 71n.3, 88–9, 98–9, 109, 111–12, 114, 117–18, 127–8, 130, 143–4, 258–9
  recapitulation 109, 192–3
  recognition as revision 132
  repetition 107–8, 117–18
  revisiting 172, 202
  self-repetition 107, 136
  sincerity/sincere verse 258–9, 261
  'There was a boy' 200
  'Thorn, The' 159–60
  translation 35–6, 114–17
  truth 113
  'Yes! Full surely' 222–3
  see also revision
Wordsworth and rhyme 10–11, 115–16, 217–18
  Home at Grasmere 176–7, 206
  internal rhyme 23, 128–9, 176–7, 222–3
  'sincere' verse 23
  'Solitary Reaper, The' 192–3
  'There was a boy' 217–18
  'Thorn, The' 161–2
  'To A Sky-Lark' 128–9
  'Yes! Full surely' 222–3
  see also rhyme
Wordsworth and sincerity 114, 254–5, 258–9, 263–4
  conjunctions and sincere verse 69, 79, 87, 262
  epitaphs 260–1
  Essays upon Epitaphs 259–60
  Prelude, The 102–3, 262
  recapitulation 37–9, 128–9, 257–9, 261–2
  repetition 43–4, 50–3, 171, 179–80
  repetition with difference 258–9, 263–4
  revision 258–9, 261
  rhyme and 23
  Romantic sincerity viii, 255
  sincerity and sense 262
  'There was a boy' 202
  'There was a spot' 194–5
  'Thorn, The' 159–60, 168–9
  see also sincerity/sincere verse
Wordsworth and sound 9–10, 190
  Home at Grasmere 206
  nonmusical sounds 190, 193–4

'Ode: Intimations of Immortality' 190
Prelude, The 195–6
recapitulation 192–3, 195–6
repeated sound 190, 193–4, 203–4, 206, 215–17, 224
silence 105–6, 190–1, 214, 216–18, 222–3
'Solitary Reaper, The' 190
'Stepping Westward' 190
'There was a boy' 190, 203–4, 215–17, 224

'There was a spot' 193–6
see also sound
Wrigley, E. A. 62–3
Wu, Duncan 80n.35, 107–8, 158–9, 206–7

Yeats, W. B. 214
'Yes! Full surely' (Wordsworth) 222–4

Zuckerkandl, Victor 12